Philosophical Problems

FIFTH EDITION

Samuel Enoch Stumpf
Late, of Vanderbilt University

James Fieser
University of Tennessee at Martin

Boston   Burr Ridge, IL   Dubuque, IA   Madison, WI   New York   San Francisco   St. Louis
Bangkok   Bogotá   Caracas   Kuala Lumpur   Lisbon   London   Madrid   Mexico City
Milan   Montreal   New Delhi   Santiago   Seoul   Singapore   Sydney   Taipei   Toronto

McGraw-Hill Higher Education

*A Division of The **McGraw-Hill** Companies*

PHILOSOPHICAL PROBLEMS: SELECTED READINGS
Published by McGraw-Hill, a business unit of The McGraw-Hill Companies, Inc., 1221 Avenue of the Americas, New York, NY, 10020. Copyright © 2003, 1994, 1989, 1983, 1971 by The McGraw-Hill Companies, Inc. All rights reserved. No part of this publication may be reproduced or distributed in any form or by any means, or stored in a database or retrieval system, without the prior written consent of The McGraw-Hill Companies, Inc., including, but not limited to, in any network or other electronic storage or transmission, or broadcast for distance learning. Some ancillaries, including electronic and print components, may not be available to customers outside the United States.

This book is printed on acid-free paper.

1 2 3 4 5 6 7 8 9 0 FGR/FGR 0 9 8 7 6 5 4 3 2

ISBN 0-07-242051-0

Publisher: *Kenneth King*
Sponsoring editor: *Jon-David Hague*
Marketing manager: *Greg Brueck*
Senior project manager: *Jean Hamilton*
Lead production supervisor: *Lori Koetters*
Senior designer: *Matthew Baldwin*
Cover design: *Georgio DiChirico, The Great Machine,* © *Superstock/ARS*
Typeface: *10/12 Palatino*
Compositor: *Shepherd Incorporated*
Printer: *Quebecor World Fairfield, Inc.*

Library of Congress Control Number: 2002105882

www.mhhe.com

About the Authors

SAMUEL ENOCH STUMPF received his Ph.D. from the University of Chicago. He was a Ford Fellow at Harvard University and a Rockefeller Fellow at Oxford University. For 15 years he was chairman of the Philosophy Department at Vanderbilt University, served a term as president of Cornell College of Iowa, and returned to Vanderbilt as Professor of the Philosophy of Law in the School of Law and as Research Professor of Medical Philosophy in the School of Medicine. He participated in various national organizations and lectured widely in the fields of philosophy, medical ethics, and jurisprudence and was Emeritus Professor of Philosophy and Law at Vanderbilt University. Professor Stumpf died in 1998.

JAMES FIESER received his Ph.D. from Purdue University and is Associate Professor of Philosophy at the University of Tennessee at Martin. He is author of *Moral Philosophy through the Ages* (2001) and coauthor, with Norman Lillegard, of *A Historical Introduction to Philosophy* (2002). He is editor of *Metaethics, Normative Ethics, and Applied Ethics* (2000), the ten-volume *Early Responses to Hume* (1999–2003), the five-volume *Scottish Common Sense Philosophy* (2000), and coeditor of *Scriptures of the World's Religions* with John Powers. Dr. Fieser is the founder and general editor of the *Internet Encyclopedia of Philosophy*.

To Jean Stumpf and Laura Roberts-Fieser

Contents

Part Three
PHILOSOPHY OF RELIGION

Part Four
EPISTEMOLOGY

Part Five
FREE WILL AND DETERMINISM

Part Six
ETHICS

Part Seven
POLITICAL PHILOSOPHY

Preface to the Fifth Edition

In the years since the first edition of *Philosophical Problems*, the book's contents have evolved based on recent developments in philosophy and the changing needs of philosophy instructors. Throughout the editions, though, there has been a consistent emphasis on the contributions of the great philosophers of the past, specifically, Plato, Aristotle, Aquinas, Descartes, Hobbes, Locke, Berkeley, Hume, Kant, Mill, Nietzsche, and James. Philosophical discussions today are not only offshoots of debates from earlier times, but recent philosophical contributions are sometimes restatements of previous theories, only in new dressing. In this Fifth Edition, the emphasis on historical figures has been retained. Perhaps the most visible change in this edition is the renaming and reordering of the parts themselves; in some cases selections have been moved from one part to another. The selections from Plato that opened previous editions have all been retained here, but are relocated according to their topics. For example, the selection from *Crito* is now placed in Part Seven, "Political Philosophy."

Within each of the seven topical parts of the text, all of the items are now sequenced chronologically, and some historical gaps are filled in. Newly included classics are Epicurus on pleasure; Epictetus on fate; Sextus Empiricus on skepticism; Pascal's wager; Hume on personal identity, determinism, miracles, and the theistic proofs; and Reid on free will. Also included are more recent discussions by Mackie on the problem of evil, Rorty on epistemology, and Fieser on cultural relativism. This edition also presents a broader range of philosophical traditions. Four new items are classic Eastern Philosophy texts, specifically from the Hindu, Buddhist, Confucian and Taoist traditions. Although these texts emerged in distinctly non-Western philosophical traditions, they nevertheless discuss universal philosophical questions and fit well within the topical divisions here. Also, two new items are historical pieces by women philosophers, namely, those by Anne Conway and Mary Wollstonecraft. These reflect the often-neglected effect that women had on philosophy during previous centuries. To make room for new items, some of the more dated selections from previous editions were removed—a necessary evil in the editing of any new edition of a book.

This edition also includes a variety of changes aimed at making this book more accessible to students. All spelling has been uniformly Americanized and, for older pieces, modernized. When appropriate, new sectional headings have been introduced into the readings, which indicate logical divisions within the pieces. Headings within square brackets are editorial additions and were not part of the original texts; headings not within square brackets reflect chapter and section titles within the original. Also, more complete bibliographical citations are given for the original sources, which should help the reader locate the selection within the complete original work itself.

James Fieser
University of Tennessee at Martin

Acknowledgments

René Descartes, *The Philosophical Works of Descartes,* translated by Elizabeth Sanderson Haldane, George Robert Thomson Ross, Cambridge: Cambridge University Press, 1911–1912. Reprinted by permission of Cambridge University Press.

Arthur Eddington, *The Nature of the Physical World* (Cambridge, England: Cambridge University Press, 1928), reprinted by permission of Cambridge University Press.

Epicturus, "Letter to Menoecius," translated by Norman Lillegard, reprinted by permission of Norman Lillegard.

James Fieser, *Moral Philosophy through the Ages* (New York: McGraw Hill, 2001), reprinted by permission of McGraw-Hill.

Carol Gilligan, "In a Different Voice: Women's Conception of Self and of Morality," *Harvard Educational Review,* 1977, vol. 47, pp. 481–517. Copyright 1977 by the President and Fellows of Harvard College. All rights reserved.

J. L. Mackie, "The Problem of Evil," *Mind,* vol. 64, 1955, pp. 200–212. Reprinted by permission of *Mind* and Oxford University Press.

John Rawls, "Justice as Fairness," in *The Journal of Philosophy,* vol. 54, 1957, pp. 653–662, reprinted by permission of *The Journal of Philosophy.*

Richard Rorty, *Philosophy and the Mirror of Nature* (Princeton, New Jersey: Princeton University Press, 1979), reprinted by permission of Princeton University Press.

Bertrand Russell, *The Problems of Philosophy* (Oxford: Oxford University Press, London, 1912). Reprinted by permission of Oxford University Press.

Jean Paul Sartre, "The Humanism of Existentialism," *The Philosophy of Existentialism,* ed. Wade Baskin (New York: Philosophical Library, 1965), reprinted by permission of Philosophical Library.

John Searle, *Minds, Brains and Science* (Cambridge, MA.: Harvard University Press, 1984). Reprinted by permission of the publisher from "Mind-Body Problem," pp. 13–27, and "The Freedom of the Will," pp. 86–98, in *Minds, Brains, and Science* by John Searle, Cambridge, MA.: Harvard University Press, Copyright 1984 by John R. Searle.

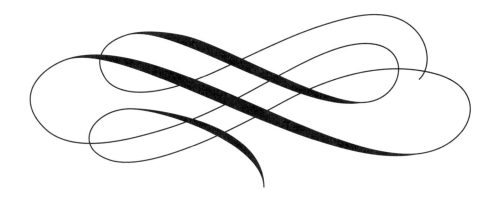

Philosophical Problems

Philosophical Problems

FIFTH EDITION

Samuel Enoch Stumpf
Late, Vanderbilt University

James Fieser
University of Tennessee at Martin

Boston   Burr Ridge, IL   Dubuque, IA   Madison, WI   New York   San Francisco   St. Louis
Bangkok   Bogotá   Caracas   Kuala Lumpur   Lisbon   London   Madrid   Mexico City
Milan   Montreal   New Delhi   Santiago   Seoul   Singapore   Sydney   Taipei   Toronto

The Meaning of Life

"*P*hilosophy" literally means the love of wisdom, and in its earliest usage it referred to all branches of knowledge, except technical skills such as art, literature, or craftsmanship. By the nineteenth century, various branches of "philosophical" learning attained their own independent identities. The natural sciences threw off their earlier designation as *natural philosophy*. Once part of a broad discipline called *moral philosophy*, psychology and economics became separate studies in their own rights. What remains of philosophy today is a variety of speculative subjects that do not fit into the usual molds of scientific inquiry, but which nevertheless demand our serious attention and reflection. This book contains selections from the principal areas of philosophical inquiry.

A theme that ties together most branches of philosophy is a concern with the overall value of human life, which German philosophers sometimes call *Lebensphilosophie*, or the *philosophy of life*. What is life's purpose or meaning? Whether there is a meaning to any person's life might depend upon whether the universe itself has some overall purpose. We sometimes feel that as our scientific knowledge of the immense galaxies in space increases, the significance of individual people becomes ever more diminished. When we look down at the earth from an airplane, we appear to be infinitesimal. It is thus natural to wonder why we take ourselves so seriously, are full of anxiety about our futures, and search earnestly for the meaning of life.

Infinitude of interstellar space is matched by yet another equally impressive infinitude that we find in the micro-world of molecular biology and particle physics. This puts human beings between twin infinities so that what is lost to human significance when viewed from vast outer space is restored when compared with the depth of microscopic reality. Moreover, the overriding fact is that our human minds are capable of grasping the structures of these two worlds so that human calculations can successfully place a machine on the moon and also successfully manipulate the world of microbiology. What this means is that while there is no overwhelming evidence of a purpose to the universe, neither is it surprising that our human minds can raise questions about the meaning of existence.

As we will see throughout this book, many philosophers offered broad visions of human existence that have clear implications on the question of life's meaning. For example, for Aristotle (384–322 B.C.E.) the concept of *purpose* is fundamental to our meaning. Everything, he said, strives to fulfill its purpose, and it is not difficult to discover what that purpose is. Purpose and function are closely related. Each part of our bodies has a function: the eyes to see, the heart to circulate the blood, and the lungs to supply oxygen. Aristotle asks whether it makes sense to say, on the one hand, that every organ of the body has a purpose but that, on the other hand, when all these organs are united into a complete person, such a unified person has no specific function or purpose. Surely, he says, our human purpose is to fulfill all our natural functions, which include not only our physical capacities but also our passions and ultimately our intellectual powers. To Aristotle's natural philosophy, Thomas Aquinas (1224–1274) added the dimension of religion, which connects our natural functions and purpose to an eternal destiny of life with God. But the optimism of these philosophical and theological definitions of the meaning of life were ultimately challenged by the impact of science and skepticism. David Hume (1711–1776) in particular rejected the notion of cause and effect upon which earlier thinkers had relied to prove that the universe has a source of order, purpose, and meaning. While Hume ended his philosophical investigations as a skeptic, he made the significant comment that "to whatever length one may push his speculative principles, he must act and live and converse like other men. . . . It is impossible for him to persevere in total skepticism, or make it appear in his conduct for a few hours."

Aside from the general picture of life's meaning that we can derive from various philosophical systems, many of civilizations' great philosophers addressed the issue head on. In *The Apology,* Plato (427–347 B.C.E.) discusses the trial of his teacher Socrates (469–399 B.C.E.). In one of the more dramatic pieces of world literature, Socrates is put on trial for atheism and corrupting the youth, and during his defense he makes the famous statement that "an unexamined life is not worth living." It could be that Socrates was brought to trial as a result of his constant use of his Socratic method—persistently questioning and answering his Athenian colleagues, often quite impolitely. Through this method, he challenged traditional ideas and showed that most people did not know what they pretended to know. According to many of his contemporaries, philosophers such as Socrates undermined the foundations of society by casting doubt on traditional ideas. The heart of Socrates' defense was that his method of philosophy was not a threat but was of the greatest value to Athens; he was in effect a useful gadfly on the body politic through his constant personal and fearless pursuit of truth. Athenian legal tradition permitted a defendant to speak at the end of a trial and suggest his own sentence. In view of his role as an important provocateur, Socrates claimed that as an alternative to the death sentence rendered by the court, he should instead be given lifelong privileges in the *prytaneum.* The prytaneum was an institution set up in Athens to honor famous people, athletes, generals, and public benefactors. Socrates asserted, "there is no reward, Athenians, so suitable for me as receiving meals in the prytaneum. It is a much more suitable reward for [me] than for any of you who has won a victory at the Olympic games with his horse or his chariots. Such a man only makes you seem happy, but I make you really happy."

Around the time of Socrates—on the other side of the world and in another cultural tradition—the Chinese philosopher Chuang-tzu (c. 250 B.C.E.) offered a different account of life's purpose. One of the founding philosophers of the Taoist tradition, Chuang-tzu argued that we must live our lives in accord with the *Tao*. The term *Tao* simply means "way" or "path" but in the context of the Taoist philosophy it means the way of nature. To live in accord with the Tao means that we should model our lives and society after the simple and spontaneous course of events in the natural world. A brilliant storyteller, Chuang-tzu illustrates the key notions of Taoism through lively tales, rather than with tedious discourses. In the "Tale of the Butcher," he describes the Taoist notion of nonaction (*wu wei*), which involves nonaggressive and spontaneous behavior. In the "Tale of the Dying Men," he tells us how we should accept the natural process of transformation in our lives, from birth, through sickness and death, and finally through our biological decay. In the "Tale of the Horses" he rejects the artificial codes of morality that politicians have imposed on us, and he recommends that we simply follow the harmonious instincts that nature has given us.

In *My Confession*, Russian novelist Leo Tolstoy (1828–1910) describes his personal history, in which he discovered that no amount of achievement, wealth, or fame can prevent a person from being concerned about the meaning of life. According to his *Confession*, Tolstoy found a meaning for himself in religious faith—although he does not describe in any detail the elements of that faith. In *Existentialism Is a Humanism*, twentieth-century French philosopher Jean Paul Sartre (1905–1980) expresses the point of view of atheistic existentialism. He argues here that we are under a duty to create our own values and meanings, but not just any values. Sartre argues that those values should be the ones that would be consistent with everyone's behaving according to them. In spite of his atheism, Sartre's prescription for behavior, if it is to be authentic, requires virtually as much choice and commitment as religion itself.

A Life Worth Living*

Plato (427–347 B.C.E.)

[SOCRATES' OLD ACCUSERS]

How you, O Athenians, have been affected by my accusers, I cannot tell; but I know that they almost made me forget who I was—so persuasively did they speak; and yet they have hardly uttered a word of truth. But of the many falsehoods told by them, there was one which quite amazed me;—I mean when they said that you should be upon your guard and not allow yourselves to be deceived by the force of my eloquence. To say this, when they were certain to be detected as soon as I opened my lips and proved myself to be anything but a great speaker, did indeed appear to me most shameless—unless by the force of eloquence they mean the force of truth; for is such is their meaning, I admit that I am eloquent. But in how different a way from theirs! Well, as I was saying, they have scarcely spoken the truth at all; but from me you shall hear the whole truth: not, however, delivered after their manner in a set oration duly ornamented with words and phrases. No, by heaven! but I shall use the words and arguments which occur to me at the moment; for I am confident in the justice of my cause (or, I am certain that I am right in taking this course): at my time of life I ought not to be appearing before you, O men of Athens, in the character of a juvenile orator—let no one expect it of me. And I must beg of you to grant me a favor:—If I defend myself in my accustomed manner, and you hear me using the words which I have been in the habit of using in the

---

*From Plato, "The Apology."

agora, at the tables of the money-changers, or anywhere else, I would ask you not to be surprised, and not to interrupt me on this account. For I am more than seventy years of age, and appearing now for the first time in a court of law, I am quite a stranger to the language of the place; and therefore I would have you regard me as if I were really a stranger, whom you would excuse if he spoke in his native tongue, and after the fashion of his country:—Am I making an unfair request of you? Never mind the manner, which may or may not be good; but think only of the truth of my words, and give heed to that: let the speaker speak truly and the judge decide justly.

And first, I have to reply to the older charges and to my first accusers, and then I will go on to the later ones. For of old I have had many accusers, who have accused me falsely to you during many years; and I am more afraid of them than of Anytus and his associates, who are dangerous, too, in their own way. But far more dangerous are the others, who began when you were children, and took possession of your minds with their falsehoods, telling of one Socrates, a wise man, who speculated about the heaven above, and searched into the earth beneath, and made the worse appear the better cause. The disseminators of this tale are the accusers whom I dread; for their hearers are apt to fancy that such enquirers do not believe in the existence of the gods. And they are many, and their charges against me are of ancient date, and they were made by them in the days when you were more impressible than you are now—in childhood, or it may have been in youth—and the cause when heard went by default, for there was none to answer. And hardest of all, I do not know and cannot tell the names of my accusers; unless in the chance case of a Comic poet. All who from envy and malice have persuaded you—some of them having first convinced themselves—all this class of men are most difficult to deal with; for I cannot have them up here, and cross-examine them, and therefore I must simply fight with shadows in my own defense, and argue when there is no one who answers. I will ask you then to assume with me, as I was saying, that my opponents are of two kinds; one recent, the other ancient: and I hope that you will see the propriety of my answering the latter first, for these accusations you heard long before the others, and much oftener.

Well, then, I must make my defense, and endeavor to clear away in a short time, a slander which has lasted a long time. May I succeed, if to succeed be for my good and yours, or likely to avail me in my cause! The task is not an easy one; I quite understand the nature of it. And so leaving the event with God, in obedience to the law I will now make my defense.

I will begin at the beginning, and ask what is the accusation which has given rise to the slander of me, and in fact has encouraged Meletus to proof this charge against me. Well, what do the slanderers say? They shall be my prosecutors, and I will sum up their words in an affidavit: "Socrates is an evil-doer, and a curious person, who searches into things under the earth and in heaven, and he makes the worse appear the better cause; and he teaches the aforesaid doctrines to others." Such is the nature of the accusation: it is just what you have yourselves seen in the comedy of Aristophanes (Aristoph., Clouds.), who has introduced a man whom he calls Socrates, going about and saying that he walks in air, and talking a deal of nonsense concerning matters of which I do not pretend to know either much or little—not that I mean to speak disparagingly of any one who is a student of natural philosophy. I should be very sorry if Meletus could bring so grave a charge against me. But the simple truth is, O Athenians, that I have nothing to do with physical speculations. Very many of those here present are witnesses to the truth of this, and to them I appeal. Speak then, you who have heard me, and tell your neighbors whether any of you have ever known me hold forth in few words or in many upon such matters . . . You hear their answer. And from what they say of this part of the charge you will be able to judge of the truth of the rest.

As little foundation is there for the report that I am a teacher, and take money; this accusation has no more truth in it than the other. Although, if a man were really able to instruct mankind, to receive money for giving instruction would, in my opinion, be an honor to him. There is Gorgias of Leontium, and Prodicus of Ceos, and Hippias of Elis, who go the round of the cities, and are able to persuade the young men to leave their own citizens by whom they might be taught for nothing, and come to them whom they not only pay, but are thankful if they may be allowed to pay them. There is at this time a Parian philosopher residing in Athens, of whom I have heard; and I came to hear of him in this way:—I came across a man who has spent a world of money on the Sophists, Callias, the son of Hipponicus, and knowing that he had sons, I asked him: "Callias," I said, "if your two sons were foals or calves, there would be no difficulty in finding some one to put over them; we should hire a trainer of horses, or a farmer probably, who would improve and perfect them in their own proper virtue and excellence; but as they are human beings, whom are you thinking of placing over them? Is there any one who understands human and political virtue? You must have thought about the matter, for you have sons; is there any one?" "There is," he said. "Who is he?" said I; "and of what country? and what does he charge?" "Evenus the Parian," he replied; "he is the man, and his charge is five minae." Happy is Evenus, I said to myself, if he really has this wisdom, and teaches at such a moderate charge. Had I the same, I should have been very proud and conceited; but the truth is that I have no knowledge of the kind.

[THE ORACLE OF DELPHI]

I dare say, Athenians, that some one among you will reply, "Yes, Socrates, but what is the origin of these accusations which are brought against you; there must have been something strange which you have been doing? All these rumors and this talk about you would never have arisen if you had been like other men: tell us, then, what is the cause of them, for we should be sorry to judge hastily of you." Now I regard this as a fair challenge, and I will endeavor to explain to you the reason why I am called wise and have such an evil fame. Please to attend then. And although some of you may think that I am joking, I declare that I will tell you the entire truth. Men of Athens, this reputation of mine has come of a certain sort of wisdom which I possess. If you ask me what kind of wisdom, I reply, wisdom such as may perhaps be attained by man, for to that extent I am inclined to believe that I am wise; whereas the persons of whom I was speaking have a superhuman wisdom which I may fail to describe, because I have it not myself; and he who says that I have, speaks falsely, and is taking away my character. And here, O men of Athens, I must beg you not to interrupt me, even if I seem to say something extravagant. For the word which I will speak is not mine. I will refer you to a witness who is worthy of credit; that witness shall be the God of Delphi—he will tell you about my wisdom, if I have any, and of what sort it is. You must have known Chaerephon; he was early a friend of mine, and also a friend of yours, for he shared in the recent exile of the people, and returned with you. Well, Chaerephon, as you know, was very impetuous in all his doings, and he went to Delphi and boldly asked the oracle to tell him whether—as I was saying, I must beg you not to interrupt—he asked the oracle to tell him whether anyone was wiser than I was, and the Pythian prophetess answered, that there was no man wiser. Chaerephon is dead himself; but his brother, who is in court, will confirm the truth of what I am saying.

Why do I mention this? Because I am going to explain to you why I have such an evil name. When I heard the answer, I said to myself, What can the god mean? and what is the interpretation of his riddle? for I know that I have no wisdom, small or great. What then can he mean when he says that I am the wisest of men? And yet he is a god, and cannot lie; that would be against his nature. After long consideration, I thought of a method of trying the question. I reflected that if I could only find a man wiser than myself, then I might go to the god with a refutation in my hand. I should say to him, "Here is a man who is wiser than I am; but you said that I was the wisest." Accordingly I went to one who had the reputation of wisdom, and observed him—his name I need not mention; he was a politician whom I selected for examination—and the result was as follows: When I began to talk with him, I could not help thinking that he was not really wise, although he was thought wise by many, and still wiser by himself; and thereupon I tried to explain to him that he thought himself wise, but was not really wise; and the consequence was that he hated me, and his enmity was shared by several who were present and heard me. So I left him, saying to myself, as I went away: Well, although I do not suppose that either of us knows anything really beautiful and good, I am better off than he is,—for he knows nothing, and thinks that he knows; I neither know nor think that I know. In this latter particular, then, I seem to have slightly the advantage of him. Then I went to another who had still higher pretensions to wisdom, and my conclusion was exactly the same. Whereupon I made another enemy of him, and of many others besides him.

Then I went to one man after another, being not unconscious of the enmity which I provoked, and I lamented and feared this: but necessity was laid upon me,—the word of God, I thought, ought to be considered first. And I said to myself, Go I must to all who appear to know, and find out the meaning of the oracle. And I swear to you, Athenians, by the dog I swear!—for I must tell you the truth—the result of my mission was just this: I found that the men most in repute were all but the most foolish; and that others less esteemed were really wiser and better. I will tell you the tale of my wanderings and of the "Herculean" labors, as I may call them, which I endured only to find at last the oracle irrefutable. After the politicians, I went to the poets; tragic, dithyrambic, and all sorts. And there, I said to myself, you will be instantly detected; now you will find out that you are more ignorant than they are. Accordingly, I took them some of the most elaborate passages in their own writings, and asked what was the meaning of them— thinking that they would teach me something. Will you believe me? I am almost ashamed to confess the truth, but I must say that there is hardly a person present who would not have talked better about their poetry than they did themselves. Then I knew that not by wisdom do poets write poetry, but by a sort of genius and inspiration; they are like diviners or soothsayers who also say many fine things, but do not understand the meaning of them. The poets appeared to me to be much in the same case; and I further observed that upon the strength of their poetry they believed themselves to be the wisest of men in other things in which they were not wise. So I departed, conceiving myself to be superior to them for the same reason that I was superior to the politicians.

At last I went to the artisans. I was conscious that I knew nothing at all, as I may say, and I was sure that they knew many fine things; and here I was not mistaken, for they did know many things of which I was ignorant, and in this they certainly were wiser than I was. But I observed that even the good artisans fell into the same error as the poets;—because they were good workmen they thought that they also knew all sorts of high matters, and this defect in them overshadowed their wisdom; and therefore I asked myself on behalf of the oracle, whether I would like to be as I was, neither having their knowledge nor their ignorance, or like them in both; and I made answer to myself and to the oracle that I was better off as I was.

This inquisition has led to my having many enemies of the worst and most dangerous kind, and has given occasion also to many calumnies. And I am called wise, for my hearers always imagine that I myself possess the wisdom which I find wanting in others: but the truth is, O men of Athens, that God only is wise; and by his answer he intends to show that the wisdom of men is worth little or nothing; he is not speaking of Socrates, he is only using my name by way of illustration, as if he said, He, O men, is the wisest, who, like Socrates, knows that his wisdom is in truth worth nothing. And so I go about the world, obedient to the god, and search and make enquiry into the wisdom of any one, whether citizen or stranger, who appears to be wise; and if he is not wise, then in vindication of the oracle I show him that he is not wise; and my occupation quite absorbs me, and I have no time to give either to any public matter of interest or to any concern of my own, but I am in utter poverty by reason of my devotion to the god.

There is another thing:—young men of the richer classes, who have not much to do, come about me of their own accord; they like to hear the pretenders examined, and they often imitate me, and proceed to examine others; there are plenty of persons, as they quickly discover, who think that they know something, but really know little or nothing; and then those who are examined by them instead of being angry with themselves are angry with me: This confounded Socrates, they say; this villainous misleader of youth!—and then if somebody asks them, Why, what evil does he practice or teach? they do not know, and cannot tell; but in order that they may not appear to be at a loss, they repeat the ready-made charges which are used against all philosophers about teaching things up in the clouds and under the earth, and having no gods, and making the worse appear the better cause; for they do not like to confess that their pretence of knowledge has been detected—which is the truth; and as they are numerous and ambitious and energetic, and are drawn up in battle array and have persuasive tongues, they have filled your ears with their loud and inveterate calumnies. And this is the reason why my three accusers, Meletus and Anytus and Lycon, have set upon me; Meletus, who has a quarrel with me on behalf of the poets; Anytus, on behalf of the craftsmen and politicians; Lycon, on behalf of the rhetoricians: and as I said at the beginning, I cannot expect to get rid of such a mass of calumny all in a moment. And this, O men of Athens, is the truth and the whole truth; I have concealed nothing, I have dissembled nothing. And yet, I know that my plainness of speech makes them hate me, and what is their hatred but a proof that I am speaking the truth?—Hence has arisen the prejudice against me; and this is the reason of it, as you will find out either in this or in any future enquiry.

[MELETUS AND THE NEW ACCUSERS]

I have said enough in my defense against the first class of my accusers; I turn to the second class. They are headed by Meletus, that good man and true lover of his country, as he calls himself. Against these, too, I must try to make a defense:—Let their affidavit be read: it contains something of this kind: It says that Socrates is a doer of evil, who corrupts the youth; and who does not believe in the gods of the state, but has other new divinities of his own. Such is the charge; and now let us examine the particular counts. He says that I am a doer of evil, and corrupt the youth; but I say, O men of Athens, that Meletus is a doer of evil, in that he pretends to be in earnest when he is only in jest, and is so eager to bring men to trial from a pretended zeal and interest about matters in which he really never had the smallest interest. And the truth of this I will endeavor to prove to you.

Come hither, Meletus, and let me ask a question of you. You think a great deal about the improvement of youth?

MELETUS: Yes, I do.

SOCRATES: Tell the judges, then, who is their improver; for you must know, as you have taken the pains to discover their corrupter, and are citing and accusing me before them. Speak, then, and tell the judges who their improver is. Observe, Meletus, that you are silent, and have nothing to say. But is not this rather disgraceful, and a very considerable proof of what I was saying, that you have no interest in the matter? Speak up, friend, and tell us who their improver is.

MELETUS: The laws.

SOCRATES: But that, my good sir, is not my meaning. I want to know who the person is, who, in the first place, knows the laws.

MELETUS: The judges, Socrates, who are present in court.

SOCRATES: What do you mean to say, Meletus, that they are able to instruct and improve youth?

MELETUS: Certainly they are.

SOCRATES: What, all of them, or some only and not others?

MELETUS: All of them.

SOCRATES: By the goddess Here, that is good news! There are plenty of improvers, then. And what do you say of the audience,—do they improve them?

MELETUS: Yes, they do.

SOCRATES: And the senators?

MELETUS: Yes, the senators improve them.

SOCRATES: But perhaps the members of the citizen assembly corrupt them?—or do they too improve them?

MELETUS: They improve them.

SOCRATES: Then every Athenian improves and elevates them; all with the exception of myself; and I alone am their corrupter? Is that what you affirm?

MELETUS: That is what I stoutly affirm.

SOCRATES: I am very unfortunate if that is true. But suppose I ask you a question: Would you say that this also holds true in the case of horses? Does one man do them harm and all the world good? Is not the exact opposite of this true? One man is able to do them good, or at least not many;—the trainer of horses, that is to say, does them good, and others who have to do with them rather injure them? Is not that true, Meletus, of horses, or any other animals? Whether you and Anytus say yes or no, that is no matter. Happy indeed would be the condition of youth if they had one corrupter only, and all the rest of the world were their improvers. And you, Meletus, have sufficiently shown that you never had a thought about the young: your carelessness is seen in your not caring about matters spoken of in this very indictment.

And now, Meletus, I must ask you another question: Which is better, to live among bad citizens, or among good ones? Answer, friend, I say; for that is a question which may be easily answered. Do not the good do their neighbors good, and the bad do them evil?

MELETUS: Certainly.

SOCRATES: And is there anyone who would rather be injured than benefited by those who live with him? Answer, my good friend; the law requires you to answer—does anyone like to be injured?

MELETUS: Certainly not.

SOCRATES: And when you accuse me of corrupting and deteriorating the youth, do you allege that I corrupt them intentionally or unintentionally?

MELETUS: Intentionally, I say.

SOCRATES: But you have just admitted that the good do their neighbors good, and the evil do them evil. Now is that a truth which your superior wisdom has recognized thus early in life, and am I, at my age, in such darkness and ignorance as not to know that if a man with whom I have to live is corrupted by me, I am very likely to be harmed by him, and yet I corrupt him, and intentionally, too;—that is what you are saying, and of that you will never persuade me or any other human being. But either I do not corrupt them, or I corrupt them unintentionally, so that on either view of the case you lie. If my offense is unintentional, the law has no cognizance of unintentional offenses: you ought to have taken me privately, and warned and admonished me; for if I had been better advised, I should have left off doing what I only did unintentionally—no doubt I should; whereas you hated to converse with me or teach me, but you indicted me in this court, which is a place not of instruction, but of punishment.

I have shown, Athenians, as I was saying, that Meletus has no care at all, great or small, about the matter. But still I should like to know, Meletus, in what I am affirmed to corrupt the young. I suppose you mean, as I infer from your indictment, that I teach them not to acknowledge the gods which the state acknowledges, but some other new divinities or spiritual agencies in their stead. These are the lessons which corrupt the youth, as you say.

MELETUS: Yes, that I say emphatically.

SOCRATES: Then, by the gods, Meletus, of whom we are speaking, tell me and the court, in somewhat plainer terms, what you mean! for I do not as yet understand whether you affirm that I teach others to acknowledge some gods, and therefore do believe in gods and am not an entire atheist—this you do not lay to my charge; but only that they are not the same gods which the city recognizes—the charge is that they are different gods. Or, do you mean to say that I am an atheist simply, and a teacher of atheism?

MELETUS: I mean the latter—that you are a complete atheist.

SOCRATES: That is an extraordinary statement, Meletus. Why do you say that? Do you mean that I do not believe in the godhead of the sun or moon, which is the common creed of all men?

MELETUS: I assure you, judges, that he does not believe in them; for he says that the sun is stone, and the moon earth.

SOCRATES: Friend Meletus, you think that you are accusing Anaxagoras; and you have but a bad opinion of the judges, if you fancy them ignorant to such a degree as not to know that those doctrines are found in the books of Anaxagoras the Clazomenian, who is full of them. And these are the doctrines which the youth are said to learn of Socrates, when there are not infrequently exhibitions of them at the theater (price of admission one drachma at the most); and they might cheaply purchase them, and laugh at Socrates if he pretends to father such eccentricities. And so, Meletus, you really think that I do not believe in any god?

MELETUS: I swear by Zeus that you believe absolutely in none at all.

SOCRATES: You are a liar, Meletus, not believed even by yourself. For I cannot help thinking, O men of Athens, that Meletus is reckless and impudent, and that he has written this indictment in a spirit of mere wantonness and youthful bravado. Has he not compounded a riddle, thinking to try me? He said to himself:—I shall see whether this wise Socrates will discover my ingenious contradiction, or whether I shall be able to deceive him and the rest of them. For he certainly does appear to me to contradict himself in the indictment as much as if he said that Socrates is guilty of not believing in the gods, and yet of believing in them—but this surely is a piece of fun.

I should like you, O men of Athens, to join me in examining what I conceive to be his inconsistency; and do you, Meletus, answer. And I must remind you that you are not to interrupt me if I speak in my accustomed manner.

Did ever man, Meletus, believe in the existence of human things, and not of human beings? . . . I wish, men of Athens, that he would answer, and not be always trying to get up an interruption. Did ever any man believe in horsemanship, and not in horses? or in flute-playing, and not in flute-players? No, my friend; I will answer to you and to the court, as you refuse to answer for yourself. There is no man who ever did. But now please to answer the next question: Can a man believe in spiritual and divine agencies, and not in spirits or demigods?

MELETUS: He cannot.

SOCRATES: I am glad that I have extracted that answer, by the assistance of the court; nevertheless you swear in the indictment that I teach and believe in divine or spiritual agencies (new or old, no matter for that); at any rate, I believe in spiritual agencies, as you say and swear in the affidavit; but if I believe in divine beings, I must believe in spirits or demigods;—is not that true? Yes, that is true, for I may assume that your silence gives assent to that. Now what are spirits or demigods? are they not either gods or the sons of gods? Is that true?

MELETUS: Yes, that is true.

SOCRATES: But this is just the ingenious riddle of which I was speaking: the demigods or spirits are gods, and you say first that I don't believe in gods, and then again that I do believe in gods; that is, if I believe in demigods. For if the demigods are the illegitimate sons of gods, whether by the Nymphs or by any other mothers, as is thought, that, as all men will allow, necessarily implies the existence of their parents. You might as well affirm the existence of mules, and deny that of horses and asses. Such nonsense, Meletus, could only have been intended by you as a trial of me. You have put this into the indictment because you had nothing real of which to accuse me. But no one who has a particle of understanding will ever be convinced by you that the same man can believe in divine and superhuman things, and yet not believe that there are gods and demigods and heroes.

[SOCRATES DEFENDS HIS COURSE OF LIFE]

I have said enough in answer to the charge of Meletus: any elaborate defense is unnecessary, but I know only too well how many are the enmities which I have incurred, and this is what will be my destruction if I am destroyed;—not Meletus, nor yet Anytus, but the envy and detraction of the world, which has been the death of many good men, and will probably be the death of many more; there is no danger of my being the last of them.

Some one will say: And are you not ashamed, Socrates, of a course of life which is likely to bring you to an untimely end? To him I may fairly answer: There you are mistaken: a man who is good for anything ought not to calculate the chance of living or dying; he ought only to consider whether in doing anything he is doing right or wrong—acting the part of a good man or of a bad. Whereas, upon your view, the heroes who fell at Troy were not good for much, and the son of Thetis above all, who altogether despised danger in comparison with disgrace; and when he was so eager to slay Hector, his goddess mother said to him, that if he avenged his companion Patroclus, and slew Hector, he would die himself—"Fate," she said, in these or the like words, "waits for you next after Hector;" he, receiving this warning, utterly despised danger and death, and instead of fearing them, feared rather to live in dishonor, and not to avenge his friend. "Let me die forthwith," he replies, "and be avenged of my enemy, rather than abide here by the beaked ships, a laughing-stock and a burden of the earth." Had Achilles any thought of death and danger? For wherever a man's place is, whether the place which he has chosen or that in which he has been placed by a commander, there he ought to remain in the hour of danger; he should not think of death or of anything but of disgrace. And this, O men of Athens, is a true saying.

Strange, indeed, would be my conduct, O men of Athens, if I who, when I was ordered by the generals whom you chose to command me at Potidaea and Amphipolis and Delium, remained where they placed me, like any other man, facing death—if now, when, as I conceive and imagine, God orders me to fulfil the philosopher's mission of searching into myself and other men, I were to desert my post through fear of death, or any other fear; that would indeed be strange, and I might justly be arraigned in court for denying the existence of the gods, if I disobeyed the oracle because I was afraid of death, fancying that I was wise when I was not wise. For the fear of death is indeed the pretence of wisdom, and not real wisdom, being a pretence of knowing the unknown; and no one knows whether death, which men in their fear apprehend to be the greatest evil, may not be the greatest good. Is not this ignorance of a disgraceful sort, the ignorance which is the conceit that a man knows what he does not know? And in this respect only I believe myself to differ from men in general, and may perhaps claim to be wiser than they are:—that whereas I know but little of the world below, I do not suppose that I know: but I do know that injustice and disobedience to a better, whether God or man, is evil and dishonorable, and I will never fear or avoid a possible good rather than a certain evil. And therefore if you let me go now, and are not convinced by Anytus, who said that since I had been prosecuted I must be put to death; (or if not that I ought never to have been prosecuted at all); and that if I escape now, your sons will all be utterly ruined by listening to my words—if you say to me, Socrates, this time we will not mind Anytus, and you shall be let off, but upon one condition, that you are not to enquire and speculate in this way any more, and that if you are caught doing so again you shall die;—if this was the condition on which you let me go, I should reply:

Men of Athens, I honor and love you; but I shall obey God rather than you, and while I have life and strength I shall never cease from the practice and teaching of philosophy, exhorting any one whom I meet and saying to him after my manner: You, my friend,—a citizen of the great and mighty and wise city of Athens,—are you not ashamed of heaping up the greatest amount of money and honor and reputation, and caring so little about wisdom and truth and the greatest improvement of the soul, which you never regard or heed at all? And if the person with whom I am arguing, says: Yes, but I do care; then I do not leave him or let him go at once; but I proceed to interrogate and examine and cross-examine him, and if I think that he has no virtue in him, but only says that he has, I reproach him with undervaluing the greater, and overvaluing the less. And I shall repeat the same words to every one whom I meet, young and old, citizen and alien, but especially to the citizens, inasmuch as they are my brethren. For know that this is the command of God; and I believe that no greater good has ever happened in the state than my service to the God. For I do nothing but go about persuading you all, old and young alike, not to take thought for your persons or your properties, but first and chiefly to care about the greatest improvement of the soul. I tell you that virtue is not given by money, but that from virtue comes money and every other good of man, public as well as private. This is my teaching, and if this is the doctrine which corrupts the youth, I am a mischievous person. But if any one says that this is not my teaching, he is speaking an untruth. Wherefore, O men of Athens, I say to you, do as Anytus bids or not as Anytus bids, and either acquit me or not; but whichever you do, understand that I shall never alter my ways, not even if I have to die many times.

Men of Athens, do not interrupt, but hear me; there was an understanding between us that you should hear me to the end: I have something more to say, at which you may be inclined to cry out; but I believe that to hear me will be good for you, and therefore I beg that you will not cry out. I would have you know, that if you kill such an one as I am, you will injure yourselves more than you will injure me. Nothing will injure me, not Meletus nor yet Anytus—they cannot, for a bad man is not permitted to injure a better than himself. I do not deny that Anytus may, perhaps, kill him, or drive him into exile, or deprive him of civil rights; and he may imagine, and others may imagine, that he is inflicting a great injury upon him: but there I do not agree. For the evil of doing as he is doing—the evil of unjustly taking away the life of another—is greater far.

And now, Athenians, I am not going to argue for my own sake, as you may think, but for yours, that you may not sin against the God by condemning me, who am his gift to you. For if you kill me you will not easily find a successor to me, who, if I may use such a ludicrous figure of speech, am a sort of gadfly, given to the state by God; and the state is a great and noble steed who is tardy in his motions owing to his very size, and requires to be stirred into life. I am that gadfly which God has attached to the state, and all day long and in all places am always fastening upon you, arousing and persuading and reproaching you. You will not easily find another like me, and therefore I would advise you to spare me. I dare say that you may feel out of temper (like a person who is suddenly awakened from sleep), and you think that you might easily strike me dead as Anytus advises, and then you would sleep on for the remainder of your lives, unless God in his care of you sent you another gadfly. When I say that I am given to you by God, the proof of my mission is this:—if I had been like other men, I should not have neglected all my own concerns or patiently seen the neglect of them during all these years, and have been doing yours, coming to you individually like a father or elder brother, exhorting you to regard virtue; such conduct, I say, would be unlike human nature. If I had gained anything, or if my exhortations had been paid, there would have been some sense in my doing so; but now, as you will perceive, not even the impudence of my accusers dares to say that I have ever exacted or sought pay of any one; of that they have no witness. And I have a sufficient witness to the truth of what I say—my poverty.

Some one may wonder why I go about in private giving advice and busy-ing myself with the concerns of others, but do not venture to come forward in public and advise the state. I will tell you why. You have heard me speak at sundry times and in divers places of an oracle or sign which comes to me, and is the divinity which Meletus ridicules in the indictment. This sign, which is a kind of voice, first began to come to me when I was a child; it always forbids but never commands me to do anything which I am going to do. This is what deters me from being a politician. And rightly, as I think. For I am certain, O men of Athens, that if I had engaged in politics, I should have perished long ago, and done no good either to you or to myself. And do not be offended at my telling you the truth: for the truth is, that no man who goes to war with you or any other multitude, honestly striving against the many lawless and unrighteous deeds which are done in a state, will save his life; he who will fight for the right, if he would live even for a brief space, must have a private station and not a public one.

I can give you convincing evidence of what I say, not words only, but what you value far more—actions. Let me relate to you a passage of my own life which will prove to you that I should never have yielded to injustice from any fear of death, and that "as I should have refused to yield" I must have died at once. I will tell you a tale of the courts, not very interesting perhaps, but nevertheless true. The only office of state which I ever held, O men of Athens, was that of senator: the tribe Antiochis, which is my tribe, had the presidency at the trial of the generals who had not taken up the bodies of the slain after the battle of Arginusae; and you proposed to try them in a body, contrary to law, as you all thought afterwards; but at the time I was the only one of the Prytanes who was opposed to the illegality, and I gave my vote against you; and when the orators threatened to impeach and arrest me, and you called and shouted, I made up my mind that I would run the risk, having law and justice with me, rather than take part in your injustice because I feared imprisonment and death. This happened in the days of the democracy. But when the oligarchy of the Thirty was in power, they sent for me and four others into the rotunda, and bade us bring Leon the Salaminian from Salamis, as they wanted to put him to death. This was a specimen of the sort of com-mands which they were always giving with the view of implicating as many as possible in their crimes; and then I showed, not in word only but in deed, that, if I may be allowed to use such an expression, I cared not a straw for death, and that my great and only care was lest I should do an unrighteous or unholy thing. For the strong arm of that oppressive power did not frighten me into doing wrong; and when we came out of the rotunda the other four went to Salamis and fetched Leon, but I went quietly home. For which I might have lost my life, had not the power of the Thirty shortly afterwards come to an end. And many will witness to my words.

Now do you really imagine that I could have survived all these years, if I had led a public life, supposing that like a good man I had always maintained the right and had made justice, as I ought, the first thing? No indeed, men of Athens, neither I nor any other man. But I have been always the same in all my actions, public as well as private, and never have I yielded any base compliance to those who are slanderously termed my disciples, or to any other. Not that I have any regular disciples. But if any one likes to come and hear me while I am pursuing my mission, whether he be young or old, he is not excluded. Nor do I converse only with those who pay; but any one, whether he be rich or poor, may ask and answer me and listen to my words; and whether he turns out to be a bad man or a good one, neither result can be justly imputed to me; for I never taught or professed to teach him anything. And if any one says that he has ever learned or heard anything from me in private which all the world has not heard, let me tell you that he is lying.

But I shall be asked, Why do people delight in continually conversing with you? I have told you already, Athenians, the whole truth about this matter: they like to hear the cross-examination of the pretenders to wisdom; there is amusement in it. Now this duty of cross-examining other men has been imposed upon me by God; and has been signified to me by oracles, visions, and in every way in which the will of divine power was ever intimated to any one. This is true, O Athenians, or, if not true, would be soon refuted. If I am or have been corrupting the youth, those of them who are now grown up and have become sensible that I gave them bad advice in the days of their youth should come forward as accusers, and take their revenge; or if they do not like to come themselves, some of their relatives, fathers, brothers, or other kinsmen, should say what evil their families have suffered at my hands. Now is their time. Many of them I see in the court. There is Crito, who is of the same age and of the same deme with myself, and there is Critobulus his son, whom I also see. Then again there is Lysanias of Sphettus, who is the father of Aeschines—he is present; and also there is Antiphon of Cephisus, who is the father of Epigenes; and there are the brothers of several who have associated with me. There is Nicostratus the son of Theosdotides, and the brother of Theodotus (now Theodotus himself is dead, and therefore he, at any rate, will not seek to stop him); and there is Paralus the son of Demodocus, who had a brother Theages; and Adeimantus the son of Ariston, whose brother Plato is present; and Aeantodorus, who is the brother of Apollodorus, whom I also see. I might mention a great many others, some of whom Meletus should have produced as witnesses in the course of his speech; and let him still produce

them, if he has forgotten—I will make way for him. And let him say, if he has
any testimony of the sort which he can produce. Nay, Athenians, the very opposite is the truth. For all these are ready to witness on behalf of the corrupter,
of the injurer of their kindred, as Meletus and Anytus call me; not the corrupted youth only—there might have been a motive for that—but their uncor-
rupted elder relatives. Why should they too support me with their testimony?
Why, indeed, except for the sake of truth and justice, and because they know
that I am speaking the truth, and that Meletus is a liar.

Well, Athenians, this and the like of this is all the defense which I have to
offer. Yet a word more. Perhaps there may be some one who is offended at
me, when he calls to mind how he himself on a similar, or even a less serious
occasion, prayed and entreated the judges with many tears, and how he produced his children in court, which was a moving spectacle, together with a
host of relations and friends; whereas I, who am probably in danger of my life,
will do none of these things. The contrast may occur to his mind, and he may
be set against me, and vote in anger because he is displeased at me on this account. Now if there be such a person among you,—mind, I do not say that
there is,—to him I may fairly reply: My friend, I am a man, and like other men,
a creature of flesh and blood, and not "of wood or stone," as Homer says; and
I have a family, yes, and sons, O Athenians, three in number, one almost a
man, and two others who are still young; and yet I will not bring any of them
hither in order to petition you for an acquittal. And why not? Not from any
self-assertion or want of respect for you. Whether I am or am not afraid of
death is another question, of which I will not now speak. But, having regard to
public opinion, I feel that such conduct would be discreditable to myself, and
to you, and to the whole state. One who has reached my years, and who has a
name for wisdom, ought not to demean himself. Whether this opinion of me
be deserved or not, at any rate the world has decided that Socrates is in some
way superior to other men. And if those among you who are said to be superior in wisdom and courage, and any other virtue, demean themselves in this
way, how shameful is their conduct! I have seen men of reputation, when they
have been condemned, behaving in the strangest manner: they seemed to
fancy that they were going to suffer something dreadful if they died, and that
they could be immortal if you only allowed them to live; and I think that such
are a dishonor to the state, and that any stranger coming in would have said of
them that the most eminent men of Athens, to whom the Athenians themselves give honor and command, are no better than women. And I say that
these things ought not to be done by those of us who have a reputation; and if
they are done, you ought not to permit them; you ought rather to show that
you are far more disposed to condemn the man who gets up a doleful scene
and makes the city ridiculous, than him who holds his peace.

But, setting aside the question of public opinion, there seems to be something wrong in asking a favor of a judge, and thus procuring an acquittal, instead of informing and convincing him. For his duty is, not to make a present
of justice, but to give judgment; and he has sworn that he will judge according
to the laws, and not according to his own good pleasure; and we ought not to

encourage you, nor should you allow yourselves to be encouraged, in this habit of perjury—there can be no piety in that. Do not then require me to do what I consider dishonorable and impious and wrong, especially now, when I am being tried for impiety on the indictment of Meletus. For if, O men of Athens, by force of persuasion and entreaty I could overpower your oaths, then I should be teaching you to believe that there are no gods, and in defending should simply convict myself of the charge of not believing in them. But that is not so—far otherwise. For I do believe that there are gods, and in a sense higher than that in which any of my accusers believe in them. And to you and to God I commit my cause, to be determined by you as is best for you and me.

[SOCRATES RESPONDS TO GUILTY VERDICT]

There are many reasons why I am not grieved, O men of Athens, at the vote of condemnation. I expected it, and am only surprised that the votes are so nearly equal; for I had thought that the majority against me would have been far larger; but now, had thirty votes gone over to the other side, I should have been acquitted. And I may say, I think, that I have escaped Meletus. I may say more; for without the assistance of Anytus and Lycon, any one may see that he would not have had a fifth part of the votes, as the law requires, in which case he would have incurred a fine of a thousand drachmae.

And so he proposes death as the penalty. And what shall I propose on my part, O men of Athens? Clearly that which is my due. And what is my due? What return shall be made to the man who has never had the wit to be idle during his whole life; but has been careless of what the many care for—wealth, and family interests, and military offices, and speaking in the assembly, and magistracies, and plots, and parties. Reflecting that I was really too honest a man to be a politician and live, I did not go where I could do no good to you or to myself; but where I could do the greatest good privately to every one of you, thither I went, and sought to persuade every man among you that he must look to himself, and seek virtue and wisdom before he looks to his private interests, and look to the state before he looks to the interests of the state; and that this should be the order which he observes in all his actions. What shall be done to such an one? Doubtless some good thing, O men of Athens, if he has his reward; and the good should be of a kind suitable to him. What would be a reward suitable to a poor man who is your benefactor, and who desires leisure that he may instruct you? There can be no reward so fitting as maintenance in the Prytaneum, O men of Athens, a reward which he deserves far more than the citizen who has won the prize at Olympia in the horse or chariot race, whether the chariots were drawn by two horses or by many. For I am in want, and he has enough; and he only gives you the appearance of happiness, and I give you the reality. And if I am to estimate the penalty fairly, I should say that maintenance in the Prytaneum is the just return. •

Perhaps you think that I am braving you in what I am saying now, as in what I said before about the tears and prayers. But this is not so. I speak rather

place (?) for heros of olympic champions.

because I am convinced that I never intentionally wronged any one, although I cannot convince you—the time has been too short; if there were a law at Athens, as there is in other cities, that a capital cause should not be decided in one day, then I believe that I should have convinced you. But I cannot in a moment refute great slanders; and, as I am convinced that I never wronged another, I will assuredly not wrong myself. I will not say of myself that I deserve any evil, or propose any penalty. Why should I? because I am afraid of the penalty of death which Meletus proposes? When I do not know whether death is a good or an evil, why should I propose a penalty which would certainly be an evil? Shall I say imprisonment? And why should I live in prison, and be the slave of the magistrates of the year—of the Eleven? Or shall the penalty be a fine, and imprisonment until the fine is paid? There is the same objection. I should have to lie in prison, for money I have none, and cannot pay. And if I say exile (and this may possibly be the penalty which you will affix), I must indeed be blinded by the love of life, if I am so irrational as to expect that when you, who are my own citizens, cannot endure my discourses and words, and have found them so grievous and odious that you will have no more of them, others are likely to endure me. No indeed, men of Athens, that is not very likely. And what a life should I lead, at my age, wandering from city to city, ever changing my place of exile, and always being driven out! For I am quite sure that wherever I go, there, as here, the young men will flock to me; and if I drive them away, their elders will drive me out at their request; and if I let them come, their fathers and friends will drive me out for their sakes.

Some one will say: Yes, Socrates, but cannot you hold your tongue, and then you may go into a foreign city, and no one will interfere with you? Now I have great difficulty in making you understand my answer to this. For if I tell you that to do as you say would be a disobedience to the God, and therefore that I cannot hold my tongue, you will not believe that I am serious; and if I say again that daily to discourse about virtue, and of those other things about which you hear me examining myself and others, is the greatest good of man, and that the unexamined life is not worth living, you are still less likely to believe me. Yet I say what is true, although a thing of which it is hard for me to persuade you. Also, I have never been accustomed to think that I deserve to suffer any harm. Had I money I might have estimated the offence at what I was able to pay, and not have been much the worse. But I have none, and therefore I must ask you to proportion the fine to my means. Well, perhaps I could afford a mina, and therefore I propose that penalty: Plato, Crito, Critobulus, and Apollodorus, my friends here, bid me say thirty minae, and they will be the sureties. Let thirty minae be the penalty; for which sum they will be ample security to you.

[SOCRATES CONSOLES HIS FRIENDS]

Not much time will be gained, O Athenians, in return for the evil name which you will get from the detractors of the city, who will say that you killed Socrates, a wise man; for they will call me wise, even although I am not wise, when they want to reproach you. If you had waited a little while, your desire would have been fulfilled in the course of nature. For I am far advanced in years, as you may perceive, and not far from death. I am speaking now not to all of you, but only to those who have condemned me to death. And I have another thing to say to them: you think that I was convicted because I had no words of the sort which would have procured my acquittal—I mean, if I had thought fit to leave nothing undone or unsaid. Not so; the deficiency which led to my conviction was not of words—certainly not. But I had not the boldness or impudence or inclination to address you as you would have liked me to do, weeping and wailing and lamenting, and saying and doing many things which you have been accustomed to hear from others, and which, as I maintain, are unworthy of me. I thought at the time that I ought not to do anything common or mean when in danger: nor do I now repent of the style of my defense; I would rather die having spoken after my manner, than speak in your manner and live. For neither in war nor yet at law ought I or any man to use every way of escaping death. Often in battle there can be no doubt that if a man will throw away his arms, and fall on his knees before his pursuers, he may escape death; and in other dangers there are other ways of escaping death, if a man is willing to say and do anything. The difficulty, my friends, is not to avoid death, but to avoid unrighteousness; for that runs faster than death. I am old and move slowly, and the slower runner has overtaken me, and my accusers are keen and quick, and the faster runner, who is unrighteousness, has overtaken them. And now I depart hence condemned by you to suffer the penalty of death,—they too go their ways condemned by the truth to suffer the penalty of villainy and wrong; and I must abide by my award—let them abide by theirs. I suppose that these things may be regarded as fated,—and I think that they are well.

And now, O men who have condemned me, I would fain prophesy to you; for I am about to die, and in the hour of death men are gifted with prophetic power. And I prophesy to you who are my murderers, that immediately after my departure punishment far heavier than you have inflicted on me will surely await you. Me you have killed because you wanted to escape the accuser, and not to give an account of your lives. But that will not be as you suppose: far otherwise. For I say that there will be more accusers of you than there are now; accusers whom hitherto I have restrained: and as they are younger they will be more inconsiderate with you, and you will be more offended at them. If you think that by killing men you can prevent some one from censuring your evil lives, you are mistaken; that is not a way of escape which is either possible or honorable; the easiest and the noblest way is not to be disabling others, but to be improving yourselves. This is the prophecy which I utter before my departure to the judges who have condemned me.

Friends, who would have acquitted me, I would like also to talk with you about the thing which has come to pass, while the magistrates are busy, and before I go to the place at which I must die. Stay then a little, for we may as well talk with one another while there is time. You are my friends, and I should like to show you the meaning of this event which has happened to me. O my judges—for you I may truly call judges—I should like to tell you of a

wonderful circumstance. Hitherto the divine faculty of which the internal oracle is the source has constantly been in the habit of opposing me even about
trifles, if I was going to make a slip or error in any matter; and now as you see
there has come upon me that which may be thought, and is generally believed
to be, the last and worst evil. But the oracle made no sign of opposition, either
when I was leaving my house in the morning, or when I was on my way to the
court, or while I was speaking, at anything which I was going to say; and yet I
have often been stopped in the middle of a speech, but now in nothing I either
said or did touching the matter in hand has the oracle opposed me. What do I
take to be the explanation of this silence? I will tell you. It is an intimation that
what has happened to me is a good, and that those of us who think that death
is an evil are in error. For the customary sign would surely have opposed me
had I been going to evil and not to good.

Let us reflect in another way, and we shall see that there is great reason to
hope that death is a good; for one of two things—either death is a state of
nothingness and utter unconsciousness, or, as men say, there is a change and
migration of the soul from this world to another. Now if you suppose that
there is no consciousness, but a sleep like the sleep of him who is undisturbed
even by dreams, death will be an unspeakable gain. For if a person were to select the night in which his sleep was undisturbed even by dreams, and were to
compare with this the other days and nights of his life, and then were to tell us
how many days and nights he had passed in the course of his life better and
more pleasantly than this one, I think that any man, I will not say a private
man, but even the great king will not find many such days or nights, when
compared with the others. Now if death be of such a nature, I say that to die is
gain; for eternity is then only a single night. But if death is the journey to another place, and there, as men say, all the dead abide, what good, O my
friends and judges, can be greater than this? If indeed when the pilgrim arrives in the world below, he is delivered from the professors of justice in this
world, and finds the true judges who are said to give judgment there, Minos
and Rhadamanthus and Aeacus and Triptolemus, and other sons of God who
were righteous in their own life, that pilgrimage will be worth making. What
would not a man give if he might converse with Orpheus and Musaeus and
Hesiod and Homer? Nay, if this be true, let me die again and again. I myself,
too, shall have a wonderful interest in there meeting and conversing with
Palamedes, and Ajax the son of Telamon, and any other ancient hero who has
suffered death through an unjust judgment; and there will be no small pleasure, as I think, in comparing my own sufferings with theirs. Above all, I shall
then be able to continue my search into true and false knowledge; as in this
world, so also in the next; and I shall find out who is wise, and who pretends
to be wise, and is not. What would not a man give, O judges, to be able to examine the leader of the great Trojan expedition; or Odysseus or Sisyphus, or
numberless others, men and women too! What infinite delight would there be
in conversing with them and asking them questions! In another world they do
not put a man to death for asking questions: assuredly not. For besides being
happier than we are, they will be immortal, if what is said is true.

Wherefore, O judges, be of good cheer about death, and know of a certainty, that no evil can happen to a good man, either in life or after death. He and his are not neglected by the gods; nor has my own approaching end happened by mere chance. But I see clearly that the time had arrived when it was better for me to die and be released from trouble; wherefore the oracle gave no sign. For which reason, also, I am not angry with my condemners, or with my accusers; they have done me no harm, although they did not mean to do me any good; and for this I may gently blame them.

Still I have a favor to ask of them. When my sons are grown up, I would ask you, O my friends, to punish them; and I would have you trouble them, as I have troubled you, if they seem to care about riches, or anything, more than about virtue; or if they pretend to be something when they are really nothing,—then reprove them, as I have reproved you, for not caring about that for which they ought to care, and thinking that they are something when they are really nothing. And if you do this, both I and my sons will have received justice at your hands.

The hour of departure has arrived, and we go our ways—I to die, and you to live. Which is better God only knows.

READING 2

Living in Accord with the Tao*

Chuang-tzu (c. 250 B.C.E.)

[THE TALE OF THE BUTCHER]

Prince Hui's cook was cutting up a bull. Every blow of his hand, every heave of his shoulders, every tread of his foot, every thrust of his knee, every whshh of cut flesh, every chhk of the knife, was in perfect harmony, rhythmical like the dance of the Mulberry Grove, simultaneous like the chords of the Ching Shou.

The prince said, "Ah! It is indeed admirable that your art has become so perfect!"

[Having finished his task], the cook laid down his knife, and replied to the remark. "I am devoted to the method of the Tao, which is superior to any skill. When I first began to cut up bulls, I saw nothing but the [entire] carcass. After three years I ceased to see it as a whole. Now I deal with it in a spirit-like manner, and do not look at it with my eyes. I discarded the use of my senses, and my spirit acts as it wills. Observing the natural lines, [my knife] slips through the great crevices and slides through the great cavities, taking advantage of

*From the *Chuang-Tzu,* Books 3, 6, and 9.

the accommodations thus presented. My skill avoids the ligaments, and much more the large bones.

A good cook changes his knife every year because he cleanly *cuts.* An ordinary cook changes his every month because he *hacks.* Now I have used my knife for nineteen years. It has cut up several thousand bulls, and yet its edge is as sharp as if it came right from the whetstone. There are crevices in the joints, and the edge of the knife has no appreciable thickness. When that which is so thin enters the crevice, how easily it moves along! The blade has more than enough room. However, whenever I come to a complicated joint and see that there will be some difficulty, I proceed with caution. I do not allow my eyes to wander from the place, and move my hand slowly. Then by a very slight movement of the knife, the part is quickly separated, and drops like a clod of earth to the ground. Then standing up with the knife in my hand, I leisurely look all round, and with an air of satisfaction, wipe it clean, and put it in its sheath."

"Excellent!" said the Prince. "I have heard the words of my cook, and learned how to care for life."

[THE TALE OF THE DYING MEN]

Masters Ssu, Yu, Li, and Lai were all four conversing together. They asked, "Who can make non-action his head, life his backbone, and death the tail of his existence? Who knows how birth and death, existence and annihilation comprise one single body? The person who understands this will be admitted to friendship with us." The four men looked at one another and laughed, but no one seized with his mind the drift of the questions. All, however, were friends together.

Not long after, Yu fell ill, and Ssu went to see him. "How great is the Creator!" said the sufferer. "He made me the deformed object that I am!" Yu was a crooked hunchback; his five viscera were squeezed into the upper part of his body; his chin bent over his navel; his shoulder was higher than his crown; on his crown was an ulcer pointing to the sky; his breath came and went in gasps. Nevertheless, he was easy in his mind, and made no trouble of his condition. He limped to a well, looked at himself in it, and said, "I can't believe that the Creator would have made me the deformed object that I am!" Ssu said, "Do you dislike your condition?" He replied, "No, why should I dislike it? If the creator transformed my left arm into a rooster, I would watch the time of the night. If he transformed my right arm into a cross-bow, I would then be looking for a duck to shoot for roasting. If he transformed my rump-bone into a wheel and my spirit into a horse, I would then be able to ride in my own chariot. I'd never have to change horses. I obtained life because it was my time. I am now parting with it in accordance with the same law. When we rest in what the time requires, and manifest that submission, neither joy nor sorrow can enter. This is what the ancients called 'loosening the rope.' Some, though, are hung up and cannot loosen themselves. They are held fast by the bonds of material existence. But it is a long-acknowledged fact that no creatures can overcome Heaven. Why, then, should I hate my condition?"

Eventually another of the four, named Tze Lai, fell ill, and lay gasping for breath, while his family stood weeping around. The fourth friend, Tze Li, went to see him. "Leave!" he cried to the wife and children; "Go away! You hinder his decomposition." Then, leaning against the door, he said, "Truly, God is great! I wonder what he will make of you now. I wonder where you will be sent. Do you think be will make you into rat's liver or into the shoulders of a snake?"

"A son," answered Tze Lai, "must go wherever his parents bid him. Nature is no other than a man's parents. If she bid me to die quickly, and I object, then I am an unfilial son. She can do me no wrong. The Tao gives me this form, this toil in adulthood, this tranquility in old age, and this rest in death. And surely that which is such a kind mediator of my life is the best mediator of my death. Suppose that the boiling metal in a smelting-pot were to bubble up and say, 'Make of me an Excalibur'; I think the caster would reject that metal as strange. And if a sinner like myself were to say to God, 'Make of me a man, make of me a man'; I think he too would reject me as strange. The universe is the smelting-pot, and God is the caster. I will go wherever I am sent, to wake unconscious of the past, as a man wakes from a dreamless sleep."

[THE TALE OF THE HORSES]

With their hoofs horses can tread on ice and snow, and with their hair withstand the wind and cold; they feed on the grass and drink water; they prance with their legs and leap. This is the true nature of horses. Even if grand towers and large dormitories were made for them, they would prefer not to use them. One day Poh Loh [i.e., the original mythical tamer of horses] said, "I know well how to manage horses," Accordingly, he clipped them, pared their hoofs, haltered their heads, bridled them and shackled their legs, and confined them in stables and corrals. [With this treatment] two or three in every ten of them died. Still, he subjected them to hunger and thirst; he galloped them and raced them, and made them prance in regular order. In front of the horses were the evils of the bit and ornamented breast bands, and behind were the terrors of the whip and switch. With this treatment more than half of them died.

The [original mythical] potter said, "I know well how to deal with clay. I can mold it into circles as exact as if made by the compass, and into squares as exact as if formed by the measuring square." The [original mythical] carpenter said, "I know well how to deal with wood. I can make it bent if I use curve, and I can make it straight if I use a plumb-line." But does the nature of clay and wood require the application of the compass and square, of a curve and line? And yet age after age people have praised Poh Loh saying, "He knew well how to manage horses," and also the [original mythical] potter and carpenter, saying, "They knew well how to deal with clay and wood." This is the same error committed by those who govern the world.

According to my idea, those who know how to properly govern hu-
mankind would not act so. People had their regular and constant nature. They
originally wove and made themselves clothes; they tilled the ground and for
food. These are common to humanity. They all agreed on this, and did not
form themselves into separate classes. In this way they were constituted and
left to their natural tendencies. Therefore in the age of perfect virtue people
walked along quietly, steadily looking forward. At that time, on the hills there
were no footpaths or excavated passages. On the lakes there were no boats or
dams. All creatures lived in groups, and the places of their settlement were
made close to one another. Birds and beasts multiplied to flocks and herds.
The grass and trees grew luxuriant and long. In this condition the birds and
beasts could led about without feeling the constrained. One could climb up to
the nest of the raven and peep into it. Yes, in the age of perfect virtue, people
lived in common with birds and beasts, and were on equal terms with all creatures, forming one family. How could they have distinctions between superior
and inferior people? As they were all without knowledge, they did not leave
their condition of natural virtue. Equally free from evil desires, they were in
the state of natural integrity. In that state of natural integrity, the nature of the
people was what it ought to be.

But when sages appeared, tripping people up with charity and constrain-
ing people with the duty to one's neighbor, then people universally began to
be perplexed. The sages went to excess in performing music and fussed over
the practice of ceremonies. Then people began to be separated from each
other. If raw materials were not cut and hacked, who could have made a sacri-
ficial vase from them? If natural jade was not broken, who could have made
the handles for the ceremonial drinking cups? If the Tao was not abandoned,
who could have introduced charity and duty to one's neighbor? If they did not
depart from the natural instincts, how could ceremonies and music have come
into use? If the five colors were not confused, who would practice decoration?
If the five notes were not confused, who would adopt the six pitched-pipes?
The cutting and hacking of the raw materials to form vessels was the crime of
the artisans. The injury done to the Tao in order to practice charity and duty to
one's neighbor was the error of the sages.

Horses, when living in the open country, eat the grass, and drink water.
When pleased, they intertwine their necks and rub one another. When en-
raged, they turn back to back and kick one another. This is all that they
know to do. But if we put a yoke on their necks with metal plates on their
foreheads, then they know to look mean, to curve their necks to bite, to rush
viciously, trying to get the bit out of their mouths, and to filch the reins
[from their driver]. This knowledge of the horse and its ability thus to act depraved is the crime of Poh Loh. In the time of Ho Hsu people did nothing in
particular when at rest. They went no where in particular when out walking.
They ate food and were glad. They slapped their stomachs to express their
satisfaction. This was all the ability which they possessed. When the sages
appeared they worried people with ceremonies and music; they instituted
governments, they dangled charity and duty to one's neighbor in order to

comfort their minds. Then people developed a taste for knowledge and struggled with each other in their pursuit of gain, and there was no stopping them. This was the error of those sages.

What Is the Aim of Life?*

Leo Tolstoy (1828–1910)

I was baptized and educated in the Orthodox Christian faith. I was taught it from childhood and through the whole time of my boyhood and youth. But when I, at eighteen years of age, left the second year's course of the university, I no longer believed any of the things I had been taught. . . .

My defection from faith took place in the same manner as it has taken place and still takes place in people of our cultivated class. . . .

I wished with all my heart to be good; but I was young, I had passions, and I was alone, completely alone, when I was trying to find the good. Every time I endeavored to give utterance to what formed my most intimate wishes, namely, that I wished to be morally good, I met with contempt and ridicule; and the moment I surrendered myself to the abominable passions, I was praised and encouraged.

Ambition, lust of power, selfishness, voluptuousness, pride, anger, revenge—all that was respected. By abandoning myself to these passions I became like a grown person, and I felt that people were satisfied with me. A good aunt of mine, a pure soul, with whom I was living, kept telling me that there was nothing she wished so much for me as that I should have a liaison with a married woman. . . . I . . . fornicated, and cheated. Lying, stealing, acts of lust of every description, drunkenness, violence, murder—there was not a crime which I did not commit, and for all that I was praised, and my contemporaries have regarded me as a comparatively moral man.

Thus I lived for ten years. . . .

When I came back [from St. Petersburg], I got married. The new conditions of my happy family life completely drew me away from all search for the general meaning of life. All my life during that time was centered in my family, my wife, my children, and, therefore, in cares for the increase of the means of existence. The striving after perfection . . . now gave way simply to the striving after making it as comfortable as possible for me and my family.

Thus another fifteen years passed.

Although I regarded authorship as a waste of time, I continued to write during those fifteen years. I had talked of the seduction of authorship, of the

*Leo N. Tolstoy, from *My Confession* (1882).

seduction of enormous monetary remunerations and applauses for my insignificant labour, and so I submitted to it, as being a means for improving my material condition and for stifling in my soul all questions about the meaning of my life and life in general.

In my writings I advocated, what to me was the only truth, that it was necessary to live in such a way as to derive the greatest comfort for oneself and one's family.

Thus I proceeded to live, but five years ago something very strange began to happen with me: I was overcome by minutes at first of perplexity and then of an arrest of life, as though I did not know how to live or what to do, and I lost myself and was dejected. But that passed, and I continued to live as before. Then those minutes of perplexity were repeated oftener and oftener, and always in one and the same form. These arrests of life found their expression in ever the same questions: "Why? Well, and then?"

At first I thought that those were simply aimless, inappropriate questions. It seemed to me that that was all well known and that if I ever wanted to busy myself with their solution, it would not cost me much labor—that now I had no time to attend to them, but that if I wanted to I should find the proper answers. But the questions began to repeat themselves oftener and oftener, answers were demanded more and more persistently, and, like dots that fall on the same spot, these questions, without any answers, thickened into one black blotch. . . .

My life came to a standstill. . . . The truth was that life was meaningless. It was as though I had just been living and walking along, and had come to an abyss, where I saw clearly that there was nothing ahead but perdition. . . .

. . . I did not know myself what it was I wanted: I was afraid of life, strove to get away from it, and, at the same time, expected something from it.

All that happened with me when I was on every side surrounded by what is considered to be complete happiness. I had a good, loving, and beloved wife, good children, and a large estate, which grew and increased without any labour on my part. I was respected by my neighbors and friends, more than ever before, was praised by strangers, and, without any self-deception, could consider my name famous. With all that, I was not deranged or mentally unsound—on the contrary, I was in full command of my mental and physical powers, such as I had rarely met with in people of my age: physically I could work in a field, mowing, without failing behind a peasant; mentally I could work from eight to ten hours in succession, without experiencing any consequences from the strain. And while in such condition I arrived at the conclusion that I could not live, and, fearing death, I had to use cunning against myself, in order that I might not take my life. . . .

Long ago has been told the Eastern story about the traveler who in the steppe is overtaken by an infuriated beast. Trying to save himself from the animal, the traveler jumps into a waterless well, but at its bottom he sees a dragon who opens his jaws in order to swallow him. And the unfortunate man does not dare climb out, lest he perish from the infuriated beast, and does not dare jump down to the bottom of the well, lest he be devoured by the dragon, and so clutches the twig of a wild bush growing in a cleft of the well and holds on to it. His hands grow weak and he feels that soon he shall have to surrender to the peril which awaits him at either side; but he still holds on and sees two mice, one white, the other black, in even measure making a circle around the main trunk of the bush to which he is clinging, and nibbling at it on all sides. Now, at any moment, the bush will break and tear off, and he will fall into the dragon's jaws. The traveler sees that and knows that he will inevitably perish; but while he is still clinging, he sees some drops of honey hanging on the leaves of the bush, and so reaches out for them with his tongue and licks the leaves. Just so I hold on to the branch of life, knowing that the dragon of death is waiting inevitably for me, ready to tear me to pieces, and I cannot understand why I have fallen on such suffering. And I try to lick that honey which used to give me pleasure; but now it no longer gives me joy, and the white and the black mouse day and night nibble at the branch to which I am holding on. I clearly see the dragon, and the honey is no longer sweet to me. I see only the inevitable dragon and the mice, and am unable to turn my glance away from them. That is not a fable, but a veritable, indisputable, comprehensible truth.

The former deception of the pleasures of life, which stifled the terror of the dragon, no longer deceives me. No matter how much one should say to me, "You cannot understand the meaning of life, do not think, live!" I am unable to do so, because I have been doing it too long before. Now I cannot help seeing day and night, which run and lead me up to death. I see that alone, because that alone is the truth. Everything else is a lie.

The two drops of honey that have longest turned my eyes away from the cruel truth, the love of family and of authorship, which I have called an art, are no longer sweet to me.

"My family," I said to myself, "but my family, my wife and children, they are also human beings. They are in precisely the same condition that I am in: they must either live in the lie or see the terrible truth. Why should they live? Why should I love them, why guard, raise, and watch them? Is it for the same despair which is in me, or for dullness of perception? Since I love them, I cannot conceal the truth from them,—every step in cognition leads them up to this truth. And the truth is death."

"Art, poetry?" For a long time, under the influence of the success of human praise, I tried to persuade myself that that was a thing which could be done, even though death should come and destroy everything, my deeds, as well as my memory of them; but soon I came to see that that, too, was a deception. It was clear to me that art was an adornment of life, a decoy of life. But life lost all its attractiveness for me. How, then, could I entrap others? So long as I did not live my own life, and a strange life bore me on its waves; so long as I believed that life had some sense, although I was not able to express it,— the reflections of life of every description in poetry and in the arts afforded me pleasure, and I was delighted to look at life through this little mirror of art; but when I began to look for the meaning of life, when I experienced the necessity of living myself, that little. mirror became either useless, superfluous, and ridiculous, or painful to me. I could no longer console myself with what I saw in the mirror, namely, that my situation was stupid and desperate. It was all right for me to rejoice so long as I believed in the depth of my soul that life had some sense. At that time the play of lights—of the comical, the tragical, the touching, the beautiful, the terrible in life—afforded me amusement. But when I knew that life was meaningless and terrible, the play in the little mirror could no longer amuse me. No sweetness of honey could be sweet to me, when I saw the dragon and the mice that were nibbling down my support.

That was not all. If I had simply comprehended that life had no meaning, I might have known that calmly, I might have known that that was my fate. But I could not be soothed by that. . . . I was like a man who had lost his way in the forest, who was overcome by terror because he had lost his way, who kept tossing about in his desire to come out on the road, knowing that every step got him only more entangled, and who could not help tossing. . . .

"But, perhaps, I overlooked something, or did not understand something right?" I said to myself several times. "It is impossible that this condition of despair should be characteristic of men!" And I tried to find an explanation for these questions in all those branches of knowledge which men had acquired. . . . and I found nothing.

For a long time I could not believe that science had no answer to give to the questions of life. . . .

. . . If you turn to the branch of knowledge which does not busy itself with the solution of the problems of life, but answers only its special, scientific questions, you are delighted at the power of the human mind, but know in advance that there will be no answers there to the questions of life. These sciences directly ignore the question of life. They say: "We have no answers to what you are and why you live, and we do not busy ourselves with that; but if you want to know the laws of light, of chemical combinations, the laws of the development of organisms, if you want to know the laws of the bodies, their forms, and the relation of numbers and quantities, if you want to know the laws of your mind, we shall give you clear, definite, incontrovertible answers to all that." . . .

No matter how strange, how incredibly incomprehensible it now seems to me that I, discussing life, should have been able to overlook all those who surrounded me on all sides, the life of humanity, that I should have been able to err in such a ridiculous manner as to think that my life, and the life of a Solomon and a Schopenhauer, was the real, the normal life, while the life of billions was a circumstance that did not deserve consideration. . . .

I lived for a long time in this madness, which, not in words, but in deeds, is particularly characteristic of us, the most liberal and learned of men. But, thanks either to my strange, physical love for the real working class, which made me understand it and see that it is not so stupid as we suppose, or to the sincerity of my conviction, which was that I could know nothing and that the best that I could do was to hang myself,—I felt that if I wanted to live and understand the meaning of life, I ought naturally to look for it, not among those who had lost the meaning of life and wanted to kill themselves, but among those billions departed and living men who had been carrying their own lives and ours upon their shoulders. And I looked around at the enormous masses of deceased and living men,—not learned and wealthy, but simple men,—and I saw something quite different. I saw that all these billions of men that lived or had lived, all, with rare exceptions, did not fit into my subdivisions, and that I could not recognize them as not understanding the question, because they themselves put it and answered it with surprising clearness. Nor could I recognize them as Epicureans, because their lives were composed rather of privations and suffering than of enjoyment. Still less could I recognize them as senselessly living out their meaningless lives, because every act of theirs and death itself was explained by them. They regarded it as the greatest evil to kill themselves. It appeared, then, that all humanity was in possession of a knowledge of the meaning of life, which I did not recognize and which I contemned. It turned out that rational knowledge did not give any meaning to life, excluded life, while the meaning which by billions of people, by all humanity, was ascribed to life was based on some despised, false knowledge.

The rational knowledge in the person of the learned and the wise denied the meaning of life, but the enormous masses of men, all humanity, recognized this meaning in an irrational knowledge. This irrational knowledge was faith, the same that I could not help but reject. That was God as one and three, the creation in six days, devils and angels, and all that which I could not accept so long as I had not lost my senses.

My situation was a terrible one. I knew that I should not find anything on the path of rational knowledge but the negation of life, and there, in faith, nothing but the negation of reason, which was still more impossible than the negation of life. From the rational knowledge it followed that life was an evil and men knew it,—it depended on men whether they should cease living, and yet they lived and continued to live, and I myself lived, though I had known long ago that life was meaningless and an evil. From faith it followed that, in order to understand life, I must renounce reason, for which alone a meaning was needed.

There resulted a contradiction, from which there were two ways out: either what I called rational was not so rational as I had thought; or that which to me appeared irrational was not so irrational as I had thought. And I began to verify the train of thoughts of my rational knowledge.

In verifying the train of thoughts of my rational knowledge, I found that it was quite correct. The deduction that life was nothing was inevitable; but I saw a mistake. The mistake was that I had not reasoned in conformity with the question put by me. The question was, "Why should I live?" that is, "What real, indestructible essence will come from my phantasmal, destructible life? What meaning has my finite existence in this infinite world?" And in order to answer this question, I studied life.

The solutions of all possible questions of life apparently could not satisfy me, because my question, no matter how simple it appeared in the beginning, included the necessity of explaining the finite through the infinite, and vice versa.

I asked, "What is the extra-temporal, extra-causal, extra-spatial meaning of life?" But I gave an answer to the question, "What is the temporal, causal, spatial meaning of my life?" The result was that after a long labour of mind I answered, "None."

In my reflections I constantly equated, nor could I do otherwise, the finite with the finite, the infinite with the infinite, and so from that resulted precisely what had to result: force was force, matter was matter, will was will, infinity was infinity, nothing was nothing,—and nothing else could come from it.

There happened something like what at times takes place in mathematics: you think you are solving an equation, when you have only an identity. The reasoning is correct, but you receive as a result the answer: $a = a$, or $x = x$, or $0 = 0$. The same happened with my reflection in respect to the question about the meaning of my life. The answers given by all science to that question are only identities.

Indeed, the strictly scientific knowledge, that knowledge which, as Descartes did, begins with a full doubt in everything, rejects all knowledge which has been taken on trust, and builds everything anew on the laws of reason and experience, cannot give any other answer to the question of life than what I received,—an indefinite answer. . . . Thus the philosophical knowledge does not negate anything, but only answers that the question cannot be solved by it, that for philosophy the solution remains insoluble.

When I saw that, I understood that it was not right for me to look for an answer to my question in rational knowledge, and that the answer given by rational knowledge was only an indication that the answer might be got if the question were differently put, but only when into the discussion of the question should be introduced the question of the relation of the finite to the infinite. I also understood that, no matter how irrational and monstrous the answers might be that faith gave, they had this advantage that they introduced into each answer the relation of the finite to the infinite, without which there could be no answer.

No matter how I may put the question, "How must I live?" the answer is, "According to God's law." "What real result will there be from my life?" "Eternal torment or eternal bliss." "What is the meaning which is not destroyed by death?"—"The union with infinite God, paradise." Thus, outside the rational knowledge, which had to me appeared as the only one, I was inevitably led to recognize that all living humanity had a certain other irrational knowledge, faith, which made it possible to live.

All the irrationality of faith remained the same for me, but I could not help recognizing that it alone gave to humanity answers to the questions of life, and, in consequence of them, the possibility of living.

The rational knowledge brought me to the recognition that life was meaningless,—my life stopped, and I wanted to destroy myself. When I looked around at people, at all humanity, I saw that people lived and asserted that they knew the meaning of life. I looked back at myself: I lived so long as I knew the meaning of life. As to other people, so even to me, did faith give the meaning of life and the possibility of living.

Looking again at the people of other countries, contemporaries of mine and those passed away, I saw again the same. Where life had been, there faith, ever since humanity had existed, had given the possibility of living, and the chief features of faith were everywhere one and the same.

No matter what answers faith may give, its every answer gives to the finite existence of man the sense of the infinite,—a sense which is not destroyed by suffering, privation, and death. Consequently in faith alone could we find the meaning and possibility of life. What, then, was faith? I understood that faith was not merely an evidence of things not seen, and so forth, not revelation (that is only the description of one of the symptoms of faith), not the relation of man to man (faith has to be defined, and then God, and not first God, and faith through him), not merely an agreement with what a man was told, as faith was generally understood,—that faith was the knowledge of the meaning of human life, in consequence of which man did not destroy himself, but lived. Faith is the power of life. If a man lives he believes in something. If he did not believe that he ought to live for some purpose, he would not live. If he does not see and understand the phantasm of the finite, he believes in that finite; if he understands the phantasm of the finite, he must believe in the infinite. Without faith one cannot live.

I was prepared now to accept any faith, so long as it did not demand from me a direct denial of reason, which would have been a lie. . . .

In order that all humanity may be able to live, in order that they may continue living, giving a meaning to life, they, those billions, must have another, a real knowledge of faith, for not the fact that I, with Solomon and Schopenhauer, did not kill myself convinced me of the existence of faith, but that these billions had lived and had borne us, me and Solomon, on the waves of life.

Then I began to cultivate the acquaintance of the believers from among the poor, the simple and unlettered folk, of pilgrims, monks, dissenters, peasants. The doctrine of these people from among the masses was also the Christian doctrine that the quasi-believers of our circle professed. With the Christian truths were also mixed in very many superstitions, but there was this difference: the superstitions of our circle were quite unnecessary to them, had no connection with their lives, were only a kind of an Epicurean amusement, while the superstitions of the believers from among the laboring classes were to such an extent blended with their life that it would have been impossible to imagine it without these superstitions,—it was a necessary condition of that life. I began to examine closely the lives and beliefs of these people, and the more I examined them, the more did I become convinced that they had the real faith, that their faith was necessary for them, and that it alone gave them a meaning and possibility of life. In contradistinction to what I saw in our circle, where life without faith was possible, and where hardly one in a thousand professed to be a believer, among them there was hardly one in a thousand who was not a believer. In contradistinction to what I saw in our circle, where all life passed in idleness, amusements, and tedium of life, I saw that the whole life of these people was passed in hard work, and that they were satisfied with life. in contradistinction to the people of our circle, who struggled and murmured against fate because of their privations and their suffering, these people accepted diseases and sorrows without any perplexity or opposition, but with the calm and firm conviction that it was all for good. In contradistinction to the fact that the more intelligent we are, the less do we understand the meaning of life and the more do we see a kind of a bad joke in our suffering and death, these people live, suffer, and approach death, and suffer in peace and more often in joy. In contradistinction to the fact that a calm death, a death without terror or despair, is the greatest exception in our circle, a restless, insubmissive, joyless death is one of the greatest exceptions among the masses. And of such people, who are deprived of everything which for Solomon and for me constitutes the only good of life, and who withal experience the greatest happiness, there is an enormous number. I cast a broader glance about me. I examined the life of past and present vast masses of men, and I saw people who in like manner had understood the meaning of life, who had known how to live and die, not two, not three, not ten, but hundreds, thousands, millions. All of them, infinitely diversified as to habits, intellect, culture, situation, all equally and quite contrary to my ignorance knew the meaning of life and of death, worked calmly, bore privations and suffering, lived and died, seeing in that not vanity, but good.

I began to love those people. The more I penetrated into their life, the life of the men now living, and the life of men departed, of whom I had read and heard, the more did I love them, and the easier it became for me to live. Thus I lived for about two years, and within me took place a transformation, which has long been working within me, and the germ of which had always been in me. What happened with me was that the life of our circle—of the rich and the learned—not only disgusted me, but even lost all its meaning. All our acts, reflections, sciences, arts—all that appeared to me in a new light. I saw that all that was mere pampering of the appetites, and that no meaning could be found in it; but the life of all the working masses, of all humanity, which created life, presented itself to me in its real significance. I saw that that was life itself and that the meaning given to this life was truth, and I accepted it.

READING 4
———————

*The Human Condition**

Jean-Paul Sartre (1905–1980)

. . . There are two kinds of existentialists; first, those who are Christian, among whom I would include Jaspers and Gabriel Marcel, both Catholic; and on the other hand the atheistic existentialists among whom I class Heidegger,

———————
*From Jean Paul Sartre, "Existentialism is a Humanism" (1946).

and then the French existentialists and myself. What they have in common is that they think that existence precedes essence, or, if you prefer, that subjectivity must be the starting point.

Just what does that mean? Let us consider some object that is manufactured, for example, a book or a paper-cutter: here is an object which has been made by an artisan whose inspiration came from a concept. He referred to the concept of what a paper-cutter is and likewise to a known method of production, which is part of the concept, something which is, by and large, a routine. Thus, the paper-cutter is at once an object produced in a certain way and, on the other hand, one having a specific use; and one cannot postulate a man who produces a paper-cutter but does not know what it is used for. Therefore, let us say that, for the paper-cutter, essence—that is, the ensemble of both the production routines and the properties which enable it to be both produced and defined—precedes existence. Thus, the presence of the paper-cutter or book in front of me is determined. Therefore, we have here a technical view of the world whereby it can be said that production precedes existence.

When we conceive God as the Creator, He is generally thought of as a superior sort of artisan. Whatever doctrine we may be considering, whether one like that of Descartes or that of Leibniz, we always grant that will more or less follows understanding or, at the very least, accompanies it, and that when God creates He knows exactly what He is creating. Thus, the concept of man in the mind of God is comparable to the concept of a paper-cutter in the mind of the manufacturer, and, following certain techniques and a conception, God produces man, just as the artisan, following a definition and a technique, makes a paper-cutter. Thus, the individual man is the realization of a certain concept in the divine intelligence.

In the eighteenth century, the atheism of the *philosophers* discarded the idea of God, but not so much for the notion that essence precedes existence. To a certain extent, this idea is found everywhere; we find it in Diderot, in Voltaire, and even in Kant. Man has a human nature; this human nature, which is the concept of the human, is found in all men, which means that each man is a particular example of a universal concept, man. In Kant, the result of this universality is that the wild-man, the natural man, as well as the bourgeois, are circumscribed by the same definition and have the same basic qualities. Thus, here too the essence of man precedes the historical existence that we find in nature.

Atheistic existentialism, which I represent, is more coherent. It states that if God does not exist, there is at least one being in whom existence precedes essence, a being who exists before he can be defined by any concept, and that this being is man, or, as Heidegger says, human reality. What is meant here by saying that existence precedes essence? It means that, first of all, man exists, turns up, appears on the scene, and, only afterwards, defines himself. If man, as the existentialist conceives him, is indefinable, it is because at first he is nothing. Only afterward will he be something, and he himself will have made what he will be. Thus, there is no human nature, since there is no God to conceive it. Not only is man what he conceives himself to be, but he is also only what he wills himself to be after his thrust toward existence.

Man is nothing else but what he makes of himself. Such is the first principle of existentialism. It is also what is called subjectivity, the name we are la-
beled with when charges are brought against us. But what do we mean by this,
if not that man has a greater dignity than a stone or table? For we mean that
man first exists, that is, that man first of all is the being who hurls himself toward a future and who is conscious of imagining himself as being in the future.
Man is at the start a plan which is aware of itself, rather than a patch of moss, a
piece of garbage, or a cauliflower; nothing exists prior to this plan; there is
nothing in heaven; man will be what he will have planned to be. Not what he
will want to be. Because by the word "will" we generally mean a conscious decision, which is subsequent to what we have already made of ourselves. I may
want to belong to a political party, write a book, get married; but all that is only
a manifestation of an earlier, more spontaneous choice that is called "will." But
if existence really does precede essence, man is responsible for what he is.
Thus, existentialism's first move is to make every man aware of what he is and
to make the full responsibility of his existence rest on him. And when we say
that a man is responsible for himself, we do not only mean that he is responsible for his own individuality, but that he is responsible for all men.

The word subjectivism means, on the one hand, that an individual
chooses and makes himself; and, on the other, that it is impossible for man to
transcend human subjectivity. The second of these is the essential meaning of
existentialism. When we say that man chooses his own self, we mean that
every one of us does likewise; but we also mean by that that in making this
choice he also chooses all men. In fact, in creating the man that we want to be,
there is not a single one of our acts which does not at the same time create an
image of man as we think he ought to be. To choose to be this or that is to affirm at the same time the value of what we choose, because we can never
choose evil. We always choose the good, and nothing can be good for us
without being good for all.

If, on the other hand, existence precedes essence, and if we grant that we
exist and fashion our image at one and the same time, the image is valid for
everybody and for our whole age. Thus, our responsibility is much greater
than we might have supposed, because it involves all mankind. If I am a
workingman and choose to join a Christian trade-union rather than be a communist, and if by being a member I want to show that the best thing for man is
resignation, that the kingdom of man is not of this world, I am not only involving my own case—I want to be resigned for everyone. As a result, my action has involved all humanity. To take a more individual matter, if I want to
marry, to have children; even if this marriage depends solely on my own circumstances or passion or wish, I am involving all humanity in monogamy and
not merely myself. Therefore, I am responsible for myself and for everyone
else. I am creating a certain image of man of my own choosing. In choosing
myself, I choose man.

This helps us understand what the actual content is of such rather grandil-
oquent words as anguish, forlornness, despair. As you will see, it's all quite
simple.

First, what is meant by anguish? The existentialists say at once that man is anguish. What that means is this: the man who involves himself and who realizes that he is not only the person he chooses to be, but also a lawmaker who is, at the same time, choosing all mankind as well as himself, can not help escape the feeling of his total and deep responsibility. Of course, there are many people who are not anxious; but we claim that they are hiding their anxiety, that they are fleeing from it. Certainly, many people believe that when they do something, they themselves are the only ones involved, and when someone says to them, "What if everyone acted that way?" they shrug their shoulders and answer, "Everyone doesn't act that way." But really, one should always ask himself, "What would happen if everybody looked at things that way?" There is no escaping this disturbing thought except by a kind of double-dealing. A man who lies and makes excuses for himself by saying "Not everybody does that," is someone with an uneasy conscience, because the act of lying implies that a universal value is conferred upon the lie.

Anguish is evident even when it conceals itself. This is the anguish that Kierkegaard called the anguish of Abraham. You know the story: an angel has ordered Abraham to sacrifice his son; if it really were an angel who has come and said, "You are Abraham, you shall sacrifice your son," everything would be all right. But everyone might first wonder, "Is it really an angel, and am I really Abraham? What proof do I have?"

There was a madwoman who had hallucinations; someone used to speak to her on the telephone and give her orders. Her doctor asked her, "Who is it who talks to you?" She answered, "He says it's God." What proof did she really have that it was God? If an angel comes to me, what proof is there that it's an angel? And if I hear voices, what proof is there that they come from heaven and not from hell, or from the subconscious, or a pathological condition? What proves that they are addressed to me? What proof is there that I have been appointed to impose my choice and my conception of man on humanity? I'll never find any proof or sign to convince me of that. If a voice addresses me, it is always for me to decide that this is the angel's voice; if I consider that such an act is a good one, it is I who will choose to say that it is good rather than bad.

Now, I'm not being singled out as an Abraham, and yet at every moment I'm obliged to perform exemplary acts. For every man, everything happens as if all mankind had its eyes fixed on him and were guiding itself by what he does. And every man ought to say to himself, "Am I really the kind of man who has the right to act in such a way that humanity might guide itself by my actions?" And if he does not say that to himself, he is masking his anguish.

There is no question here of the kind of anguish which would lead to quietism, to inaction. It is a matter of a simple sort of anguish that anybody who has had responsibilities is familiar with. For example, when a military officer takes the responsibility for an attack and sends a certain number of men to death, he chooses to do so, and in the main he alone makes the choice. Doubtless, orders come from above, but they are too broad; he interprets them, and on this interpretation depend the lives of ten or fourteen or twenty men. In making a decision he can not help having a certain anguish. All leaders know this anguish. That doesn't keep them from acting; on the contrary, it is the very condition of their action. For it implies that they envisage a number of possibilities, and when they choose one, they realize that it has value only because it is chosen. We shall see that this kind of anguish, which is the kind that existentialism describes, is explained, in addition, by a direct responsibility to the other men whom it involves. It is not a curtain separating us from action, but is part of action itself.

When we speak of forlornness, a term Heidegger was fond of, we mean only that God does not exist and that we have to face all the consequences of this. The existentialist is strongly opposed to a certain kind of secular ethics which would like to abolish God with the least possible expense. About 1880, some French teachers tried to set up a secular ethics which went something like this: God is a useless and costly hypothesis; we are discarding it; but, meanwhile, in order for there to be an ethics, a society, a civilization, it is essential that certain values be taken seriously and that they be considered as having an *a priori* existence. It must be obligatory, *a priori*, to be honest, not to fie, not to beat your wife, to have children, etc., etc. So we're going to try a little device which will make it possible to show that values exist all the same, inscribed in a heaven of ideas, though otherwise God does not exist. In other words—and this, I believe, is the tendency of everything called reformism in France—nothing will be changed if God does not exist. We shall find ourselves with the same norms of honesty, progress, and humanism, and we shall have made of God an outdated hypothesis which will peacefully die off by itself.

The existentialist, on the contrary, thinks it very distressing that God does not exist, because all possibility of finding values in a heaven of ideas disappears along with Him; there can no longer be an *a priori* Good, since there is no infinite and perfect consciousness to think it. Nowhere is it written that the Good exists, that we must be honest, that we must not lie; because the fact is we are on a plane where there are only men. Dostoievsky said, "If God didn't exist, everything would be permitted." That is the very starting point of existentialism. Indeed, everything is permissible if God does not exist, and as a result man is forlorn, because neither within him nor without does he find anything to cling to. He can't start making excuses for himself.

If existence really does precede essence, there is no explaining things away by reference to a fixed and given human nature. In other words, there is no determinism, man is free, man is freedom. On the other hand, if God does not exist, we find no values or commands to turn to which legitimize our conduct. So, in the bright realm of values, we have no excuse behind us, nor justification before us. We are alone, with no excuses.

That is the idea I shall try to convey when I say that man is condemned to be free. Condemned, because he did not create himself, yet, in other respects is free; because, once thrown into the world, he is responsible for everything he does. The existentialist does not believe in the power of passion. He will never agree that a sweeping passion is a ravaging torrent which fatally leads a man to certain acts and is ~~therefore an excuse~~. He thinks that ~~man is responsible for his passion.~~

The existentialist does not think that man is going to help himself by finding in the world some omen by which to orient himself. Because he thinks that man will interpret the omen to suit himself. Therefore, he thinks that man, with no support and no aid, is condemned every moment to invent man. Ponge, in a very fine article, has said, "Man is the future of man." That's exactly it. But if it is taken to mean that this future is recorded in heaven, that God sees it, then it is false, because it would really no longer be a future. If it is taken to mean that, whatever a man may be, there is a future to be forged, a virgin future before him, then this remark is sound. But then we are forlorn. . . .   *keeping yourself to yourself*

Actually, things will be as man will have decided they are to be. Does that mean that ~~I should abandon myself to quietism?~~ No. First, I should involve myself; then, act on the old saw, "Nothing ventured, nothing gained." Nor does it mean that I shouldn't belong to a party, but rather that I shall have no illusions and shall do what I can. For example, suppose I ask myself, "Will socialization, as such, ever come about?" I know nothing about it. All I know is that I'm going to do everything in my power to bring it about. Beyond that, I can't count on anything. Quietism is the attitude of people who say, "Let others do what I can't do." The doctrine I am presenting is the very opposite of quietism, since it declares, "There is no reality except in action." Moreover, it goes further, since it adds, "Man is nothing else than his plan; he exists only to the extent that he fulfills himself; he is therefore nothing else than the ensemble of his acts, nothing else than his life."

According to this, we can understand why our doctrine horrifies certain people. Because often the only way they can bear their wretchedness is to think, "Circumstances have been against me. What I've been and done doesn't show my true worth. To be sure, I've had no great love, no great friendship, but that's because I haven't met a man or woman who was worthy. The books I've written haven't been very good because I haven't had the proper leisure. I haven't had children to devote myself to because I didn't find a man with whom I could have spent my life. So there remains within me, unused and quite viable, a host of propensities, inclinations, possibilities, that one wouldn't guess from the mere series of things I've done."

Now, for the existentialist there is really no love other than one which manifests itself in a person's being in love. There is no genius other than one which is expressed in works of art; the genius of Proust is the sum of Proust's works; the genius of Racine is his series of tragedies. Outside of that, there is nothing. Why say that Racine could have written another tragedy, when he didn't write it? A man is involved in life, leaves his impress on it, and outside of that there is nothing. To be sure, this may seem a harsh thought to someone whose life hasn't been a success. But, on the other hand, it prompts people to understand that reality alone is what counts, that dreams, expectations, and hopes warrant no more than to define a man as a disappointed dream, as miscarried hopes, as vain expectations. In other words, to define him negatively and not positively. However, when we say, "You are nothing else than your life," that does not imply that the artist will be judged solely on the basis of his works of art; a thousand other things will contribute toward summing him up. What we mean is that a man is nothing else than a series of undertakings, that he is the sum, the organization, the ensemble of the relationships which make up these undertakings.

When all is said and done, what we are accused of, at bottom, is not our pessimism, but an optimistic toughness. If people throw up to us our works of fiction in which we write about people who are soft, weak, cowardly, and sometimes even downright bad, it's not because these people are soft, weak, cowardly, or bad; because if we were to say, as Zola did, that they are that way because of heredity, the workings of environment, society, because of biological or psychological determinism, people would be reassured. They would say, "Well, that's what we're like, no one can do anything about it." But when the existentialist writes about a coward, he says that this coward is responsible for his cowardice. He's not like that because he has a cowardly heart or lung or brain; he's not like that on account of his physiological make-up; but he's like that because he has made himself a coward by his acts. There's no such thing as a cowardly constitution; there are nervous constitutions; there is poor blood, as the common people say, or there are strong constitutions. But the man whose blood is poor is not a coward on that account, for what makes cowardice is the act of renouncing or yielding. A constitution is not an act; the coward is defined on the basis of the acts he performs. People feel, in a vague sort of way, that this coward we're talking about is guilty of being a coward, and the thought frightens them. What people would like is that a coward or a hero be born that way.

One of the complaints most frequently made about *The Ways of Freedom* can be summed up as follows: "After all, these people are so spineless, how are you going to make heroes out of them?" This objection almost makes me laugh, for it assumes that people are born heroes. That's what people really want to think. If you're born cowardly, you may set your mind perfectly at rest; there's nothing you can do about it; you'll be cowardly all your life, whatever you may do. If you're born a hero, you may set your mind just as much at rest; you'll be a hero all your life; you'll drink like a hero and eat like a hero. What the existentialist says is that the coward makes himself cowardly, that the hero makes himself heroic. There's always a possibility for the coward not to be cowardly any more and for the hero to stop being heroic. What counts is total involvement; some one particular action or set of circumstances is not total involvement.

. . . [Existentialism] defines man in terms of action there is no doctrine more optimistic, since man's destiny is within himself; it tells him that the only hope is in his acting and that action is the only thing that enables a man to live.

PART TWO

Philosophy of Mind

[handwritten annotations:]
- some think we are mere physical beings → materialists (the mind is just brain working)
- others think the mind is distinct from the brain → dualists (mind & body interact)
- states of mind aren't physical — intentions
- memory
- will
- emotions
- perceptions

*F*rom earliest times, philosophers have reflected on the question "What is there?" Sometimes they rephrased the question to ask "What is real?" or "What really is?" They were puzzled by the fact that things come and go—they come into being, exist, and then cease to be. They were fascinated to discover that things are not what they appear to be. Answers to these questions involve the subject of *metaphysics*, or the study of the fundamental nature of reality. The origin of the term "metaphysics" is unclear, but it rests on two Greek words: *meta* (beyond) and *phusis* (nature). It may be helpful to see it as the study of things that exist—apart from or beyond what is immediately apparent in the physical world around us. Part of the job of metaphysics is to take an inventory of all the kinds of things that exist, and philosophers disagree widely about how many kinds of things there are. *Monism* is the view that there is one fundamental type of thing. Even here, though, there are disputes about what this one thing might be. Monistic *materialism* is the view that everything in the universe is made of material stuff. We might think that some sorts of nonmaterial spirits might exist—such as human or divine spirits. However, materialists deny this and suggest that even whatever human or divine elements we consider must ultimately be made of material stuff. Monistic *idealism*, by contrast, is the view that everything in the universe is made of spiritual stuff, and nothing is actually material in nature. The term "idealism" is based on the word "idea" insofar as ideas are thought to be spiritual in nature. Both types of monism have a simple conclusion: Says the materialist, "Never mind"; says the idealist, "No matter."

Against both of these types of materialism, the theory of *dualism* is the view that there are two basic types of stuff that exist in the world, namely, matter and spirit. Dualism acknowledges what appears to be obvious to at least some philosophers, namely that there is both a physical component to the world and a realm of spiritual things, such as human minds and divine spirits. Yet another position called *pluralism* holds that there are *many* different types of things that exist. On this view, both monism and dualism are far too simplistic, and pluralists argue that we should recognize that many things—and perhaps even *everything* out there—differs from other things in some major respect.

When philosophers investigate the issues of monism, dualism and pluralism, they typically cast their eyes on one of two fields: (1) the broad makeup of things in the universe or (2) the more narrow makeup of human existence. The broader issue usually focuses on the possible existence of a spiritual realm, the nature of God, and how God interrelates with things in the universe. The more narrow issue of human existence attempts to discover whether human beings are composed of one, two, or many types of things. Our focus in this part is on the more narrow issue of the metaphysical components of human existence—although even here the narrow issue often interweaves with the broader concerns about the makeup of the universe as a whole. The narrow issue typically involves investigating the relation between the human *mind* and the human *body*. The dualistic presumption is that the human mind is spiritual in nature, and that the body is physical. Monistic materialists, though, argue that the human mind is ultimately grounded in physical brain activity, and there is nothing spiritual about our thinking process. Idealists, on the other hand, deny that humans really have any physical bodies at all and, instead, they hold that perceptions of our physical selves is sort of like a divinely imposed hallucination. Today, the study of the mind–body problem is the cornerstone of the subject area known as the *philosophy of mind.*

The selections in this chapter cover a wide range of metaphysical positions in the philosophy of mind. In the *Phaedo,* Plato (427–347 B.C.E.) offers the classic dualistic position and argues that we have an immortal human soul that survives the death of our physical bodies. The Hindu philosophical tradition in India has a completely different perspective on the nature of the human mind. Throughout most of our lives, Hindus believe, we are preoccupied with a superficial aspect of our selves that emphasizes individual identity. Presumably, these are *my* unique thoughts and feelings, which no one else shares. This is *my* body, and these are *my* things. At around 500 B.C.E., Hindu philosophers challenged this commonsense notion of human identity and suggested instead that our true and innermost self is actually the ultimate God of the cosmos—the divine existence that pervades every existing thing. They expressed this in the notion of the *Self-God* (*Atman-Brahman*). A collection of writings from around this time called the *Upanishads* develops this concept. The selection below from the *Katha Upanishad* (c. 500 B.C.E.) describes how difficult it is to discover the true God-Self within each of us, as we are continually distracted by our empirical thinking processes. But, with the right teacher and the right reflective attitude, we may discover our true inner and divine identity. This analysis of the human makeup is largely dualistic, although not quite the same as Plato's theory. For Plato, the two distinct components of my existence are my physical mortal body, and my spiritual immortal soul. However, the *Katha Upanishad* draws a distinction between a person's outermost empirical components (which includes the body and some mental phenomena), and a person's hidden inner divine Self.

Influenced by the Hindu tradition, Buddhist philosophers in India also questioned basic assumptions about our commonsense notions of personal identity. According to Buddhist philosophers, when we attempt to articulate the key features of our commonsense notions of ourselves, we will never find any single concrete self to describe. Technically speaking, then, we have *no self*. An early Buddhist text titled *Questions of King Milinda* (c. 100 C.E.) explores the no-self doctrine. In a dialog between King Milinda and a Buddhist monk named Nagasena, the King feels that the no-self doctrine is absurd, and he starts to ridicule it. Nagasena responds with an analogy. Imagine that we examine a chariot, piece by piece, attempting to find the true nature of the chariot. In the end, we will not be able to identify the chariot with any of its constituent parts. Instead, the term "chariot" is only a name that we use to refer to a collection of parts. In the same way, we cannot identify our commonsense notion of the self with any of our specific mental or physical features. The "self" too is just a name that we use in reference to a fluctuating collection of mental and physical attributes.

The Roman philosopher Lucretius (c. 94–55 B.C.E.) defends monistic materialism in his poem *On the Nature of Things*. He describes how our senses deceive us when we see a solid white mass on a distant hill: "Often the fleecy flock cropping the glad pasture on a hill creep on whither each is called and tempted by the grass bejeweled with fresh dew, and the lambs fed full gambol and butt playfully; yet all this seems blurred to us afar, and to lie like a white mass on a green hill." What appears to be a solid white mass from a distance turns out to be a flock of sheep. Lucretius uses this analogy of the flock of sheep to say that everything in nature is similarly composed of small particles. His poem is an elaboration of earlier ideas of nature, especially the theory taught by Democritus, who said that everything is composed of tiny bits of solid matter, which he called "atoms." These tiny atoms are, he said, invisible, eternal, indestructible, and come in different sizes and shapes. Everything can be explained by the movement and arrangement of these atoms. Atoms not only account for the nature of physical things but also explain the operation of our senses and feelings as well as the functioning of our minds. Although Democritus and Lucretius offered no scientific proof of this atomic theory, which they arrived at simply intuitively, in time renowned scientists such as Isaac Newton accepted this theory as the basis of the science of physics. Although contemporary scientists have made modified this atomic theory, they have nevertheless preserved it in principle.

Many centuries after Lucretius, in his *Meditations* and *The Passions of the Soul*, French philosopher René Descartes (1569–1650) offered a view that we now call *interactive dualism*. As a dualist, Descartes argued that a human being is composed of two distinct substances, namely, thought and extension, or mind and body. This distinction is intuitively understandable as a way of separating our various experiences, which alternately focus on physical things and our bodies on the one hand and on our ideas of thought and imagination on the other. However, when we try to specify the exact nature of mind or thought as compared with body, many difficulties arise. The main problem is understanding how information transfers between our conscious spirit and our unconscious physical bodies. Even though my mind and body are distinct, the two must somehow interact. Suppose, for example, that a mosquito bites my foot; that sensory information must eventually make its way up through my brain, and out of my body into my spiritual mind. Similarly, if I decide to swat the mosquito with my hand, my spirit must issue a command that first flows back into my brain, then down through my hand. Descartes believed that the interactive gateway between these two realms was the pineal gland in the brain.

Descartes offered his pineal gland theory to explain how two radically different things—spirit and physical matter—could interact with each other. In her *Principles of the Most Ancient and Modern Philosophy* (1692), British philosopher Anne Conway (1631–1678) was not impressed with Descartes' solution, and she felt that the entire mind–body problem rested on the mistaken assumption that mind and body are fundamentally different kinds of things. Conway suggests instead that matter and mind do not really differ in kind but only in degree. That is, we should picture a graded spectrum of stuff, beginning with the heaviest matter at one end and with the lightest spirit at the other. In the middle of this spectrum there is light matter and heavy spirit. It is in this middle ground that heavy spirit, which is slightly physical itself, can physically push light matter such as air.

In his *Three Dialogues*, Irish philosopher George Berkeley (1685–1753) defends monistic idealism and, accordingly, denied what seemed obvious to Democritus, Descartes, and most of us. Who can deny that physical things have an external existence independent of our thoughts? Berkeley argued that there is no material world—and consequently that we have no physical bodies! The only things that exist are spiritual minds and the perceptions that these minds experience. And, the perceptions that we have of external things—such as trees, other people, and our physical bodies—are interjected into our minds by God. According to Berkeley, for something *to be* means simply that we have a perception. His formula is that "to be is to be perceived" (*esse est percipi*). Take the example of a cherry. We normally think that there is a cherry and that it has certain qualities. It is soft, red, round, sweet, and fragrant. All these qualities are ideas in our minds that the cherry has the power to produce through the senses, so that the softness is felt, the color is seen, the roundness is either felt or seen, the sweetness is tasted, and the fragrance is smelled. The very existence of these qualities consists in their being perceived. Apart from these qualities, there is no sensed something, in short, there is nothing else. The cherry, and everything else in our experience, consists of the qualities we perceive and therefore only represents a complex of sensations or ideas. In the selection included here, Berkeley defends his view that matter does not exist.

Scottish philosopher David Hume (1711–1776) rejected the view of both Descartes and Berkeley that our minds are spiritual in nature; for Hume, it is just an aspect of our physical bodies. In his *Treatise of Human Nature* he also rejected the common presumption that a person's mind is a unified thing that continues intact over time. According to Hume, "there are some philosophers, who imagine we are every moment intimately conscious of what we call our Self." But he says that "for my part, when I enter most intimately into what I call *myself*, I always stumble on some particular perception or other, of heat or cold, light or shade, love or hatred, pain or pleasure. I never can catch *myself* at any time without a perception and can never observe anything but the perception." Similar to the Buddhist discussion in *Questions of King Milinda*, Hume argued that our minds consist simply of a bundle of transient and fluctuation perceptions. However, unlike Buddhists who believed that spiritual exercise can bring us to enlightenment, Hume remained skeptical regarding the "Self" and other issues.

In his book the *Concept of Mind* (1949), British philosopher Gilbert Ryle (1900–1976) argued that Descartes created philosophical difficulties regarding the mind–body problem because he made a serious mistake—a "category mistake"—in accounting for the nature of the mind. Almost as a modern-day Hume, Ryle sees no evidence for something called the "self" or "mind." There is, he says, no "ghost in the machine." To say that various forms of human behavior, including emotions, point to an inner intelligence or mind is an unwarranted inference. "To find that most people have minds," says Ryle, "is simply to find that they are able and prone to do certain sorts of things, and this we do by witnessing the sorts of things they do." Ryle's position became known as logical behaviorism. Ryle solves the mind–body problem by rejecting spirit, as Hume did, but the mind as well. In *Minds, Brains and Science* (1984) John Searle (b. 1932) similarly rejects the notion of spirit, but nevertheless retains the concept of mind. He argues that mental phenomena are simply higher features of the brain and that a study of the mind is ultimately a study of the brain. Thus, mentalism (mind) and naive physicalism (body) are "perfectly consistent with each other. Indeed, as far as we know anything about how the world works, they are not only consistent, they are both true."

Do Minds Survive after Death?*

Plato (427–347 B.C.E.)

SOCRATES: I desire to prove to you that the real philosopher has reason to be of good cheer when he is about to die, and that after death he may hope to obtain the greatest good in the other world. And how this may be, Simmias and Cebes, I will endeavour to explain. For I deem that the true votary of philosophy is likely to be misunderstood by other men; they do not perceive that he is always pursuing death and dying; and if this be so, and he has had the desire of death all his life long, why when his time comes should he repine at that which he has been always pursuing and desiring?

SIMMIAS: Simmias said laughingly: Though not in a laughing humour, you have made me laugh, Socrates; for I cannot help thinking that the many when they hear your words will say how truly you have described philosophers, and our people at home will likewise say that the life which philosophers desire is in reality death, and that they have found them out to be deserving of the death which they desire.

SOCRATES: And they are right, Simmias, in thinking so, with the exception of the words "they have found them out"; for they have not found out either what is the nature of that death which the true philosopher deserves, or how he deserves or desires death. But enough of them:—let us discuss the matter among ourselves: Do we believe that there is such a thing as death?

SIMMIAS: To be sure, replied Simmias.

*From Plato, "Phaedo."

SOCRATES: Is it not the separation of soul and body? And to be dead is the completion of this; when the soul exists in herself, and is released from the body and the body is released from the soul, what is this but death?

SIMMIAS: Just so, he replied.

SOCRATES: There is another question, which will probably throw light on our present inquiry if you and I can agree about it:—Ought the philosopher to care about the pleasures—if they are to be called pleasures—of eating and drinking?

SIMMIAS: Certainly not, answered Simmias.

SOCRATES: And what about the pleasures of love—should he care for them?

SIMMIAS: By no means.

SOCRATES: And will he think much of the other ways of indulging the body, for example, the acquisition of costly raiment, or sandals, or other adornments of the body? Instead of caring about them, does he not rather despise anything more than nature needs? What do you say?

SIMMIAS: I should say that the true philosopher would despise them.

SOCRATES: Would you not say that he is entirely concerned with the soul and not with the body? He would like, as far as he can, to get away from the body and to turn to the soul.

SIMMIAS: Quite true.

SOCRATES: In matters of this sort philosophers, above all other men, may be observed in every sort of way to dissever the soul from the communion of the body.

SIMMIAS: Very true.

SOCRATES: Whereas, Simmias, the rest of the world are of opinion that to him who has no sense of pleasure and no part in bodily pleasure, life is not worth having; and that he who is indifferent about them is as good as dead.

SIMMIAS: That is also true.

SOCRATES: What again shall we say of the actual acquirement of knowledge?— is the body, if invited to share in the enquiry, a hinderer or a helper? I mean to say, have sight and hearing any truth in them? Are they not, as the poets are always telling us, inaccurate witnesses? and yet, if even they are inaccurate and indistinct, what is to be said of the other senses?—for you will allow that they are the best of them?

SIMMIAS: Certainly, he replied.

SOCRATES: Then when does the soul attain truth?—for in attempting to consider anything in company with the body she is obviously deceived.

SIMMIAS: True.

SOCRATES: Then must not true existence be revealed to her in thought, if at all?

SIMMIAS: Yes.

SOCRATES: And thought is best when the mind is gathered into herself and none of these things trouble her—neither sounds nor sights nor pain nor any pleasure,—when she takes leave of the body, and has as little as possible to do with it, when she has no bodily sense or desire, but is aspiring after true being?

SIMMIAS: Certainly.

SOCRATES: And in this the philosopher dishonors the body; his soul runs away from his body and desires to be alone and by herself?

SIMMIAS: That is true.   → Soul wants to be alone.

SOCRATES: Well, but there is another thing, Simmias: Is there or is there not an absolute justice?

SIMMIAS: Assuredly there is.

SOCRATES: And an absolute beauty and absolute good?

SIMMIAS: Of course.

SOCRATES: But did you ever behold any of them with your eyes?

SIMMIAS: Certainly not.

SOCRATES: Or did you ever reach them with any other bodily sense?—and I speak not of these alone, but of absolute greatness, and health, and strength, and of the essence or true nature of everything. Has the reality of them ever been perceived by you through the bodily organs? or rather, is not the nearest approach to the knowledge of their several natures made by him who so orders his intellectual vision as to have the most exact conception of the essence of each thing which he considers?

SIMMIAS: Certainly.

SOCRATES: And he attains to the purest knowledge of them who goes to each with the mind alone, not introducing or intruding in the act of thought sight or any other sense together with reason, but with the very light of the mind in her own clearness searches into the very truth of each; he who has got rid, as far as he can, of eyes and ears and, so to speak, of the whole body, these being in his opinion distracting elements which when they infect the soul hinder her from acquiring truth and knowledge—who, if not he, is likely to attain the knowledge of true being?

SIMMIAS: What you say has a wonderful truth in it, Socrates, replied Simmias.

SOCRATES: And when real philosophers consider all these things, will they not be led to make a reflection which they will express in words something like the following? "Have we not found," they will say, "a path of thought which seems to bring us and our argument to the conclusion, that while we are in the body, and while the soul is infected with the evils of the body, our desire will not be satisfied? and our desire is of the truth. For the body is a source of endless trouble to us by reason of the mere requirement of food; and is liable also to diseases which overtake and impede us in the search after true being: it fills us full of loves, and lusts, and fears, and fancies of all kinds, and endless foolery, and in fact, as men say, takes away from us the power of thinking at all. Whence come wars, and fightings, and factions? whence but from the body and the lusts of the body? wars are occasioned by the love of money, and money has to be acquired for the sake and in the service of the body; and by reason of all these impediments we have no time to give to philosophy; and, last and worst of all, even if we are at leisure and betake ourselves to some speculation, the body is always breaking in upon us, causing turmoil and confusion in our enquiries, and so amazing us that we are prevented from seeing the truth.

body is a constant distraction

—*Socrates calls abstract & intangible things — FORMS*

It has been proved to us by experience that if we would have pure knowledge of anything we must be quit of the body—the soul in herself must
behold things in themselves: and then we shall attain the wisdom which
we desire, and of which we say that we are lovers, not while we live, but
after death; for if while in company with the body, the soul cannot have
pure knowledge, one of two things follows—either knowledge is not to be
attained at all, or, if at all, after death. For then, and not till then, the soul
will be parted from the body and exist in herself alone. In this present life,
I reckon that we make the nearest approach to knowledge when we have
the least possible intercourse or communion with the body, and are not
surfeited with the bodily nature, but keep ourselves pure until the hour
when God himself is pleased to release us. And thus having got rid of the
foolishness of the body we shall be pure and hold converse with the pure,
and know of ourselves the clear light everywhere, which is no other than
the light of truth." For the impure are not permitted to approach the pure.
These are the sort of words, Simmias, which the true lovers of knowledge
cannot help saying to one another, and thinking. You would agree; would
you not?

SIMMIAS: Undoubtedly, Socrates.

SOCRATES: But, O my friend, if this is true, there is great reason to hope that,
going whither I go, when I have come to the end of my journey, I shall attain that which has been the pursuit of my life. And therefore I go on my
way rejoicing, and not I only, but every other man who believes that his
mind has been made ready and that he is in a manner purified.

SIMMIAS: Certainly, replied Simmias.

SOCRATES: And what is purification but the separation of the soul from the
body, as I was saying before; the habit of the soul gathering and collecting
herself into herself from all sides out of the body; the dwelling in her own
place alone, as in another life, so also in this, as far as she can;—the release
of the soul from the chains of the body?

SIMMIAS: Very true, he said.

SOCRATES: And this separation and release of the soul from the body is termed
death?

SIMMIAS: To be sure, he said.

SOCRATES: And the true philosophers, and they only, are ever seeking to release the soul. Is not the separation and release of the soul from the body
their especial study?

SIMMIAS: That is true.

SOCRATES: And, as I was saying at first, there would be a ridiculous contradiction in men studying to live as nearly as they can in a state of death, and
yet repining when it comes upon them.

SIMMIAS: Clearly.

SOCRATES: And the true philosophers, Simmias, are always occupied in the
practice of dying, wherefore also to them least of all men is death terrible.
Look at the matter thus:—if they have been in every way the enemies of
the body, and are wanting to be alone with the soul, when this desire of

theirs is granted, how inconsistent would they be if they trembled and re-pined, instead of rejoicing at their departure to that place where, when they arrive, they hope to gain that which in life they desired—and this was wisdom—and at the same time to be rid of the company of their enemy. Many a man has been willing to go to the world below animated by the hope of seeing there an earthly love, or wife, or son, and conversing with them. And will he who is a true lover of wisdom, and is strongly per-suaded in like manner that only in the world below he can worthily enjoy her, still repine at death? Will he not depart with joy? Surely he will, O my friend, if he be a true philosopher. For he will have a firm conviction that there and there only, he can find wisdom in her purity. And if this be true, he would be very absurd, as I was saying, if he were afraid of death.

The All-Pervading Self-God*

Many are not even able to hear the Self, and many, even when they hear of it, do not comprehend it. Wonderful is the person, who when found, is able to teach the Self. Wonderful also is the person who comprehends it when taught by an able teacher. The Self, when taught by an inferior person, is not easy to understand, even when one frequently thinks about it. Unless another teaches it, there is no way to it, for it is inconceivably smaller than what is small. That doctrine cannot be obtained by argument, but when someone else declares it, then it is easy to understand. You have obtained this knowledge now, and you are truly a person of genuine determination. May we always have an inquirer like you! . . . Indeed, the wise person leaves joy and sorrow far behind when he meditates on his Self and recognizes the primordial, who is difficult to see, who has entered into the dark, who is hidden in the cave, and who dwells in the abyss. A mortal rejoices when he hears this, embraces it, separates it from all qualities, and thus reaches the subtle Being, because he has obtained what is a cause for rejoicing. I believe that the house of God is open.

That word is *Om*, which all the Vedas [i.e., Hindu scriptures] record, which all prayers proclaim, which people desire when they live as religious students. That imperishable syllable means God, that syllable means the high-est God. If a person knows that syllable, then he obtains whatever he desires. This is the best support, this is the highest support; he who knows that sup-port is magnified in the world of God.

The knowing Self is not born, and it does not die. It sprang from nothing, and nothing sprang from it. The primordial is unborn, eternal, everlasting. He is not killed, though the body is killed. If the killer thinks that he kills, if the

*From *Katha Upanishad* (c. 500 B.C.E.).

killed think that he is killed, they do not understand. For this one does not kill, nor is that one killed. The Self, smaller than small, greater than great, is hidden in the heart of that creature. A person who is free from desires and free from grief sees the majesty of the Self by the grace of the Creator. Though sitting still, he walks far. Though lying down, he goes everywhere. Who, except myself, is able to know the God who rejoices yet who also does not rejoice? The wise person never grieves who knows the Self as bodiless within the bodies, as unchanging among changing things, as great and all-pervading.

That Self cannot be gained by the Vedas, nor by understanding, nor by much learning. Whoever the Self chooses can gain knowledge of the Self. The Self chooses him as his own. However, a person cannot obtain knowledge of the Self if he has not first turned away from his wickedness. He must be tranquil, subdued, and have his mind at rest. . . .

We may understand that the Self is sitting in the chariot, the body is the chariot, the intellect is the charioteer, and the mind is the reins. The senses are the horses, the objects of the senses are their roads. When he [i.e., the highest Self] is in union with the body, the senses, and the mind, then wise people call him the Enjoyer. If someone has no understanding and his mind [i.e., the reins] is never firmly held, then his senses, like vicious horses, are unmanageable. But if someone has understanding and his mind is always firmly held, then his senses are under control, like good horses of a charioteer. If someone has no understanding and is unmindful and always impure, then he never reaches that place, but enters into the cycle of births. But if someone has understanding and is mindful and always pure, then he indeed reaches that place, and from there he is not born again. And if someone has understanding for his charioteer, and who holds the reins of the mind, then he reaches the end of his journey, and that is the highest place of Vishnu.

Beyond the senses there are the objects, beyond the objects there is the mind, and beyond the mind there is the intellect. The Great self [i.e., the ego] is beyond the intellect. Beyond the Great there is the Undeveloped, beyond the Undeveloped there is the Person. Beyond the Person there is nothing. This is the goal, and is the highest road.

That Self is hidden in all beings and does not shine forth, although astute seers see it through their sharp and subtle intellects. A wise person should keep down speech and mind. He should keep them within the Self, which is knowledge. He should keep knowledge within the Self, which is the Great. And he should keep that [the Great] within the Self, which is the Quiet. Wake up and rise, having obtained your wishes. Understand them! The wise say that, like the sharp edge of a razor, the path [to the Self] is difficult to travel and obtain. We are freed from the jaws of death when we perceive that which is without sound, without touch, without form, without decay, without taste, eternal, without smell, without beginning, without end, beyond the Great, and unchangeable.

The existent Self pierced the openings [of the senses] so that they turn outward; and so one [wrongly] looks outward, and not within himself. A certain wise person, however, wishing for immortality, closed his eyes and saw the

Self directly [within himself]. Children follow outward pleasures, and fall into the snare of widespread death. Only the wise, knowing the nature of what is immortal, do not look for anything stable here among unstable things. Through that [i.e. the Self] we know form, taste, smell, sounds, and loving touches; through that we also know what else exists [within us]. This is that [for which you seek]. By knowing the great all-pervading Self, the wise person knows things while asleep and awake, and he grieves no more. Those who know that this living soul which eats honey [i.e., perceives objects] is the Self—which is always near, the Lord of the past and the future—[those people] have no more fears. This is that [for which you seek].

READING 7

No Permanent Self*

[THE SELF AS A NAME FOR A COLLECTION OF PROPERTIES]

NAGASENA: I am known as Nagasena, your majesty, and it is by this name that my associates address me. But although parents give us names such as "Nagasena" . . . it is, however, only a generally understood term, a designation in common use. For there is no permanent self involved in the matter.

KING MILINDA: . . . If there is no self to be found, who is it then that furnishes you priests with the priestly requisites,—robes, food, bedding, and medicine, the reliance of the sick? Who is it makes use of the same? Who is it that keeps the precepts? Who is it that applies himself to meditation? Who is it that realizes the Paths, the Fruits, and Nirvana? Who is it that destroys life? Who is it that takes what is not given him? Who is it that commits immorality? Who is it that tells lies? Who is it that drinks intoxicating liquor? Who is it that commits the five crimes that constitute "proximate karma" [i.e., actions that have consequences in the next life]? In that case, there is no merit; there is no demerit; there is no one who does or causes to be done meritorious or demeritorious deeds; neither good nor evil deeds can have any fruit or result. Nagasena, neither is he a murderer who kills a priest, nor can you priests, Nagasena, have any teacher, preceptor, or ordination. When you say, "My fellow-priests, your majesty, address me as 'Nagasena,' what then is this 'Nagesena'? Please, revered one, is the hair of the head 'Nagasena'?"

NAGASENA: No, truly, your majesty.

KING MILINDA: Is the hair of the body "Nagasena"?

*From *Questions of King Milinda* (c. 100 C.E.), 2.1.1, 2, 6.

NAGASENA: No, truly, your majesty.

KING MILINDA: Are nails . . . teeth . . . skin . . . flesh . . . sinews . . . bones . . . marrow of the bones . . . kidneys . . . heart . . . liver . . . pleura . . . spleen . . . lungs . . . intestines . . . mesentery . . . stomach . . . feces . . . bile . . . phlegm . . . pus . . . blood . . . sweat . . . fat . . . tears . . . lymph . . . saliva . . . snot . . . synovial fluid . . . urine . . . brain of the head . . . form . . . sensation . . . perception . . . predispositions . . . consciousness . . . form, "Nagasena"?

KING MILINDA: Are, then, form, sensation, perception, the predispositions, and consciousness unitedly "Nagasena"?

NAGASENA: No, truly, your majesty.

KING MILINDA: Is it, then, something besides form, sensation, perception, the predispositions, and consciousness, which is "Nagasena"?

NAGASENA: No, truly, your majesty.

KING MILINDA: Although I question you very closely, I fail to discover any "Nagasena". Truly, now, "Nagasena" is a mere empty sound. What "Nagasena" is there here? You speak a falsehood, a lie: there is no "Nagasena".

NAGASENA: Your majesty . . . did you come on foot, or riding?

KING MILINDA: I do not go on foot; I came in a chariot.

NAGASENA: If you came in a chariot, indicate this chariot to me. Is the pole the chariot?

KING MILINDA: No, truly.

NAGASENA: Is the axle . . . wheels . . . chariot-body . . . bannerstaff . . . yoke . . . reins . . . goading-stick the chariot?

KING MILINDA: No, truly, Nagasena.

NAGASENA: Please, your majesty, are pole, axle, wheels, chariot-body, bannerstaff, yoke, reins, and goad unitedly the chariot?

KING MILINDA: No, truly, Nagasena.

NAGASENA: Is it, then, something else besides pole, axle, wheels, chariot-body, banner-staff, yoke, reins, and goad which is the chariot?

KING MILINDA: No, truly, Nagasena.

NAGASENA: Although I question you very closely, I fail to discover any chariot. Truly now, your majesty, the word "chariot" is a mere empty sound. What chariot is there here? Your majesty, you speak a falsehood, a lie: there is no chariot. Your majesty, you are the chief king in all the continent of India. Of whom are you afraid that you speak a lie? Listen to me, my lords, you five hundred High priests, and you eighty thousand priests! Milinda the king here says this: "I came in a chariot," and when I request, "If you came in a chariot, indicate that chariot to me," he fails to produce any chariot. Is it possible for me to agree with what he says?

NARRATOR: When he had thus spoken, the five hundred High priests applauded the venerable Nagasena. The priests then spoke to King Milinda as follows: "Now, your majesty, answer, if you can." Then King Milinda spoke to the venerable Nagasena as follows.

KING MILINDA: Speaking truthfully, Nagasena, the word "chariot" is only a way of counting, a term, a label, a convenient designation, and a name for pole, axle, wheels, chariot-body, and banner-staff.

NAGASENA: You understand a chariot very well. In exactly the same way, in regards to me, [the word] "Nagasena" is only a way of counting, a term, a label, a convenient designation, or a mere name for the hair of my head, hair of my body . . . brain of the head, form, sensation, perception, the predispositions, and consciousness. But in the absolute sense there is no self here to be found. And the priestess Vajira said the following in the presence of The Blessed One: "Even as the word of 'chariot' means that members join to frame a whole; so when the groups appear to view, we use the phrase, 'A living being.' "

KING MILINDA: This is wonderful, Nagasena! This is marvelous! The wit of your replies is brilliant and prompt. If the Buddha were alive, he would applaud.

[THE SELF IS NOT AN INDISCRIMINATE LIVING PRINCIPLE WITHIN US]

KING MILINDA: Is there, Nagasena, such a thing as the soul?

NAGASENA: What is this "soul" your majesty?

KING MILINDA: It is the *living principle* within which sees forms through the eye, hears sounds through the ear, experiences tastes through the tongue, smells odors through the nose, feels touch through the body, and discerns things through the mind. It is just as we—sitting here in the palace—can look out of any window out of which we wish to look, the east window or the west, or the north or the south.

NAGASENA: I will tell you about the five doors, great king. Listen attentively. If the [so-called] *living principle* within sees forms through the eye in the manner that you mention, choosing its window as it likes, can it not then see forms not only through the eye, but also through each of the other five organs of sense? And in like manner can it not then as well hear sounds, and experience taste, and smell odors, and feel touch, and discern conditions through each of the other five organs of sense, besides the one you have in each case specified?

KING MILINDA: No, Sir.

NAGASENA: Then these powers are not united one to another indiscriminately [through a so-called "living principle"], the latter sense to the former organ, and so on. Now—as we are seated here in the palace, with these windows all thrown open, and in full daylight—if we only stretch forth our heads, we will see all kinds of objects plainly. Can the *living principle* do the same when the doors of the eyes are thrown open? When the doors of the ear are thrown open, can it do so? Can it then not only hear sounds, but see sights, experience tastes, smell odors, feel touch, and discern conditions? And so with each of its windows?

KING MILINDA: No, Sir.

NAGASENA: Then these powers are not united one to another indiscriminately [through a so-called "living principle"]. Now again, great king, if Dinna here were to go outside and stand in the gateway, would you be aware that he had done so?

KING MILINDA: Yes, I should know it.

NAGASENA: And if the same Dinna were to come back again, and stand before you, would you be aware of his having done so?

KING MILINDA: Yes, I should know it.

NAGASENA: Well, great king, would the living principle within discern, in like manner, if anything possessing flavor were laid upon the tongue, its sourness, or its saltness, or its acidity, or its pungency, or its astringency, or its sweetness?

KING MILINDA: Yes, it would know it.

NAGASENA: But when the flavor had passed into the stomach would it still discern these things?

KING MILINDA: Certainly not.

NAGASENA: Then these powers are not united one to the other indiscriminately [through a so-called "living principle"]. Now suppose, your majesty, a man were to have a hundred vessels of honey brought and poured into one trough, and then, having had another man's mouth closed over and tied up, were to have him cast into the trough full of honey. Would he know whether that into which he had been thrown was sweet or whether it was not?

KING MILINDA: No, Sir.

NAGASENA: But why not?

KING MILINDA: Because the honey could not get into his mouth.

NAGASENA: Then, great king, these powers are not united one to another indiscriminately.

KING MILINDA: I am not capable of discussing with such a reasoner. Be pleased, Sir, to explain to me how the matter stands.

NAGASENA: It is by reason, your majesty, of the eye and of forms that sight arises, and those other conditions—contact, sensation, idea, thought, abstraction, sense of vitality, and attention—arise each simultaneously with its predecessor. And a similar succession of cause and effect arises when each of the other five organs of sense is brought into play. And so herein there is no such thing as soul.

READING 8

*The Mind as Body**

Lucretius (c. 94–55 B.C.E.)

[BODIES AND THE VOID]

All nature then, as it exists by itself, is founded on two things; there are bodies and there is void in which these bodies are placed and through which they move about. For that body exists by itself the general feeling of mankind declares; and unless at the very first belief in this be firmly grounded, there will be nothing to which we can appeal on hidden things in order to prove anything by reasoning of mind. Then again, if room and space which we call void did not exist, bodies could not be placed anywhere nor move about at all to any side; . . . Therefore beside void and bodies no third nature taken by itself can be left in the number of things, either such as to fall at any time under the ken of our senses or such as any one can grasp by the reason of his mind. . . .

First of all then since there has been found to exist a two-fold and widely dissimilar nature of two things, that is to say of body and of place in which things severally go on, each of the two must exist for and by itself and quite unmixed. For wherever there is empty space which we call void, there body is not; wherever again body maintains itself, there empty void no wise exists. First bodies therefore are solid and without void. . . . These can neither be broken in pieces by the stroke of blows from without nor have their texture undone by aught piercing to their core nor give way before any other kind of assault; as we have proved to you a little before. For without void nothing seems to admit of being crushed in or broken up or split in two by cutting, or of taking in wet or permeating cold or penetrating fire, by which all things are destroyed. And the more anything contains within it of void, the more thoroughly it gives way to the assault of these things. Therefore if first bodies are as I have shown solid and without void, they must be everlasting. Again unless matter had been eternal, all things before this would have utterly returned to nothing and whatever things we see would have been born anew from nothing. But since I have proved above that nothing can be produced from nothing, and that what is begotten cannot be recalled to nothing, first-beginnings must be of an imperishable body into which all things can be dissolved at their last hour, that there may be a supply of matter for the reproduction of things. Therefore first-beginnings are of solid singleness, and in no other way can they have been preserved through ages during infinite time past in order to reproduce things.

*From Lucretius, *On the Nature of Things*, Books 1–3.

But since I have taught that most solid bodies of matter fly about forever unvanquished through all time, mark now, let us unfold whether there is or is not any limit to their sum; likewise let us clearly see whether that which has been found to be void, or room and space, in which things severally go on, is all of it altogether finite or stretches without limits and to an unfathomable depth.

Well then the existing universe is bounded in none of its dimensions; for then it must have had an outside. Again it is seen that there can be an outside of nothing, unless there be something beyond to bound it, so that that is seen, farther than which the nature of this our sense does not follow the thing. Now since we must admit that there is nothing outside the sum, it has no outside, and therefore is without end and limit. And it matters not in which of its regions you take your stand; so invariably, whatever position any one has taken up, he leaves the universe just as infinite as before in all directions. Again if for the moment all existing space be held to be bounded, supposing a man runs forward to its outside borders, and stands on the utmost verge and then throws a winged javelin, do you choose that when hurled with vigorous force it, shall advance to the point to which it has been sent and fly to a distance, or do you decide that something can get in its way and stop it? for you must admit and adopt one of the two suppositions; either of which shuts you out from all escape and compels you to grant that the universe stretches without end.

[THE "SWERVE" AS ATOMS MOVE IN SPACE: THE RANDOM CAUSE OF ALL THINGS]

This point too herein we wish you to apprehend: when bodies are borne downwards sheer through void by their own weights, at quite uncertain times and uncertain spots they push themselves a little from their course: you just and only just can call it a change of inclination. If they were not used to swerve, they would all fall down, like drops of rain, through the deep void, and no clashing would have been begotten nor blow produced among the first-beginnings: thus nature never would have produced anything.

But if haply any one believes that heavier bodies, as they are carried more quickly sheer through space, can fall from above on the lighter and so beget blows able to produce begetting motions, he goes most widely astray from true reason. For whenever bodies fall through water and thin air, they must quicken their descents in proportion to their weights, because the body of water and subtle nature of air cannot retard everything in equal degree, but more readily give way, overpowered by the heavier: on the other hand empty void cannot offer resistance to anything in any direction at any time, but must, as its nature craves, continually give way; and for this reason all things must be moved and borne along with equal velocity though of unequal weights through the unresisting void. Therefore heavier things will never be able to fall from above on lighter nor of themselves to beget blows sufficient to produce the varied motions by which nature carries on things. Wherefore again and again I say bodies must swerve a little; and yet not more than the least possible—lest we be found to be imagining oblique motions and this the reality should refute. For this we see to be plain and evident, that weights, so far as in them is, cannot travel obliquely, when they fall from above, at least so far as you can perceive; but that nothing swerves in any case from the straight course, who is there that can perceive? . . .

And herein you need not wonder at this, that though the first-beginnings of things are all in motion, yet the sum is seen to rest in supreme repose, unless where a thing exhibits motions with its individual body. For all the nature of first things lies far away from our senses beneath their ken; and therefore since they are themselves beyond what you can see, they must withdraw from sight their motion as well; and the more so that the things which we can see, do yet often conceal their motions when a great distance off. Thus often the woolly flocks as they crop the glad pastures on a hill, creep on whither the grass jewelled with fresh dew summons and invites each, and the lambs fed to the full gambol and playfully butt; all which objects appear to us from a distance to be blended together and to rest like a white spot on a green hill. . . .

Now mark and next in order apprehend of what kind and how widely differing in their forms are the beginnings of all things, how varied by manifold diversities of shape; not that a scanty number are possessed of a like form, but because as a rule they do not all resemble one the other. . . . Again things which look to us hard and dense must consist of particles more hooked together, and be held in union because welded all through with branch-like elements. In this class first of all diamond stones stand in foremost line inured to despise blows, and stout blocks of basalt and the strength of hard iron and brass bolts which scream out as they hold fast to their staples. . . .

[MATTER: THE ORIGIN OF SENSATION AND THOUGHT]

Then again what is that which strikes your mind, affects that mind and constrains it to give utterance to many different thoughts, to save you from believing that the sensible is begotten out of senseless things? Sure enough it is because stones and wood and earth however mixed together are yet unable to produce vital sense. This therefore it will be well to remember herein, that I do not assert that the sensible and sensations are forthwith begotten out of all elements without exception which produce things; but that it is of great moment first how minute the particles are which make up the sensible thing and then what shape they possess and what in short they are in their motions, arrangements and positions. . . .

Above all senses cannot exist in any body before the nature itself of the living thing has been begotten, because sure enough the matter remains scattered about in air, rivers, earth, and things produced from earth, and has not met together and combined in appropriate fashion the vital motions by which the all-discerning senses are kindled into action in each living thing.

Again a blow more severe than its nature can endure, prostrates at once any living thing and goes on to stun all the senses of body and mind. For the positions of the first-beginnings are broken up and the vital motions entirely stopped, until the matter, disordered by the shock through the whole frame, unties from the body the vital fastenings of the soul and scatters it abroad and forces it out through all the pores. For what more can we suppose the infliction of a blow can do, than shake from their place and break up the union of the several elements?

In the first place we see that round in all directions, about, above, and underneath, throughout the universe there is no bound. . . .

Again when much matter is at hand, when room is there and there is no thing, no cause to hinder, things sure enough must go on and be completed. Well then if on the one hand there is so great a store of seeds as the whole life of living creatures cannot reckon up, and if the same force and nature abide in them and have the power to throw the seeds of things together into their several places in the same way as they are thrown together into our world, you must admit that in other parts of space there are other earths and various races of men and kinds of wild beasts.

And now since I have shown what-like the beginnings of all things are and how diverse with varied shapes as they fly spontaneously driven on in everlasting motion, and how all things can be severally produced out of these, next after these questions the nature of the mind and soul should I think be cleared up by my verses.

[THE NATURE OF THE HUMAN MIND]

First then I say that the mind which we often call the understanding, in which dwells the directing and governing principle of life, is no less part of the man, than hand and foot and eyes are parts of the whole living creature. . . . Now that you may know that the soul as well is in the limbs and that the body is not wont to have sense by any harmony, this is a main proof: when much of the body has been taken away, still life often stays in the limbs. . . .

Now I assert that the mind and the soul are kept together in close union and make up a single nature, but that the directing principle which we call mind and understanding, is the head so to speak and reigns paramount in the whole body. It has a fixed seat in the middle region of the breast: here throb fear and apprehension, about these spots dwell soothing joys; therefore here is the understanding or mind. All the rest of the soul disseminated through the whole body obeys and moves at the will and inclination of the mind. It by itself alone knows for itself, rejoices for itself, at times when the impression does not move either soul or body together with it. And as when some part of us, the head or the eye, suffers from an attack of pain, we do not feel the anguish at the same time over the whole body, thus the mind sometimes suffers pain by itself or is inspirited with joy, when all the rest of the soul throughout the limbs and frame is stirred by no novel sensation. . . .

This same principle teaches that the nature of the mind and soul is bodily; for when it is seen to push the limbs, rouse the body from sleep, and alter the countenance and guide and turn about the whole man, and when we see that none of these effects can take place without touch nor touch without body, must we not admit that the mind and the soul are of a bodily nature? . . .

I will now go on to explain in my verses of what kind of body the mind consists and out of what it is formed. First of all I say that it is extremely fine and formed of exceedingly minute bodies. That this is so you may, if you please to attend, clearly perceive from what follows: nothing that is seen takes place with a velocity equal to that of the mind when it starts some suggestion and actually sets it going; the mind therefore is stirred with greater rapidity than any of the things whose nature stands out visible to sight. . . . Since then the nature of the mind has been found to be eminently easy to move, it must consist of bodies exceedingly small, smooth, and round. The knowledge of which fact, my good friend, will on many accounts prove useful and be serviceable to you. The following fact too likewise demonstrates how fine the texture is of which its nature is composed, and how small the room is in which it can be contained, could it only be collected into one mass: soon as the un-troubled sleep of death has gotten hold of a man and the nature of the mind and soul has withdrawn, you can perceive then no diminution of the entire body either in appearance or weight: death makes all good save the vital sense and heat. Therefore the whole soul must consist of very small seeds and be in-woven through veins and flesh and sinews; inasmuch as, after it has all with-drawn from the whole body, the exterior contour of the limbs preserves itself entire and not a tittle of the weight is lost. Just in the same way when the flavour of wine is gone or when the delicious aroma of a perfume has been dispersed into the air or when the savour has left some body, yet the thing it-self does not therefore look smaller to the eye. . . .

Again we perceive that the mind is begotten along with the body and grows up together with it and becomes old along with it. For even as children go about with a tottering and weakly body, so slender sagacity of mind fol-lows along with it; then when their life has reached the maturity of confirmed strength, the judgement too is greater and the Power of the mind more devel-oped. Afterwards when the body has been shattered by the mastering might of time and the frame has drooped with its forces dulled, then the intellect halts, the tongue dotes, the mind gives way, all faculties fail and are found wanting at the same time. It naturally follows then that the whole nature of the soul is dissolved, like smoke, into the high air; since we see it is begotten along with the body and grows up along with it and, as I have shown, breaks down at the same time worn out with age.

The Distinction between Mind and Body*

René Descartes (1569–1650)

MEDITATION 6: OF THE EXISTENCE OF MATERIAL THINGS, AND OF THE REAL DISTINCTION BETWEEN THE SOUL AND BODY OF MAN

. . . First of all, then, I perceived that I had a head, hands, feet, and all other members of which this body—which I considered as a part, or possibly even as the whole, of myself—is composed. Further I was sensible that this body was placed amidst many others, from which it was capable of being affected in many different ways, beneficial and hurtful, and I remarked that a certain feeling of pleasure accompanied those that were beneficial, and pain those which were harmful. And in addition to this pleasure and pain, I also experienced hunger, thirst, and other similar appetites, as also certain corporeal inclinations towards joy, sadness, anger, and other similar passions. And outside myself, in addition to extension, figure, and motions of bodies, I remarked in them hardness, heat, and all other tactile qualities, and, further, light and color, and scents and sounds, the variety of which gave me the means of distinguishing the sky, the earth, the sea, and generally all the other bodies, one from the other.

And certainly, considering the ideas of all these qualities which presented themselves to my mind, and which alone I perceived properly or immediately, it was not without reason that I believed myself to perceive objects quite different from my thought, to wit, bodies from which those ideas proceeded; for I found by experience that these ideas presented themselves to me without my consent being requisite, so that I could not perceive any object, however desirous I might be, unless it were present to the organs of sense; and it was not in my power not to perceive it, when it was present. . . .

Nor was it without some reason that I believed that this body (which be a certain special right I call my own) belonged to me more properly and more strictly than any other; for in fact I could never be separated from it as from other bodies; I experienced in it and on account of it all my appetites and affections, and finally I was touched by the feeling of pain and the titillation of pleasure in its parts, and not in the parts of other bodies which were separated from it.

But when I inquired, why, from some, I know not what, painful sensation, there follows sadness of mind, and from the pleasurable sensation there arises

*From René Descartes, *Meditations on the First Philosophy* (1641), Meditation 6; *The Passions of the Soul* (1649).

joy, or why this mysterious pinching of the stomach which I call **hunger** causes me to desire to eat, and dryness of throat causes a desire to drink, and so on, I could give no reason excepting that nature taught me so . . .

But there is nothing which this nature teaches me more expressly nor more sensibly than that I have a body which is adversely affected when I feel pain, which has need of food or drink when I experience the feelings of hunger and thirst, and so on; nor can I doubt there being some truth in all this.

Nature also teaches me by these sensations of pain, hunger, thirst, etc., that I am not only lodged in my body as a pilot in a vessel, but that I am not only lodged in my body as a pilot in a vessel, but that I am very closely united to it, and so to speak so intermingled with it that I seem to compose with it one whole. For if that were not the case, when my body is hurt, I, who am merely a thinking thing, should not feel pain, for I should perceive this wound by the understanding only, just as the sailor perceives by sight when something is damaged in his vessel; and when my body has need of drink or food, I should clearly understand the fact without being warned of it by confused feelings of hunger and thirst. For all these sensations of hunger, thirst, pain, etc. are in truth none other than certain confused modes of thought which are produced by the union and apparent intermingling of mind and body.

Moreover, nature teaches me that many other bodies exist around mine, of which some are to be avoided, and others sought after. And certainly from the fact that I am sensible of different sorts of colors, sounds, scents, tastes, heat, hardness, etc., I very easily conclude that there are in the bodies from which all these diverse sense-perceptions proceed certain variations which answer to them, although possibly these are not really at all similar to them. And also from the fact that amongst these different sense-perceptions some are very agreeable to me and others disagreeable, it is quite certain that my body (or rather myself in my entirety, inasmuch as I am formed of body and soul) may receive different impressions agreeable and disagreeable from the other bodies which surround it. . . .

In this sum [of my existence] many things are comprehended which only pertain to mind (and to these I do not refer in speaking of nature) such as the notion which I have of the fact that what has once been done cannot ever be undone and an infinitude of such things which I know by the light of nature without the help of the body; and seeing that it comprehends many other matters besides which only pertain to body, and are no longer here contained under the name of nature, such as the quality of weight which it possesses and the like, with which I also do not deal; for in talking of nature I only treat of those things given by God to me as a being composed of mind and body. But the nature here described truly teaches me to flee from things which cause the sensation of pain, and seek after the things which communicate to me the sentiment of pleasure and so forth; but I do not see that beyond this it teaches me that from those diverse sense-perceptions we should ever form any conclusion regarding things outside of us, without having carefully and maturely mentally examined them beforehand. For it seems to me that it is mind alone, and not mind and body in conjunction, that is requisite to a knowledge of the truth in regard to such things. . . .

In order to begin this examination, then, I here say, in the first place, that there is a great difference between mind and body, inasmuch as body is by nature always divisible, and the mind is entirely indivisible. For, as a matter of fact, when I consider the mind, that is to say, myself inasmuch as I am only a thinking thing, I cannot distinguish in myself any parts, but apprehend myself to be clearly one and entire; and although the whole mind seems to be united to the whole body, yet if a foot, or an arm, or some other part, is separated from my body, I am aware that nothing has been taken away from my mind. And the faculties of willing, feeling, conceiving, etc., cannot be properly speaking said to be its parts, for it is one and the same mind which employs itself in willing and in feeling and understanding. But it is quite otherwise with corporeal or extended objects, for there is not one of these imaginable by me which my mind cannot easily divide into parts, and which consequently I do not recognize as being divisible; this would be sufficient to teach me that the mind or soul of man is entirely different from the body, if I had not already learned it from other sources.

I further notice that the mind does not receive the impressions from all parts of the body immediately, but only from the brain, or perhaps even from one of its smallest parts, to wit, from that in which the common sense is said to reside, which, whenever it is disposed in the same particular way, conveys the same thing to the mind, although meanwhile the other portions of the body may be differently disposed, as is testified by innumerable experiments which it is unnecessary here to recount.

I notice, also, that the nature of body is such that none of its parts can be moved by another part a little way off which cannot also be moved in the same way by each one of the parts which are between the two, although this more remote part does not act at all. As, for example, in the cord ABCD which is in tension if we pull the last part D, the first part A will not be moved in any way differently from what would be the case if one of the intervening parts B or C were pulled, and the last part D were to remain unmoved. And in the same way, when I feel pain in my foot, my knowledge of physics teaches me that this sensation is communicated by means of nerves dispersed through the foot, which, being extended like cords from there to the brain, when they are contracted in the foot, at the same time contract the inmost portions of the brain which is their extremity and place of origin, and then excite a certain movement which nature has established in order to cause the mind to be affected by a sensation of pain represented as existing in the foot. But because these nerves must pass through the tibia, the thigh, the loins, the back and the neck, in order to reach from the leg to the brain, it may happen that although their extremities which are in the foot are not affected, but only certain ones of their intervening parts which pass by the loins or the neck, this action will excite the same movement in the brain that might have been excited there by a hurt received in the foot, in consequence of which the mind will necessarily feel in the foot the same pain as if it had received a hurt. And the same holds good of all the other perceptions of our senses. . . .

THE PASSIONS OF THE SOUL

31. That there is a small gland in the brain in which the soul exercises its function more particularly than in the other parts.   It is likewise necessary to know that although the soul is joined to the whole body, there is yet in that a certain part in which it exercises its functions more particularly than in all the others. And it is usually believed that this part is the brain, or possibly the heart. It is believed to be the brain because it is with it that the organs of sense are connected. And it is believed to be the heart because it is apparently in it that we experience the passions. But, in examining the matter with care, it seems as though I had clearly ascertained that the part of the body in which the soul exercises its functions immediately is in nowise the heart, nor the whole of the brain. Instead, it is merely the most inward of all its parts, namely, a certain very small gland which is situated in the middle of its substance and so suspended above the duct whereby the animal spirits in its anterior cavities have communication with those in the posterior. It is such that the slightest movements which take place in it may alter very greatly the course of these spirits. And, reciprocally, the smallest changes which occur in the course of the spirits may do much to change the movements of this gland.

32. How we know that this gland is the main seat of the soul.   The reason which persuades me that the soul cannot have any other seat in all the body than this gland wherein to exercise its functions immediately, is that I reflect that the other parts of our brain are all of them double, just as we have two eyes, two hands, two ears, and finally all the organs of our outside senses are double. And inasmuch as we have but one solitary and simple thought of one particular thing at one and the same moment, it must necessarily be the case that there must somewhere be a place where the two images which come to us by the two eyes, where the two other impressions which proceed from a single object by means of the double organs of the other senses, can unite before arriving at the soul, in order that they may not represent to it two objects instead of one. And it is easy to see how these images or other impressions might unite in this gland by the intermission of the spirits which fill the cavities of the brain. But there is no other place in the body where they can be thus united unless they are so in this gland.

34. How the soul and the body act on one another.   Let us then conceive here that the soul has its principal seat in the little gland which exists in the middle of the brain. For, from this spot it radiates forth through all the remainder of the body by means of the animal spirits, nerves, and even the blood, which, participating in the impressions of the spirits, can carry them by the arteries into all the members. Recall what has been said above about the machine of our body, that is, that the little filaments of our nerves are so distributed in all its parts, that on the occasion of the diverse movements which are there excited by sensible objects, they open in different ways the pores of the brain. This, in turn, causes the animal spirit contained in these cavities to enter in different ways into the muscles, by which means they can move the members in all the different ways in which they are capable of being moved. And also, recall all the other causes which are capable of moving the spirits in different ways and which suffice to conduct them into different muscles. Let us here add that the small gland which is the main seat of the soul is so suspended between the cavities which contain the spirits that it can be moved by them in as many different ways as there are sensible differences in the object. Further, it may also be moved in different ways by the soul, whose nature is such that it receives in itself as many different impressions, that is to say, that it possesses as many different perceptions as there are different movements in this gland. Reciprocally, likewise, the machine of the body is so formed that from the simple fact that this gland is differently moved by the soul (or by such other cause, whatever it is) it thrusts the spirits which surround it towards the pores of the brain, which conduct them by the nerves into the muscles, by which means it causes them to move the limbs.

READING 10

*Blurring the Distinction between Mind and Body**

Anne Conway (1631–1678)

[BODY AND SOUL DIFFER ONLY IN DEGREE, NOT IN KIND]

To prove that spirit and body differ not essentially, but gradually, I shall deduce my fourth argument from the intimate band or union, which intercedes between bodies and spirits. [It is] by means whereof the spirits have dominion over the bodies with which they are united, that they move them from one place to another, and use them as instruments in their various operations. For if spirit and body are so contrary one to another (so that a spirit is only life, or a living and sensible substance, but a body a certain mass merely dead; a spirit penetrable and indiscerpible [i.e., indivisible into parts], which are all contrary attributes) what (I pray you) is that which does so join or unite them together? Or, what are those links or chains, whereby they have so firm a connection, and that for so long a space of time? Moreover also, when the spirit or soul is separated from the body, so that it has no longer dominion or power over it to move it as it had before, what is the cause of this separation?

  If it be said, that the vital agreement ([which] the soul has to the body) is the cause of the said union, and that the body being corrupted that vital

*From Anne Conway, *The Principles of the Most Ancient and Modern Philosophy* (1692), Chapters 8 and 9.

agreement ceases, I answer, we must first inquire in what this vital agreement does consist. For if they cannot tell us wherein it does consist, they only trifle with empty words, which give a sound, but want a signification. For certainly in the sense which they take body and spirit in, there is no agreement at all between them. For a body is always a dead thing, void of life and sense, no less when the spirit is in it, than when it is gone out of it. Hence there is no agreement at all between them. And if there is any agreement, that certainly will remain the same, both when the body is sound, and when it is corrupted.

If they deny this, because a spirit requires an organized body (y means whereof it performs its vital acts of the external senses—moves a d transports the body from place to place, which organical action ceases when the body is corrupted) certainly by this the difficulty is never the better solved. For why does the spirit require such an organized body? For example, Why does it require a corporeal eye so wonderfully formed and organized, that I can see by it? Why does it need a corporeal light to see corporeal objects? Or, why is it requisite that the image of the object should be sent to it, through the eye, that I may see it? If the same were entirely nothing but a spirit, and no way corporeal, why does it need so many several corporeal organs, so far different from the nature of it?

Furthermore, how can a spirit move its body, or any of its members, if a spirit (as they affirm) is of such a nature, that no part of its body can in the least resist it, even as one body is wont to resist another, when it is moved by it, by reason of its impenetrability? For if a spirit could also easily penetrate all bodies, wherefore does it not leave the body behind it when it is moved from place to place, seeing it can so easily pass out without the least resistance? For certainly this is the cause of all motions which we see in the world, where one thing moves another, *viz.* because both are impenetrable in the sense aforesaid. For, were it not for this impenetrability, one creature could not move another, because this would not oppose that, nor at all resist it. An example whereof we have in the sails of a ship, by which the wind drives the ship, and that so much the more vehemently, by how much the fewer holes, vents, and passages, the same finds in the sails against which it drives. When on the contrary, if, instead of sails, nets were expanded, through which the wind would have a freer passage, certainly by these the ship would be but little moved, although it blew with great violence. Hence we see how this impenetrability causes resistance, and this makes motion. But if there were no impenetrability, as in the case of body and spirit, then there would be no resistance, and by consequence the spirit could make no motion in the body. . . . .

For we may easily understand how one body is united with another, by that true agreement that one has with another in its own nature. And so the most subtle and spiritual body may be united with a body that is very gross and thick, namely, by means of certain bodies partaking of subtlety and grossness, according to divers degrees consisting between two extremes. And these middle bodies are indeed the links and chains by which the soul, which is so subtle and spiritual, is conjoined with a body so gross—which middle spirits (if they cease, or are absent) the union is broken or dissolved. So from the same foundation we may easily understand how the soul moves the body, *viz.* as one subtle body can move another gross and thick body. And seeing body itself is a sensible life, or an intellectual substance, it is no less clearly conspicuous how one body can wound, or grieve, or gratify, or please another. [It is] because things of one, or alike nature can easily affect each other. . . .

I shall draw a fifth argument from what we observe in all visible bodies, as in earth, water, stones, wood, etc. What abundance of spirits is in all these things? For earth and water continually produce animals, as they have done from the beginning, so that a pool filled with water may produce fishes though none were ever put there to increase or breed. And seeing that all other things do more originally proceed from earth and water, it necessarily follows, that the spirits of all animals were in the water. And therefore it is said in *Genesis,* that the spirit of God moved upon the face of the waters, *viz.* that from hence he might produce whatsoever was afterwards created.

But if it be said, this argument does not prove that all spirits are bodies, but that all bodies have in them the spirits of all animals (so that every body has a spirit in it, and likewise a spirit and body, and although they are thus united, yet they still remain different in nature one from another, and so cannot be changed one into another) to this I answer. If every body, even the least, has in it the spirits of all animals, and other things, even as matter is said to have in it all forms, now I demand, whether a body has actually all those spirits in it, or potentially only? If actually, how is it possible that so many spirits essentially distinct from body can actually exist in their distinct essences in so small a body (even in the least that can be conceived) unless it be by intrinsic presence, which is not communicable to any creature, as already proved. For if all kinds of spirits are in any, even the least body, how comes it to pass that such an animal is produced of this body and not another? Yea, how comes it to pass that all kinds of animals are not immediately produced out of one and the same body, which experience denies. For we see that nature keeps her order in all operations, whence one animal is formed of another, and one species proceeds from another, as well when it ascends to a farther perfection, as when it descends to a viler state and condition.

But if they say, all spirits are contained in any body, not actually in their distinct essences, but only potentially as they term it, then it must be granted, that the body and all those spirits are one and the same thing. That is, that a body may be turned into them, as when we say wood is potentially fire (that is, can be turned into fire), water is potentially air (that is, may be changed into air) . . .

[AGAINST DESCARTES, HOBBES, AND SPINOZA]

From what has been lately said, and from divers reasons alleged, that spirit and body are originally in their first substance but one and the same thing, it evidently appears that the philosophers (so called) which have taught otherwise, whether ancient or modern, have generally erred . . .

And none can object, that all this philosophy is no other than that of Descartes or Hobbes under a new mask. For, first, as touching the Cartesian philosophy, this says that every body is a mere dead mass, not only void of all kind of life and sense, but utterly incapable thereof to all eternity. This grand error also is to be imputed to all those who affirm body and spirit to be contrary things, and inconvertible one into another, so as to deny a body all life and sense, but utterly incapable thereof to all eternity. This grand error also is to be imputed to all those who affirm body and spirit to be contrary things, and inconvertible one into another, so as to deny a body all life and sense, which is quite contrary to the grounds of this our philosophy. Wherefore it is so far from being a *Cartesian* principle, under a new mask, that it may be truly said it is *anti-Cartesian,* in regard of their fundamental principles—although, it cannot be denied that Descartes taught many excellent and ingenious things concerning the mechanical part of natural operations, and how all natural motions proceed according to rules and laws mechanical, even as indeed nature herself, i.e., the creature, as an excellent mechanical skill and wisdom in itself (given it from God, who is the fountain of all wisdom) by which it operates. But yet in nature, and her operations, they are far more than merely mechanical, and the same is not a mere organical body, like a clock, wherein there is not a vital principle of motion, but a living body, having life and sense, which body is far more sublime than a mere mechanism, or mechanical motion.

But, secondly, as to what pertains to Hobbes's opinion, this is more contrary to this our philosophy, than that of Descartes. For Descartes acknowledged God to be plainly immaterial, and an incorporeal spirit. Hobbes affirms God himself to be material and corporeal—yea, nothing else but matter and body—and so confounds God and the creatures in their essences, and denies that there is any essential distinction between them. These and many more the worst of consequences are the dictates of Hobbes's philosophy, to which may be added that of Spinoza, for this Spinoza also confounds God and the creatures together, and makes but one being of both, all which are diametrically opposite to the philosophy here delivered by us.

READING 11

Consciousness, not Matter, the True Reality*

George Berkeley (1685–1753)

HYLAS: You were represented, in last night's conversation, as one who maintained the most extravagant opinion that ever entered into the mind of man, to wit, that there is no such thing as *material substance* in the world.

PHILONOUS: That there is no such thing as what *philosophers call material substance*, I am seriously persuaded: but, if I were made to see anything absurd or skeptical in this, I should then have the same reason to renounce this that I imagine I have now to reject the contrary opinion.

HYLAS: What I can anything be more fantastical, more repugnant to Common Sense, or a more manifest piece of Skepticism, than to believe there is no such thing as *matter?*

PHILONOUS: Softly, good Hylas. What if it should prove that you, who hold there is, are, by virtue of that opinion, a greater skeptic, and maintain more paradoxes and repugnances to Common Sense, than I who believe no such thing?

HYLAS: You may as soon persuade me, the part is greater than the whole, as that, in order to avoid absurdity and Skepticism, I should ever be obliged to give up my opinion in this point.

PHILONOUS: Well then, are you content to admit that opinion for true, which upon examination shall appear most agreeable to Common Sense, and remote from Skepticism?

HYLAS: With all my heart. Since you are for raising disputes about the plainest things in nature, I am content for once to hear what you have to say. . . .

[NO MATERIAL SUBSTRATUM]

PHILONOUS: Make me to understand the difference between what is immediately perceived and a sensation.

HYLAS: The sensation I take to be an act of the mind perceiving; besides which, there is something perceived; and this I call the *object.* For example, there is red and yellow on that tulip. But then the act of perceiving those colors is in me only, and not in the tulip.

PHILONOUS: What tulip do you speak of? Is it that which you see?

HYLAS: The same.

PHILONOUS: And what do you see beside color, figure, and extension? . . .

*From George Berkeley, *Three Dialogues between Hylas and Philonous,* (1713), Dialogue 1.

HYLAS: I acknowledge, Philonous, that, upon a fair observation of what passes in my mind, I can discover nothing else but that I am a thinking being, affected with variety of sensations; neither is it possible to conceive how a sensation should exist in an unperceiving substance. But then, on the other hand, when I look on sensible things in a different view, considering them as so many modes and qualities, I find it necessary to suppose a *material substratum,* without which they cannot be conceived to exist.

PHILONOUS: *Material substratum* call you it? Pray, by which of your senses came you acquainted with that being?

HYLAS: It is not itself sensible; its modes and qualities only being perceived by the senses.

PHILONOUS: I presume then it was by reflexion and reason you obtained the idea of it?

HYLAS: I do not pretend to any proper positive *idea* of it. However, I conclude it exists, because qualities cannot be conceived to exist without a support.

PHILONOUS: It seems then you have only a relative *notion* of it, or that you conceive it not otherwise than by conceiving the relation it bears to sensible qualities?

HYLAS: Right.

PHILONOUS: Be pleased therefore to let me know wherein that relation consists.

HYLAS: Is it not sufficiently expressed in the term *substratum,* or *substance?*

PHILONOUS: If so, the word *substratum* should import that it is spread under the sensible qualities or accidents?

HYLAS: True.

PHILONOUS: And consequently under extension?

HYLAS: I own it.

PHILONOUS: It is therefore somewhat in its own nature entirely distinct from extension?

HYLAS: I tell you, extension is only a mode, and matter is something that supports modes. And is it not evident the thing supported is different from the thing supporting?

PHILONOUS: So that something distinct from, and exclusive of, extension is supposed to be the *substratum* of extension?

HYLAS: Just so.

PHILONOUS: Answer me, Hylas. Can a thing be spread without extension? Or is not the idea of extension necessarily included in *spreading?*

HYLAS: It is.

PHILONOUS: Whatsoever therefore you suppose spread under anything must have in itself an extension distinct from the extension of that thing under which it is spread?

HYLAS: It must.

PHILONOUS: Consequently, every corporeal substance, being the *substratum* of extension, must have in itself another extension, by which it is qualified to be a *substratum:* and so on to infinity. And I ask whether this be not absurd in itself, and repugnant to what you granted just now, to wit, that the *substratum* was something distinct from and exclusive of extension?

[NO MATERIAL SUBSTANCE WITH ACCIDENTS]

HYLAS: Aye but, Philonous, you take me wrong. I do not mean that matter is *spread* in a gross literal sense under extension. The word *substratum* is used only to express in general the same thing with *substance.*

PHILONOUS: Well then, let us examine the relation implied in the term *substance.* Is it not that it stands under accidents?

HYLAS: The very same.

PHILONOUS: But, that one thing may stand under or support another, must it not be extended?

HYLAS: It must.

PHILONOUS: Is not therefore this supposition liable to the same absurdity with the former?

HYLAS: You still take things in a strict literal sense. That is not fair, Philonous.

PHILONOUS: I am not for imposing any sense on your words: you are at liberty to explain them as you please. Only, I beseech you, make me understand something by them. You tell me matter supports or stands under accidents. How! is it as your legs support your body?

HYLAS: No; that is the literal sense.

PHILONOUS: Pray let me know any sense, literal or not literal, that you understand it in.—How long must I wait for an answer, Hylas?

HYLAS: I declare I know not what to say. I once thought I understood well enough what was meant by matter's supporting accidents. But now, the more I think on it the less can I comprehend it: in short I find that I know nothing of it.

PHILONOUS: It seems then you have no idea at all, neither relative nor positive, of matter; you know neither what it is in itself, nor what relation it bears to accidents?

HYLAS: I acknowledge it.

PHILONOUS: And yet you asserted that you could not conceive how qualities or accidents should really exist, without conceiving at the same time a material support of them?

HYLAS: I did.

PHILONOUS: That is to say, when you conceive the real existence of qualities, you do withal conceive something which you cannot conceive?

HYLAS: It was wrong, I own. But still I fear there is some fallacy or other. Pray what think you of this? It is just come into my head that the ground of all our mistake lies in your treating of each quality by itself. Now, I grant that each quality cannot singly subsist without the mind. Color cannot without extension, neither can figure without some other sensible quality. But, as the several qualities united or blended together form entire sensible things, nothing hinders why such things may not be supposed to exist without the mind.

PHILONOUS: Either, Hylas, you are jesting, or have a very bad memory. Though indeed we went through all the qualities by name one after another, yet my arguments or rather your concessions, nowhere tended to prove that the Secondary Qualities did not subsist each alone by itself; but, that they were not *at all* without the mind. Indeed, in treating of figure and motion we concluded they could not exist without the mind, because it was impossible even in thought to separate them from all secondary qualities, so as to conceive them existing by themselves. But then this was not the only argument made use of upon that occasion. But (to pass by all that has been hitherto said, and reckon it for nothing, if you will have it so) I am content to put the whole upon this issue. If you can conceive it possible for any mixture or combination of qualities, or any sensible object whatever, to exist without the mind, then I will grant it actually to be so.

[WE CANNOT CONCEIVE OF THINGS EXISTING INDEPENDENTLY OF MINDS]

HYLAS: If it comes to that the point will soon be decided. What more easy than to conceive a tree or house existing by itself, independent of, and unperceived by, any mind whatsoever? I do at this present time conceive them existing after that manner.

PHILONOUS: How say you, Hylas, can you see a thing which is at the same time unseen?

HYLAS: No, that were a contradiction.

PHILONOUS: Is it not as great a contradiction to talk of *conceiving* a thing which is *unconceived?*

HYLAS: It is.

PHILONOUS: The tree or house therefore which you think of is conceived by you?

HYLAS: How should it be otherwise?

PHILONOUS: And what is conceived is surely in the mind?

HYLAS: Without question, that which is conceived is in the mind.

PHILONOUS: How then came you to say, you conceived a house or tree existing independent and out of all minds whatsoever?

HYLAS: That was I own an oversight; but stay, let me consider what led me into it.—It is a pleasant mistake enough. As I was thinking of a tree in a solitary place, where no one was present to see it, methought that was to conceive a tree as existing unperceived or unthought of; not considering that I myself conceived it all the while. But now I plainly see that all I can do is to frame ideas in my own mind. I may indeed conceive in my own thoughts the idea of a tree, or a house, or a mountain, but that is all. And this is far from proving that I can conceive them *existing out of the minds of all Spirits.*

PHILONOUS: You acknowledge then that you cannot possibly conceive how any one corporeal sensible thing should exist otherwise than in the mind?

HYLAS: I do.

PHILONOUS: And yet you will earnestly contend for the truth of that which you cannot so much as conceive?

HYLAS: I profess I know not what to think; but still there are some scruples remain with me. Is it not certain I *see things at* a distance? Do we not perceive the stars and moon, for example, to be a great way off? Is not this, I say, manifest to the senses?

PHILONOUS: Do you not in a dream too perceive those or the like objects?

HYLAS: I do.

PHILONOUS: And have they not then the same appearance of being distant?

HYLAS: They have.

PHILONOUS: But you do not thence conclude the apparitions in a dream to be without the mind?

HYLAS: By no means.

PHILONOUS: You ought not therefore to conclude that sensible objects are without the mind, from their appearance, or manner wherein they are perceived.

HYLAS: I acknowledge it. But does not my sense deceive me in those cases?

PHILONOUS: By no means. The idea or thing which you immediately perceive, neither sense nor reason informs you that it actually exists without the mind. By sense you only know that you are affected with such certain sensations of light and colors, etc. And these you will not say are without the mind.

HYLAS: True: but, beside all that, do you not think the sight suggests something of *outness or distance?*

PHILONOUS: Upon approaching a distant object, do the visible size and figure change perpetually, or do they appear the same at all distances?

HYLAS: They are in a continual change.

PHILONOUS: Sight therefore does not suggest, or any way inform you, that the visible object you immediately perceive exists at a distance, or will be perceived when you advance farther onward; there being a continued series of visible objects succeeding each other during the whole time of your approach.

HYLAS: It does not; but still I know, upon seeing an object, what object I shall perceive after having passed over a certain distance: no matter whether it be exactly the same or no: there is still something of distance suggested in the case.

PHILONOUS: Good Hylas, do but reflect a little on the point, and then tell me whether there be any more in it than this: from the ideas you actually perceive by sight, you have by experience learned to collect what other ideas you will (according to the standing order of nature) be affected with, after such a certain succession of time and motion.

HYLAS: Upon the whole, I take it to be nothing else.

PHILONOUS: Now, is it not plain that if we suppose a man born blind was on a sudden made to see, he could at first have no experience of what may be *suggested* by sight?

HYLAS: It is.

PHILONOUS: He would not then, according to you, have any notion of distance annexed to the things he saw; but would take them for a new set of sensations, existing only in his mind?

HYLAS: It is undeniable.

PHILONOUS: But, to make it still more plain: is not *distance* a line turned end-wise to the eye?

HYLAS: It is.

PHILONOUS: And can a line so situated be perceived by sight?

HYLAS: It cannot.

PHILONOUS: Does it not therefore follow that distance is not properly and immediately perceived by sight?

HYLAS: It should seem so.

PHILONOUS: Again, is it your opinion that colors are at a distance?

HYLAS: It must be acknowledged they are only in the mind.

PHILONOUS: But do not colors appear to the eye as coexisting in the same place with extension and figures?

HYLAS: They do.

PHILONOUS: How can you then conclude from sight that figures exist without, when you acknowledge colors do not; the sensible appearance being the very same with regard to both?

HYLAS: I know not what to answer.

PHILONOUS: But, allowing that distance was truly and immediately perceived by the mind, yet it would not thence follow it existed out of the mind. For, whatever is immediately perceived is an idea: and can any idea exist out of the mind?

HYLAS: To suppose that were absurd: but, inform me, Philonous, can we perceive or know nothing beside our ideas?

PHILONOUS: As for the rational deducing of causes from effects, that is beside our inquiry. And, by the senses you can best tell whether you perceive anything which is not immediately perceived. And I ask you, whether the things immediately perceived are other than your own sensations or ideas? You have indeed more than once, in the course of this conversation, declared yourself on those points; but you seem, by this last question, to have departed from what you then thought.

[NO MEDIATELY PERCEIVED OBJECTS]

HYLAS: To speak the truth, Philonous, I think there are two kinds of objects:— the one perceived immediately, which are likewise called *ideas;* the other are real things or external objects, perceived by the mediation of ideas, which are their images and representations. Now, I own ideas do not exist without the mind; but the latter sort of objects do. I am sorry I did not think of this distinction sooner; it would probably have cut short your discourse.

PHILONOUS: Are those external objects perceived by sense or by some other faculty?

HYLAS: They are perceived by sense.

PHILONOUS: How! Is there any thing perceived by sense which is not immediately perceived?

HYLAS: Yes, Philonous, in some sort there is. For example, when I look on a picture or statue of Julius Caesar, I may be said after a manner to perceive him (though not immediately) by my senses.

PHILONOUS: It seems then you will have our ideas, which alone are immediately perceived, to be pictures of external things: and that these also are perceived by sense, inasmuch as they have a conformity or resemblance to our ideas?

HYLAS: That is my meaning.

PHILONOUS: And, in the same way that Julius Caesar, in himself invisible, is nevertheless perceived by sight; real things, in themselves imperceptible, are perceived by sense.

HYLAS: In the very same.

PHILONOUS: Tell me, Hylas, when you behold the picture of Julius Caesar, do you see with your eyes any more than some colors and figures, with a certain symmetry and composition of the whole?

HYLAS: Nothing else.

PHILONOUS: And would not a man who had never known anything of Julius Caesar see as much?

HYLAS: He would.

PHILONOUS: Consequently he has his sight, and the use of it, in as perfect a degree as you?

HYLAS: I agree with you.

PHILONOUS: Whence comes it then that your thoughts are directed to the Roman emperor, and his are not? This cannot proceed from the sensations or ideas of sense by you then perceived; since you acknowledge you have no advantage over him in that respect. It should seem therefore to proceed from reason and memory: should it not?

HYLAS: It should.

PHILONOUS: Consequently, it will not follow from that instance that anything is perceived by sense which is not immediately perceived. Though I grant we may, in one acceptation, be said to perceive sensible things mediately by sense: that is, when, from a frequently perceived connection, the immediate perception of ideas by one sense *suggests* to the mind others, perhaps belonging to another sense, which are wont to be connected with them. For instance, when I hear a coach drive along the streets, immediately I perceive only the sound; but, from the experience I have had that such a sound is connected with a coach, I am said to hear the coach. It is nevertheless evident that, in truth and strictness, nothing can be heard but sound; and the coach is not then properly perceived by sense, but suggested from experience. So likewise when we are said to see a red-hot bar of iron; the solidity and heat of the iron are not the objects of sight, but suggested to the imagination by the color and figure which are properly perceived by that sense. In short, those things alone are actually and strictly perceived by any sense, which would have been perceived in case that same sense had then been first conferred on us. As for other things, it is plain they are only suggested to the mind by experience, grounded on former perceptions. But, to return to your comparison of Caesar's picture, it is plain, if you keep to that, you must hold the real things, or archetypes of our ideas, are not perceived by sense, but by some internal faculty of the soul, as reason or memory. I would therefore fain know what arguments you can draw from reason for the existence of what you call *real things* or *material objects.* Or, whether you remember to have seen them formerly as they are in themselves; or, if you have heard or read of any one that did.

HYLAS: I see, Philonous, you are disposed to raillery; but that will never convince me.

PHILONOUS: My aim is only to learn from you the way to come at the knowledge of *material beings.* Whatever we perceive is perceived immediately or mediately: by sense, or by reason and reflexion. But, as you have excluded sense, pray shew me what reason you have to believe their existence; or what *medium* you can possibly make use of to prove it, either to mine or your own understanding.

HYLAS: To deal ingenuously, Philonous, now I consider the point, I do not find I can give you any good reason for it. But, thus much seems pretty plain, that it is at least possible such things may really exist. And, as long as there is no absurdity in supposing them, I am resolved to believe as I did, till you bring good reasons to the contrary.

PHILONOUS: What! Is it come to this, that you only *believe* the existence of material objects, and that your belief is founded barely on the possibility of its being true? Then you will have me bring reasons against it: though another would think it reasonable the proof should lie on him who holds the affirmative. And, after all, this very point which you are now resolved to maintain, without any reason, is in effect what you have more than once during this discourse seen good reason to give up. But, to pass over all this; if I understand you rightly, you say our ideas do not exist without the mind, but that they are copies, images, or representations, of certain originals that do?

HYLAS: You take me right.

PHILONOUS: They are then like external things?

HYLAS: They are.

PHILONOUS: Have those things a stable and permanent nature, independent of our senses; or are they in a perpetual change, upon our producing any motions in our bodies—suspending, exerting, or altering, our faculties or organs of sense?

HYLAS: Real things, it is plain, have a fixed and real nature, which remains the same notwithstanding any change in our senses, or in the posture and motion of our bodies; which indeed may affect the ideas in our minds, but it were absurd to think they had the same effect on things existing without the mind.

PHILONOUS: How then is it possible that things perpetually fleeting and variable as our ideas should be copies or images of anything fixed and constant? Or, in other words, since all sensible qualities, as size, figure, color, etc., that is, our ideas, are continually changing, upon every alteration in the distance, medium, or instruments of sensation; how can any determinate material objects be properly represented or painted forth by several distinct things, each of which is so different from and unlike the rest? Or, if you say it resembles some one only of our ideas, how shall we be able to distinguish the true copy from all the false ones?

HYLAS: I profess, Philonous, I am at a loss. I know not what to say to this.

PHILONOUS: But neither is this all. Which are material objects in themselves—perceptible or imperceptible?

HYLAS: Properly and immediately nothing can be perceived but ideas. All material things, therefore, are in themselves insensible, and to be perceived only by our ideas.

PHILONOUS: Ideas then are sensible, and their archetypes or originals insensible?

HYLAS: Right.

PHILONOUS: But how can that which is sensible be like that which is insensible? Can a real thing, in itself *invisible,* be like a *color;* or a real thing, which is not *audible,* be like a *sound?* In a word, can anything be like a sensation or idea, but another sensation or idea?

HYLAS: I must own, I think not.

PHILONOUS: Is it possible there should be any doubt on the point? Do you not perfectly know your own ideas?

HYLAS: I know them perfectly; since what I do not perceive or know can be no part of my idea.

PHILONOUS: Consider, therefore, and examine them, and then tell me if there be anything in them which can exist without the mind: or if you can conceive anything like them existing without the mind.

HYLAS: Upon inquiry, I find it is impossible for me to conceive or understand how anything but an idea can be like an idea. And it is most evident that *no idea can exist without the mind.*

PHILONOUS: You are therefore, by your principles, forced to deny the *reality* of sensible things; since you made it to consist in an absolute existence exterior to the mind. That is to say, you are a downright skeptic. So I have gained my point, which was to shew your principles led to Skepticism.

HYLAS: For the present I am, if not entirely convinced, at least silenced.

READING 12

The Mind as a Bundle of Perceptions*

David Hume (1711–1776)

[INITIAL WORRIES ABOUT THE SELF]

There are some philosophers who imagine we are every moment intimately conscious of what we call our *self*; that we feel its existence and its continuance in existence; and are certain, beyond the evidence of a demonstration, both of its perfect identity and simplicity. The strongest sensation, the most violent passion, say they, instead of distracting us from this view, only fix it the more intensely, and make us consider their influence on *self* either by their pain or pleasure. To attempt a further proof of this were to weaken its evidence; since no proof can be derived from any fact of which we are so intimately conscious; nor is there any thing of which we can be certain if we doubt of this.

Unluckily all these positive assertions are contrary to that very experience which is pleaded for them; nor have we any idea of *self*, after the manner it is here explained. For, from what impression could this idea be derived? This question it is impossible to answer without a manifest contradiction and absurdity; and yet it is a question which must necessarily be answered, if we would have the idea of self pass for clear and intelligible. It must be some one impression that gives rise to every real idea. But self or person is not any one impression, but that to which our several impressions and ideas are supposed to have a reference. If any impression gives rise to the idea of self, that impression must continue invariably the same, through the whole course of our lives; since self is supposed to exist after that manner. But there is no impression constant and invariable. Pain and pleasure, grief and joy, passions and sensations succeed each other, and never all exist at the same time. It cannot therefore be from any of these impressions, or from any other, that the idea of self is derived; and consequently there is no such idea.

But further, what must become of all our particular perceptions upon this hypothesis? All these are different, and distinguishable, and separable from each other, and may be separately considered, and may exist separately, and have no need of any thing to support their existence. After what manner therefore do they belong to self, and how are they connected with it? For my part, when I enter most intimately into what I call *myself*, I always stumble on some particular perception or other, of heat or cold, light or shade, love or hatred, pain or pleasure. I never can catch *myself* at any time without a perception, and never can observe any thing but the perception. When my perceptions are removed for any time, as by sound sleep, so long am I insensible of *myself*, and may truly be said not to exist. And were all my perceptions removed by death,

*From David Hume, *Treatise of Human Nature* (1739–1740), 1.4.6 and Appendix.

and could I neither think, nor feel, nor see, nor love, nor hate, after the dissolution of my body, I should be entirely annihilated, nor do I conceive what is further requisite to make me a perfect nonentity. If any one, upon serious and unprejudiced reflection, thinks he has a different notion of *himself*, I must confess I can reason no longer with him. All I can allow him is, that he may be in the right as well as I, and that we are essentially different in this particular. He may, perhaps, perceive something simple and continued, which he calls *himself;* though I am certain there is no such principle in me.

But setting aside some metaphysicians of this kind, I may venture to affirm of the rest of mankind, that they are nothing but a bundle or collection of different perceptions, which succeed each other with an inconceivable rapidity, and are in a perpetual flux and movement. Our eyes cannot turn in their sockets without varying our perceptions. Our thought is still more variable than our sight; and all our other senses and faculties contribute to this change: nor is there any single power of the soul, which remains unalterably the same, perhaps for one moment. The mind is a kind of theatre, where several perceptions successively make their appearance; pass, repass, glide away, and mingle in an infinite variety of postures and situations. There is properly no *simplicity* in it at one time, nor *identity* in different, whatever natural propension we may have to imagine that simplicity and identity. The comparison of the theatre must not mislead us. They are the successive perceptions only, that constitute the mind; nor have we the most distant notion of the place where these scenes are represented, or of the materials of which it is composed.

[MORE WORRIES ABOUT THE SELF]

I had entertained some hopes, that however deficient our theory of the intellectual world might be, it would be free from those contradictions and absurdities which seem to attend every explication that human reason can give of the material world. But upon a more strict review of the section concerning *personal identity*, I find myself involved in such a labyrinth that, I must confess, I neither know how to correct my former opinions, nor how to render them consistent. If this be not a good *general* reason for skepticism, it is at least a sufficient one (if I were not already abundantly supplied) for me to entertain a diffidence and modesty in all my decisions. I shall propose the arguments on both sides, beginning with those that induced me to deny the strict and proper identity and simplicity of a self or thinking being.

When we talk of *self* or *subsistence*, we must have an idea annexed to these terms, otherwise they are altogether unintelligible. Every idea is derived from preceding impressions; and we have no impression of self or substance, as something simple and individual. We have, therefore, no idea of them in that sense.

Whatever is distinct is distinguishable, and whatever is distinguishable is separable by the thought or imagination. All perceptions are distinct. They are, therefore, distinguishable, and separable, and may be conceived as separately existent, and may exist separately, without any contradiction or absurdity.

When I view this table and that chimney, nothing is present to me but particular perceptions, which are of a like nature with all the other perceptions. This is the doctrine of philosophers. But this table, which is present to me, and that chimney, may, and do exist separately. This is the doctrine of the vulgar, and implies no contradiction. There is no contradiction, therefore, in extending the same doctrine to all the perceptions.

In general, the following reasoning seems satisfactory. All ideas are borrowed from preceding perceptions. Our ideas of objects, therefore, are derived from that source. Consequently no proposition can be intelligible or consistent with regard to objects, which is not so with regard to perceptions. But it is intelligible and consistent to say, that objects exist distinct and independent, without any common simple substance or subject of inhesion. This proposition, therefore, can never be absurd with regard to perceptions.

When I turn my reflection on *myself*, I never can perceive this *self* without some one or more perceptions; nor can I ever perceive any thing but the perceptions. It is the composition of these, therefore, which forms the self.

We can conceive a thinking being to have either many or few perceptions. Suppose the mind to be reduced even below the life of an oyster. Suppose it to have only one perception, as of thirst or hunger. Consider it in that situation. Do you conceive any thing but merely that perception? Have you any notion of *self* or *substance?* If not, the addition of other perceptions can never give you that notion.

The annihilation which some people suppose to follow upon death, and which entirely destroys this self, is nothing but an extinction of all particular perceptions; love and hatred, pain and pleasure, thought and sensation. These, therefore, must be the same with self, since the one cannot survive the other.

Is *self* the same with *substance?* If it be, how can that question have place, concerning the substance of self, under a change of substance? If they be distinct, what is the difference betwixt them? For my part, I have a notion of neither, when conceived distinct from particular perceptions.

Philosophers begin to be reconciled to the principle, *that we have no idea of external substance, distinct from the ideas of particular qualities.* This must pave the way for a like principle with regard to the mind, *that we have no notion of it, distinct from the particular perception.*

So far I seem to be attended with sufficient evidence. But having thus loosened all our particular perceptions, when I proceed to explain the principle of connections, which binds them together, and makes us attribute to them a real simplicity and identity, I am sensible that my account is very defective, and that nothing but the seeming evidence of the precedent reasonings could have induced me to receive it. If perceptions are distinct existences, they form a whole only by being connected together. But no connections among distinct existences are ever discoverable by human understanding. We only *feel* a connections or determination of the thought to pass from one object to another. It follows, therefore, that the thought alone feels personal identity, when reflecting on the train of past perceptions that compose a mind, the ideas of them are felt to be connected together, and naturally introduce each other. However extraordinary this conclusion may seem, it need not surprise us. Most philosophers seem inclined to think, that personal identity *arises* from consciousness, and consciousness is nothing but a reflected thought or perception. The present philosophy, therefore, has so far a promising aspect. But all my hopes vanish when I come to explain the principles that unite our successive perceptions in our thought or consciousness. I cannot discover any theory which gives me satisfaction on this head.

In short, there are two principles which I cannot render consistent, nor is it in my power to renounce either of them, viz. *that all our distinct perceptions are distinct existences, and that the mind never perceives any real connections among distinct existences.* Did our perceptions either inhere in something simple and individual, or did the mind perceive some real connections among them, there would be no difficulty in the case. For my part, I must plead the privilege of a skeptic, and confess that this difficulty is too hard for my understanding. I pretend not, however, to pronounce it absolutely insuperable. Others, perhaps, or myself, upon more mature reflections, may discover some hypothesis that will reconcile those contradictions.

READING 13

*Descartes' Myth**

Gilbert Ryle (1900–1976)

(1) THE OFFICIAL DOCTRINE

There is a doctrine about the nature and place of minds which is so prevalent among theorists and even among laymen that it deserves to be described as the official theory. Most philosophers, psychologists and religious teachers subscribe, with minor reservations, to its main articles and, although they admit certain theoretical difficulties in it, they tend to assume that these can be overcome without serious modifications being made to the architecture of the theory. It will be argued here that the central principles of the doctrine are unsound and conflict with the whole body of what we know about minds when we are not speculating about them.

The official doctrine, which hails chiefly from Descartes, is something like this. With the doubtful exceptions of idiots and infants in arms every human being has both a body and a mind. Some would prefer to say that every human being is both a body and a mind. His body and his mind are ordinarily harnessed together, but after the death of the body his mind may continue to exist and function.

*From Gilbert Ryle, *The Concept of Mind.*

Human bodies are in space and are subject to the mechanical laws which govern all other bodies in space. Bodily processes and states can be inspected by external observers. So a man's bodily life is as much a public affair as are the lives of animals and reptiles and even as the careers of trees, crystals and planets.

But minds are not in space, nor are their operations subject to mechanical laws. The workings of one mind are not witnessable by other observers; career is private. Only I can take direct cognizance of the states and processes of my own mind. A person therefore lives through two collateral histories, one consisting of what happens in and to his body, the other consisting of what happens in and to his mind. The first is public, the second private. The events in the first history are events in the physical world, those in the second are events in the mental world.

It has been disputed whether a person does or can directly monitor all or only some of the episodes of his own private history; but, according to the official doctrine, of at least some of these episodes he has direct and unchallengeable cognizance. In consciousness, self-consciousness and introspection he is directly and authentically apprised of the present states and operations of his mind. He may have great or small uncertainties about concurrent and adjacent episodes in the physical world, but he can have none about at least part of what is momentarily occupying his mind.

It is customary to express this bifurcation of his two lives and of his two worlds by saying that the things and events which belong to the physical world, including his own body, are external, while the workings of his own mind are internal. This antithesis of outer and inner is of course meant to be construed as a metaphor, since minds, not being in space, could not be described as being spatially inside anything else, or as having things going on spatially inside themselves. But relapses from this good intention are common and theorists are found speculating how stimuli, the physical sources of which are yards or miles outside a person's skin, can generate mental responses inside his skull, or how decisions framed inside his cranium can set going movements of his extremities. *how the mind influences the body.*

Even when "inner" and "outer" are construed as metaphors, the problem how a person's mind and body influence one another is notoriously charged with theoretical difficulties. What the mind wills, the legs, arms and the tongue execute; what affects the ear and the eye has something to do with what the mind perceives; grimaces and smiles betray the mind's moods and bodily castigations lead, it is hoped, to moral improvement. But the actual transactions between the episodes of the private history and those of the public history remain mysterious, since by definition they can belong to neither series. They could not be reported among the happenings described in a person's autobiography of his inner life, but nor could they be reported among those described in some one else's biography of that person's overt career. They can be inspected neither by introspection nor by laboratory experiment. They are theoretical shuttlecocks which are forever being bandied from the physiologist back to the psychologist and from the psychologist back to the physiologist.

Underlying this partly metaphorical representation of the bifurcation of a person's two lives there is a seemingly more profound and philosophical assumption. It is assumed that there are two different kinds of existence or status. What exists or happens may have the status of physical existence, or it may have the status of mental existence. Somewhat as the faces of coins are either heads or tails, or somewhat as living creatures are either male or female, so, it is supposed, some existing is physical existing, other existing is mental existing. It is a necessary feature of what has physical existence that it is in space and time; it is a necessary feature of what has mental existence that it is in time but not in space. What has physical existence is composed of matter, or else is a function of matter; what has mental existence consists of consciousness, or else is a function of consciousness.

There is thus a polar opposition between mind and matter, an opposition which is often brought out as follows. Material objects are situated in a common field, known as "space," and what happens to one body in one part of space is mechanically connected with what happens to other bodies in other parts of space. But mental happenings occur in insulated fields, known as "minds," and there is, apart maybe from telepathy, no direct causal connection between what happens in one mind and what happens in another. Only through the medium of the public physical world can the mind of one person make a difference to the mind of another. The mind is its own place and in his inner life each of us lives the life of a ghostly Robinson Crusoe. People can see, hear and jolt one another's bodies, but they are irremediably blind and deaf to the workings of one another's minds and inoperative upon them.

What sort of knowledge can be secured of the workings of a mind? On the one side, according to the official theory, a person has direct knowledge of the best imaginable kind of the workings of his own mind. Mental states and processes are (or are normally) conscious states and processes, and the consciousness which irradiates them can engender no illusions and leaves the door open for no doubts. A person's present thinkings, feelings and willings, his perceivings, rememberings and imaginings are intrinsically "phosphorescent"; their existence and their nature are inevitably betrayed to their owner. The inner life is a stream of consciousness of such a sort that it would be absurd to suggest that the mind whose life is that stream might be unaware of what is passing down it.

True, the evidence adduced recently by Freud seems to show that there exist channels tributary to this stream, which run hidden from their owner. People are actuated by impulses the existence of which they vigorously disavow; some of their thoughts differ from the thoughts which they acknowledge; and some of the actions which they think they will to perform they do not really will. They are thoroughly gulled by some of their own hypocrisies and they successfully ignore facts about their mental lives which on the official theory ought to be patent to them. Holders of the official theory tend, however, to maintain that anyhow in normal circumstances a person must be directly and authentically seized of the present state and workings of his own mind.

Besides being currently supplied with these alleged immediate data of consciousness, a person is also generally supposed to be able to exercise from time to time a special kind of perception, namely inner perception, or introspection. He can take a (non-optical) "look" at what is passing in his mind.

Not only can he view and scrutinize a flower through his sense of sight and listen to and discriminate the notes of a bell through his sense of hearing; he can also reflectively or introspectively watch, without any bodily organ of sense, the current episodes of his inner life. This self-observation is also commonly supposed to be immune from illusion, confusion or doubt. A mind's reports of its own affairs have a certainty superior to the best that is possessed by its reports of matters in the physical world. Sense-perceptions can, but consciousness and introspection cannot, be mistaken or confused.

On the other side, one person has no direct access of any sort to the events of the inner life of another. He cannot do better than make problematic inferences from the observed behavior of the other person's body to the states of mind which, by analogy from his own conduct, he supposes to be signalized by that behavior. Direct access to the workings of a mind is the privilege of that mind itself; in default of such privileged access, the workings of one mind are inevitably occult to everyone else. For the supposed arguments from bodily movements similar to their own to mental workings similar to their own would lack any possibility of observational corroboration. Not unnaturally, therefore, an adherent of the official theory finds it difficult to resist this consequence of his premises, that he has no good reason to believe that there do exist minds other than his own. Even if he prefers to believe that to other human bodies there are harnessed minds not unlike his own, he cannot claim to be able to discover their individual characteristics, or the particular things that they undergo and do. Absolute solitude is on this showing the ineluctable destiny of the soul. Only our bodies can meet.

As a necessary corollary of this general scheme there is implicitly prescribed a special way of construing our ordinary concepts of mental powers and operations. The verbs, nouns and adjectives, with which in ordinary life we describe the wits, characters and higher-grade performances of the people with whom we have do, are required to be construed as signifying special episodes in their secret histories, or else as signifying tendencies for such episodes to occur. When someone is described as knowing, believing or guessing something, as hoping, dreading, intending or shirking something, as designing this or being amused at that, these verbs are supposed to denote the occurrence of specific modifications in his (to us) occult stream of consciousness. Only his own privileged access to this stream in direct awareness and introspection could provide authentic testimony that these mental-conduct verbs were correctly or incorrectly applied. The onlooker, be he teacher, critic, biographer or friend, can never assure himself that his comments have any vestige of truth. Yet it was just because we do in fact all know how to make such comments, make them with general correctness and correct them when they turn out to be confused or mistaken, that philosophers found it necessary to construct their theories of the nature and place of minds. Finding mental-conduct concepts being regularly and effectively used, they properly sought to fix their logical geography. But the logical geography officially recommended would entail that there could be no regular or effective use of these mental-conduct concepts in our descriptions of, and prescriptions for, other people's minds.

(2) THE ABSURDITY OF THE OFFICIAL DOCTRINE

Such in outline is the official theory. I shall often speak of it, with deliberate abusiveness, as "the dogma of the Ghost in the Machine." I hope to prove that it is entirely false, and false not in detail but in principle. It is not merely an assemblage of particular mistakes. It is one big mistake and a mistake of a special kind. It is, namely, a category-mistake. It represents the facts of mental life as if they belonged to one logical type or category (or range of types or categories), when they actually belong to another. The dogma is therefore a philosopher's myth. In attempting to explode the myth I shall probably be taken to be denying well-known facts about the mental life of human beings, and my plea that I aim at doing nothing more than rectify the logic of mental-conduct concepts will probably be disallowed as mere subterfuge.

I must first indicate what is meant by the phrase "Category-mistake." This I do in a series of illustrations.

A foreigner visiting Oxford or Cambridge for the first time is shown a number of colleges, libraries, playing fields, museums, scientific departments and administrative offices. He then asks "But where is the University? I have seen where the members of the Colleges live, where the Registrar works, where the scientists experiment and the rest. But I have not yet seen the University in which reside and work the members of your University." It has then to be explained to him that the University is not another collateral institution, some ulterior counterpart to the colleges, laboratories and offices which he has seen. The University is just the way in which all that he has already seen is organized. When they are seen and when their co-ordination is understood, the University has been seen. His mistake lay in his innocent assumption that it was correct to speak of Christ Church, the Bodleian Library, the Ashmolean Museum *and* the University, to speak, that is, as if "the University" stood for an extra member of the class of which these other units are members. He was mistakenly allocating the University to the same category as that to which the other institutions belong.

The same mistake would be made by a child witnessing the march-past of a division, who, having had pointed out to him such and such battalions, batteries, squadrons, etc., asked when the division was going to appear. He would be supposing that a division was a counterpart to the units already seen, partly similar to them and partly unlike them. He would be shown his mistake by being told that in watching the battalions, batteries and squadrons marching past he had been watching the division marching past. The march-past was not a parade of battalions, batteries, squadrons *and* a division; it was a parade of the battalions, batteries, and squadrons *of* a division.

One more illustration. A foreigner watching his first game of cricket learns what the functions of the bowlers, the batsmen, the fielders, the umpires and the scorers. He then says "But there is no one left on the field to contribute the famous element of team-spirit. I see who does the bowling, the batting and the wicket-keeping; but I do not see whose role it is to exercise *esprit de corps.*"

Once more, it would have to be explained that he was looking for the wrong type of thing. Team-spirit is not another cricketing-operation supplementary to all of the other special tasks. It is, roughly, the keenness with which each of the special tasks is performed, and performing a task keenly is not performing two tasks. Certainly exhibiting team-spirit is not the same thing as bowling or catching, but nor is it a third thing such that we can say that the bowler first bowls *and* then exhibits team-spirit or that a fielder is at a given moment *either* catching or displaying *esprit de corps*.

These illustrations of category-mistakes have a common feature which must be noticed. The mistakes were made by people who did not know how to wield the concepts *University, division* and *team-spirit*. Their puzzles arose from inability to use certain items in the English vocabulary.

The theoretically interesting category-mistakes are those made by people who are perfectly competent to apply concepts, at least in the situations with which they are familiar, but are still liable in their abstract thinking to allocate those concepts to logical types to which they do not belong. An instance of a mistake of this sort would be the following story. A student of politics has learned the main differences between the British, the French and the American Constitutions, and has learned also the differences and connections between the Cabinet, Parliament, the various Ministries, the Judicature and the Church of England. But he still becomes embarrassed when asked questions about the connections between the Church of England, the Home Office and the British Constitution. For while the Church and the Home Office are institutions, the British Constitution is not another institution in the same sense of that noun. So inter-institutional relations which can be asserted or denied to hold between the Church and the Home Office cannot be asserted or denied to hold between either of them and the British Constitution. "The British Constitution" is not a term of the same logical type as "the Home Office" and "the Church of England." In a partially similar way, John Doe may be a relative, a friend, an enemy or a stranger to Richard Roe; but he cannot be any of these things to the Average Taxpayer. He knows how to talk sense in certain sorts of discussions about the Average Taxpayer, but he is baffled to say why he could not come across him in the street as he can come across Richard Roe.

It is pertinent to our main subject to notice that, so long as the student of politics continues to think of the British Constitution as a counterpart to the other institutions, he will tend to describe it as a mysteriously occult institution; and so long as John Doe continues to think of the Average Taxpayer as a fellow-citizen, he will tend to think of him as an elusive insubstantial man, a ghost who is everywhere yet nowhere.

My destructive purpose is to show that a family of radical category-mistakes is the source of the double-life theory. The representation of a person as a ghost mysteriously ensconced in a machine derives from this argument. Because, as is true, a person's thinking, feeling and purposive doing cannot be described solely in the idioms of physics, chemistry and physiology, therefore they must be described in counterpart idioms. As the human body is a complex organized unit, so the human mind must be another complex organized unit, though one made of a different sort of stuff and with a different sort of structure. Or, again, as the human body, like any other parcel of matter, is a field of causes and effects, so the mind must be another field of causes and effects, though not (Heaven be praised) mechanical causes and effects.

(3) THE ORIGIN OF THE CATEGORY-MISTAKE

One of the chief intellectual origins of what I have yet to prove to be the Cartesian category-mistake seems to be this. When Galileo showed that his methods of scientific discovery were competent to provide a mechanical theory which should cover every occupant of space, Descartes found in himself two conflicting motives. As a man of scientific genius he could not but endorse the claims of mechanics, yet as a religious and moral man he could not accept, as Hobbes accepted, the discouraging rider to those claims, namely that human nature differs only in degree of complexity from clockwork. The mental could not be just a variety of the mechanical.

He and subsequent philosophers naturally but erroneously availed themselves of the following escape-route. Since mental-conduct words are not to be construed as signifying the occurrence of mechanical processes, they must be construed as signifying the occurrence of non-mechanical processes; since mechanical laws explain movements in space as the effects of other movements in space, other laws must explain some of the non-spatial workings of minds as the effects of other non-spatial workings of minds. The difference between the human behaviors which we describe as intelligent and those which we describe as unintelligent must be a difference in their causation; so, while some movements of human tongues and limbs are the effects of mechanical causes, others must be the effects of non-mechanical causes, i.e., some issue from movements of particles of matter, others from workings of the mind.

The differences between the physical and the mental were thus represented as differences inside the common framework of the categories of "thing," "stuff," "attribute," "state," "process," "change," "cause" and "effect." Minds are things, but different sorts of things from bodies; mental processes are causes and effects, but different sorts of causes and effects from bodily movements. And so on. Somewhat as the foreigner expected the University to be an extra edifice, rather like a college but also considerably different, so the repudiators of mechanism represented minds as extra centers of causal processes, rather like machines but also considerably different from them. Their theory was a para-mechanical hypothesis.

That this assumption was at the heart of the doctrine is shown by the fact that there was from the beginning felt to be a major theoretical difficulty in explaining how minds can influence and be influenced by bodies. How can a mental process, such as willing, cause spatial movements like the movements of the tongue? How can a physical change in the optic nerve have among its effects a mind's perception of a flash of light? This notorious crux by itself shows the logical mould into which Descartes pressed his theory of the mind. It was the self-same mould into which he and Galileo set their mechanics. Still unwittingly adhering to the grammar of mechanics, he tried to avert disaster

[handwritten marginalia: — couldn't provide a real explanation of what mind is, only what it is not — opp./counterpart of fact/truth]

by describing minds in what was merely an obverse vocabulary. The work-ings of minds had to be described by the mere negatives of the specific de-scriptions given to bodies; they are not in space, they are not motions, they are not modifications of matter, they are not accessible to public observation. Minds are not bits of clockwork, they are just bits of not-clockwork.

As thus represented, minds are not merely ghosts harnessed to machines, they are themselves just spectral machines. Though the human body is an en-gine, it is not quite an ordinary engine, since some of its workings are gov-erned by another engine inside it—this interior governor—engine being one of a very special sort. It is invisible, inaudible and it has no size or weight. It can-not be taken to bits and the laws it obeys are not those known to ordinary en-gineers. Nothing is known of how it governs the bodily engine.

A second major crux points the same moral. Since, according to the doc-trine, minds belong to the same category as bodies and since bodies are rigidly governed by mechanical laws, it seemed to many theorists to follow that minds must be similarly governed by rigid non-mechanical laws. The physical world is a deterministic system, so the mental world must be a deterministic system. Bodies cannot help the modifications that they undergo, so minds can-not help pursuing the careers fixed for them. *Responsibility, choice, merit* and *de-merit* are therefore inapplicable concepts—unless the compromise solution is adopted of saying that the laws governing mental processes, unlike those gov-erning physical processes, have the congenial attribute of being only rather rigid. The problem of the Freedom of the Will was the problem how to recon-cile the hypothesis that minds are to be described in terms drawn from the cat-egories of mechanics with the knowledge that higher-grade human conduct is not of a piece with the behavior of machines.

It is an historical curiosity that it was not noticed that the entire argument was broken-backed. Theorists correctly assumed that any sane man could al-ready recognize the differences between, say, rational and non-rational utter-ances or between purposive and automatic behavior. Else there would have been nothing requiring to be saved from mechanism. Yet the explanation given presupposed that one person could in principle never recognize the dif-ference between the rational and the irrational utterances issuing from other human bodies, since he could never get access to the postulated immaterial causes of some of their utterances. Save for the doubtful exception of himself, he could never tell the difference between a man and a Robot. It would have to be conceded, for example, that, for all that we can tell, the inner lives of per-sons who are classed as idiots or lunatics are as rational as those of anyone else. Perhaps only their overt behavior is disappointing; that is to say, perhaps "idiots" are not really idiotic, or "lunatics" lunatic. Perhaps, too, some of those who are classed as sane are really idiots. According to the theory, external ob-servers could never know how the overt behavior of others is correlated with their mental powers and processes and so they could never know or even plausibly conjecture whether their applications of mental-conduct concepts to these other people were correct or incorrect. It would then be hazardous or impossible for a man to claim sanity or logical consistency even for himself, since he would be debarred from comparing his own performances with those of others. In short, our characterizations of persons and their performances as intelligent, prudent and virtuous or as stupid, hypocritical and cowardly could never have been made, so the problem of providing a special causal hypothesis to serve as the basis of such diagnoses would never have arisen. The question, "How do persons differ from machines?" arose just because everyone already knew how to apply mental-conduct concepts before the new causal hypothesis was introduced. This causal hypothesis could not therefore be the source of the criteria used in those applications. Nor, of course, has the causal hypothesis in any degree improved our handling of those criteria. We still distinguish good from bad arithmetic, politic from impolitic conduct and fertile from infertile imaginations in the ways in which Descartes himself distinguished them before and after he speculated how the applicability of these criteria was compatible with the principle of mechanical causation.

He had mistaken the logic of his problem. Instead of asking by what criteria intelligent behavior is actually distinguished from non-intelligent behavior, he asked "Given that the principle of mechanical causation does not tell us the difference, what other causal principle will tell it us?" He realized that the problem was not one of mechanics and assumed that it must therefore be one of some counterpart to mechanics. Not unnaturally psychology is often cast for just this role.

When two terms belong to the same category, it is proper to construct conjunctive propositions embodying them. Thus a purchaser may say that he bought a left-hand glove and a right-hand glove, but not that he bought a left-hand glove, a right-hand glove and a pair of gloves. "She came home in a flood of tears and a sedan-chair" is a well-known joke based on the absurdity of conjoining terms of different types. It would have been equally ridiculous to construct the disjunction "She came home either in a flood of tears or else in a sedan-chair." Now the dogma of the Ghost in the Machine does just this. It maintains that there exist both bodies and minds; that there occur physical processes and mental processes; that there are mechanical causes of corporeal movements and mental causes of corporeal movements. I shall argue that these and other analogous conjunctions are absurd; but, it must be noticed, the argument will not show that either of the illegitimately conjoined propositions is absurd in itself. I am not, for example, denying that there occur mental processes. Doing long division is a mental process and so is making a joke. But I am saying that the phrase "there occur mental processes" does not mean the same sort of thing as "there occur physical processes," and, therefore, that it makes no sense to conjoin or disjoin the two.

If my argument is successful, there will follow some interesting consequences. First, the hallowed contrast between Mind and Matter will be dissipated, but dissipated not by either of the equally hallowed absorptions of Mind by Matter or of Matter by Mind, but in quite a different way. For the seeming contrast of the two will be shown to be as illegitimate as would be the contrast of "she came home in a flood of tears" and "she came home in a sedan-chair." The belief that there is a polar opposition between Mind and Matter is the belief that they are terms of the same logical type.

It will also follow that both Idealism and Materialism are answers to an improper question. The "reduction" of the material world to mental states and processes, as well as the "reduction" of mental states and processes to physical states and processes, presuppose the legitimacy of the disjunction "Either there exist minds or there exist bodies (but not both)." It would be like saying, "Either she bought a left-hand and a right-hand glove or she bought a pair of gloves (but not both)."

It is perfectly proper to say, in one logical tone of voice, that there exist minds and to say, in another logical tone of voice, that there exist bodies. But these expressions do not indicate two different species of existence, for "existence" is not a generic word like "colored" or "sexed." They indicate two different senses of "exist," somewhat as "rising" has different senses in "the tide is rising," "hopes are rising," and "the average age of death is rising." A man would be thought to be making a poor joke who said that three things are now rising, namely the tide, hopes and the average age of death. It would be just as good or bad a joke to say that there exist prime numbers and Wednesdays and public opinions and navies; or that there exist both minds and bodies.

READING 14

The Mind–Body Problem*

John Searle (b. 1932)

[THE NATURE OF THE MIND–BODY PROBLEM]

For thousands of years, people have been trying to understand their relationship to the rest of the universe. For a variety of reasons many philosophers today are reluctant to tackle such big problems. Nonetheless, the problems remain, and in this book I am going to attack some of them.

At the moment, the biggest problem is this: We have a certain common-sense picture of ourselves as human beings which is very hard to square with our overall "scientific" conception of the physical world. We think of ourselves as *conscious, free, mindful, rational* agents in a world that science tells us consists entirely of mindless, meaningless physical particles. Now, how can we square these two conceptions? How, for example, can it be the case that the world contains nothing but unconscious physical particles, and yet that it also contains

---

*From John Searle, "The Mind-Body Problem," in *Minds, Brains and Science,* (1984).

consciousness? How can a mechanical universe contain intentionalistic human beings—that is, human beings that can represent the world to themselves? How, in short, can an essentially meaningless world contain meanings?

Such problems spill over into other more contemporary-sounding issues: How should we interpret recent work in computer science and artificial intelligence—work aimed at making intelligent machines? Specifically, does the digital computer give us the right picture of the human mind? And why is it that the social sciences in general have not given us insights into ourselves comparable to the insights that the natural sciences have given us into the rest of nature? What is the relation between the ordinary, commonsense explanations we accept of the way people behave and scientific modes of explanation?

In this first chapter, I want to plunge right into what many philosophers think of as the hardest problem of all: What is the relation of our minds to the rest of the universe? This, I am sure you will recognize, is the traditional mind–body or mind–brain problem. In its contemporary version it usually takes the form: how does the mind relate to the brain? I believe that the mind–body problem has a rather simple solution, one that is consistent both with what we know about neurophysiology and with our commonsense conception of the nature of mental states—pains, beliefs, desires, and so on. But before presenting that solution, I want to ask why the mind–body problem seems so intractable. Why do we still have in philosophy and psychology after all these centuries a "mind–body problem" in a way that we do not have, say, a "digestion–stomach problem"? Why does the mind seem more mysterious than other biological phenomena?

I am convinced that part of the difficulty is that we persist in talking about a twentieth-century problem in an outmoded seventeenth-century vocabulary. When I was an undergraduate, I remember being dissatisfied with the choices that were apparently available in the philosophy of mind: you could be either a monist or a dualist. If you were a monist, you could be either a materialist or an idealist. If you were a materialist, you could be either a behaviorist or a physicalist. And so on. One of my aims in what follows is to try to break out of these tired old categories. Notice that nobody feels he has to choose between monism and dualism where the "digestion–stomach problem" is concerned. Why should it be any different with the "mind–body problem"?

But, vocabulary apart, there is still a problem or family of problems. Since Descartes, the mind–body problem has taken the following form: how can we account for the relationships between two apparently completely different kinds of things? On the one hand, there are mental things, such as our thoughts and feelings; we think of them as subjective, conscious, and immaterial. On the other hand, there are physical things; we think of them as having mass, as extended in space, and as causally interacting with other physical things. Most attempted solutions to the mind–body problem wind up by denying the existence of, or in some way downgrading the status of, one or the other of these types of things. Given the successes of the physical sciences, it is not surprising that in our stage of intellectual development the temptation is to downgrade the status of mental entities. So, most of the recently fashion-able materialist conceptions of the mind—such as behaviorism, functionalism, and physicalism—end up by denying, implicitly or explicitly, that there are any such things as minds as we ordinarily think of them. That is, they deny that we do really *intrinsically* have subjective, conscious, mental states and that they are as real and irreducible as anything else in the universe.

Now, why do they do that? Why is it that so many theorists end up deny-ing the intrinsically mental character of mental phenomena? If we can answer that question, I believe that we will understand why the mind–body problem has seemed so intractable for so long.

[FOUR FEATURES OF MENTAL PHENOMENA]

There are four features of mental phenomena which have made them seem impossible to fit into our "scientific" conception of the world as made up of material things. And it is these four features that have made the mind–body problem really difficult. They are so embarrassing that they have led many thinkers in philosophy, psychology, and artificial intelligence to say strange and implausible things about the mind.

The most important of these features is consciousness. I, at the moment of writing this, and you, at the moment of reading it, are both conscious. It is just a plain fact about the world that it contains such conscious mental states and events, but it is hard to see how mere physical systems could have conscious-ness. How could such a thing occur? How, for example, could this grey and white gook inside my skull be conscious?

I think the existence of consciousness ought to seem amazing to us. It is easy enough to imagine a universe without it, but if you do, you will see that you have imagined a universe that is truly meaningless. Consciousness is the central fact of specifically human existence because without it all of the other specifically human aspects of our existence—language, love, humor, and so on—would be impossible. I believe it is, by the way, something of a scandal that contemporary discussions in philosophy and psychology have so little of interest to tell us about consciousness.

The second intractable feature of the mind is what philosophers and psy-chologists call "intentionality," the feature by which our mental states are di-rected at, or about, or refer to, or are of objects and states of affairs in the world other than themselves. "Intentionality," by the way, doesn't just refer to intentions, but also to beliefs, desires, hopes, fears, love, hate, lust, disgust, shame, pride, irritation, amusement, and all of those mental states (whether conscious or unconscious) that refer to, or are about, the world apart from the mind. Now the question about intentionality is much like the question about consciousness. How can this stuff inside my head be *about* anything? How can it *refer* to anything? After all, this stuff in the skull consists of "atoms in the void," just as all of the rest of material reality consists of atoms in the void. Now how, to put it crudely, can atoms in the void represent anything?

The third feature of the mind that seems difficult to accommodate within a scientific conception of reality is the subjectivity of mental states. This subjectivity is marked by such facts as that I can feel my pains, and you can't. I see the world from my point of view; you see it from your point of view. I am aware of myself and my internal mental states, as quite distinct from the selves and mental states of other people. Since the seventeenth century we have come to think of reality as something which must be equally accessible to all competent observers—that is, we think it must be objective. Now, how are we to accommodate the reality of *subjective* mental phenomena with the scientific conception of reality as totally *objective*?

Finally, there is a fourth problem, the problem of mental causation. We all suppose, as part of common sense, that our thoughts and feelings make a real difference to the way we behave, that they actually have some *causal* effect on the physical world. I decide, for example, to raise my arm and—lo and behold—my arm goes up. But if our thoughts and feelings are truly mental, how can they affect anything physical? How could something mental make a physical difference? Are we supposed to think that our thoughts and feelings can somehow produce chemical effects on our brains and the rest of our nervous system? How could such a thing occur? Are we supposed to think that thoughts can wrap themselves around the axons or shake the dendrites or sneak inside the cell wall and attack the cell nucleus?

But unless some such connection takes place between the mind and the brain, aren't we just left with the view that the mind doesn't matter, that it is as unimportant causally as the froth on the wave is to the movement of the wave? I suppose if the froth were conscious, it might think to itself: "What a tough job it is pulling these waves up on the beach and then pulling them out again, all day long!" But we know the froth doesn't make any important difference. Why do we suppose our mental life is any more important than a froth on the wave of physical reality?

These four features, consciousness, intentionality, subjectivity, and mental causation are what make the mind–body problem seem so difficult. Yet, I want to say, they are all real features of our mental lives. Not every mental state has all of them. But any satisfactory account of the mind and of mind–body relations must take account of all four features. If your theory ends up by denying any one of them, you know you must have made a mistake somewhere.

[ALL MENTAL PHENOMENA ARE CAUSED BY BRAIN ACTIVITY]

The first thesis I want to advance toward "solving the mind–body problem" is this:

> Mental phenomena, all mental phenomena whether conscious or unconscious, visual or auditory, pains, tickles, itches, thoughts, indeed, all of our mental life, are caused by processes going on in the brain.

To get a feel for how this works, let's try to describe the causal processes in some detail for at least one kind of mental state. For example, let's consider pains. Of course, anything we say now may seem wonderfully quaint in a generation, as our knowledge of how the brain works increases. Still, the *form* of the explanation can remain valid even though the *details* are altered. On current views, pain signals are transmitted from sensory nerve endings to the spinal cord by at least two types of fibers—there are Delta A fibers, which are specialized for prickling sensations, and C fibers, which are specialized for burning and aching sensations. In the spinal cord, they pass through a region called the tract of Lissauer and terminate on the neurons of the cord. As the signals go up the spine, they enter the brain by two separate pathways: the prickling pain pathway and the burning pain pathway. Both pathways go through the thalamus, but the prickling pain is more localized afterwards in the somato-sensory cortex, whereas the burning pain pathway transmits signals, not only upwards into the cortex, but also laterally into the hypothalamus and other regions at the base of the brain. Because of these differences, it is much easier for us to localize a prickling sensation—we can tell fairly accurately where someone is sticking a pin into our skin, for example—whereas burning and aching pains can be more distressing because they activate more of the nervous system. The actual sensation of pain appears to be caused both by the stimulation of the basal regions of the brain, especially the thalamus, and the stimulation of the somato-sensory cortex.

Now for the purposes of this discussion, the point we need to hammer home is this: our sensations of pains are caused by a series of events that begin at free nerve endings and end in the thalamus and in other regions of the brain. Indeed, as far as the actual sensations are concerned, the events inside the central nervous system are quite sufficient to cause pains—we know this both from the phantom-limb pains felt by amputees and the pains caused by artificially stimulating relevant portions of the brain. I want to suggest that what is true of pain is true of mental phenomena generally. To put it crudely, and counting all of the central nervous system as part of the brain for our present discussion, everything that matters for our mental life, all of our thoughts and feelings, are caused by processes inside the brain. As far as causing mental states is concerned, the crucial step is the one that goes on inside the head, not the external or peripheral stimulus. And the argument for this is simple. If the events outside the central nervous system occurred, but nothing happened in the brain, there would be no mental events. But if the right things happened in the brain, the mental events would occur even if there was no outside stimulus. (And that, by the way, is the principle on which surgical anaesthesia works: the outside stimulus is prevented from having the relevant effects on the central nervous system.)

But if pains and other mental phenomena are caused by processes in the brain, one wants to know: what are pains? What are they really? Well, in the case of pains, the obvious answer is that they are unpleasant sorts of sensations. But that answer leaves us unsatisfied because it doesn't tell us how pains fit into our overall conception of the world.

Once again, I think the answer to the question is obvious, but it will take some spelling out. To our first claim—that pains and other mental phenomena are caused by brain processes, we need to add a second claim:

Pains and other mental phenomena just are features of the brain (and perhaps the rest of the central nervous system).

One of the primary aims of this chapter is to show how *both* of these propositions can be true together. How can it be both the case that brains cause minds and yet minds just are features of brains? I believe it is the failure to see how both these propositions can be true together that has blocked a solution to the mind-body problem for so long. There are different levels of confusion that such a pair of ideas can generate. If mental and physical phenomena have cause and effect relationships, how can one be a feature of the other? Wouldn't that imply that the mind caused itself—the dreaded doctrine of *causa sui?* But at the bottom of our puzzlement is a misunderstanding of causation. It is tempting to think that whenever A causes B there must be two discrete events, one identified as the cause, the other identified as the effect; that all causation functions in the same way as billiard balls hitting each other. This crude model of the causal relationships between the brain and the mind inclines us to accept some kind of dualism; we are inclined to think that events in one material realm, the "physical," cause events in another insubstantial realm, the "mental." But that seems to me a mistake. And the way to remove the mistake is to get a more sophisticated concept of causation. To do this, I will turn away from the relations between mind and brain for a moment to observe some other sorts of causal relationships in nature.

A common distinction in physics is between micro- and macro-properties of systems—the small and large scales. Consider, for example, the desk at which I am now sitting, or the glass of water in front of me. Each object is composed of micro-particles. The micro-particles have features at the level of molecules and atoms as well as the deeper level of subatomic particles. But each object also has certain properties such as the solidity of the table, the liquidity of the water, and the transparency of the glass, which are surface or global features of the physical systems. Many such surface or global properties can be causally explained by the behavior of elements at the micro-level. For example, the solidity of the table in front of me is explained by the lattice structure occupied by the molecules of which the table is composed. Similarly, the liquidity of the water is explained by the nature of the interactions between the H_2O molecules. Those macro-features are causally explained by the behavior of elements at the micro-level.

I want to suggest that this provides a perfectly ordinary model for explaining the puzzling relationships between the mind and the brain. In the case of liquidity, solidity, and transparency, we have no difficulty at all in supposing that the surface features are *caused by* the behavior of elements at the micro-level, and at the same time we accept that the surface phenomena *just are* features of the very systems in question. I think the clearest way of stating this point is to say that the surface feature is both *caused by* the behavior of micro-elements, and at the same time is *realized in* the system that is made up of the micro-elements. There is a cause and effect relationship, but at the same time the surface features are just higher level features of the very system whose behavior at the micro-level causes those features.

In objecting to this someone might say that liquidity, solidity, and so on are identical with features of the micro-structure. So, for example, we might just define solidity as the lattice structure of the molecular arrangement, just as heat often is identified with the mean kinetic energy of molecule movements. This point seems to me correct but not really an objection to the analysis that I am proposing. It is a characteristic of the progress of science that an expression that is originally defined in terms of surface features, features accessible to the senses, is subsequently defined in terms of the micro-structure that causes the surface features. Thus, to take the example of solidity, the table in front of me is solid in the ordinary sense that it is rigid, it resists pressure, it supports books, it is not easily penetrable by most other objects such as other tables, and so on. Such is the commonsense notion of solidity. And in a scientific vein one can define solidity as whatever micro-structure causes these gross observable features. So one can then say either that solidity just is the lattice structure of the system of molecules and that solidity so defined causes, for example, resistance to touch and pressure. Or one can say that solidity consists of such high level features as rigidity and resistance to touch and pressure and that it is caused by the behavior of elements at the micro-level.

If we apply these lessons to the study of the mind, it seems to me that there is no difficulty in accounting for the relations of the mind to the brain in terms of the brain's functioning to cause mental states. Just as the liquidity of the water is caused by the behavior of elements at the micro-level, and yet at the same time it is a feature realized in the system of micro-elements, so in exactly that sense of "caused by" and "realized in" mental phenomena are caused by processes going on in the brain at the neuronal or modular level, and at the same time they are realized in the very system that consists of neurons. And just as we need the micro/macro distinction for any physical system, so for the same reasons we need the micro/macro distinction for the brain. And though we can say of a system of particles that it is 10° C or it is solid or it is liquid, we cannot say of any given particle that this particle is solid, this particle is liquid, this particle is 10° C. I can't for example reach into this glass of water, pull out a molecule and say: "This one's wet."

In exactly the same way, as far as we know anything at all about it, though we can say of a particular brain: "This brain is conscious," or: "This brain is experiencing thirst or pain," we can't say of any particular neuron in the brain: "This neuron is in pain, this neuron is experiencing thirst." To repeat this point, though there are enormous empirical mysteries about how the brain works in detail, there are no logical or philosophical or metaphysical obstacles to accounting for the relation between the mind and the brain in terms that are quite familiar to us from the rest of nature. Nothing is more common in nature than for surface features of a phenomenon to be both caused by and realized in a micro-structure, and those are exactly the relationships that are exhibited by the relation of mind to brain.

[EXPLAINING THE FOUR FEATURES
OF MENTAL PHENOMENA]

Let us now return to the four problems that I said faced any attempt to solve the mind–brain problem.

First, how is consciousness possible?

The best way to show how something is possible is to show how it actually exists. We have already given a sketch of how pains are actually caused by neurophysiological processes going on in the thalamus and the sensory cortex. Why is it then that many people feel dissatisfied with this sort of answer? I think that by pursuing an analogy with an earlier problem in the history of science we can dispel this sense of puzzlement. For a long time many biologists and philosophers thought it was impossible, in principle, to account for the existence of *life* on purely biological grounds. They thought that in addition to the biological processes some other element must be necessary, some *élan vital* must be postulated in order to lend life to what was otherwise dead and inert matter. It is hard today to realize how intense the dispute was between vitalism and mechanism even a generation ago, but today these issues are no longer taken seriously. Why not? I think it is not so much because mechanism won and vitalism lost, but because we have come to understand better the biological character of the processes that are characteristic of living organisms. Once we understand how the features that are characteristic of living beings have a biological explanation, it no longer seems mysterious to us that matter should be alive. I think that exactly similar considerations should apply to our discussions of consciousness. It should seem no more mysterious, in principle, that this hunk of matter, this grey and white oatmeal-textured substance of the brain, should be conscious than it seems mysterious that this other hunk of matter, this collection of nucleo-protein molecules stuck onto a calcium frame, should be alive. The way, in short, to dispel the mystery is to understand the processes. We do not yet fully understand the processes, but we understand their general *character*, we understand that there are certain specific electro-chemical activities going on among neurons or neuron-modules and perhaps other features of the brain and these processes cause consciousness.

Our second problem was, how can atoms in the void have intentionality? How can they be about something?

As with our first question, the best way to show how something is possible is to show how it actually exists. So let's consider thirst. As far as we know anything about it, at least certain kinds of thirst are caused in the hypothalamus by sequences of nerve firings. These firings are in turn caused by the action of angiotensin in the hypothalamus, and angiotensin, in turn, is synthesized by renin, which is secreted by the kidneys. Thirst, at least of these kinds, is caused by a series of events in the central nervous system, principally the hypothalamus, and it is realized in the hypothalamus. To be thirsty is to have, among other things, the desire to drink. Thirst is therefore an intentional state: it has content; its content determines under what conditions it is satisfied, and it has all the rest of the features that are common to intentional states.

As with the "mysteries" of life and consciousness, the way to master the mystery of intentionality is to describe in as much detail as we can how the phenomena are caused by biological processes while being at the same time realized in biological systems. Visual and auditory experiences, tactile sensations, hunger, thirst, and sexual desire, are all caused by brain processes and they are realized in the structure of the brain, and they are all intentional phenomena.

I am not saying we should lose our sense of the mysteries of nature. On the contrary, the examples I have cited are all in a sense astounding. But I am saying that they are neither more nor less mysterious than other astounding features of the world, such as the existence of gravitational attraction, the process of photosynthesis, or the size of the Milky Way.

Our third problem: how do we accommodate the subjectivity of mental states within an objective conception of the real world?

It seems to me a mistake to suppose that the definition of reality should exclude subjectivity. If "science" is the name of the collection of objective and systematic truths we can state about the world, then the existence of subjectivity is an objective scientific fact like any other. If a scientific account of the world attempts to describe how things are, then one of the features of the account will be the subjectivity of mental states, since it is just a plain fact about biological evolution that it has produced certain sorts of biological systems, namely human and certain animal brains, that have subjective features. My present state of consciousness is a feature of my brain, but its conscious aspects are accessible to me in a way that they are not accessible to you. And your present state of consciousness is a feature of your brain and its conscious aspects are accessible to you in a way that they are not accessible to me. Thus the existence of subjectivity is an objective fact of biology. It is a persistent mistake to try to define "science" in terms of certain features of existing scientific theories. But once this provincialism is perceived to be the prejudice it is, then any domain of facts whatever is a subject of systematic investigation. So, for example, if God existed, then that fact would be a fact like any other. I do not know whether God exists, but I have no doubt at all that subjective mental states exist, because I am now in one and so are you. If the fact of subjectivity runs counter to a certain definition of "science," then it is the definition and not the fact which we will have to abandon.

Fourth, the problem of mental causation for our present purpose is to explain how mental events can cause physical events. How, for example, could anything as "weightless" and "ethereal" as a thought give rise to an action?

The answer is that thoughts are not weightless and ethereal. When you have a thought, brain activity is actually going on. Brain activity causes bodily movements by physiological processes. Now, because mental states are features of the brain, they have two levels of descriptions higher level in mental terms, and a lower level in physiological terms. The very same causal powers of the system can be described at either level.

Once again, we can use an analogy from physics to illustrate these relationships. Consider hammering a nail with a hammer. Both hammer and nail have a certain kind of solidity. Hammers made of cottonwool or butter will be quite useless, and hammers made of water or steam are not hammers at all. Solidity is a real causal property of the hammer. But the solidity itself is caused by the behavior of particles at the micro-level and it is realized in the system which consists of micro-elements. The existence of two causally real levels of description in the brain, one a macro-level of mental processes and the other a micro-level of neuronal processes is exactly analogous to the existence of two causally real levels of description of the hammer. Consciousness, for example, is a real property of the brain that can cause things to happen. My conscious attempt to perform an action such as raising my arm causes the movement of the arm. At the higher level of description, the intention to raise my arm causes the movement of the arm. But at the lower level of description, a series of neuron firings starts a chain of events that results in the contraction of the muscles. As with the case of hammering a nail, the same sequence of events has two levels of description. Both of them are causally real, and the higher level causal features are both caused by and realized in the structure of the lower level elements.

To summarize: on my view, the mind and the body interact, but they are not two different things, since mental phenomena just are features of the brain. One way to characterize this position is to see it as an assertion of both physicalism and mentalism. Suppose we define "naive physicalism" to be the view that all that exists in the world are physical particles with their properties and relations. The power of the physical model of reality is so great that it is hard to see how we can seriously challenge naive physicalism. And let us define "naive mentalism" to be the view that mental phenomena really exist. There really are mental states; some of them are conscious; many have intentionality; they all have subjectivity; and many of them function causally in determining physical events in the world. The thesis of this first chapter can now be stated quite simply. Naive mentalism and naive physicalism are perfectly consistent with each other. Indeed, as far as we know anything about how the world works, they are not only consistent, they are both true.

PART THREE

Philosophy of Religion

We noted in the previous part that the field of metaphysics wrestles with the fundamental nature of reality, and this typically involves speculation about a spirit-component of existence beyond the immediate physical world around us. Part of that speculation involves narrowly focused discussions about our human makeup—the relation between our allegedly spiritual minds and physical bodies. Another aspect of metaphysics looks more broadly around the universe and attempts to discover a possible spiritual realm beyond this physical realm. In contemporary philosophy the *philosophy of religion* deals with this part of metaphysics.

Of the many subjects commanding the attention of philosophers of religion, few have received more careful treatment than the questions of the *existence* of God and the *nature* of God. Throughout the centuries, theologians and philosophers have attempted to prove the existence of God in a variety of ways, as we will see in the selections below. Even if we might demonstrate the existence of a divine being, though, a question immediately arises about the nature or attributes of that being. First and foremost, theologians argue that God is the all-powerful creator of things. He is also all-knowing, all-good, and a personal being who acts with a purpose. For believers, understanding God's existence and nature not only explains the origin of all things but also illuminates the purpose of human existence.

One of the first attempts to systematically prove God's existence was made by British monastic theologian Anselm of Canterbury (1033–1109). He personally believed in the existence of God and felt no need of a proof. But he wanted to provide an intellectual basis for belief in God for those who were unwilling to accept God's existence solely as a matter of faith. The proof he formulated is now known as the *ontological argument*. Anselm begins with the concept of "that than which nothing greater can be conceived"—or more simply, the greatest possible being. What type of qualities must this being possess? By definition, the greatest possible being must possess every great-making quality. Anselm then argues that *existence* is a great-making attribute: If a being lacked existence, then it would have been greater if it actually possessed existence. Thus, the greatest possible being must possess the attribute of existence since, if it lacked existence, then it would not be the *greatest* possible being. Shortly after, a monk named Gaunilo challenged Anselm's reasoning. Suppose, he argued, that we replace the notion of "the greatest possible being" with "the greatest possible island." Anselm's argument would then show that the greatest possible island actually exists, which is of course absurd. Thus, Anselm's logic is somewhere flawed. Responding to Gaunilo, Anselm contended that the ontological argument only works with the notion of the greatest possible *being*, since only "being" (and not islands) can have infinitely great qualities, without lapsing into logical contradiction. The principle difference is that an island is only a contingent being, whereas the notion of God is that of a necessary being.

In his *Summa Theologica*, Thomas Aquinas (1224–1274) offers five proofs for God's existence. Unlike Anselm's argument, which based on the logical implications of a mental concept, Aquinas's arguments are based on information found in our actual experience. The first three of Aquinas's arguments rely upon the notion of cause and effect, and today are referred to as *cosmological arguments* for God's existence. Take, for example, his first argument, which is based on the motion that we see around us. Starting from the simple fact that we perceive by our senses that in the world some things are in motion, we also observe that things tend to stay at rest unless they are moved. For every motion, then, there must be a mover. Although, say, a billiard ball, is potentially in motion, it will not move unless it is moved by something that is actually in motion. If you lined up all the billiard balls behind each other on the table, not one of them would move until the first one was struck by the cue, even though potentially they could all move. The argument, then, comes to this: What if *everything* in the universe is of this kind, namely, that it will move only if it is moved? The word "motion," in this context, signifies more than simply locomotion as suggested by billiard balls; motion also means generation or coming into being. If everything were only potentially in motion, then even now nothing would be in motion. Actual motion cannot be derived from potential motion. Yet the fact is that there is motion in the world. To explain this fact, Aquinas concludes, there must be some being that is capable of moving others but does not require to be moved, a being that actually is that is capable of bringing others into being. That is, there must be a first mover, which is God.

Although this argument is short and to the point, its brevity creates problems. We might think that Aquinas is simply saying that we cannot trace a causal sequence of motion back through infinity past. However, in another part of his *Summa Theologica* (also contained herein), he states very explicitly that there is nothing logically contradictory in the idea that the world existed from eternity past. That is, we might in theory trace the causal sequences of motion back to infinity. Aquinas then distinguishes between *accidental causes* (causes *per accidens*) that happen over a period of time, and *essential causes* (causes *per se*) that occur simultaneously. An example of accidental causes over time is Abraham begetting Isaac, who in turn begets Jacob. An example of simultaneous essential causes is a hand that moves a stick, which in turn moves a stone, all at the same time. Aquinas's point is that, yes, we can trace accidental motion back to infinity past, but simultaneous essential motion—which occurs here and now—traces immediately back to a first mover.

Aside from the three cosmological arguments that Aquinas offers, in his fifth proof he proposes an argument that in later years was dubbed the *design argument* or the *teleological argument* for God's existence. The central intuition behind this argument is clear: We see obvious signs of intelligent design in the natural world, and this implies that there must be an intelligent designer of the world. Aquinas observes that many things in nature are directed toward a purpose or final goal, and so we must conclude that an intelligent being orchestrates this purposeful direction.

French monastic theologian Blaise Pascal (1623–1662) was well aware of previous efforts to prove God's existence, but he was not convinced of their success. In his *Thoughts,* he argued that reason is neutral on the whole matter of God's existence, and we cannot conclusively demonstrate that God does or does not exist. Where, then, does this leave us? According to Pascal, the issue of belief in God is purely a matter of faith, and our faith might only be sparked when we embrace a faith-tradition, such as his own Catholic Christian tradition. The issue, then, becomes one of psychologically motivating us to adopt a faith tradition. To this end, he proposes that we take a wager, consider the possible positive benefits of belief in God, and weigh them against the possible benefits of disbelief in God. His assessment is that, by affirming God's existence, we have everything to gain and nothing to lose. We should then enter into our faith tradition and have this initiate our faith.

During the sixteenth and seventeenth centuries, the European intellectual community made dramatic advances in scientific discoveries, which had a direct impact on the discipline of philosophy and philosophical proofs for God's existence—specifically the cosmological and design arguments. But with improved theistic arguments came improved religious critiques, a champion of which was the skeptical Scottish philosopher David Hume (1711–1776). In his *An Enquiry Concerning Human Understanding* (1748), Hume included a chapter that criticized belief in miracles. Hume's central point is that uniform experience of natural law outweighs the testimony of any alleged miracle. The issue involves a competition between conflicting evidence. On the one hand, we might amass the best evidence that we can in favor of a reported miraculous event, such as the credibility of the various witnesses. However, on the other hand, we have our life-long and consistent experience of natural laws—laws that are unvarying. The strong evidence of natural laws, then, will always outweigh the weaker evidence in support of miraculous events. In his *Dialogues Concerning Natural Religion* (1779), Hume challenges both the design and cosmological arguments for God's existence. As to the design argument, Hume offers two key criticisms. First, he argues that the design argument rests on a faulty analogy between objects of human design, such as watches, and the alleged order of the universe. Because two are so dissimilar we cannot reasonably draw a conclusion about a natural designer. Second, Hume argues that we must proportion the cause of a thing to the effects that we actually see; so, since the universe (as an effect) is limited, diverse, and imperfect, we cannot infer that the designer (the cause) is unlimited, single, and perfect.

As to the cosmological argument, Hume examines a modern version of this as articulated by British philosopher Samuel Clarke (1675–1729). Clarke grants that, in theory, we might trace the various causes of the world back to infinity past. We might envision an infinitely long sequence of dependent beings, each of which relies for its existence on the previous thing—such as Jacob depending on his father Isaac, who depends on his father Abraham, and so on. Even though each thing in this sequence is adequately explained by its previous member, there is one huge fact that remains unexplained: why the entire infinite series exists to begin with. Clarke concludes that there must be a self-existent being to explain this huge fact. Against Clarke, Hume argues that once we adequately explain each individual item in an infinite series of dependent beings, then we have thus given a full explanation of the entire series.

The presence of human suffering has always raised skepticism about the goodness and the all-powerful nature of God. How is it possible to reconcile an overall design and purpose in nature when there is so much physical pain, mental suffering, and moral wickedness? Philosophers distinguish between two types of human suffering. First, *moral evil* is the suffering that humans willfully inflict on each other, such as rapes and murders. Second, *natural evil* is the suffering that results from purely natural causes, apart from human choice, such as diseases and natural disasters. Both of these present special theological challenges. Australian philosopher J. L. Mackie (1917–1981) presented what is now called the *logical problem of evil*—an attempt to show that the presence of evil is logically incompatible with the existence of God.

The Ontological Argument*

Anselm (1033–1109)

CHAPTER 2: TRULY THERE IS A GOD

And so, Lord, do you, who gives understanding to faith, give me, so far as you know it to be profitable, to understand that you are as we believe; and that you are that which we believe. And indeed, we believe that you are a being than which nothing greater can be conceived. Or is there no such nature, since the fool hath said in his heart, there is no God? (Psalms 14:1). But, at any rate, this very fool, when he hears of this being of which I speak—a being than which nothing greater can be conceived—understands what he hears, and what he understands is in his understanding; although he does not understand it to exist.

For, it is one thing for an object to be in the understanding, and another to understand that the object exists. When a painter first conceives of what he will afterwards perform, he has it in his understanding, but he does not yet understand it to be, because he has not yet performed it. But after he has made the painting, he both has it in his understanding, and he understands that it exists, because he has made it.

Hence, even the fool is convinced that something exists in the understanding, at least, than which nothing greater can be conceived. For, when he hears of this, he understands it. And whatever is understood, exists in the understanding. And assuredly that, than which nothing greater can be conceived,

*From Anselm, *Proslogium*.

cannot exist in the understanding alone. For, suppose it exists in the understanding alone: then it can be conceived to exist in reality; which is greater.

Therefore, if that, than which nothing greater can be conceived, exists in the understanding alone, the very being, than which nothing greater can be conceived, is one, than which a greater can be conceived. But obviously this is impossible. Hence, there is no doubt that there exists a being, than which nothing greater can be conceived, and it exists both in the understanding and in reality.

CHAPTER 3: GOD CANNOT
BE CONCEIVED NOT TO EXIST

And it assuredly exists so truly, that it cannot be conceived not to exist. For, it is possible to conceive of a being which cannot be conceived not to exist; and this is greater than one which can be conceived not to exist. Hence, if that, than which nothing greater can be conceived, can be conceived not to exist, it is not that, than which nothing greater can be conceived. But this is an irreconcilable contradiction. There is, then, so truly a being than which nothing greater can be conceived to exist, that it cannot even be conceived not to exist; and this being you are, O Lord, our God.

So truly, therefore, do you exist, O Lord, my God, that you can not be conceived not to exist; and rightly. For, if a mind could conceive of a being better than you, the creature would rise above the Creator; and this is most absurd. And, indeed, whatever else there is, except you alone, can be conceived not to exist. To you alone, therefore, it belongs to exist more truly than all other beings, and hence in a higher degree than all others. For, whatever else exists does not exist so truly, and hence in a less degree it belongs to it to exist. Why, then, has the fool said in his heart, there is no God (Psalms 14:1), since it is so evident, to a rational mind, that you do exist in the highest degree of all? Why, except that he is dull and a fool?

CHAPTER 4: HOW THE FOOL HAS SAID
IN HIS HEART WHAT CANNOT BE CONCEIVED

But how has the fool said in his heart what he could not conceive; or how is it that he could not conceive what he said in his heart? since it is the same to say in the heart, and to conceive.

But, if really, nay, since really, he both conceived, because he said in his heart; and did not say in his heart, because he could not conceive; there is more than one way in which a thing is said in the heart or conceived. For, in one sense, an object is conceived, when the word signifying it is conceived; and in another, when the very entity, which the object is, is understood.

In the former sense, then, God can be conceived not to exist; but in the latter, not at all. For no one who understands what fire and water are can conceive fire to be water, in accordance with the nature of the facts themselves, although this is possible according to the words. So, then, no one who understands what God is can conceive that God does not exist; although he says these words in his heart, either without any or with some foreign, signification. For, God is that than which a greater cannot be conceived. And he who thoroughly understands this, assuredly understands that this being so truly exists, that not even in concept can it be non-existent. Therefore, he who understands that God so exists, cannot conceive that he does not exist.

I thank you, gracious Lord, I thank you; because what I formerly believed by your bounty, I now so understand by your illumination, that if I were unwilling to believe that you do exist, I should not be able not to understand this to be true.

CHAPTER 5: GOD IS WHATEVER IT IS BETTER TO BE THAN NOT TO BE

What are you, then, Lord God, than whom nothing greater can be conceived? But what are you, except that which, as the highest of all beings, alone exists through itself, and creates all other things from nothing? For, whatever is not this is less than a thing which can be conceived of. But this cannot be conceived of you. What good, therefore, does the supreme Good lack, through which every good is? Therefore, you are just, truthful, blessed, and whatever it is better to be than not to be. For it is better to be just than not just; better to be blessed than not blessed.

[GAUNILON'S ANSWER TO ANSELM'S ARGUMENT]

For example: it is said that somewhere in the ocean is an island, which, because of the difficulty, or rather the impossibility, of discovering what does not exist, is called the lost island. And they say that this island has an inestimable wealth of all manner of riches and delicacies in greater abundance than is told of the Islands of the Blest; and that having no owner or inhabitant, it is more excellent than all other countries, which are inhabited by mankind, in the abundance with which it is stored.

Now if some one should tell me that there is such an island, I should easily understand his words, in which there is no difficulty. But suppose that he went on to say, as if by a logical inference: "You can no longer doubt that this island which is more excellent than all lands exists somewhere, since you have no doubt that it is in your understanding. And since it is more excellent not to be in the understanding alone, but to exist both in the understanding and in reality, for this reason it must exist. For if it does not exist, any land which really exists will be more excellent than it; and so the island already understood by you to be more excellent will not be more excellent."

If a man should try to prove to me by such reasoning that this island truly exists, and that its existence should no longer be doubted, either I should believe that he was jesting, or I know not which I ought to regard as the greater fool: myself, supposing that I should allow this proof; or him, if he should suppose that he had established with any certainty the existence of this island. For he ought to show first that the hypothetical excellence of this island exists as a real and indubitable fact, and in no wise as any unreal object, or one whose existence is uncertain, in my understanding.

[ANSELM'S REPLY TO GAUNILON]

But, you say, it is as if one should suppose an island in the ocean, which surpasses all lands in its fertility, and which, because of the difficulty, or the impossibility, of discovering what does not exist, is called a lost island; and should say that there can no doubt that this island truly exists in reality, for this reason, that one who hears it described easily understands what he hears.

Now I promise confidently that if any man shall devise anything existing either in reality or in concept alone (except that than which a greater be conceived) to which he can adapt the sequence of my reasoning, I will discover that thing, and will give him his lost island, not to be lost again.

But it now appears that this being than which a greater is inconceivable cannot be conceived not to be, because it exists on so assured a ground of truth; for otherwise it would not exist at all.

Hence, if any one says that he conceives this being not to exist, I say that at the time when he conceives of this either he conceives of a being than which a greater is inconceivable, or he does not conceive at all. If he does not conceive, he does not conceive of the non-existence of that of which he does not conceive. But if he does conceive, he certainly conceives of a being which cannot be even conceived not to exist. For if it could be conceived not to exist, it could be conceived to have a beginning and an end. But this is impossible.

He, then, who conceives of this being conceives of a being which cannot be even conceived not to exist; but he who conceives of this being does not conceive that it does not exist; else he conceives what is inconceivable. The non-existence, then, of that than which a greater cannot be conceived is inconceivable.

You say, moreover, that whereas I assert that this supreme being cannot be conceived not to exist, it might better be said that its non-existence, or even the possibility of its non-existence, cannot be understood.

But it was more proper to say, it cannot be conceived. For if I had said that the object itself cannot be understood not to exist, possibly you yourself, who say that in accordance with the true meaning of the term what is unreal cannot be understood, would offer the objection that nothing which is can be understood not to be, for the non-existence of what exists is unreal: hence God would not be the only being of which it could be said, it is impossible to understand its non-existence. For thus one of those beings which most certainly exist can be understood not to exist in the same way in which certain other real objects can be understood not to exist.

But this objection, assuredly, cannot be urged against the term conception, if one considers the matter well. For although no objects which exist can be understood not to exist, yet all objects, except that which exists in the highest degree, can be conceived not to exist. For all those objects, and those alone, can be conceived not to exist, which have a beginning or end or composition of parts: also, as I have already said, whatever at any place or at any time does not exist as a whole.

That being alone, on the other hand, cannot be conceived not to exist, in which any conception discovers neither beginning nor end nor composition of parts, and which any conception finds always and everywhere as a whole.

Be assured, then, that you can conceive of your own non-existence, although you are most certain that you exist. I am surprised that you should have admitted that you are ignorant of this. For we conceive of the non-existence of many objects which we know to exist, and of the existence of many which we know not to exist; not by forming the opinion that they so exist, but by imagining that they exist as we conceive of them.

And indeed, we can conceive of the non-existence of an object, although we know it to exist, because at the same time we can conceive of the former and know the latter. And we cannot conceive of the nonexistence of an object, so long as we know it to exist, because we cannot conceive at the same time of existence and non-existence.

If, then, one will thus distinguish these two senses of this statement, he will understand that nothing, so long as it is known to exist, can be conceived not to exist; and that whatever exists, except that being than which a greater cannot be conceived, can be conceived not to exist, even when it is known to exist.

So, then, of God alone it can be said that it is impossible to conceive of his non-existence; and yet many objects, so long as they exist, in one sense cannot be conceived not to exist. But in what sense God is to be conceived not to exist, I think has been shown clearly enough in my book.

READING 16

Five Ways of Proving God's Existence[*]

Thomas Aquinas (1224–1274)

WHETHER GOD EXISTS?

Objection 1   It seems that God does not exist; because if one of two contraries be infinite, the other would be altogether destroyed. But the word "God" means that He is infinite goodness. If, therefore, God existed, there would be no evil discoverable; but there is evil in the world. Therefore God does not exist.

---

*From Thomas Aquinas, *Summa Theologica*, First Part, Question 2: The Existence of God, Article 3; Question 46: The Beginning of the Duration of Creatures, Article 2.

Objection 2   Further, it is superfluous to suppose that what can be accounted for by a few principles has been produced by many. But it seems that everything we see in the world can be accounted for by other principles, supposing God did not exist. For all natural things can be reduced to one principle which is nature; and all voluntary things can be reduced to one principle which is human reason, or will. Therefore there is no need to suppose God's existence.

On the contrary, It is said in the person of God: "I am Who am."

I answer that, The existence of God can be proved in five ways.

The first and more manifest way is the argument from motion. It is certain, and evident to our senses, that in the world some things are in motion. Now whatever is in motion is put in motion by another, for nothing can be in motion except it is in potentiality to that towards which it is in motion; whereas a thing moves inasmuch as it is in act. For motion is nothing else than the reduction of something from potentiality to actuality. But nothing can be reduced from potentiality to actuality, except by something in a state of actuality. Thus that which is actually hot, as fire, makes wood, which is potentially hot, to be actually hot, and thereby moves and changes it. Now it is not possible that the same thing should be at once in actuality and potentiality in the same respect, but only in different respects. For what is actually hot cannot simultaneously be potentially hot; but it is simultaneously potentially cold. It is therefore impossible that in the same respect and in the same way a thing should be both mover and moved, i.e., that it should move itself. Therefore, whatever is in motion must be put in motion by another. If that by which it is put in motion be itself put in motion, then this also must needs be put in motion by another, and that by another again. But this cannot go on to infinity, because then there would be no first mover, and, consequently, no other mover; seeing that subsequent movers move only inasmuch as they are put in motion by the first mover; as the staff moves only because it is put in motion by the hand. Therefore it is necessary to arrive at a first mover, put in motion by no other; and this everyone understands to be God.

The second way is from the nature of the efficient cause. In the world of sense we find there is an order of efficient causes. There is no case known (neither is it, indeed, possible) in which a thing is found to be the efficient cause of itself; for so it would be prior to itself, which is impossible. Now in efficient causes it is not possible to go on to infinity, because in all efficient causes following in order, the first is the cause of the intermediate cause, and the intermediate is the cause of the ultimate cause, whether the intermediate cause be several, or only one. Now to take away the cause is to take away the effect. Therefore, if there be no first cause among efficient causes, there will be no ultimate, nor any intermediate cause. But if in efficient causes it is possible to go on to infinity, there will be no first efficient cause, neither will there be an ultimate effect, nor any intermediate efficient causes; all of which is plainly false. Therefore it is necessary to admit a first efficient cause, to which everyone gives the name of God.

The third way is taken from possibility and necessity, and runs thus. We find in nature things that are possible to be and not to be, since they are found to be generated, and to corrupt, and consequently, they are possible to be and not to be. But it is impossible for these always to exist, for that which is possible not to be at some time is not. Therefore, if everything is possible not to be, then at one time there could have been nothing in existence. Now if this were true, even now there would be nothing in existence, because that which does not exist only begins to exist by something already existing. Therefore, if at one time nothing was in existence, it would have been impossible for anything to have begun to exist, and thus even now nothing would be in existence—which is absurd. Therefore, not all beings are merely possible, but there must exist something the existence of which is necessary. But every necessary thing either has its necessity caused by another, or not. Now it is impossible to go on to infinity in necessary things which have their necessity caused by another, as has been already proved in regard to efficient causes. Therefore we cannot but postulate the existence of some being having of itself its own necessity, and not receiving it from another, but rather causing in others their necessity. This all men speak of as God.

The fourth way is taken from the gradation to be found in things. Among beings there are some more and some less good, true, noble and the like. But "more" and "less" are predicated of different things, according as they resemble in their different ways something which is the maximum, as a thing is said to be hotter according as it more nearly resembles that which is hottest; so that there is something which is truest, something best, something noblest and, consequently, something which is uttermost being; for those things that are greatest in truth are greatest in being, as it is written in Metaphysics. ii. Now the maximum in any genus is the cause of all in that genus; as fire, which is the maximum heat, is the cause of all hot things. Therefore there must also be something which is to all beings the cause of their being, goodness, and every other perfection; and this we call God.

The fifth way is taken from the governance of the world. We see that things which lack intelligence, such as natural bodies, act for an end, and this is evident from their acting always, or nearly always, in the same way, so as to obtain the best result. Hence it is plain that not fortuitously, but designedly, do they achieve their end. Now whatever lacks intelligence cannot move towards an end, unless it be directed by some being endowed with knowledge and intelligence; as the arrow is shot to its mark by the archer. Therefore some intelligent being exists by whom all natural things are directed to their end; and this being we call God.

Reply to Objection 1   As Augustine says: "Since God is the highest good, He would not allow any evil to exist in His works, unless His omnipotence and goodness were such as to bring good even out of evil." This is part of the infinite goodness of God, that He should allow evil to exist, and out of it produce good.

Reply to Objection 2   Since nature works for a determinate end under the direction of a higher agent, whatever is done by nature must needs be traced back to God, as to its first cause. So also whatever is done voluntarily must also be traced back to some higher cause other than human reason or will, since these can change or fail; for all things that are changeable and capable of defect must be traced back to an immovable and self-necessary first principle, as was shown in the body of the Article.

WHETHER IT IS AN ARTICLE
OF FAITH THAT THE WORLD BEGAN?

Objection 1   It would seem that it is not an article of faith but a demonstrable conclusion that the world began. For everything that is made has a beginning of its duration. But it can be proved demonstratively that God is the effective cause of the world; indeed this is asserted by the more approved philosophers. Therefore it can be demonstratively proved that the world began.

Objection 2   Further, if it is necessary to say that the world was made by God, it must therefore have been made from nothing or from something. But it was not made from something; otherwise the matter of the world would have preceded the world; against which are the arguments of Aristotle, who held that heaven was ungenerated. Therefore it must be said that the world was made from nothing; and thus it has being after not being. Therefore it must have begun.

Objection 3   Further, everything which works by intellect works from some principle, as appears in all kinds of craftsmen. But God acts by intellect: therefore His work has a principle. The world, therefore, which is His effect, did not always exist.

Objection 4   Further, it appears manifestly that certain arts have developed, and certain countries have begun to be inhabited at some fixed time. But this would not be the case if the world had been always. Therefore it is manifest that the world did not always exist.

Objection 5   Further, it is certain that nothing can be equal to God. But if the world had always been, it would be equal to God in duration. Therefore it is certain that the world did not always exist.

Objection 6   Further, if the world always was, the consequence is that infinite days preceded this present day. But it is impossible to pass through an infinite medium. Therefore we should never have arrived at this present day; which is manifestly false.

Objection 7   Further, if the world was eternal, generation also was eternal. Therefore one man was begotten of another in an infinite series. But the father is the efficient cause of the son. Therefore in efficient causes there could be an infinite series, which is disproved.

Objection 8   Further, if the world and generation always were, there have been an infinite number of men. But man's soul is immortal: therefore an infinite number of human souls would actually now exist, which is impossible. Therefore it can be known with certainty that the world began, and not only is it known by faith.

On the contrary, The articles of faith cannot be proved demonstratively, because faith is of things "that appear not." But that God is the Creator of the world: hence that the world began, is an article of faith; for we say, "I believe in one God," etc. And again, Gregory says, that Moses prophesied of the past, saying, "In the beginning God created heaven and earth": in which words the newness of the world is stated. Therefore the newness of the world is known only by revelation; and therefore it cannot be proved demonstratively.

I answer that, By faith alone do we hold, and by no demonstration can it be proved, that the world did not always exist, as was said above of the mystery of the Trinity. The reason of this is that the newness of the world cannot be demonstrated on the part of the world itself. For the principle of demonstration is the essence of a thing. Now everything according to its species is abstracted from "here" and "now"; whence it is said that universals are everywhere and always. Hence it cannot be demonstrated that man, or heaven, or a stone were not always. Likewise neither can it be demonstrated on the part of the efficient cause, which acts by will. For the will of God cannot be investigated by reason, except as regards those things which God must will of necessity; and what He wills about creatures is not among these, as was said above. But the divine will can be manifested by revelation, on which faith rests. Hence that the world began to exist is an object of faith, but not of demonstration or science. And it is useful to consider this, lest anyone, presuming to demonstrate what is of faith, should bring forward reasons that are not cogent, so as to give occasion to unbelievers to laugh, thinking that on such grounds we believe things that are of faith.

Reply to Objection 1   As Augustine says, the opinion of philosophers who asserted the eternity of the world was twofold. For some said that the substance of the world was not from God, which is an intolerable error; and therefore it is refuted by proofs that are cogent. Some, however, said that the world was eternal, although made by God. For they hold that the world has a beginning, not of time, but of creation, so that in a certain hardly intelligible way it was always made. "And they try to explain their meaning thus: for as, if the foot were always in the dust from eternity, there would always be a footprint which without doubt was caused by him who trod on it, so also the world always was, because its maker always existed." To understand this we must consider that the efficient cause, which acts by motion, of necessity precedes its effect in time; because the effect is only in the end of the action, and every agent must be the principle of action. But if the action is instantaneous and not successive, it is not necessary for the maker to be prior to the thing made in duration as appears in the case of illumination. Hence they say that it does not follow necessarily if God is the active cause of the world, that He should be prior to the world in duration; because creation, by which He produced the world, is not a successive change, as was said above.

Reply to Objection 2   Those who would say that the world was eternal, would say that the world was made by God from nothing, not that it was made after nothing, according to what we understand by the word creation, but that it was not made from anything; and so also some of them do not reject the word creation, as appears from Avicenna.

Reply to Objection 3   This is the argument of Anaxagoras. But it does not lead to a necessary conclusion, except as to that intellect which deliberates in order to find out what should be done, which is like movement. Such is the human intellect, but not the divine intellect.

Reply to Objection 4   Those who hold the eternity of the world hold that some region was changed an infinite number of times, from being uninhabitable to being inhabitable and "vice versa," and likewise they hold that the arts, by reason of various corruptions and accidents, were subject to an infinite variety of advance and decay. Hence Aristotle says (Meteor. i), that it is absurd from such particular changes to hold the opinion of the newness of the whole world.

Reply to Objection 5   Even supposing that the world always was, it would not be equal to God in eternity, as Boethius says; because the divine Being is all being simultaneously without succession; but with the world it is otherwise.

Reply to Objection 6   Passage is always understood as being from term to term. Whatever bygone day we choose, from it to the present day there is a finite number of days which can be passed through. The objection is founded on the idea that, given two extremes, there is an infinite number of mean terms.

Reply to Objection 7   In efficient causes it is impossible to proceed to infinity "*per se*"—thus, there cannot be an infinite number of causes that are "*per se*" required for a certain effect; for instance, that a stone be moved by a stick, the stick by the hand, and so on to infinity. But it is not impossible to proceed to infinity "accidentally" as regards efficient causes; for instance, if all the causes thus infinitely multiplied should have the order of only one cause, their multiplication being accidental, as an artificer acts by means of many hammers accidentally, because one after the other may be broken. It is accidental, therefore, that one particular hammer acts after the action of another; and likewise it is accidental to this particular man as generator to be generated by another man; for he generates as a man, and not as the son of another man. For all men generating hold one grade in efficient causes—viz. the grade of a particular generator. Hence it is not impossible for a man to be generated by man to infinity; but such a thing would be impossible if the generation of this man depended upon this man, and on an elementary body, and on the sun, and so on to infinity.

Reply to Objection 8   Those who hold the eternity of the world evade this reason in many ways. For some do not think it impossible for there to be an actual infinity of souls, as appears from the Metaphysics of Algazel, who says that such a thing is an accidental infinity. But this was disproved above. Some say that the soul is corrupted with the body. And some say that of all souls only one will remain. But others, as Augustine says, asserted on this account a circuit of souls—viz. that souls separated from their bodies return again thither after a course of time; a fuller consideration of which matters will be given later. But be it noted that this argument considers only a particular case. Hence one might say that the world was eternal, or least some creature, as an angel, but not man. But we are considering the question in general, as to whether any creature can exist from eternity.

Wagering on Belief in God*

Blaise Pascal (1623–1662)

By faith we know God's existence. In the glorious state of heaven we will know his nature. Now, I have already shown that we may easily know the existence of a thing without knowing its nature. Let us speak now according to the light of nature. If there is a God he is infinitely incomprehensible, since, having neither parts nor limits, he has no proportion to us. We are then incapable of knowing either what he is, or whether he is. This being true, who will dare to undertake to resolve this question? It cannot be we who have no proportion to him.

Who, then, will blame those Christians who are not able to give a reason for their belief insofar as they profess a religion for which they can give no reason? In exposing it to the world, they declare that it is a folly *stultitiam* (1 Corinthians, 1:18). And then you complain that they do not prove it! If they proved it, they would not keep their word. It is in lacking proofs that they do not lack sense. Yes, but though this may excuse those who offer it such, and take away the blame for producing it without reason, this does not excuse those who receive it. Let us examine this point then, and say "God is, or he is not." But to which side shall we incline? Reason cannot decide it at all. There is an infinite chaos that separates us. A game is being played at the extremity of this infinite distance in which heads or tails must come up. Which will you take? By reason you can wager on neither. By reason you can hinder neither from winning.

*From Blaise Pascal, *Thoughts* (1670).

Do not, then, charge those with falsehood who have made a choice. For you know nothing about it. "No. But I blame them for having made, not *this* choice, but *a* choice. For although he who takes heads, and the other, are in the same fault, they are both in fault. The proper way is simply not to wager." Yes, but you must wager. This is not voluntary. You have set sail. Which will you take? Let's see. Since a choice must be made, let's see which interests you the least. You have two things to lose: the true and the good. And you have two things to stake: your reason and your will; that is, your knowledge and your complete happiness. And your nature has two things to shun: error and misery. Your reason is not more wounded, since a choice must necessarily be made in choosing one rather than the other. Here a point is eliminated. But what about your happiness?

Let us weigh the gain and the loss in taking heads that God exists. Let us weigh these two cases. If you gain, you gain all. If you lose, you lose nothing. Wager without hesitation, then, that he is. "This is admirable. Yes, it is necessary to wager, but perhaps I wager too much." Let us see. Since there is equal risk of gaining or losing, if you had to gain but two lives for one, still you might wager. But if there were three lives to gain, it would be required to play (since you are under the necessity of playing). And, when you are forced to play, you would be imprudent not to risk your life in order to gain three in a play where there is equal hazard of loss and gain. But there is an eternity of life and happiness. And this being true, even if there were an infinity of chances (only one of which might be for you) you would still be right in wagering one in order to have two. And being obliged to play, if there was an infinity of life infinitely happy to gain, you would act foolishly to refuse to play one life against three in a game where among an infinity of chances there is one for you. But there is here an infinity of life infinitely happy to gain. And there is a chance of gain against a finite number of chances of loss, and what you play is finite. This [the balance of gain over loss] is quite settled. Wherever the infinite is, and where there is not an infinity of chances of loss against the chance of gain, there is nothing to weigh, and we must give all. And thus, when we are forced to play, we must renounce reason in order to keep life, rather than to risk it for the infinite gain, which is as likely to occur as the loss of nothingness.

For there is no use in saying that it is uncertain whether we shall gain, and that it is certain that we risk. And there is no use in saying that, [a] the infinite distance between the certainty of what we risk and, [b] the uncertainty of what we shall gain, raises the finite good which we certainly risk to a level of equality with the uncertain infinite gain. It is not so. Every player, without violating reason, risks a certainty to gain uncertainty, and nevertheless he risks a finite certainty to gain a finite uncertainty. The distance is not infinite between this certainty of what we risk, and the uncertainty of gain. This is false. There is, in truth, an infinity between the certainty of gaining and the certainty of losing. But the uncertainty of gaining is proportioned to the certainty of what we risk, according to the proportion of the chances of gain and loss. It follows from this that if there are as many chances on one side as there are on the other, the game is playing even. And then the certainty of what we risk is equal to the uncertainty of the gain. This is quite far from being infinitely distant. And thus our proposition [of infinite gain] is of infinite force when there is the finite to hazard in a play where the chances of gain and loss are equal, and the infinite to gain. This is demonstrative, and if people are capable of any truths, this is one of them.

"I confess it, I admit it. But, still, are there no means of seeing the truth behind the game?" Yes, the scriptures and the rest.

"Yes, but my hands are tied and my mouth is dumb. I am forced to wager, and I am not free. I am chained and so constituted that I cannot believe. What will you have me do then?" It is true. But at least learn your inability to believe, since reason brings you to such belief [given the above reasoning], and yet you cannot believe. Try then to convince yourself not by the addition of proofs for the existence of God, but by the reduction of your own passions. You would have recourse to faith, but don't know the ways. You wish to be cured of infidelity, and you ask for the remedy. Learn it from those who have been bound like yourself, and who would wager now all their goods. These know the road that you wish to follow, and are cured of a disease that you wish to be cured of. Follow their course, then, from its beginning. It consisted in doing all things *as if* they believed in them, in using holy water, in having masses said, etc. Naturally this will make you believe and stupefy you at the same time. "But this is what I fear." And why? What have you to lose?

But to show you that this leads to it [i.e., belief], this will diminish the passions, which are your great obstacles. Now, what harm will come to you in taking this course? You would be faithful, virtuous, humble, grateful, beneficent, a sincere friend, truthful. Truly, you would not be given up to poisonous pleasures, to false glory, or false joys. But would you not have other pleasures?

I say to you that you will gain by it in this life. And, each step you take in this direction, you will see so much of the certainty of gain, and so much of the nothingness of what you hazard, that you will acknowledge in the end that you have wagered something certain, infinite for which you have given nothing.

READING 18

The Irrationality of Believing in Miracles*

David Hume (1711–1776)

[EVIDENCE FROM NATURE VERSUS MIRACLE TESTIMONIES]

Though experience be our only guide in reasoning concerning matters of fact; it must be acknowledged, that this guide is not altogether infallible, but in some cases is apt to lead us into errors. One, who in our climate, should expect

*From David Hume, *An Enquiry Concerning Human Understanding* (1748), Section 10 "Of Miracles."

better weather in any week of June than in one of December, would reason justly, and conformably to experience; but it is certain, that he may happen, in the event, to find himself mistaken. However, we may observe, that, in such a case, he would have no cause to complain of experience; because it commonly informs us beforehand of the uncertainty, by that contrariety of events, which we may learn from a diligent observation. All effects follow not with like certainty from their supposed causes. Some events are found, in all countries and all ages, to have been constantly conjoined together: Others are found to have been more variable, and sometimes to disappoint our expectations; so that, in our reasonings concerning matter of fact, there are all imaginable degrees of assurance, from the highest certainty to the lowest species of moral evidence.

A wise man, therefore, proportions his belief to the evidence. In such conclusions as are founded on an infallible experience, he expects the event with the last degree of assurance, and regards his past experience as a full *proof* of the future existence of that event. In other cases, he proceeds with more caution: He weighs the opposite experiments: He considers which side is supported by the greater number of experiments: To that side he inclines, with doubt and hesitation; and when at last he fixes his judgment, the evidence exceeds not what we properly call *probability*. All probability, then, supposes an opposition of experiments and observations, where the one side is found to overbalance the other, and to produce a degree of evidence, proportioned to the superiority. A hundred instances or experiments on one side, and fifty on another, afford a doubtful expectation of any event; though a hundred uniform experiments, with only one that is contradictory, reasonably beget a pretty strong degree of assurance. In all cases, we must balance the opposite experiments, where they are opposite, and deduct the smaller number from the greater, in order to know the exact force of the superior evidence.

To apply these principles to a particular instance; we may observe, that there is no species of reasoning more common, more useful, and even necessary to human life, than that which is derived from the testimony of men, and the reports of eye-witnesses and spectators. This species of reasoning, perhaps, one may deny to be founded on the relation of cause and effect. I shall not dispute about a word. It will be sufficient to observe that our assurance in any argument of this kind is derived from no other principle than our observation of the veracity of human testimony, and of the usual conformity of facts to the reports of witnesses. It being a general maxim, that no objects have any discoverable connection together, and that all the inferences, which we can draw from one to another, are founded merely on our experience of their constant and regular conjunction; it is evident, that we ought not to make an exception to this maxim in favor of human testimony, whose connection with any event seems, in itself, as little necessary as any other. Were not the memory tenacious to a certain degree; had not men commonly an inclination to truth and a principle of probity; were they not sensible to shame, when detected in a falsehood: Were not these, I say, discovered by *experience* to be qualities, inherent in human nature, we should never repose the least confidence in human testimony. A man delirious, or noted for falsehood and villainy, has no manner of authority with us.

And as the evidence, derived from witnesses and human testimony, is founded on past experience, so it varies with the experience, and is regarded either as a *proof* or a *probability,* according as the conjunction between any particular kind of report and any kind of object has been found to be constant or variable. There are a number of circumstances to be taken into consideration in all judgments of this kind; and the ultimate standard, by which we determine all disputes, that may arise concerning them, is always derived from experience and observation. Where this experience is not entirely uniform on any side, it is attended with an unavoidable contrariety in our judgments, and with the same opposition and mutual destruction of argument as in every other kind of evidence. We frequently hesitate concerning the reports of others. We balance the opposite circumstances, which cause any doubt or uncertainty; and when we discover a superiority on any side, we incline to it; but still with a diminution of assurance, in proportion to the force of its antagonist.

This contrariety of evidence, in the present case, may be derived from several different causes; from the opposition of contrary testimony; from the character or number of the witnesses; from the manner of their delivering their testimony; or from the union of all these circumstances. We entertain a suspicion concerning any matter of fact, when the witnesses contradict each other; when they are but few, or of a doubtful character; when they have an interest in what they affirm; when they deliver their testimony with hesitation, or on the contrary, with too violent asseverations. There are many other particulars of the same kind, which may diminish or destroy the force of any argument, derived from human testimony.

Suppose, for instance, that the fact, which the testimony endeavors to establish, partakes of the extraordinary and the marvelous; in that case, the evidence, resulting from the testimony, admits of a diminution, greater or less, in proportion as the fact is more or less unusual. The reason why we place any credit in witnesses and historians, is not derived from any *connection,* which we perceive *a priori,* between testimony and reality, but because we are accustomed to find a conformity between them. But when the fact attested is such a one as has seldom fallen under our observation, here is a contest of two opposite experiences; of which the one destroys the other, as far as its force goes, and the superior can only operate on the mind by the force, which remains. The very same principle of experience, which gives us a certain degree of assurance in the testimony of witnesses, gives us also, in this case, another degree of assurance against the fact, which they endeavor to establish; from which contradiction there necessarily arises a counterpoize, and mutual destruction of belief and authority.

I should not believe such a story were it told me by Cato; was a proverbial saying in Rome, even during the lifetime of that philosophical patriot. The incredibility of a fact, it was allowed, might invalidate so great an authority.

The Indian prince, who refused to believe the first relations concerning the effects of frost, reasoned justly; and it naturally required very strong testimony to engage his assent to facts, that arose from a state of nature, with which he was unacquainted, and which bore so little analogy to those events, of which he had had constant and uniform experience. Though they were not contrary to his experience, they were not conformable to it.

But in order to increase the probability against the testimony of witnesses, let us suppose, that the fact, which they affirm, instead of being only marvelous, is really miraculous; and suppose also, that the testimony considered apart and in itself, amounts to an entire proof; in that case, there is proof against proof, of which the strongest must prevail, but still with a diminution of its force, in proportion to that of its antagonist.

A miracle is a violation of the laws of nature; and as a firm and unalterable experience has established these laws, the proof against a miracle, from the very nature of the fact, is as entire as any argument from experience can possibly be imagined. Why is it more than probable, that all men must die; that lead cannot, of itself, remain suspended in the air; that fire consumes wood, and is extinguished by water; unless it be, that these events are found agreeable to the laws of nature, and there is required a violation of these laws, or in other words, a miracle to prevent them? Nothing is esteemed a miracle, if it ever happen in the common course of nature. It is no miracle that a man, seemingly in good health, should die on a sudden: Because such a kind of death, though more unusual than any other, has yet been frequently observed to happen. But it is a miracle, that a dead man should come to life; because that has never been observed in any age or country. There must, therefore, be a uniform experience against every miraculous event, otherwise the event would not merit that appellation. And as a uniform experience amounts to a proof, there is here a direct and full *proof*, from the nature of the fact, against the existence of any miracle; nor can such a proof be destroyed, or the miracle rendered credible, but by an opposite proof, which is superior.

The plain consequence is (and it is a general maxim worthy of our attention), 'That no testimony is sufficient to establish a miracle, unless the testimony be of such a kind, that its falsehood would be more miraculous, than the fact, which it endeavors to establish: And even in that case there is a mutual destruction of arguments, and the superior only gives us an assurance suitable to that degree of force, which remains, after deducting the inferior.' When any one tells me, that he saw a dead man restored to life, I immediately consider with myself, whether it be more probable, that this person should either deceive or be deceived, or that the fact, which he relates, should really have happened. I weigh the one miracle against the other; and according to the superiority, which I discover, I pronounce my decision, and always reject the greater miracle. If the falsehood of his testimony would be more miraculous, than the event which he relates; then, and not till then, can he pretend to command my belief or opinion.

[FOUR FACTORS AGAINST MOST MIRACLES]

In the foregoing reasoning we have supposed, that the testimony, upon which a miracle is founded, may possibly amount to an entire proof, and that the falsehood of that testimony would be a real prodigy: But it is easy to shew, that we have been a great deal too liberal in our concession, and that there never was a miraculous event established on so full an evidence.

For *first*, there is not to be found, in all history, any miracle attested by a sufficient number of men, of such unquestioned good-sense, education, and learning, as to secure us against all delusion in themselves; of such undoubted integrity, as to place them beyond all suspicion of any design to deceive others; of such credit and reputation in the eyes of mankind, as to have a great deal to lose in case of their being detected in any falsehood; and at the same time, attesting facts performed in such a public manner and in so celebrated a part of the world, as to render the detection unavoidable: All which circumstances are requisite to give us a full assurance in the testimony of men.

Secondly. We may observe in human nature a principle which, if strictly examined, will be found to diminish extremely the assurance which we might, from human testimony, have in any kind of prodigy. The maxim by which we commonly conduct ourselves in our reasonings is that the objects, of which we have no experience, resembles those of which we have; that what we have found to be most usual is always most probable; and that where there is an opposition of arguments, we ought to give the preference to such as are founded on the greatest number of past observations. But though in proceeding by this rule we readily reject any fact which is unusual and incredible in an ordinary degree; yet in advancing farther, the mind observes not always the same rule; but when anything is affirmed utterly absurd and miraculous, it rather the more readily admits of such a fact, upon account of that very circumstance, which ought to destroy all its authority. The passion of surprise and wonder arising from miracles, being an agreeable emotion, gives a sensible tendency towards the belief of those events from which it is derived. And this goes so far, that even those who cannot enjoy this pleasure immediately, nor can believe those miraculous events, of which they are informed, yet love to partake of the satisfaction at second-hand or by rebound, and place a pride and delight in exciting the admiration of others.

With what greediness are the miraculous accounts of travelers received, their descriptions of sea and land monsters, their relations of wonderful adventures, strange men, and uncouth manners? But if the spirit of religion join itself to the love of wonder, there is an end of common sense; and human testimony, in these circumstances, loses all pretensions to authority. A religionist may be an enthusiast, and imagine he sees what has no reality: He may know his narrative to be false, and yet persevere in it, with the best intentions in the world, for the sake of promoting so holy a cause: Or even where this delusion has not place, vanity, excited by so strong a temptation, operates on him more powerfully than on the rest of mankind in any other circumstances; and self-interest with equal force. His auditors may not have, and commonly have not, sufficient judgment to canvass his evidence: What judgment they have, they renounce by principle, in these sublime and mysterious subjects: Or if they were ever so willing to employ it, passion and a heated imagination disturb the regularity of its operations. Their credulity increases his impudence: And his impudence overpowers their credulity. . . .

Thirdly. It forms a strong presumption against all supernatural and miraculous relations, that they are observed chiefly to abound among ignorant and barbarous nations; or if a civilized people has ever given admission to any of them, that people will be found to have received them from ignorant and barbarous ancestors, who transmitted them with that inviolable sanction and authority, which always attend received opinions. When we peruse the first histories of all nations, we are apt to imagine ourselves transported into some new world; where the whole frame of nature is disjointed, and every element performs its operations in a different manner, from what it does at present. Battles, revolutions, pestilence, famine and death, are never the effect of those natural causes, which we experience. Prodigies, omens, oracles, judgments, quite obscure the few natural events, that are intermingled with them. But as the former grow thinner every page, in proportion as we advance nearer the enlightened ages, we soon learn, that there is nothing mysterious or supernatural in the case, but that all proceeds from the usual propensity of mankind towards the marvelous, and that, though this inclination may at intervals receive a check from sense and learning, it can never be thoroughly extirpated from human nature. . . .

I may add as a *fourth* reason, which diminishes the authority of prodigies, that there is no testimony for any, even those which have not been expressly detected, that is not opposed by an infinite number of witnesses; so that not only the miracle destroys the credit of testimony, but the testimony destroys itself. To make this the better understood, let us consider, that, in matters of religion, whatever is different is contrary; and that it is impossible the religions of ancient Rome, of Turkey, of Siam, and of China should, all of them, be established on any solid foundation. Every miracle, therefore, pretended to have been wrought in any of these religions (and all of them abound in miracles), as its direct scope is to establish the particular system to which it is attributed; so has it the same force, though more indirectly, to overthrow every other system. In destroying a rival system, it likewise destroys the credit of those miracles, on which that system was established; so that all the prodigies of different religions are to be regarded as contrary facts, and the evidences of these prodigies, whether weak or strong, as opposite to each other. According to this method of reasoning, when we believe any miracle of Mahomet or his successors, we have for our warrant the testimony of a few barbarous Arabians: And on the other hand, we are to regard the authority of Titus Livius, Plutarch, Tacitus, and, in short, of all the authors and witnesses, Grecian, Chinese, and Roman Catholic, who have related any miracle in their particular religion; I say, we are to regard their testimony in the same light as if they had mentioned that Mahometan miracle, and had in express terms contradicted it, with the same certainty as they have for the miracle they relate. This argument may appear over subtle and refined; but is not in reality different from the reasoning of a judge, who supposes, that the credit of two witnesses, maintaining a crime against any one, is destroyed by the testimony of two others, who affirm him to have been two hundred leagues distant, at the same instant when the crime is said to have been committed. . . .

[MIRACLES AND CHRISTIANITY]

Upon the whole, then, it appears, that no testimony for any kind of miracle has ever amounted to a probability, much less to a proof; and that, even supposing it amounted to a proof, it would be opposed by another proof; derived from the very nature of the fact, which it would endeavor to establish. It is experience only, which gives authority to human testimony; and it is the same experience, which assures us of the laws of nature. When, therefore, these two kinds of experience are contrary, we have nothing to do but subtract the one from the other, and embrace an opinion, either on one side or the other, with that assurance which arises from the remainder. But according to the principle here explained, this subtraction, with regard to all popular religions, amounts to an entire annihilation; and therefore we may establish it as a maxim, that no human testimony can have such force as to prove a miracle, and make it a just foundation for any such system of religion. . . .

I am the better pleased with the method of reasoning here delivered, as I think it may serve to confound those dangerous friends or disguised enemies to the *Christian Religion,* who have undertaken to defend it by the principles of human reason. Our most holy religion is founded on *Faith,* not on reason; and it is a sure method of exposing it to put it to such a trial as it is, by no means, fitted to endure. To make this more evident, let us examine those miracles, related in scripture; and not to lose ourselves in too wide a field, let us confine ourselves to such as we find in the *Pentateuch,* which we shall examine, according to the principles of these pretended Christians, not as the word or testimony of God himself, but as the production of a mere human writer and historian. Here then we are first to consider a book, presented to us by a barbarous and ignorant people, written in an age when they were still more barbarous, and in all probability long after the facts which it relates, corroborated by no concurring testimony, and resembling those fabulous accounts, which every nation gives of its origin. Upon reading this book, we find it full of prodigies and miracles. It gives an account of a state of the world and of human nature entirely different from the present: Of our fall from that state: Of the age of man, extended to near a thousand years: Of the destruction of the world by a deluge: Of the arbitrary choice of one people, as the favorites of heaven; and that people the countrymen of the author: Of their deliverance from bondage by prodigies the most astonishing imaginable: I desire any one to lay his hand upon his heart, and after a serious consideration declare, whether he thinks that the falsehood of such a book, supported by such a testimony, would be more extraordinary and miraculous than all the miracles it relates; which is, however, necessary to make it be received, according to the measures of probability above established.

What we have said of miracles may be applied, without any variation, to prophecies; and indeed, all prophecies are real miracles, and as such only, can be admitted as proofs of any revelation. If it did not exceed the capacity of human nature to foretell future events, it would be absurd to employ any prophecy as an argument for a divine mission or authority from heaven. So that, upon the whole, we may conclude, that the *Christian Religion* not only was at first attended with miracles, but even at this day cannot be believed by any reasonable person without one. Mere reason is insufficient to convince us of its veracity: And whoever is moved by *Faith* to assent to it, is conscious of a continued miracle in his own person, which subverts all the principles of his understanding, and gives him a determination to believe what is most contrary to custom and experience.

READING 19

Against the Design and Cosmological Arguments for God's Existence*

David Hume (1711–1776)

Hume's Dialogues Concerning Natural Religion *is a conversation among three principal characters. Cleanthes defends the design argument but rejects the cosmological argument. Demea defends the cosmological argument but rejects the design argument. Philo—the philosophical skeptic in the dialog—rejects both the design and cosmological arguments.*

[CRITICISM OF THE DESIGN ARGUMENT]

[The Design Argument Presented]

CLEANTHES: . . . I shall briefly explain how I conceive this matter. Look round the world: contemplate the whole and every part of it: You will find it to be nothing but one great machine, subdivided into an infinite number of lesser machines, which again admit of subdivisions to a degree beyond what human senses and faculties can trace and explain. All these various machines, and even their most minute parts, are adjusted to each other with an accuracy which ravishes into admiration all men who have ever contemplated them. The curious adapting of means to ends, throughout all nature, resembles exactly, though it much exceeds, the productions of human contrivance; of human designs, thought, wisdom, and intelligence. Since, therefore, the effects resemble each other, we are led to infer, by all the rules of analogy, that the causes also resemble; and that the Author of Nature is somewhat similar to the mind of man, though possessed of much larger faculties, proportioned to the grandeur of the work which he

*From David Hume, *Dialogues Concerning Natural Religion* (1779), Parts 2, 5, and 9.

has executed. By this argument *a posteriori,* and by this argument alone, do we prove at once the existence of a Deity, and his similarity to human mind and intelligence.

[The Failure of the Analogy]

PHILO: . . . That a stone will fall, that fire will burn, that the earth has solidity, we have observed a thousand and a thousand times; and when any new instance of this nature is presented, we draw without hesitation the accustomed inference. The exact similarity of the cases gives us a perfect assurance of a similar event; and a stronger evidence is never desired nor sought after. But wherever you depart, in the least, from the similarity of the cases, you diminish proportionably the evidence; and may at last bring it to a very weak *analogy,* which is confessedly liable to error and uncertainty. After having experienced the circulation of the blood in human creatures, we make no doubt that it takes place in Titius and Maevius. But from its circulation in frogs and fishes, it is only a presumption, though a strong one, from analogy, that it takes place in men and other animals. The analogical reasoning is much weaker, when we infer the circulation of the sap in vegetables from our experience that the blood circulates in animals; and those, who hastily followed that imperfect analogy, are found, by more accurate experiments, to have been mistaken.

If we see a house, Cleanthes, we conclude, with the greatest certainty, that it had an architect or builder; because this is precisely that species of effect which we have experienced to proceed from that species of cause. But surely you will not affirm, that the universe bears such a resemblance to a house, that we can with the same certainty infer a similar cause, or that the analogy is here entire and perfect. The dissimilitude is so striking, that the utmost you can here pretend to is a guess, a conjecture, a presumption concerning a similar cause; and how that pretension will be received in the world, I leave you to consider.

CLEANTHES: It would surely be very ill received, replied Cleanthes; and I should be deservedly blamed and detested, did I allow, that the proofs of a Deity amounted to no more than a guess or conjecture. But is the whole adjustment of means to ends in a house and in the universe so slight a resemblance? The economy of final causes? The order, proportion, and arrangement of every part? Steps of a stair are plainly contrived, that human legs may use them in mounting; and this inference is certain and infallible. Human legs are also contrived for walking and mounting; and this inference, I allow, is not altogether so certain, because of the dissimilarity which you remark; but does it, therefore, deserve the name only of presumption or conjecture?

PHILO: That all inferences, Cleanthes, concerning fact, are founded on experience; and that all experimental reasonings are founded on the supposition that similar causes prove similar effects, and similar effects similar causes; I shall not at present much dispute with you. But observe, I entreat you, with what extreme caution all just reasoners proceed in the transferring of experiments to similar cases. Unless the cases be exactly similar, they repose no perfect confidence in applying their past observation to any particular phenomenon. Every alteration of circumstances occasions a doubt concerning the event; and it requires new experiments to prove certainly, that the new circumstances are of no moment or importance. A change in bulk, situation, arrangement, age, disposition of the air, or surrounding bodies; any of these particulars may be attended with the most unexpected consequences: And unless the objects be quite familiar to us, it is the highest temerity to expect with assurance, after any of these changes, an event similar to that which before fell under our observation. The slow and deliberate steps of philosophers here, if any where, are distinguished from the precipitate march of the vulgar, who, hurried on by the smallest similitude, are incapable of all discernment or consideration.

But can you think, Cleanthes, that your usual phlegm and philosophy have been preserved in so wide a step as you have taken, when you compared to the universe houses, ships, furniture, machines, and, from their similarity in some circumstances, inferred a similarity in their causes? Thought, design, intelligence, such as we discover in men and other animals, is no more than one of the springs and principles of the universe, as well as heat or cold, attraction or repulsion, and a hundred others, which fall under daily observation. It is an active cause, by which some particular parts of nature, we find, produce alterations on other parts. But can a conclusion, with any propriety, be transferred from parts to the whole? Does not the great disproportion bar all comparison and inference? From observing the growth of a hair, can we learn any thing concerning the generation of a man? Would the manner of a leaf's blowing, even though perfectly known, afford us any instruction concerning the vegetation of a tree?

But, allowing that we were to take the operations of one part of nature upon another, for the foundation of our judgment concerning the *origin* of the whole, (which never can be admitted,) yet why select so minute, so weak, so bounded a principle, as the reason and design of animals is found to be upon this planet? What peculiar privilege has this little agitation of the brain which we call thought, that we must thus make it the model of the whole universe? Our partiality in our own favor does indeed present it on all occasions; but sound philosophy ought carefully to guard against so natural an illusion.

So far from admitting, continued Philo, that the operations of a part can afford us any just conclusion concerning the origin of the whole, I will not allow any one part to form a rule for another part, if the latter be very remote from the former. Is there any reasonable ground to conclude, that the inhabitants of other planets possess thought, intelligence, reason, or any thing similar to these faculties in men? When nature has so extremely diversified her manner of operation in this small globe, can we imagine that she incessantly copies herself throughout so immense a universe? And if thought, as we may well suppose, be confined merely to this narrow corner, and has even there so limited a sphere of action, with what propriety can we assign it for the original cause of all things? The narrow views of a peasant, who makes his domestic economy the rule for the government of kingdoms, is in comparison a pardonable sophism.

But were we ever so much assured, that a thought and reason, resembling the human, were to be found throughout the whole universe, and were its activity elsewhere vastly greater and more commanding than it appears in this globe; yet I cannot see, why the operations of a world constituted, arranged, adjusted, can with any propriety be extended to a world which is in its embryo state, and is advancing towards that constitution and arrangement. By observation, we know somewhat of the economy, action, and nourishment of a finished animal; but we must transfer with great caution that observation to the growth of a fetus in the womb, and still more to the formation of an animalcule in the loins of its male parent. Nature, we find, even from our limited experience, possesses an infinite number of springs and principles, which incessantly discover themselves on every change of her position and situation. And what new and unknown principles would actuate her in so new and unknown a situation as that of the formation of a universe, we cannot, without the utmost temerity, pretend to determine.

A very small part of this great system, during a very short time, is very imperfectly discovered to us; and do we thence pronounce decisively concerning the origin of the whole?

Admirable conclusion! Stone, wood, brick, iron, brass, have not, at this time, in this minute globe of earth, an order or arrangement without human art and contrivance; therefore the universe could not originally attain its order and arrangement, without something similar to human art. But is a part of nature a rule for another part very wide of the former? Is it a rule for the whole? Is a very small part a rule for the universe? Is nature in one situation, a certain rule for nature in another situation vastly different from the former?

And can you blame me, Cleanthes, if I here imitate the prudent reserve of Simonides, who, according to the noted story, being asked by Hiero, *What God was?* desired a day to think of it, and then two days more; and after that manner continually prolonged the term, without ever bringing in his definition or description? Could you even blame me, if I had answered at first, *that I did not know,* and was sensible that this subject lay vastly beyond the reach of my faculties? You might cry out skeptic and railler, as much as you pleased: but having found, in so many other subjects much more familiar, the imperfections and even contradictions of human reason, I never should expect any success from its feeble conjectures, in a subject so sublime, and so remote from the sphere of our observation. When two *species* of objects have always been observed to be conjoined together, I can *infer,* by custom, the existence of one wherever I *see* the existence of the other; and this I call an argument from experience. But how this argument can have place, where the objects, as in the present case, are single, individual, without parallel, or specific resemblance, may be difficult to explain. And will any man tell me with a serious countenance, that an orderly universe must arise from some thought and art like the human, because we have experience of it? To ascertain this reasoning, it were requisite that we had experience of the origin of worlds; and it is not sufficient, surely, that we have seen ships and cities arise from human art and contrivance.

[Concerning the Infinity, Perfection, Unity of the Creator]

PHILO: *First,* By this method of reasoning, you renounce all claim to infinity in any of the attributes of the Deity. For, as the cause ought only to be proportioned to the effect, and the effect, so far as it falls under our cognizance, is not infinite; what pretensions have we, upon your suppositions, to ascribe that attribute to the Divine Being? You will still insist, that, by removing him so much from all similarity to human creatures, we give in to the most arbitrary hypothesis, and at the same time weaken all proofs of his existence.

Secondly, You have no reason, on your theory, for ascribing perfection to the Deity, even in his finite capacity, or for supposing him free from every error, mistake, or incoherence, in his undertakings. There are many inexplicable difficulties in the works of Nature, which, if we allow a perfect author to be proved *a priori,* are easily solved, and become only seeming difficulties, from the narrow capacity of man, who cannot trace infinite relations. But according to your method of reasoning, these difficulties become all real; and perhaps will be insisted on, as new instances of likeness to human art and contrivance. At least, you must acknowledge, that it is impossible for us to tell, from our limited views, whether this system contains any great faults, or deserves any considerable praise, if compared to other possible, and even real systems. Could a peasant, if the *Aneid* were read to him, pronounce that poem to be absolutely faultless, or even assign to it its proper rank among the productions of human wit, he, who had never seen any other production?

But were this world ever so perfect a production, it must still remain uncertain, whether all the excellences of the work can justly be ascribed to the workman. If we survey a ship, what an exalted idea must we form of the ingenuity of the carpenter who framed so complicated, useful, and beautiful a machine? And what surprise must we feel, when we find him a stupid mechanic, who imitated others, and copied an art, which, through a long succession of ages, after multiplied trials, mistakes, corrections, deliberations, and controversies, had been gradually improving? Many worlds might have been botched and bungled, throughout an eternity, ere this system was struck out; much labor lost, many fruitless trials made; and a slow, but continued improvement carried on during infinite ages in the art of world-making. In such subjects, who can determine, where the truth; nay, who can conjecture where the probability lies, amidst a great number of hypotheses which may be proposed, and a still greater which may be imagined?

And what shadow of an argument, continued Philo, can you produce, from your hypothesis, to prove the unity of the Deity? A great number of men join in building a house or ship, in rearing a city, in framing a commonwealth; why may not several deities combine in contriving and framing a world? This is only so much greater similarity to human affairs. By sharing the work among several, we may so much further limit the attributes of each, and get rid of that extensive power and knowledge, which must be supposed in one deity, and which, according to you, can only serve to weaken the proof of his existence. And if such foolish, such vicious creatures as man, can yet often unite in framing and executing one plan, how much more those deities or demons, whom we may suppose several degrees more perfect!

To multiply causes without necessity, is indeed contrary to true philosophy: but this principle applies not to the present case. Were one deity antecedently proved by your theory, who were possessed of every attribute requisite to the production of the universe; it would be needless, I own, (though not absurd,) to suppose any other deity existent. But while it is still a question, Whether all these attributes are united in one subject, or dispersed among several independent beings, by what phenomena in nature can we pretend to decide the controversy? Where we see a body raised in a scale, we are sure that there is in the opposite scale, however concealed from sight, some counterpoising weight equal to it; but it is still allowed to doubt, whether that weight be an aggregate of several distinct bodies, or one uniform united mass. And if the weight requisite very much exceeds any thing which we have ever seen conjoined in any single body, the former supposition becomes still more probable and natural. An intelligent being of such vast power and capacity as is necessary to produce the universe, or, to speak in the language of ancient philosophy, so prodigious an animal exceeds all analogy, and even comprehension.

But further, Cleanthes: men are mortal, and renew their species by generation; and this is common to all living creatures. The two great sexes of male and female, says Milton, animate the world. Why must this circumstance, so universal, so essential, be excluded from those numerous and limited deities? Behold, then, the theogony of ancient times brought back upon us.

And why not become a perfect Anthropomorphite? Why not assert the deity or deities to be corporeal, and to have eyes, a nose, mouth, ears, etc.? Epicurus maintained, that no man had ever seen reason but in a human figure; therefore the gods must have a human figure. And this argument, which is deservedly so much ridiculed by Cicero, becomes, according to you, solid and philosophical.

In a word, Cleanthes, a man who follows your hypothesis is able perhaps to assert, or conjecture, that the universe, sometime, arose from something like design: but beyond that position he cannot ascertain one single circumstance; and is left afterwards to fix every point of his theology by the utmost license of fancy and hypothesis. This world, for aught he knows, is very faulty and imperfect, compared to a superior standard; and was only the first rude essay of some infant deity, who afterwards abandoned it, ashamed of his lame performance: it is the work only of some dependent, inferior deity; and is the object of derision to his superiors: it is the production of old age and dotage in some superannuated deity; and ever since his death, has run on at adventures, from the first impulse and active force which it received from him.

[CRITICISM OF THE COSMOLOGICAL ARGUMENT]

[The Cosmological Argument Presented]

DEMEA: The argument, replied Demea, which I would insist on, is the common one. Whatever exists must have a cause or reason of its existence; it being absolutely impossible for any thing to produce itself, or be the cause of its own existence. In mounting up, therefore, from effects to causes, we must either go on in tracing an infinite succession, without any ultimate cause at all; or must at last have recourse to some ultimate cause, that is *necessarily* existent: Now, that the first supposition is absurd, may be thus proved. In the infinite chain or succession of causes and effects, each single effect is determined to exist by the power and efficacy of that cause which immediately preceded; but the whole eternal chain or succession, taken together, is not determined or caused by any thing; and yet it is evident that it requires a cause or reason, as much as any particular object which begins to exist in time. The question is still reasonable, why this particular succession of causes existed from eternity, and not any other succession, or no succession at all. If there be no necessarily existent being, any supposition which can be formed is equally possible; nor is there any more absurdity in Nothing's having existed from eternity, than there is in that succession of causes which constitutes the universe. What was it, then, which determined Something to exist rather than Nothing, and bestowed being on a particular possibility, exclusive of the rest? *External causes*, there are supposed to be none. *Chance* is a word without a meaning. Was it *Nothing*? But that can never produce any thing. We must, therefore, have recourse to a necessarily existent Being, who carries the *reason* of his existence in himself, and who cannot be supposed not to exist, without an express contradiction. There is, consequently, such a Being; that is, there is a Deity.

[The Failure of *A Priori* Arguments]

CLEANTHES: I shall not leave it to Philo, said Cleanthes, though I know that the starting objections is his chief delight, to point out the weakness of this metaphysical reasoning. It seems to me so obviously ill-grounded, and at the same time of so little consequence to the cause of true piety and religion, that I shall myself venture to show the fallacy of it.

I shall begin with observing, that there is an evident absurdity in pretending to demonstrate a matter of fact, or to prove it by any arguments *a priori*. Nothing is demonstrable, unless the contrary implies a contradiction. Nothing, that is distinctly conceivable, implies a contradiction. Whatever we conceive as existent, we can also conceive as non-existent. There is no being, therefore, whose non-existence implies a contradiction. Consequently there is no being, whose existence is demonstrable. I propose this argument as entirely decisive, and am willing to rest the whole controversy upon it.

It is pretended that the Deity is a necessarily existent being; and this necessity of his existence is attempted to be explained by asserting, that if we knew his whole essence or nature, we should perceive it to be as impossible for him not to exist, as for twice two not to be four. But it is evident that this can never happen, while our faculties remain the same as at present. It will still be possible for us, at any time, to conceive the non-existence of what we formerly conceived to exist; nor can the mind ever lie under a necessity of supposing any object to remain always in being; in the same manner as we lie under a necessity of always conceiving twice two to be four. The words, therefore, *necessary existence,* have no meaning; or, which is the same thing, none that is consistent.

But further, why may not the material universe be the necessarily existent Being, according to this pretended explication of necessity? We dare not affirm that we know all the qualities of matter; and for aught we can determine, it may contain some qualities, which, were they known, would make its non-existence appear as great a contradiction as that twice two is five. I find only one argument employed to prove, that the material world is not the necessarily existent Being: and this argument is derived from the contingency both of the matter and the form of the world. "Any particle of matter," it is said, "may be *conceived* to be annihilated; and any form may be *conceived* to be altered. Such an annihilation or alteration, therefore, is not impossible." But it seems a great partiality not to perceive, that the same argument extends equally to the Deity, so far as we have any conception of him; and that the mind can at least imagine him to be non-existent, or his attributes to be altered. It must be some unknown, inconceivable qualities, which can make his non-existence appear impossible, or his attributes unalterable: And no reason can be assigned, why these qualities may not belong to matter. As they are altogether unknown and inconceivable, they can never be proved incompatible with it.

Add to this, that in tracing an eternal succession of objects, it seems absurd to inquire for a general cause or first author. How can any thing, that exists from eternity, have a cause, since that relation implies a priority in time, and a beginning of existence?

In such a chain, too, or succession of objects, each part is caused by that which preceded it, and causes that which succeeds it. Where then is the difficulty? But the *whole,* you say, wants a cause. I answer, that the uniting of these parts into a whole, like the uniting of several distinct countries into one kingdom, or several distinct members into one body, is performed merely by an arbitrary act of the mind, and has no influence on the nature of things. Did I show you the particular causes of each individual in a collection of twenty particles of matter, I should think it very unreasonable, should you afterwards ask me, what was the cause of the whole twenty. This is sufficiently explained in explaining the cause of the parts.

READING 20

The Logical Problem of Evil[*]

J. L. Mackie (1917–1981)

The traditional arguments for the existence of God have been fairly thoroughly criticized by philosophers. But the theologian can, if he wishes, accept this criticism. He can admit that no rational proof of God's existence is possible. And he can still retain all that is essential to his position, by holding that God's existence is known in some other, non-rational way. I think, however, that a more telling criticism can be made by way of traditional problem of evil. Here it can be shown, not that religious beliefs lack rational support, but that they are positively irrational, that the several parts of the essential theological doctrine are inconsistent with one another, so that the theologian can maintain his position as a whole only by a much more extreme rejection of reason than in the former case. He must now be prepared to believe, not merely what cannot be proved, but what can be *disproved* from other beliefs that he also holds.

The problem of evil, in the sense in which I shall be using the phrase, is a problem only for someone who believes that there is a God who is both omnipotent and wholly good. And it is a logical problem, the problem of clarifying and reconciling a number of beliefs: it is not a scientific problem that might be solved by further observations, or a practical problem that might be solved by a decision or an action. These points are obvious; I mention them only because they are sometimes ignored by theologians, who sometimes parry a statement of the problem with such remarks as "Well, can you solve the problem yourself?" or "This is a mystery which may be revealed to us later" or "Evil is something to be faced and overcome, not to be merely discussed."

In its simplest form the problem is this: God is omnipotent; God is wholly good; and yet evil exists. There seems to be some contradiction between these

[*]From J. L. Mackie, "Evil and Omnipotence," *Mind,* vol. 64, 1955, pp. 200–212.

three propositions, so that if any two of them were true the third would be false. But at the same time all three are essential parts of most theological positions: the theologian, it seems, at once must adhere and *cannot consistently* adhere to all three. (The problem does not arise only for theists, but I shall discuss it in the form in which it presents itself for ordinary theism.)

However, the contradiction does not arise immediately; to show it we need some additional premises, or perhaps some quasi-logical rules connecting the terms 'good,' 'evil,' and 'omnipotent.' These additional principles are that good is opposed to evil, in such a way that a good thing always eliminates evil as far as it can, and that there are no limits to what an omnipotent thing can do. From these it follows that a good omnipotent thing eliminates evil completely, and then the propositions that a good omnipotent thing exists, and the evil exists, are incompatible.

ADEQUATE SOLUTIONS

Now once the problem is fully stated it is clear that it can be solved, in the sense that the problem will not arise if one gives up at least one of the propositions that constitute it. If you are prepared to say that God is not wholly good, or not quite omnipotent, or that evil does not exist, or that good is not opposed to the kind of evil that exists, or that there are limits to what an omnipotent thing can do, then the problem of evil will not arise for you.

There are, then, quite a number of adequate solutions of the problem of evil, and some of these have been adopted, Dr almost adopted, by various thinkers. For example, a few have been prepared to deny God's omnipotence, and rather more have been prepared to keep the term 'omnipotence' but severely to restrict its meaning, recording quite a number of things that an omnipotent being cannot do. Some have said that evil is an illusion, perhaps because they held that the whole world of temporal, changing things is an illusion, and that what we call evil belongs only to this world, or perhaps because they held that although temporal things are much as we see them, those that we call evil are not really evil. Some have said that what we call evil is merely the privation of good, that evil in a positive sense, evil that would really be opposed to good, does not exist. Many have agreed with Pope that disorder is harmony not understood, and that partial evil is universal good. Whether any of these views is *true* is, of course, another question. But each of them gives an adequate solution of the problem of evil in the sense that if you accept it this problem does not arise for you, though you may, of course, have *other* problems to face.

But often enough these adequate solutions are only *almost* adopted. The thinkers who restrict God's power, but keep the term 'omnipotence,' may reasonably be suspected of thinking, in other contexts, that his power is really unlimited. Those who say that evil is an illusion may also be thinking, inconsistently, that this illusion is itself an evil. Those who say that "evil" is merely privation of good may also be thinking, inconsistently, that privation of good is an evil. (The fallacy here is akin to some forms of the "naturalistic fallacy" in ethics, where some think, for example, that "good" is just what contributes to evolutionary progress, and that evolutionary progress is itself good.) If Pope meant what he said in the first line of his couplet, that "disorder" is only harmony not understood, the "partial evil" of the second line must, for consistency, mean "that which, taken in isolation, falsely appears to be evil" but it would more naturally mean "that which, in isolation, really is evil." The second line, in fact, hesitates between two views, that "partial evil" isn't really evil, since only the universal quality is real, and that "partial evil" is really an evil, but only a little one.

In addition, therefore, to adequate solutions, we must recognize unsatisfactory inconsistent solutions, in which there is only a half-hearted or temporary rejection of one of the propositions which together constitute the problem. In these, one of the constituent propositions is explicitly rejected, but it is covertly re-asserted or assumed elsewhere in the system.

FALLACIOUS SOLUTIONS

Besides these half-hearted solutions, which explicitly reject but implicitly assert one of the constituent propositions, there are definitely fallacious solutions which explicitly maintain all the constituent propositions, but implicitly reject at least one of them in the course of the argument that explains away the problem of evil.

There are, in fact, many so-called solutions which purport to remove the contradiction without abandoning any of its constituent propositions. These must be fallacious, as we can see from the very statement of the problem, but it is not so easy to see in each case precisely where the fallacy lies. I suggest that in all cases the fallacy has the general form suggested above: in order to solve the problem one (or perhaps more) of its constituent propositions is given up, but in such a way that it appears to have been retained, and can therefore be asserted without qualification in other contexts. Sometimes there is a further complication: the supposed solution moves to and fro between, say, two of the constituent propositions, at one point asserting the first of these but covertly abandoning the second, at another point asserting the second but covertly abandoning the first. These fallacious Solutions often turn upon some equivocation with the words "good" and "evil," or upon some vagueness about the way in which good and evil are opposed to one another, or about how much is meant by "omnipotence." I propose to examine some of these so-called solutions, and to exhibit their fallacies iii detail. Incidentally, I shall also be considering whether an adequate solution could be reached by a minor modification of one or more of the constituent propositions, which would, however, still satisfy all the essential requirements of ordinary theism.

1. "Good Cannot Exist without Evil" or "Evil Is Necessary as a Counterpart to Good"

It is sometimes suggested that evil is necessary as a counterpart to good, that if there were no evil there could be no good either, and that this solves the problem of evil. It is true that it points to an answer to the question "Why should there be evil?" But it does so only by qualifying some of the propositions that constitute the problem.

First, it sets a limit to what God can do, saying that God *cannot* create good without simultaneously creating evil, and this means either that God is not omnipotent or that there are *some* limits to what an omnipotent thing can do. It may be replied that these limits are always presupposed, that omnipotence has never meant the power to do what is logically impossible, and on the present view the existence of good without evil would be a logical impossibility. This interpretation of omnipotence may, indeed, be accepted as a modification of our original account which does not reject anything that is essential to theism, and I shall in general assume it in the subsequent discussion. It is, perhaps, the most common theistic view, but I think that some theists at least have maintained that God can do what is logically impossible. Many theists, at any rate, have held that logic itself is created or laid down by God, that logic is the way in which God arbitrarily chooses to think. (This is, of course, parallel to the ethical view that morally right actions are those which God arbitrarily chooses to command, and the two views encounter similar difficulties.) And *this* account of logic is clearly inconsistent with the view that God is bound by logical necessities-unless it is possible for an omnipotent being to bind himself, an issue which we shall consider later, when we come to the Paradox of Omnipotence. This solution of the problem of evil cannot, therefore, be consistently adopted along with the view that logic is itself created by God.

But, secondly, this solution denies that evil is opposed to good in our original sense. If good and evil are counterparts, a good thing will not "eliminate evil as far as it can." Indeed, this view suggests that good and evil are not strictly qualities of things at all. Perhaps the suggestion is that good and evil are related in much the same way as great and small. Certainly, when the term "great" is used relatively as a condensation of "greater than so-and-so," and "small" is used correspondingly, greatness and smallness are counterparts and cannot exist without each other. But in this sense greatness is not a quality, not an intrinsic feature of anything; and it would be absurd to think of a movement in favor of greatness and against smallness in this sense. Such a movement would be self-defeating, since relative greatness can be promoted only by a simultaneous promotion of relative smallness. I feel sure that no theists would be content to regard God's goodness as analogous to this-as if what he supports were not the *good* but the *better*, and as if he had the paradoxical aim that all things should be better than other things.

This point is obscured by the fact that "great" and "small" seem to have an absolute as well as a relative sense. I cannot discuss here whether there is absolute magnitude or not, but if there is, there could be an absolute sense for "great," it could mean of at least a certain size, and it would make sense to speak of all things getting bigger, of a universe that was expanding all over, and therefore it would make sense to speak of promoting greatness. But in *this* sense great and small are not logically necessary counterparts: either quality could exist without the other. There would be no logical impossibility in everything's being small or in everything's being great.

Neither in the absolute nor in the relative sense, then, of "great" and "small" do these terms provide an analogy of the sort that would be needed to support this solution of the problem of evil. In neither case are greatness and smallness *both* necessary counterparts and mutually opposed forces or possible objects for support and attack.

It may be replied that good and evil are necessary counterparts in the same way as any quality and its logical opposite: redness can occur, it is suggested, only if non-redness also occurs. But unless evil is merely the privation of good, they are not logical opposites, and some further argument would be needed to show that they are counterparts in the same way as genuine logical opposites. Let us assume that this could be given. There is still doubt of the correctness of the metaphysical principle that a quality must have a real opposite: I suggest that it is not really impossible that everything should be, say, red, that the truth is merely that if everything were red we should not notice redness, and so we should have no word "red"; we observe and give names to qualities only if they have real opposites. If so, the principle that a term must have an opposite would belong only to our language or to our thought, and would not be an ontological principle, and, correspondingly, the rule that good cannot exist without evil would not state a logical necessity of a sort that God would just have to put up with. God might have made everything good, though *we* should not have noticed it if he had.

But, finally, even if we concede that this *is* an ontological principle, it will provide a solution for the problem of evil only if one is prepared to say, "Evil exists, but only just enough evil to serve as the counterpart of good." I doubt whether any theist will accept this. After all, the *ontological* requirement that non-redness should occur would be satisfied even if all the universe, except for a minute speck, were red, and, if there were a corresponding requirement for evil as a counterpart to good, a minute dose of evil would presumably do. But theists are not usually willing to say, in all contexts, that all the evil that occurs is a minute and necessary dose.

2. "Evil Is Necessary as a Means to Good"

It is sometimes suggested that evil is necessary for good not as a counterpart but as a means. In its simple form this has little plausibility as a solution of the problem of evil, since it obviously implies a severe restriction of God's power. It would be a *causal* law that you cannot have a certain end without a certain means, so that if God has to introduce evil as a means to good, he must be subject to at least some causal laws. This certainly conflicts with what a theist normally means by omnipotence. This view of God as limited by causal laws also conflicts with the view that causal laws are themselves made by God, which is more widely held than the corresponding view about the laws of logic. This conflict, would, indeed, be resolved if it were possible for an omnipotent being to bind himself, and this possibility has still to be considered. Unless a favorable answer can be given to this question, the suggestion that evil is necessary as a means to good solves the problem of evil only by denying one of its constituent propositions, either that God is omnipotent or that "omnipotent" means what it says.

3. "The Universe Is Better with Some Evil in It Than It Could Be If There Were No Evil"

Much more important is a solution which at first seems to be a mere variant of the previous one, that evil may contribute to the goodness of a whole in which it is found, so that the universe as a whole is better as it is, with some evil in it, than it would be if there were no evil. This solution may be developed in either of two ways. It may be supported by an aesthetic analogy, by the fact that contrasts heighten beauty, that in a musical work, for example, there may occur discords which somehow add to the beauty of the work as a whole. Alternatively, it may be worked out in connection with the notion of progress, that the best possible organization of the universe will not be static, but progressive, that the gradual overcoming of evil by good is really a finer thing than would be the eternal unchallenged supremacy of good.

In either case, this solution usually starts from the assumption that the evil whose existence gives rise to the problem of evil is primarily what is called physical evil, that is to say, pain. In Hume's rather half-hearted presentation of the problem of evil, the evils that he stresses are pain and disease, and those who reply to him argue that the existence of pain and disease makes possible the existence of sympathy, benevolence, heroism, and the gradually successful struggle of doctors and reformers to overcome these evils. In fact, theists often seize the opportunity to accuse those who stress the problem of evil of taking a low, materialistic view of good and evil, equating these with pleasure and pain, and of ignoring the more spiritual goods which can arise in the struggle against evils.

But let us see exactly what is being done here. Let us call pain and misery 'first order evil' or 'evil (1).' What contrasts with this, namely, pleasure and happiness, will be called 'first order good' or 'good (1).' Distinct from this is 'second order good' or 'good (2)' which somehow emerges in a complex situation in which evil (1) is a necessary component-logically, not merely causally, necessary. (Exactly *how* it emerges does not matter: in the crudest version of this solution good (2) is simply the heightening of happiness by the contrast with misery, in other versions it includes sympathy with suffering, heroism in facing danger, and the gradual decrease of first order evil and increase of first order good.) It is also being assumed that second order good is more important than first order good or evil, in particular that it more than outweighs the first order evil it involves.

Now that is a particularly subtle attempt to solve the problem of evil. It defends God's goodness and omnipotence on the ground that (on a sufficiently long view) this is the best of all logically possible worlds, because it includes the important second order goods, and yet it admits that real evils, namely first order evils, exist. But does it still hold that good and evil are opposed? Not, clearly, in the sense that we set out originally: good does not tend to eliminate evil in general. Instead, we have a modified, a more complex pattern. First order good (*e.g.,* happiness) *contrasts with* first order evil (*e.g.,* misery): these two are opposed in a fairly mechanical way; some second order goods (*e.g.*, benevolence) try to maximize first order good and minimize first order evil; but God's goodness is not this, it is rather the will to maximize *second* order good. We might, therefore, call God's goodness an example of a third order goodness, or good (3). While this account is different from our original one, it might well be held to be an improvement on it, to give a more accurate description of the way in which good is opposed to evil, and to be consistent with the essential theist position.

There might, however, be several objections to this solution.

First, some might argue that such qualities as benevolence—and a *fortiori* the third order goodness which promotes benevolence—have a merely derivative value, that they are not higher sorts of good, but merely means to good (1), that is, to happiness, so that it would be absurd for God to keep misery in existence in order to make possible the virtues of benevolence, heroism, etc. The theist who adopts the present solution must, of course, deny this, but he can do so with some plausibility, so I should not press this objection.

Secondly, it follows from this solution that God is not in our sense benevolent or sympathetic: he is not concerned to minimize evil (1), but only to promote good (2); and this might be a disturbing conclusion for some theists.

But, thirdly, the fatal objection is this. Our analysis shows clearly the possibility of the existence of a *second* order evil, an evil (2) contrasting with good (2) as evil (1) contrasts with good (1). This would include malevolence, cruelty, callousness, cowardice, and states in which good (1) is decreasing an evil (1) increasing. And just as good (2) is held to be the important kind of good, the kind that God is concerned to promote, so evil (2) will, by analogy, be the important kind of evil, the kind which God, if he were wholly good and omnipotent, would eliminate. And yet evil (2) plainly exists, and indeed most theists (in other contexts) stress its existence more than that of evil (1). We should, therefore, state the problem of evil in terms of second order evil, and against this form of the problem the present solution is useless.

An attempt might be made to use this solution again, at a higher level, to explain the occurrence of evil (2): indeed the next main solution that we shall examine does just this, with the help of some new notions. Without any fresh notions, such a solution would have little plausibility: for example, we could hardly say that the really important good was a good (3), such as the increase of benevolence in proportion to cruelty, which logically required for its occurrence the occurrence of some second order evil. But even if evil (2) could be explained in this way, it is fairly clear that there would be third order evils contrasting with this third order good: and we should be well on the way to an infinite regress, where the solution of a problem of evil, stated in terms of evil (n), indicated the existence of an evil (n + 1), and a further problem to be solved.

4. "Evil Is Due to Human Freewill"

Perhaps the most important proposed solution of the problem of evil is that evil is not to be ascribed to God at all, but to the independent actions of human beings, supposed to have been endowed by God with freedom of the

will. This solution may be combined with the preceding one: first order evil
(*e.g.,* pain) may be justified as a logically necessary component in second order
good (*e.g.,* sympathy) while second order evil (*e.g.,* cruelty) is not *justified,* but
is so ascribed to human beings that God cannot be held responsible for it. This
combination evades my third criticism of the preceding solution.

The freewill solution also involves the preceding solution at a higher level.
To explain why a wholly good God gave men freewill although it would lead
to some important evils, it must be argued that it is better on the whole that
men should act freely, and sometimes err, than that they should be innocent
automata, acting rightly in a wholly determined way. Freedom, that is to say,
is now treated as a third order good, and as being more valuable than second
order goods (such as sympathy and heroism) would be if they were determin-
istically produced, and it is being assumed that second order evils, such as
cruelty, are logically necessary accompaniments of freedom, just as pain is a
logically necessary pre-condition of sympathy.

I think that this solution is unsatisfactory primarily because of the incoherence of the notion of freedom of the will: but I cannot discuss this topic adequately here, although some of my criticisms will touch upon it.

First I should query the assumption that second order evils are logically
necessary accompaniments of freedom. I should ask this: if God has made
men such that in their free choices they sometimes prefer what is good and
sometimes what is evil, why could He not have made men such that they always freely choose the good? If there is no logical impossibility in a man's
freely choosing the good on one, or on several, occasions, there cannot be a
logical impossibility in his freely choosing the good on every occasion. God
was not, then, faced with a choice between making innocent automata and
making beings who, in acting freely, would sometimes go wrong: there was
open to him the obviously better possibility of making beings who would act
freely but always go right. Clearly, his failure to avail himself of this possibility is inconsistent with his being both omnipotent and wholly good.

If it is replied that this objection is absurd, that the making of some wrong
choices is logically necessary for freedom, it would seem that 'freedom' must
here mean complete randomness or indeterminacy, including randomness
with regard to the alternatives good and evil, in other words that men's
choices and consequent actions can be "free" only if they are not determined
by their characters. Only on this assumption can God escape the responsibility
for men's actions; for if he made them as they are, but did not determine their
wrong choices, this can only be because the wrong choices are not determined
by men as they are. But then if freedom is randomness, how can it be a characteristic of *will?* And, still more, how can it be the most important good? What
value or merit would there be in free choices if these were random actions
which were not determined by the nature of the agent?

I conclude that to make this solution plausible two different senses of
'freedom' must be confused, one sense which will justify the view that freedom is a third order good, more valuable than other goods would be without
it, and another sense, sheer randomness, to prevent us from ascribing to God a

decision to make men such that they sometimes go wrong when he might have made them such that they would always freely go right.

This criticism is sufficient to dispose of this solution. But besides this there is a fundamental difficulty in the notion of an omnipotent God creating men with free will, for if men's wills are really free this must mean that even God cannot control them, that is, that God is no longer omnipotent. It may be objected that God's gift of freedom to men does not mean that he *cannot* control their wills, but that he always *refrains* from controlling their wills. But why, we may ask, should God refrain from controlling evil wills? Why should he not leave men free to will rightly, but intervene when he sees them beginning to will wrongly? If God could do this, but does not, and if he is wholly good, the only explanation could be that even a wrong free act of will is not really evil, that its freedom is a value which outweighs its wrongness, so that there would be a loss of value if God took away the wrongness and the freedom together. But this is utterly opposed to what theists say about sin in other contexts. The present solution of the problem of evil, then, can be maintained only in the form that God has made men so free that he *cannot* control their wills.

This leads us to what I call the Paradox of Omnipotence: can an omnipotent being make things which he cannot subsequently control? Or, what is practically equivalent to this, can an omnipotent being make rules which then bind himself? (These are practically equivalent because any such rules could be regarded as setting certain things beyond his control, and *vice versa.*) The second of these formulations is relevant to the suggestions that we have already met, that an omnipotent God creates the rules of logic or causal laws, and is then bound by them.

It is clear that this is a paradox: the questions cannot be answered satisfactorily either in the affirmative or in the negative. If we answer "Yes," it follows that if God actually makes things which he cannot control, or makes rules which bind himself, he is not omnipotent once he has made them: there are then things which he cannot do. But if we answer "No," we are immediately asserting that there are things which he cannot do, that is to say that he is already not omnipotent.

It cannot be replied that the question which sets this paradox is not a proper question. It would make perfectly good sense to say that a human mechanic has made a machine which he cannot control: if there is any difficulty about the question it lies in the notion of omnipotence itself.

This, incidentally, shows that although we have approached this paradox from the free will theory, it is equally a problem for a theological determinist. No one thinks that machines have free will, yet they may well be beyond the control of their makers. The determinist might reply that anyone who makes anything determines its ways of acting, and so determines its subsequent behavior: even the human mechanic does this by his *choice of* materials and structure for his machine, though he does not know all about either of these: the mechanic thus determines, though he may not foresee, his machine's actions. And since God is omniscient, and since his creation of things is total, he both determines and foresees the ways in which his creatures will act. We may grant this, but it is beside the point. The question is not whether God *originally* determined the future actions of his creatures, but whether he can *subsequently* control their actions, or whether he was able in his original creation to put things beyond his subsequent control. Even on determinist principles the answers "Yes" and "No" are equally irreconcilable with God's omnipotence.

Before suggesting a solution of this paradox, I would point out that there is a parallel Paradox of Sovereignty. Can a legal sovereign make a law restricting its own future legislative power? For example, could the British parliament make a law forbidding any future parliament to socialize banking, and also forbidding the future repeal of this law itself? Or could the British parliament, which was legally sovereign in Australia in, say, 1899, pass a valid law, or series of laws, which made it no longer sovereign in 1933? Again, neither the affirmative nor the negative answer is really satisfactory. If we were to answer "Yes," we should be admitting the validity of a law which, if it were actually made, would mean that parliament was no longer sovereign. If we were to answer "No," we should be admitting that there is a law, not logically absurd, which parliament cannot validly make, that is, that parliament is not now a legal sovereign. This paradox can be solved in the following way. We should distinguish between first order laws, that is laws governing the actions of individuals and bodies other than the legislature, and second order laws, that is laws about laws, laws governing the actions of the legislature itself. Correspondingly, we should distinguish two orders of sovereignty, first order sovereignty (sovereignty (1)) which is unlimited authority to make first order laws, and second order sovereignty (sovereignty (2)) which is unlimited authority to make second order laws. If we say that parliament is sovereign we might mean that any parliament at any time has sovereignty (1), or we might mean that parliament has both sovereignty (1) and sovereignty (2) at present, but we cannot without contradiction mean both that the present parliament has sovereignty (2) and that every parliament at every time has sovereignty (1), for if the present parliament has sovereignty (2) it may use it to take away the sovereignty (1) of later parliaments. What the paradox shows is that we cannot ascribe to any continuing institution legal sovereignty in an inclusive sense.

The analogy between omnipotence and sovereignty shows that the paradox of omnipotence can be solved in a similar way. We must distinguish between first order omnipotence (omnipotence (1)), that is unlimited power to act, and second order omnipotence (omnipotence (2)), that is unlimited power to determine what powers to act things shall have. Then we could consistently say that God all the time has omnipotence (1), but if so no beings at any time have powers to act independently of God. Or we could say that God at one time had omnipotence (2), and used it to assign independent powers to act to certain things, so that God thereafter did not have omnipotence (1). But what the paradox shows is that we cannot consistently ascribe to any continuing being omnipotence is an inclusive sense.

An alternative solution of this paradox would be simply to deny that God is a continuing being, that any times can be assigned to his actions at all. But on this assumption (which also has difficulties of its own) no meaning can be given to the assertion that God made men with wills so free that he could not control them. The paradox of omnipotence can be avoided by putting God outside time, but the freewill solution of the problem of evil cannot be saved in this way, and equally it remains impossible to hold that an omnipotent God *binds himself* by causal or logical laws.

CONCLUSION

Of the proposed solutions of the problem of evil which we have examined, none has stood up to criticism. There may be other solutions which require examination, but this study strongly suggests that there is no valid solution of the problem which does not modify at least one of the constituent propositions in a way which would seriously affect the essential core of the theistic position.

Quite apart from the problem of evil, the paradox of omnipotence has shown that God's omnipotence must in any case be restricted in one way or another, that unqualified omnipotence cannot be ascribed to any being that continues through time. And if God and his actions are not in time, can omnipotence, or power of any sort, be meaningfully ascribed to him?

PART FOUR

Epistemology

*E*pistemology, or the theory of knowledge, focuses on the fundamental question, "What can I know?" What occurs when we perceive something, say, an apple? Do we *know* that it is an apple? Do we know that it *is* an apple? What does it mean to *know* anything? What does it mean to say that something *is?* Suppose I says that "I know that it is an apple because I recognize its shape and color." There can be no question that when I perceive an apple I in fact have the psychological experience of shape and color. But is that experience what we call knowledge? Does it follow, for example, when I perceive a certain shape and color—which appears identical to the apple I ate yesterday—that the present object will taste the same or even be an apple? Perhaps, unlike the apple I ate yesterday, the present object is something made of wax or paper or clay. If the object I perceive turns out differently from what you thought it was, then I did not have true knowledge about the object. True knowledge assumes that we know what reality is. But the problem philosophers have tried to solve is whether there is any reliable way to distinguish between appearance and reality.

In his *Republic,* Greek philosopher Plato (427–347 B.C.E.) illustrates the contrast between appearance and reality by using two vivid illustrations, namely, (1) the divided line and (2) the cave. These two illustrations describe how Plato viewed the steps the mind takes on its way to true knowledge. The imaginary line is divided into two major parts; the lower part refers to the "visible" world and the upper part to the "intelligible" world. In the visible world we encounter things that are constantly changing; in the intelligible world we recognize ideas and ideals that Plato calls "real." Similarly, the illustration of the cave describes how individuals who dwell in the cave have a very distorted idea of what they are experiencing. Not until they come up out of the cave do they discover, step by step, how limited their knowledge was in the cave. These two illustrations of the divided line and the cave are meant by Plato to say the same thing, namely, that there is a basic difference between appearance and reality.

Plato had a quite optimistic view about our ability to acquire knowledge. Not all philosophers, though, agreed with him, and a school of philosophy arose that specifically emphasized our inability to know *anything.* The founder of this school was an eccentric Greek philosopher named Pyrrho (c. 365–275). Although Pyrrho wrote nothing and we know very little of his actual teaching, we have a detailed account of the school's later views in a work titled *Outlines of Pyrrhonism* by Greek philosopher Sextus Empiricus (c. 200 C.E.). According to Sextus, we do not doubt just for the sake of doubting. Instead, we achieve a kind of psychological tranquility when we set aside our dogmatic views of everything—including metaphysics, religion, and morality. He explains a skeptical method of argumentation called the Ten Modes of Skepticism, by which we can come to doubt every subject of inquiry. The underlying reasoning behind most of the ten modes is that there are vastly different ways of perceiving things, and we cannot prefer any one of these ways to another.

During the sixteenth and seventeenth centuries, Europe experienced an intellectual Renaissance—or rebirth—which was sparked by a rediscovery of ancient Greek writings. This included a reacquaintance with Sextus Empiricus, and many Renaissance writers advanced his skeptical views. French philosopher René Descartes (1569–1650) was disturbed by this resurgence of skepticism and, in his *Meditations* he attempts to refute skepticism and ground knowledge on a secure foundation. Descartes opens his *Meditations* by tentatively adopting a skeptical view point and pushing it as far as he can. He asks himself whether he can, for example, ever be certain that he is sitting by his fireplace or whether he is just dreaming that he was. After all, he had from time to time had dreams in which he appeared to be doing things similar to his behavior during his waking moments. How can he now be certain that he is not dreaming? He finds it possible to doubt virtually everything and wonders whether he can ever discover anything that he cannot doubt. One thing he *cannot* doubt, says Descartes, is *that he doubts.* To doubt is to think, and "to think that I am something is necessarily true every time I propound it or mentally apprehend it even though I do not yet know in any adequate manner what I am." From this preliminary certainty Descartes set out to construct his theory of knowledge, now called *rationalism,* which emphasizes the ability of human reason to grasp fundamental truth about the world without the aid of sense impressions.

Although a variety of philosophers adopted Descartes's rationalist view of knowledge, others—particularly in Great Britain and now called Empiricists— quickly opposed this view. In his *Essay Concerning Human Understanding,* John Locke (1632–1704) argued that our knowledge is in fact based solely upon our experiences—upon the information supplied by our senses. Locke takes pains first of all to reject the notion that there are in our minds some "innate ideas or principles" as if implanted there at birth. Take, for example, how we know colors or taste. Locke says, "I would have anyone try to fancy any taste, which had never affected his palate; or frame the idea of a scent he had never smelt: and when he could do this, I will also conclude that a blind man hath ideas of colors, and a deaf man true distinct notions of sounds." The mind, says Locke, is originally "an empty cabinet" and "it is the senses that at first let in particular ideas." Using another metaphor, Locke asks us to "suppose the mind to be . . . white paper, void of all characters, without any ideas: how comes it to be furnished?" His answer to this question gives us Locke's theory of knowledge.

Locke's empiricist view of knowledge was adopted by Scottish skeptical philosopher David Hume (1711–1776). In his *Enquiry Concerning Human Understanding* (1748) Hume argues that the objects of human reason may be divided into two kinds, namely, relations of ideas and matters of fact—a view now called "Hume's fork." For example, "three times five equals fifteen" expresses a relation between these numbers. We discover this by the mere operation of thought without any reference to anything that exists anywhere in the universe. As for matters of fact, knowledge of these is grounded in cause and effect. And, knowledge of cause/effect connections is in turn grounded in *experience*, rather than in *a priori* reasoning. For example, suppose that I swallow an aspirin tablet and my headache disappears. I believe that the aspirin is the cause of my headache's disappearance. But the only way that I know this is through repeated experience. This, though, raises another puzzle, which today is called the *problem of induction*—namely, how do I know that my experiences in the past will hold true for my future experiences? We know only that I swallowed the aspirin and that subsequently my headache ceased. It is logically possible that this sequence will not occur next time. Hume explores several possible explanations for inductive reasoning. Perhaps, he speculates, we logically deduce our inductive inference from the past to the future. Perhaps, instead, it is grounded in some kind of experiential reasoning. However, Hume rejects all of these speculations. Ultimately, he argues, inductive inferences from the past to the future are based on instinctive abilities to form mental habits when we repeatedly see two things associated with each other.

German philosopher Immanuel Kant (1724–1804) forged a middle position between rationalists such as Descartes (who believed that knowledge was based on innate concepts) and empiricists such as Locke (who believed that knowledge comes from sensory experience). In his *Critique of Pure Reason* (1781) Kant says, "There can be no doubt that all our knowledge begins with experience. . . . But although all our knowledge begins with experience, it does not follow that it all arises out of experience." Kant acknowledges that our faculty of knowledge is awakened into action by the objects affecting our senses. But having been awakened by sense impressions, our faculty of knowledge *supplies from itself* significant ingredients to the raw material of these impressions. The mind organizes the elements of our experiences by bringing to them its "ways of thinking." The human mind, he argued, is structured in such a way that as impressions enter it, the mind processes them. It is as though the mind possesses the capability of imposing its structure upon the impressions received, just as a pair of colored lenses give that particular color to the objects perceived. It is the mind's way of functioning that brings to experience the elements of cause and effect. Thus, we have some knowledge that is not immediately derived from experience, even though it is experience that triggers such knowledge.

A distinctively American approach to philosophy called *pragmatism* emerged in the late nineteenth and early twentieth centuries. One of its chief proponents was Harvard professor William James (1842–1910), who made significant contributions in the fields of both philosophy and psychology. In *Pragmatism: A New Name for Some Old Ways of Thinking* (1907), James presents the radical view that "truth is made," that is, that "truth is what happens to an idea." What was so radical about this was that James rejected the conventional definition of truth—now called the *correspondence theory of truth*—that truth is the agreement of an idea with "reality." On this view, a true idea is something like a mental copy of an external thing. James found fault with this notion of truth because he did not know with any clarity what it means for an idea to "agree" with or "copy" reality, and he certainly could not be sure what in every case was meant by "reality." For him, the essential question is this: What practical value is there in saying that something is true? He asks, "What concrete difference will [an idea's] being true make in one's actual life?" Or, "What experience will be different from those which would obtain if the belief were false?" Finally, "What, in short, is the truth's cash-value in experiential terms?" An idea is true "if it works." Truth is made true by events. And, says James, "True ideas are those that we can assimilate, validate, corroborate, and verify."

As early as Plato and Sextus Empiricus, philosophers were troubled with distinguishing between appearance and reality. This same epistemological problem continues right on up to contemporary times. In his short book *Problems of Philosophy* (1912), British philosopher Bertrand Russell (1872–1970) uses the example of a table to demonstrate that almost every appearance produced by the table turns out to raise questions about the table's true reality. To our eyes it is oblong, brown, shiny, hard, smooth, and cool. Each of us looking at the table will agree with these appearances of the shape, size, color, and texture, but only if each of us looks at it from the same position. But when viewed from a different point of view, the shape and color will appear different. This raises the question of whether we can ever *see* the real shape or color. Bertrand Russell draws the conclusion that "the real table, if there is one, is not *immediately* known to us at all, but must be an inference from what is immediately known." In *The Nature of the Physical World* (1928), British astronomer Arthur Eddington (1882–1944) adds another twist to the problem of appearance and reality. For Eddington, we must distinguish between common sense knowledge and scientific knowledge. On the one hand, there is a common sense table before my eyes that I see and understand. On the other, though, there is the scientific table of electric charges, quanta, or electrons.

In *Philosophy and the Mirror of Nature* (1979) American philosopher Richard Rorty (b. 1931), examines and rejects a key assumption in traditional epistemology that began with Descartes. The assumption is that knowledge involves mental representations—that is, pictures or images—of things in the world. As such the mind *mirrors* nature. Philosophers perpetuated this view over the centuries, and philosophy progressively became more scientific as writers searched for the proper foundations of representational knowledge. Rorty notes that some recent philosophers abandoned the theory of knowledge as representation, and he too abandons this theory. He suggests that philosophical convictions are actually based on metaphors, rather than on propositions and statements that allegedly represent reality.

The Ascent to True Knowledge: The Divided Line and Cave*

Plato (427–347 B.C.E.)

[FOUR STAGES OF COGNITION: THE ALLEGORY OF THE DIVIDED LINE]

According to Plato, there are four main kinds of human cognition; the weakest of these involves our imagination, and the strongest involves our intelligence and knowledge. He describes the differences between these using an example of a line that is divided into four segments. The details of the divisions are charted on the next page.

THE DIVIDED LINE

SOCRATES: Now take a line which has been cut into two unequal parts, and divide each of them again in the same proportion, and suppose the two main divisions to answer, one to the visible and the other to the intelligible, and then compare the subdivisions in respect of their clearness and want of clearness, and you will find that the first section in the sphere of the visible consists of images. And by images I mean, in the first place, shadows, and in the second place, reflections in water and in solid, smooth and polished bodies and the like: Do you understand?

---

*From Plato, *The Republic*, Books 6 and 7.

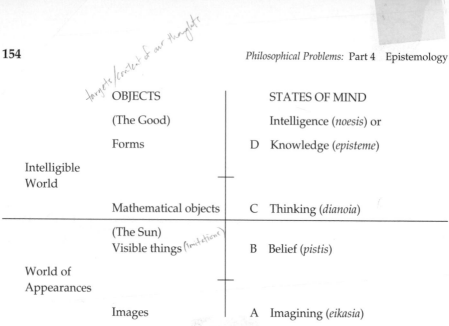

targets/content of our thoughts

OBJECTS	STATES OF MIND
(The Good)	Intelligence (*noesis*) or
Forms	D Knowledge (*episteme*)
Intelligible World	
Mathematical objects	C Thinking (*dianoia*)
(The Sun) Visible things (imitations)	B Belief (*pistis*)
World of Appearances	
Images	A Imagining (*eikasia*)

GLAUCON: Yes, I understand.

SOCRATES: You have to imagine, then, that there are two ruling powers, and that one of them is set over the intellectual world, the other over the visible. I do not say heaven, lest you should fancy that I am making a play on words. May I suppose that you have this distinction of the visible and intelligible fixed in your mind?

GLAUCON: I have.

SOCRATES: Imagine, now, the other section (B), of which this is only the resemblance, to include the animals which we see, and everything that grows or is made.

GLAUCON: Very good.

SOCRATES: Would you not admit that both the sections of this division have different degrees of truth, and that the copy is to the original as the sphere of opinion is to the sphere of knowledge?

GLAUCON: Most undoubtedly.

SOCRATES: Next proceed to consider the manner in which the sphere of the intellectual is to be divided.

GLAUCON: In what manner?

SOCRATES: Thus, there are two subdivisions. In the lower of the two (C), the soul uses the figures given by the former division as images; the inquiry can only be hypothetical, and instead of going upwards to a principle descends to the other end. In the higher of the two (D), the soul passes out of hypotheses, and goes up to a principle which is above hypotheses, making no use of images as in the former case, but proceeding only in and through the ideas themselves.

GLAUCON: I do not quite understand your meaning, he said.

SOCRATES: Then I will try again. (C) You will understand me better when I have made some preliminary remarks. You are aware that students of geometry, arithmetic, and the kindred sciences assume the odd and the even and the figures and three kinds of angles and the like in their several branches of science; these are their hypotheses, which they and everybody are supposed to know, and therefore they do not deign to give any account of them either to themselves or others; but they begin with them, and go on until they arrive at last, and in a consistent manner, at their conclusion?

GLAUCON: Yes, he said, I know.

SOCRATES: And do you not know also that although they make use of the visible forms and reason about them, they are thinking not of these, but of the ideals which they resemble; not of the figures which they draw, but of the absolute square and the absolute diameter, and so on—the forms which they draw or make, and which have shadows and reflections in water of their own, are converted by them into images, but they are really seeking to behold the things themselves, which can only be seen with the eye of the mind?

GLAUCON: That is true.

SOCRATES: And of this kind I spoke as the intelligible, although in the search after it the soul is compelled to use hypotheses; not ascending to a first principle, because she is unable to rise above the region of hypothesis, but employing the objects of which the shadows below are resemblances in their turn as images, they having in relation to the shadows and reflections of them a greater distinctness, and therefore a higher value.

GLAUCON: I understand, he said, that you are speaking of the province of geometry and the sister arts.

SOCRATES: And when I speak of the other division (D) of the intelligible, you will understand me to speak of that other sort of knowledge which reason herself attains by the power of dialectic, using the hypotheses not as first principles, but only as hypotheses—that is to say, as steps and points of departure into a world which is above hypotheses, in order that she may soar beyond them to the first principle of the whole; and clinging to this and then to that which depends on this, by successive steps she descends again without the aid of any sensible object, from ideas, through ideas, and in ideas she ends.

GLAUCON: I understand you, he replied; not perfectly, for you seem to me to be describing a task which is really tremendous; but, at any rate, I understand you to say that knowledge and being, which the science of dialectic contemplates, are clearer than the notions of the arts, as they are termed, which proceed from hypotheses only: these are also contemplated by the understanding, and not by the senses: yet, because they start from hypotheses and do not ascend to a principle, those who contemplate them appear to you not to exercise the higher reason upon them, although when a first principle is added to them they are cognizable by the higher reason. And the habit which is concerned with geometry and the cognate sciences I suppose that you would term understanding and not reason, as being intermediate between opinion and reason.

SOCRATES: You have quite conceived my meaning, I said; and now, corresponding to these four divisions, let there be four faculties in the soul—reason answering to the highest, understanding to the second, faith (or conviction) to the third, and perception of shadows to the last—and let there be a scale of them, and let us suppose that the several faculties have clearness in the same degree that their objects have truth.

GLAUCON: I understand, he replied, and give my assent, and accept your arrangement.

THE ALLEGORY OF THE CAVE

SOCRATES: And now, I said, let me show in a figure how far our nature is enlightened or unenlightened:—Behold! human beings living in a underground den, which has a mouth open towards the light and reaching all along the den; here they have been from their childhood, and have their legs and necks chained so that they cannot move, and can only see before them, being prevented by the chains from turning round their heads. Above and behind them a fire is blazing at a distance, and between the fire and the prisoners there is a raised way; and you will see, if you look, a low wall built along the way, like the screen which marionette players have in front of them, over which they show the puppets.

GLAUCON: I see.

SOCRATES: And do you see, I said, men passing along the wall carrying all sorts of vessels, and statues and figures of animals made of wood and stone and various materials, which appear over the wall? Some of them are talking, others silent.

GLAUCON: You have shown me a strange image, and they are strange prisoners.

SOCRATES: Like ourselves, I replied; and they see only their own shadows, or the shadows of one another, which the fire throws on the opposite wall of the cave?

GLAUCON: True, he said; how could they see anything but the shadows if they were never allowed to move their heads?

SOCRATES: And of the objects which are being carried in like manner they would only see the shadows?

GLAUCON: Yes, he said.

SOCRATES: And if they were able to converse with one another, would they not suppose that they were naming what was actually before them?

GLAUCON: Very true.

SOCRATES: And suppose further that the prison had an echo which came from the other side, would they not be sure to fancy when one of the passers-by spoke that the voice which they heard came from the passing shadow?

GLAUCON: No question, he replied.

SOCRATES: To them, I said, the truth would be literally nothing but the shadows of the images.

GLAUCON: That is certain.

SOCRATES: And now look again, and see what will naturally follow if the prisoners are released and disabused of their error. At first, when any of them is liberated and compelled suddenly to stand up and turn his neck round and walk and look towards the light, he will suffer sharp pains; the glare will distress him, and he will be unable to see the realities of which in his former state he had seen the shadows; and then conceive some one saying to him, that what he saw before was an illusion, but that now, when he is approaching nearer to being and his eye is turned towards more real existence, he has a clearer vision,—what will be his reply? And you may further imagine that his instructor is pointing to the objects as they pass and requiring him to name them,—will he not be perplexed? Will he not fancy that the shadows which he formerly saw are truer than the objects which are now shown to him?

GLAUCON: Far truer.

SOCRATES: And if he is compelled to look straight at the light, will he not have a pain in his eyes which will make him turn away and take in the objects of vision which he can see, and which he will conceive to be in reality clearer than the things which are now being shown to him?

GLAUCON: True, he said.

SOCRATES: And suppose once more, that he is reluctantly dragged up a steep and rugged ascent, and held fast until he 's forced into the presence of the sun himself, is he not likely to be pained and irritated? When he approaches the light his eyes will be dazzled, and he will not be able to see anything at all of what are now called realities.

GLAUCON: Not all in a moment, he said.

SOCRATES: He will require to grow accustomed to the sight of the upper world. And first he will see the shadows best, next the reflections of men and other objects in the water, and then the objects themselves; then he will gaze upon the light of the moon and the stars and the spangled heaven; and he will see the sky and the stars by night better than the sun or the light of the sun by day?

GLAUCON: Certainly.

SOCRATES: Last of he will be able to see the sun, and not mere reflections of him in the water, but he will see him in his own proper place, and not in another; and he will contemplate him as he is.

GLAUCON: Certainly.

SOCRATES: He will then proceed to argue that this is he who gives the season and the years, and is the guardian of all that is in the visible world, and in a certain way the cause of all things which he and his fellows have been accustomed to behold?

GLAUCON: Clearly, he said, he would first see the sun and then reason about him.

SOCRATES: And when he remembered his old habitation, and the wisdom of the den and his fellow-prisoners, do you not suppose that he would felicitate himself on the change, and pity them?

GLAUCON: Certainly, he would.

SOCRATES: And if they were in the habit of conferring honors among themselves on those who were quickest to observe the passing shadows and to remark which of them went before, and which followed after, and which were together; and who were therefore best able to draw conclusions as to the future, do you think that he would care for such honors and glories, or envy the possessors of them? Would he not say with Homer, "Better to be the poor servant of a poor master," and to endure anything, rather than think as they do and live after their manner?

GLAUCON: Yes, he said, I think that he would rather suffer anything than entertain these false notions and live in this miserable manner.

SOCRATES: Imagine once more, I said, such an one coming suddenly out of the sun to be replaced in his old situation; would he not be certain to have his eyes full of darkness?

GLAUCON: To be sure, he said.

SOCRATES: And if there were a contest, and he had to compete in measuring the shadows with the prisoners who had never moved out of the den, while his sight was still weak, and before his eyes had become steady (and the time which would be needed to acquire this new habit of sight might be very considerable) would he not be ridiculous? Men would say of him that up he went and down he came without his eyes; and that it was better not even to think of ascending; and if any one tried to loose another and lead him up to the light, let them only catch the offender, and they would put him to death.

GLAUCON: No question, he said.

SOCRATES: This entire allegory, I said, you may now append, dear Glaucon, to the previous argument; the prison-house is the world of sight, the light of the fire is the sun, and you will not misapprehend me if you interpret the journey upwards to be the ascent of the soul into the intellectual world according to my poor belief, which, at your desire, I have expressed whether rightly or wrongly God knows. But, whether true or false, my opinion is that in the world of knowledge the idea of good appears last of all, and is seen only with an effort; and, when seen, is also inferred to be the universal author of all things beautiful and right, parent of light and of the lord of light in this visible world, and the immediate source of reason and truth in the intellectual; and that this is the power upon which he who would act rationally, either in public or private life must have his eye fixed.

GLAUCON: I agree, he said, as far as I am able to understand you.

SOCRATES: Moreover, I said, you must not wonder that those who attain to this beatific vision are unwilling to descend to human affairs; for their souls are ever hastening into the upper world where they desire to dwell; which desire of theirs is very natural, if our allegory may be trusted.

GLAUCON: Yes, very natural.

SOCRATES: And is there anything surprising in one who passes from divine contemplations to the evil state of man, misbehaving himself in a ridiculous manner; if, while his eyes are blinking and before he has become accustomed to the surrounding darkness, he is compelled to fight in courts of law, or in other places, about the images or the shadows of images of justice, and is endeavouring to meet the conceptions of those who have never yet seen absolute justice?

GLAUCON: Anything but surprising, he replied.

SOCRATES: Any one who has common sense will remember that the bewilderments of the eyes are of two kinds, and arise from two causes, either from coming out of the light or from going into the light, which is true of the mind's eye, quite as much as of the bodily eye; and he who remembers this when he sees any one whose vision is perplexed and weak, will not be too ready to laugh; he will first ask whether that soul of man has come out of the brighter life, and is unable to see because unaccustomed to the dark, or having turned from darkness to the day is dazzled by excess of light. And he will count the one happy in his condition and state of being, and he will pity the other; or, if he have a mind to laugh at the soul which comes from below into the light, there will be more reason in this than in the laugh which greets him who returns from above out of the light into the den.

GLAUCON: That, he said, is a very just distinction.

SOCRATES: But then, if I am right, certain professors of education must be wrong when they say that they can put a knowledge into the soul which was not there before, like sight into blind eyes.

GLAUCON: They undoubtedly say this, he replied.

SOCRATES: Whereas, our argument shows that the power and capacity of learning exists in the soul already; and that just as the eye was unable to turn from darkness to light without the whole body, so too the instrument of knowledge can only by the movement of the whole soul be turned from the world of becoming into that of being, and learn by degrees to endure the sight of being, and of the brightest and best of being, or in other words, of the good.

GLAUCON: Very true.

SOCRATES: And must there not be some art which will effect conversion in the easiest and quickest manner; not implanting the faculty of sight, for that exists already, but has been turned in the wrong direction, and is looking away from the truth?

READING 22

The Goals and Methods of Skepticism*

Sextus Empiricus (c. 200 C.E.)

BOOK 1

1. *The Principal Differences between Philosophers.* It is probable that those who seek after anything whatever, will either find it as they continue the search, will deny that it can be found and confess it to be out of reach, or

*From Sextus Empiricus, *Outlines of Pyrrhonism*, Book 1.

will go on seeking it. Some have said, accordingly, in regard to the things sought in philosophy, that they have found the truth, while others have declared it impossible to find, and still others continue to seek it. Those who think that they have found it are those who are especially called Dogmatics, as for example, the Schools of Aristotle and Epicurus, the Stoics and some others. Those who have declared it impossible to find are Clitomachus, Carneades, with their respective followers, and other Academicians. Those who still seek it are the Skeptics. It appears therefore, reasonable to conclude that the three principal kinds of philosophy are the Dogmatic, the Academic, and the Skeptic. Others may suitably treat of the other Schools, but as for the Skeptical School, we shall now give an outline of it, remarking in advance that in respect to nothing that will be said do we speak positively, that it must be absolutely so, but we shall state each thing historically as it now appears to us.

2. ***Ways of Treating Skepticism.*** One way of treating the Skeptical philosophy is called general, and the other special. The general method is that by which we set forth the character of Skepticism, declaring what its idea is, what its principles are, its mode of reasoning its criterion, and its aim. It presents also, the modes of doubt, and the way in which we should understand the Skeptical formulae, and the distinction between Skepticism and the related Schools of philosophy. The special method, on the contrary, is that by which we speak against each part of so-called philosophy. Let us then treat Skepticism at first in the general way, beginning our delineation with the nomenclature of the Skeptical School.

3. ***The Nomenclature of Skepticism.*** The Skeptical School is also called the "Seeking School," from its spirit of research and examination; the "Suspending School," from the condition of mind in which one is left after the search, in regard to the things that he has examined; and the "Doubting School," either because, as some say, the Skeptics doubt and are seeking in regard to everything, or because they never know whether to deny or affirm. It is also called the Pyrrhonian School, because Pyrrho appears to us the best representative of Skepticism, and is more prominent than all who before him occupied themselves with it.

4. ***What Is Skepticism?*** The way of the Skeptical School is an *ability to place appearances in opposition to judgments in any way whatever, and thus through the equilibrium of the reasons and things opposed to each other, to reach, first the state of suspension of judgment, and afterwards that of tranquility.* We do not use the word "ability" in any unusual sense, but simply, meaning the force of the system. By the "appearances" we understand the sensible, hence we place the intellectual in opposition to it. The phrase "in any way whatever" may refer to the word "ability" in order that we may understand that word in a simple sense as we said, or it may refer to the "placing appearances in opposition to judgments." For we place these in opposition to each other in a variety of ways, appearances to appearances, and judgments to judgments, or reciprocally, and we say "in any way whatever," in order that all methods of opposition may be included. Or "in any way whatever" may refer to

appearances and judgments, so that we need not ask how does appearances appear, or how are the thoughts are judged, but that we may understand these things in a simple sense. By "reasons opposed to each other," we do not by any means understand that they deny or affirm anything, but simply that they offset each other. By "equilibrium" we mean equality in regard to trustworthiness and untrustworthiness, so that of the reasons that are placed in opposition to each other, one should not excel another in trustworthiness. "Suspension of judgment" is a holding back of the opinion, in consequence of which we neither deny nor affirm anything. "Tranquility" is repose and calmness of soul. We shall explain how tranquility accompanies suspension of judgment when we speak of the aim.

5. *The Skeptic.* What is meant by a Pyrrhonian philosopher cannot be understood from the idea of the Skeptical School. He is Pyrrhonian, namely, who identifies himself with this ability.

6. *The Origin of Skepticism.* Skepticism arose in the beginning from the hope of attaining tranquility; for men of the greatest talent were perplexed by the contradiction of things, and being at a loss what to believe, began to question what things are true, and what false, hoping to attain tranquility as a result of the decision. The fundamental principle of the Skeptical system is especially this, namely, to oppose every argument by one of equal weight, for it seems to us that in this way we finally reach the position where we have no dogmas.

7. *Does the Skeptic Dogmatize?* We say that the Skeptic does not dogmatize. We do not say this, meaning by the word dogma the popular assent to certain things rather than others (for the Skeptic does assent to feelings that are a necessary result of sensation, as for example, when he is warm or cold, he cannot say that he thinks he is not warm or cold), but we say this, meaning by dogma the acceptance of any opinion in regard to the unknown things investigated by science. For the Pyrrhonian assents to nothing that is unknown. Furthermore, he does not dogmatize even when he utters the skeptical formula in regard to things that are unknown, such as "Nothing more," or "I decide nothing," or any of the others which we shall speak later. For the one who dogmatizes regards the thing about which he is said to dogmatize, as existing in itself; the Skeptic does not regard these formula in an absolute sense, for he assumes that the saying "All is false" includes itself with other things as false, and likewise the saying "Nothing is true." In the same way "Nothing more" states that together with other things it itself is nothing more, and cancels itself therefore, as well as other things. We say the same also in regard to the other Skeptical expressions. In short, if he who dogmatizes assumes as existing in itself that about which he dogmatizes, the Skeptic, on the contrary, expresses his sayings in such a way that they are understood to be themselves included, and it cannot be said that he dogmatizes in saying these things. The principal thing in uttering these formula is that he says what appears to him, and communicates his own feelings in an unprejudiced way, without asserting anything in regard to external objects.

8. *Is Skepticism a System?* We respond in a similar way if we are asked whether Skepticism is a sect or not. If the word "system" is defined as meaning a body of persons who hold dogmas which are in conformity with each other, and also with appearances, and dogma means an assent to anything that is unknown, then we reply that we have no sect. If, however, one means by sect, a school which follows a certain line of reasoning based on appearances, and that reasoning shows how it is possible to apparently live rightly, not understanding "rightly" as referring to virtue only, but in a broader sense; if, also, it leads one to be able to suspend the judgment, then we reply that we have a system. For we follow a certain kind of reasoning which is based upon appearances, and which shows us how to live according to the habits, laws, and teachings of our country, and our own feelings.

9. *Does the Skeptic Study Natural Science?* We reply similarly also to the question whether the Skeptic should study natural science. For we do not study natural science in order to express ourselves with confidence regarding any of the dogmas that it teaches, but we take it up in order to be able to meet every argument by one of equal weight, and also for the sake of tranquility. In the same way we study the logical and ethical part of so-called philosophy.

10. *Do the Skeptics Deny Appearances?* Those who say that the Skeptics deny appearances appear to me to be in ignorance of our teachings. For as we said before, we do not deny the sensations which we think we have, and which lead us to assent involuntarily to them, and these are the appearances. When, however, we ask whether the object is such as it appears to be, while we concede that it appears so and so, we question, not the phenomenon, but in regard to that which is asserted of the phenomenon, and that is different from doubting the phenomenon itself. For example, it appears to us that honey is sweet. This we concede, for we experience sweetness through sensation. We doubt, however, whether it is sweet by reason of its essence, which is not a question of the phenomenon, but of that which is asserted of the phenomenon. Should we, however, argue directly against the appearances, it is not with the intention of denying their existence, but to show the rashness of the Dogmatics. For if reasoning is such a deceiver that it well nigh snatches away the appearances from before your eyes, how should we not distrust it in regard to things that are unknown, so as not to rashly follow it?

11. *The Criterion of Skepticism.* It is evident that we pay careful attention to appearances from what we say about the criterion of the Skeptical School. The word criterion is used in two ways. First, it is understood as a proof of existence or non-existence, in regard to which we shall speak in the opposing argument. Secondly, when it refers to action, meaning the criterion to which we give heed in life, in doing some things and refraining from doing others, and it is about this that we shall now speak. We say, consequently, that the criterion of the Skeptical School is the appearance, and in calling it

so, we mean the idea of it. It cannot be doubted, as it is based upon susceptibility and involuntary feeling. Hence no one doubts, perhaps, that an object appears so and so, but one questions if it is as it appears. Therefore, as we cannot be entirely inactive as regards the observances of daily life, we live by giving heed to appearances, and in an unprejudiced way. But this observance of what pertains to the daily life, appears to be of four different kinds. Sometimes it is directed by the guidance of nature, sometimes by the necessity of the feelings, sometimes by the tradition of laws and of customs, and sometimes by the teaching of the arts. It is directed by the guidance of nature, for by nature we are capable of sensation and thought; by the necessity of the feelings, for hunger leads us to food, and thirst to drink; by the traditions of laws and customs, for according to them we consider piety a good in daily life, and impiety an evil; by the teaching of the arts, for we are not inactive in the arts we undertake. We say all these things, however, without expressing a decided opinion.

12. *What Is the Aim of Skepticism?* It follows naturally in order to treat of the aim of the Skeptical School. An aim is that for which as an end all things are done or thought, itself depending on nothing, or in other words, it is the ultimatum of things to be desired. We say, then, that the aim of the Skeptic is tranquility in those things which pertain to the opinion, and moderation in the things that life imposes. For as soon as he began to philosophize he wished to discriminate between ideas, and to understand which are true and which are false, in order to attain tranquility. He met, however, with contradictions of equal weight, and, being unable to judge, he withheld his opinion; and while his judgment was in suspension tranquility followed, as if by chance, in regard to matters of opinion. For he who is of the opinion that anything is either good or bad by nature is always troubled, and when he does not possess those things that seem to him good he thinks that he is tortured by the things which are by nature bad, and pursues those that he thinks to be good. Having acquired them, however, he falls into greater perturbation, because he is excited beyond reason and without measure from fear of a change, and he does everything in his power to retain the things that seem to him good. But he who is undecided, on the contrary, regarding things that are good and bad by nature, neither seeks nor avoids anything eagerly, and is therefore in a state of tranquility. For that which is related of Apelles the painter happened to the Skeptic. It is said that as he was once painting a horse he wished to represent the foam of his mouth in the picture, but he could not succeed in doing so, and he gave it up and threw the sponge at the picture with which he had wiped the colors from the painting. As soon, however, as it touched the picture it produced a good copy of the foam. The Skeptics likewise hoped to gain tranquility by forming judgments in regard to the anomaly between appearances and the things of thought, but they were unable to do this, and so they suspended their judgment; and while their judgment was in suspension tranquility followed, as if by chance, as the shadow follows a body. Nevertheless, we do not consider the Skeptic wholly undisturbed, but he is disturbed by some things that are inevitable.

We confess that sometimes he is cold and thirsty, and that he suffers in such ways. But in these things even the ignorant are beset in two ways, from the feelings themselves, and not less also from the fact that they think these conditions are bad by nature. The Skeptic, however, escapes more easily, as he rejects the opinion that anything is in itself bad by nature. Therefore we say that the aim of the Skeptic is tranquility in matters of opinion, and moderation of feeling in those things that are inevitable. Some notable Skeptics have added also suspension of judgment in investigation.

13. *The General Modes of Suspending Judgment.* Since we have said that tranquility follows the suspension of judgment in regard to everything, it behooves us to explain how the suspension of judgment takes place. Speaking in general it takes place through placing things in opposition to each other. We either place appearances in opposition to appearances, or the intellectual in opposition to the intellectual, or reciprocally. For example, we place appearances in opposition to appearances when we say that this tower appears round from a distance but square near by; the intellectual in opposition to the intellectual, when to the one who from the order of the heavens builds a tower of reasoning to prove that a providence exists, we oppose the fact that adversity often falls to the good and prosperity to the evil, and that therefore we draw the conclusion that there is no providence. The intellectual is placed in opposition to appearances, as when Anaxagoras opposed the fact that snow is white, by saying that snow is frozen water, and, as water is black, snow must also be black. Likewise we sometimes place the present in opposition to the present, similarly to the abovementioned cases, and sometimes also the present in opposition to the past or the future. As for example, when someone proposes an argument to us that we cannot refute, we say to him, "Before the founder of the sect to which you belong was born, the argument which you propose in accordance with it had not appeared as a valid argument, but was dormant in nature, so in the same way it is possible that its refutation also exists in nature, but has not yet appeared to us, so that it is not at all necessary for us to agree with an argument that now seems to be strong." In order to make it clearer to us what we mean by these oppositions, I will proceed to give the Modes, through which the suspension of judgment is produced, without asserting anything about their meaning or their number, because they may be unsound, or there may be more than I shall enumerate.

14. *The Ten Modes.* Certain Modes were commonly handed down by the older Skeptics, by means of which suspend judgment seems to take place. They are ten in number, and are called synonymously arguments and points. They are these: The first is based upon the differences in animals; the second upon the differences in men; the third upon the difference in the constitution of the organs of sense; the fourth upon circumstances; the fifth upon position, distance, and place; the sixth upon mixtures; the seventh upon the quantity and constitution of objects; the eighth upon relation; the ninth upon frequency or rarity of occurrences; the tenth upon systems, customs, laws, mythical beliefs, and dogmatic opinions. We

make this order ourselves. These Modes come under three general beads: the standpoint of the judge, the standpoint of the thing judged, and the standpoint of both together. Under the standpoint of the judge come the first four, for the judge is either an animal, or a man, or a sense, and exists under certain circumstances. Under the standpoint of that which is judged, come the seventh and the tenth. Under the one composed of both together, come the fifth and the sixth, the eighth and the ninth. Again, these three divisions are included under the Mode of relation, because that is the most general one; it includes the three special divisions, and these in turn include the ten. We say these things in regard to their probable number, and we proceed in the following chapter to speak of their meaning.

The first Mode, we said, is the one based upon the differences in animals, and according to this Mode, different animals do not get the same ideas of the same objects through the senses. This we conclude from the different origin of the animals, and also from the difference in the constitution of their bodies. . . .

We may see this more clearly in the things that are sought for and avoided by animals. For example, myrrh appears very agreeable to men and intolerable to beetles and bees. Oil also, which is useful to men, destroys wasps and bees if sprinkled on them; and sea-water, while it is unpleasant and poisonous to men if they drink it, is most agreeable and sweet to fishes. Swine also prefer to wash in vile filth rather than in pure clean water. Furthermore, some animals cat grass and some eat herbs; some live in the woods, others eat seeds; some are carnivorous, and others lactivorous; some enjoy putrefied food, and others fresh food; some raw food, and others that which is prepared by cooking; and in general that which is agreeable to some is disagreeable and fatal to others, and should be avoided by them. Thus hemlock makes the quail fat, and henbane the hogs, and these, as it is known, enjoy eating lizards; deer also eat poisonous animals, and swallows, the cantharid. Moreover, ants and flying ants, when swallowed by men, cause discomfort and colic, but the bear, on the contrary, whatever sickness he may have, becomes stronger by devouring them. The viper is benumbed if one twig of the oak touches it, as is also the bat by a leaf of the plane-tree. The elephant flees before the ram, and the lion before the cock, and seals from the rattling of beans that are being pounded, and the tiger from the sound of the drum. Many other examples could be given, but that we may not seem to dwell longer than is necessary on this subject, we conclude by saying that since the same things are pleasant to some and unpleasant to others, and the pleasure and displeasure depend on the ideas, it must be that different animals have different ideas of objects.

And since the same things appear different according to the difference in the animals, it will be possible for us to say how the external object appears to us, but as to how it is in reality we shall suspend our judgment. For we cannot ourselves judge between our own ideas and those of other animals, being ourselves involved in the difference, and therefore much more in need of being judged than being ourselves able to judge. And furthermore, we cannot give the preference to our own mental representations over those of other animals, either without evidence or with evidence, for besides the fact that perhaps there is no evidence, as we shall show, the evidence so called will be either manifest to us or not. If it is not manifest to us, then we cannot accept it with conviction; if it is manifest to us, since the question is in regard to what is manifest to animals, and we use as evidence that which is manifest to us who are animals, then it is to be questioned if it is true as it is manifest to us. It is absurd, however, to try to base the questionable on the questionable, because the same thing is to be believed and not to be believed, which is certainly impossible. The evidence is to be believed insofar as it will furnish a proof, and disbelieved insofar as it is itself to be proved. We shall therefore have no evidence according to which we can give preference to our own ideas over those of so-called irrational animals. Since therefore ideas differ according to the difference in animals, and it is impossible to judge them, it is necessary to suspend the judgment in regard to external objects.

READING 23

*Certainty and the Limits of Doubt**

René Descartes (1569–1650)

MEDITATION 1: OF THE THINGS WHICH MAY BE BROUGHT WITHIN THE SPHERE OF THE DOUBTFUL

It is now some years since I detected how many were the false beliefs that I had from my earliest youth admitted as true, and how doubtful was everything I had since constructed on this basis; and from that time I was convinced that I must once for all seriously undertake to rid myself of all the opinions which I had formerly accepted, and commence to build anew from the foundation, if I wanted to establish any firm and permanent structure in the sciences. But as this enterprise appeared to be a very great one, I waited until I had attained an age so mature that I could not hope that at any later date I should be better fitted to execute my design. This reason caused me to delay so long that I should feel that I was doing wrong were I to occupy in deliberation the time that yet remains to me for action. Today, then, since very oppor-

---

*From René Descartes, Meditations on the First Philosophy (1641), 1 and 2.

tunely for the plan I have in view I have delivered my mind from every care and am happily agitated by no passions and since I have procured for myself an assured leisure in a peaceable retirement, I shall at last seriously and freely address myself to the general upheaval of all my former opinions.

Now for this object it is not necessary that I should show that all of these are false; I shall perhaps never arrive at this end. But inasmuch as reason already persuades me that I ought no less carefully to withhold my assent from matters which are not entirely certain and indubitable than from those which appear to me manifestly to be false, if I am able to find in each one some reason to doubt, this will suffice to justify my rejecting the whole. And for that end it will not be requisite that I should examine each in particular, which would be an endless undertaking; for owing to the fact that the destruction of the foundations of necessity brings with it the downfall of the rest of the edifice, I shall only in the first place attack those principles upon which all my former opinions rested.

All that up to the present time I have accepted as most true and certain I have learned either from the senses or through the senses; but it is sometimes proved to me that these senses are deceptive, and it is wiser not to trust entirely to anything by which we have once been deceived.

But it may be that although the senses sometimes deceive us concerning things which are hardly perceptible, or very far away, there are yet many others to be met with as to which we cannot reasonably have any doubt, although we recognize them by their means. For example, there is the fact that I am here, seated by the fire, attired in a dressing gown, having this paper in my hands and other similar matters. And how could I deny that these hands and this body are mine, were it not perhaps that I compare myself to certain persons, devoid of sense, whose cerebella are so troubled and clouded by the violent vapors of black bile, that they constantly assure us that they think they are kings when they are really quite poor, or that they are clothed in purple when they are really without covering, or who imagine that they have an earthenware head or are nothing but pumpkins or are made of glass. But they are mad, and I should not be any the less insane were I to follow examples so extravagant.

At the same time I must remember that I am a man, and that consequently I am in the habit of sleeping, and in my dreams representing to myself the same things or sometimes even less probable things, than do those who are insane in their waking moments. How often has it happened to me that in the night I dreamt that I found myself in this particular place, that I was dressed and seated near the fire, while in reality I was lying undressed in bed! At this moment it does indeed seem to me that it is with eyes awake that I am looking at this paper; that this head which I move is not asleep, that it is deliberately and of set purpose that I extend my hand and perceive it; what happens in sleep does not appear so clear nor so distinct as does all this. But in thinking over this I remind myself that on many occasions I have in sleep been deceived by similar illusions, and in dwelling carefully on this reflection I see so manifestly that there are no certain indications by which we may clearly distinguish wakefulness from sleep that I am lost in astonishment. And my astonishment is such that it is almost capable of persuading me that I now dream.

Now let us assume that we are asleep and that all these particulars, e.g., that we open our eyes, shake our head, extend our hands, and so on, are but false delusions; and let us reflect that possibly neither our hands nor our whole body are such as they appear to us to be. At the same time we must at least confess that the things which are represented to us in sleep are like painted representations which can only have been formed as the counterparts of something real and true, and that in this way those general things at least, i.e., eyes, a head, hands, and a whole body, are not imaginary things, but things really existent. For, as a matter of fact, painters, even when they study with the greatest skill to represent sirens and satyrs by forms the most strange and extraordinary, cannot give them natures which are entirely new, but merely make a certain medley of the members of different animals; or if their imagination is extravagant enough to invent something so novel that nothing similar has ever before been seen, and that then their work represents a thing purely fictitious and absolutely false, it is certain all the same that the colors of which this is composed are necessarily real. And for the same reason, although these general things, to with, a body, eyes, a head, hands, and such like, may be imaginary, we are bound at the same time to confess that there are at least some other objects yet more simple and more universal, which are real and true; and of these just in the same way as with certain real colors, all these images of things which dwell in our thoughts, whether true and real or false and fantastic, are formed.

To such a class of things pertains corporeal nature in general, and its extension, the figure of extended things, their quantity or magnitude and number, as also the place in which they are, the time which measures their duration, and so on.

That is possibly why our reasoning is not unjust when we conclude from this that Physics, Astronomy, Medicine, and all other sciences which have as their end the consideration of composite things, are very dubious and uncertain; but that Arithmetic, Geometry, and other sciences of that kind which only treat of things that are very simple and very general, without taking great trouble to ascertain whether they are actually existent or not, contain some measure of certainty and an element of the indubitable. For whether I am awake or asleep, two and three together always form five, and the square can never have more than four sides, and it does not seem possible that truths so clear and apparent can be suspected of any falsity or uncertainty.

Nevertheless I have long had fixed in my mind the belief that an all-powerful God existed by whom I have been created such as I am. But how do I know that He has not brought it to pass that there is no earth, no heaven, no extended body, no magnitude, no place, and that nevertheless I possess the perceptions of all these things and that they seem to me to exist just exactly as I now see them? And, besides, as I sometimes imagine that others deceive themselves in the things which they think they know best, how do I know that I am not deceived every time that I add two and three, or count the sides of a square, or judge of things yet simpler, if anything simpler can be imagined? But possibly God has not desired that I should be thus deceived, for He is said to be supremely good. If, however, it is contrary to His goodness to have made me such that I constantly deceive myself, it would also appear to be contrary to His goodness to permit me to be sometimes deceived, and nevertheless I cannot doubt that He does permit this.

There may indeed be those who would prefer to deny the existence of a God so powerful, rather than believe that all other things are uncertain. But let us not oppose them for the present, and grant that all that is here said of a God is a fable; nevertheless in whatever way they suppose that I have arrived at the state of being that I have reached—whether they attribute it to fate or to accident, or make out that it is by a continual succession of antecedents, or by some other method—since to err and deceive oneself is a defect, it is clear that the greater will be the probability of my being so imperfect as to deceive myself ever, as is the Author to whom they assign my origin the less powerful. To these reasons I have certainly nothing to reply, but at the end I feel constrained to confess that there is nothing in all that I formerly believed to be true, of which I cannot in some measure doubt, and that not merely through want of thought or through levity, but for reasons which are very powerful and maturely considered; so that henceforth I ought not the less carefully to refrain from giving credence to these opinions than to that which is manifestly false, if I desire to arrive at any certainty in the sciences.

But it is not sufficient to have made these remarks, we must also be careful to keep them in mind. For these ancient and commonly held opinions still revert frequently to my mind, long and familiar custom having given them the right to occupy my mind against my inclination and rendered them almost masters of my belief; nor will I ever lose the habit of deferring to them or of placing my confidence in them, so long as I consider them as they really are, i.e., opinions in some measure doubtful, as I have just shown, and at the same time highly probable, so that there is much more reason to believe in than to deny them. That is why I consider that I shall not be acting amiss, if, taking of set purpose a contrary belief, I allow myself to be deceived, and for a certain time pretend that all these opinions are entirely false and imaginary, until at last, having thus balanced my former prejudices with my latter so that they cannot divert my opinions more to one side than to the other, my judgment will no longer be dominated by bad usage or turned away from the right knowledge of the truth. For I am assured that there can be neither peril nor error in this course, and that I cannot at present yield too much to distrust, since I am not considering the question of action, but only of knowledge.

I shall then suppose, not that God who is supremely good and the fountain of truth, but some evil genius not less powerful than deceitful, has employed his whole energies in deceiving me; I shall consider that the heavens, the earth, colors, figures, sound, and all other external things are nothing but the illusions and dreams of which this genius has availed himself in order to lay traps for my credulity; I shall consider myself as having no hands, no eyes, no flesh, no blood, nor any senses, yet falsely believing myself to possess all these things; I shall remain obstinately attached to this idea, and if by this means it is not in my power to arrive at the knowledge of any truth, I may at least do what is in my power, i.e., suspend my judgment, and with firm purpose avoid giving credence to any false thing, or being imposed upon by this arch deceiver, however powerful and deceptive he may be. But this task is a laborious one, and insensibly a certain lassitude leads me into the course of my ordinary life. And just as a captive who in sleep enjoys an imaginary liberty, when he begins to suspect that his liberty is but a dream, fears to awaken, and conspires with these agreeable illusions that the deception may be prolonged, so insensibly of my own accord I fall back into my former opinions, and I dread awakening from this slumber, lest the laborious wakefulness which would follow the tranquillity of this repose should have to be spent not in daylight, but in the excessive darkness of the difficulties which have just been discussed.

MEDITATION 2: OF THE NATURE
OF THE HUMAN MIND; AND THAT
IT IS MORE EASILY KNOWN THAN THE BODY

The Meditation of yesterday filled my mind with so many doubts that it is no longer in my power to forget them. And yet I do not see in what manner I can resolve them; and, just as if I had all of a sudden fallen into very deep water, I am so disconcerted that I can neither make certain of setting my feet on the bottom, nor can I swim and so support myself on the surface. I shall nevertheless make an effort and follow anew the same path as that on which I yesterday entered, i.e., I shall proceed by setting aside all that in which the least doubt could be supposed to exist, just as if I had discovered that it was absolutely false; and I shall ever follow in this road until I have met with something which is certain, or at least, if I can do nothing else, until I have learned for certain that there is nothing in the world that is certain. Archimedes, in order that he might draw the terrestrial globe out of its place, and transport it elsewhere, demanded only that one point should be fixed and immoveable; in the same way I shall have the right to conceive high hopes if I am happy enough to discover one thing only which is certain and indubitable.

I suppose, then, that all the things that I see are false; I persuade myself that nothing has ever existed of all that my fallacious memory represents to me. I consider that I possess no senses; I imagine that body, figure, extension, movement and place are but the fictions of my mind. What, then, can be esteemed as true? Perhaps nothing at all, unless that there is nothing in the world that is certain.

But how can I know there is not something different from those things that I have just considered, of which one cannot have the slightest doubt? Is there not some God, or some other being by whatever name we call it, who puts these reflections into my mind? That is not necessary, for is it not possible that I am capable of producing them myself? I myself, am I not at least something?

But I have already denied that I had senses and body. Yet I hesitate, for what follows from that? Am I so dependent on body and senses that I cannot exist without these? But I was persuaded that there was nothing in all the world, that there was no heaven, no earth, that there were no minds, nor any bodies: was I not then likewise persuaded that I did not exist? Not at all; of a surety I myself did exist since I persuaded myself of something or merely because I thought of something. But there is some deceiver or other, very powerful and very cunning, who ever employs his ingenuity in deceiving me. Then without doubt I exist also if he deceives me, and let him deceive me as much as he will, he can never cause me to be nothing so long as I think that I am something. So that after having reflected well and carefully examined all things, we must come to the definite conclusion that this proposition: I am, I exist, is necessarily true each time that I pronounce it, or that I mentally conceive it.

But I do not yet know clearly enough what I am, I who am certain that I am; and hence I must be careful to see that I do not imprudently take some other object in place of myself, and thus that I do not go astray in respect of this knowledge that I hold to be the most certain and most evident of all that I have formerly learned. That is why I shall now consider anew what I believed myself to be before I embarked upon these last reflections; and of my former opinions I shall withdraw all that might even in a small degree be invalidated by the reasons which I have just brought forward, in order that there may be nothing at all left beyond what is absolutely certain and indubitable.

What then did I formerly believe myself to be? Undoubtedly I believed myself to be a man. But what is a man? Shall I say a reasonable animal? Certainly not; for then I should have to inquire what an animal is, and what is reasonable; and thus from a single question I should insensibly fall into an infinitude of others more difficult; and I should not wish to waste the little time and leisure remaining to me in trying to unravel subtleties like these. But I shall rather stop here to consider the thoughts which of themselves spring up in my mind, and which were not inspired by anything beyond my own nature alone when I applied myself to the consideration of my being. In the first place, the, I considered myself as having a face, hands, arms, and all that system of members composed on bones and flesh as seen in a corpse which I designated by the name of body. In addition to this I considered that I was nourished, that I walked, that I felt, and that I thought, and I referred all these actions to the soul: but I did not stop to consider what the soul was, or if I did stop, I imagined that it was something extremely are and subtle like a wind, a flame, or an ether, which was spread throughout my grosser parts. As to body I had no manner of doubt about its nature, but thought I had a very clear knowledge of it; and if I had desired to explain it according to the notions that I had then formed of it, I should have described it thus: By the body I understand all that which can be defined by a certain figure: something which can be confined in a certain place, and which can fill a given space in such a way that every other body will be excluded from it; which can be perceived either by tough, or by sight, or by hearing, or by taste, or by smell: which can be moved in many ways not, in truth, by itself, but by something which is foreign to it, by which it is touched and from which it receives impressions: for to have the power of self-movement, as also of feeling or of thinking, I did not consider to appertain to the nature of body: on the contrary, I was rather astonished to find that faculties similar to them existed in some bodies.

But what am I, now that I suppose that there is a certain genius which is extremely powerful, and, if I may say so, malicious, who employs all his powers in deceiving me? Can I affirm that I possess the least of all those things which I have just said pertain to the nature of body? I pause to consider, I revolve all these things in my mind, and I find none of which I can say that it pertains to me. It would be tedious to stop to enumerate them. Let us pass to the attributes of soul and see if there is any one which is in me? What of nutrition or walking the first mentioned? But if it is so that I have no body it is also true that I can neither walk nor take nourishment. Another attribute is sensation. But one cannot feel without body, and besides I have thought I perceived many things during sleep that I recognized in my waking moments as not having been experienced at all. What of thinking? I find here that thought is an attribute that belongs to me; it alone cannot be separated from me. I am, I exist, that is certain. But how often? Just when I think; for it might possibly be the case if I ceased entirely to think, that I should likewise cease altogether to exist. I do not now admit anything which is not necessarily true: to speak accurately I am not more than a thing which thinks, that is to say a mind or a soul, or an understanding, or a reason, which are terms whose significance was formerly unknown to me. I am, however, a real thing and really exist; but what thing? I have answered: a thing which thinks.

And what more? I shall exercise my imagination in order to see if I am not something more. I am not a collection of members which we call the human body: I am not a subtle air distributed through these members, I am not a wind, a fire, a vapor, a breath, nor anything at all which I can imagine or conceive; because I have assumed that all these were nothing. Without changing that supposition I find that I only leave myself certain of the fact that I am somewhat. But perhaps it is true that these same things which I supposed were non-existent because they are unknown to me, are really not different from the self which I know. I am not sure about this, I shall not dispute about it now; I can only give judgment on things that are known to me. I know that I exist, and I inquire what I am, I whom I know to exist. But it is very certain that the knowledge of my existence taken in its precise significance does not depend on things whose existence is not yet known to me; consequently it does not depend on those which I can feign in imagination. And indeed the very term *feign* in imagination proves to me my error, for I really do this if I image myself a something, since to imagine is nothing else than to contemplate the figure or image of a corporeal thing. But I already know for certain that I am, and that it may be that all these images, and, speaking generally, all things that relate to the nature of body are nothing but dreams and chimeras. For this reason I see clearly that I have as little reason to say, "I shall stimulate my imagination in order to know more distinctly what I am," than if I were to say, "I am now awake, and I perceive somewhat that is real and true: but because I do not yet perceive it distinctly enough, I shall go to sleep of express purpose, so that my dreams may represent the perception with greatest truth and evidence." And, thus, I know for certain that nothing of all that I can understand by means of my imagination belongs to this knowledge which I have of myself, and that it is necessary to recall the mind from this mode of thought with the utmost diligence in order that it may be able to know its own nature with perfect distinctness.

But what then am I? A thing which thinks. What is a thing which thinks? It is a thing which doubts, understands, conceives, affirms, denies, wills, refuses, which also imagines and feels.

Certainly it is no small matter if all these things pertain to my nature. But why should they not so pertain? Am I not that being who now doubts nearly everything, who nevertheless understands certain things, who affirms that one only is true, who denies all the others, who desires to know more, is averse from being deceived, who imagines many things, sometimes indeed despite his will, and who perceives many likewise, as by the intervention of the bodily organs? Is there nothing in all this which is as true as it is certain that I exist, even though I should always sleep and though he who has given me being employed all his ingenuity in deceiving me? Is there likewise any one of these attributes which can be distinguished from my thought, or which might be said to be separated from myself? For it is so evident of itself that it is I who doubts, who understands, and who desires, that there is no reason here to add anything to explain it. And I have certainly the power of imagining likewise; for although it may happen (as I formerly supposed) that none of the things which I imagine are true, nevertheless this power of imagining does not cease to be really in use, and it forms part of my thought. Finally, I am the same who feels, that is to say, who perceives certain things, as by the organs of sense, since it truth I see light, I hear noise, I feel heat. But it will be said that these phenomena are false and that I am dreaming. Let it be so; still it is at least quite certain that it seems to me that I see light, that I hear noise and that I feel heat. That cannot be false; properly speaking it is what is in me called feeling; and used in this precise sense that is no other thing than thinking.

From this time I begin to know what I am with a little more clearness and distinction than before; but nevertheless it still seems to me, and I cannot prevent myself from thinking, that corporeal things, whose images are framed by thought, which are tested by the senses, are much more distinctly known than that obscure part of me which does not come under the imagination. Although really it is very strange to say that I know and understand more distinctly these things whose existence seems to me dubious, which are unknown to me, and which do not belong to me, than others of the truth of which I am convinced, which are known to me and which pertain to my real nature, in a word, than myself. But I see clearly how the case stands: my mind loves to wander, and cannot yet suffer itself to be retained within the just limits of truth. Very good, let us once more give it the freest rein, so that, when afterwards we seize the proper occasion for pulling up, it may the more easily be regulated and controlled.

Let us begin by considering the commonest matters, those which we believe to be the most distinctly comprehended, to wit, the bodies which we touch and see; not indeed bodies in general, for these general ideas are usually a little more confused, but let us consider one body in particular. Let us take, for example, this piece of wax: it has been taken quite freshly from the hive, and it has not yet lost the sweetness of the honey which it contains; it still retains somewhat of the odor of the flowers from which it has been culled; its color, its figure, its size are apparent; it is hard, cold, easily handled, and if you strike it with the finger, it will emit a sound. Finally all the things which are requisite to cause us distinctly to recognize a body, are met with in it. But notice that while I speak and approach the fire what remained of the taste is exhaled, the smell evaporates, the color alters, the figure is destroyed, the size increases, it becomes liquid, it heats, scarcely can one handle it, and when one strikes it, now sound is emitted. Does the same wax remain after this change? We must confess that it remains; none would judge otherwise. What then did I know so distinctly in this piece of wax? It could certainly be nothing of all that the senses brought to my notice, since all these things which fall under taste, smell, sight, touch, and hearing, are found to be changed, and yet the same wax remains.

Perhaps it was what I now think, viz. that this wax was not that sweetness of honey, nor that agreeable scent of flowers, nor that particular whiteness, nor that figure, nor that sound, but simply a body which a little while before appeared tome as perceptible under these forms, and which is now perceptible under others. But what, precisely, is it that I imagine when I form such conceptions? Let us attentively consider this, and, abstracting from all that does not belong to the wax, let us see what remains. Certainly nothing remains excepting a certain extended thing which is flexible and movable. But what is the meaning of flexible and movable? Is it not that I imagine that this piece of wax being round is capable of becoming square and of passing from a square to a triangular figure? No, certainly it is not that, since I imagine it admits of an infinitude of similar changes, and I nevertheless do not know how to compass the infinitude by my imagination, and consequently this conception which I have of the wax is not brought about by the faculty of imagination. What now is this extension? Is it not also unknown? For it becomes greater when the wax is melted, greater when it is boiled, and greater still when the heat increases; and I should not conceive clearly according to truth what wax is, if I did not think that even this piece that we are considering is capable of receiving more variations in extension than I have ever imagined. We must then grant that I could not even understand through the imagination what this piece of wax is, and that it is my mind alone which perceives it. I say this piece of wax in particular, for as to wax in general it is yet clearer. But what is this piece of wax which cannot be understood excepting by the understanding or mind? It is certainly the same that I see, touch, imagine, and finally it is the same which I have always believed it to be from the beginning. But what must particularly be observed is that its perception is neither an act of vision, nor of touch, nor of imagination, and has never been such although it may have appeared formerly to be so, but only an intuition of the mind, which may be imperfect and confused as it was formerly, or clear and distinct as it is at present, according as my attention is more or less directed to the elements which are found in it, and of which it is composed.

Yet in the meantime I am greatly astonished when I consider the great feebleness of mind and its proneness to fall insensibly into error; for although without giving expression to my thought I consider all this in my own mind, words often impede me and I am almost deceived by the terms of ordinary language. For we say that we see the same wax, if it is present, and not that we simply judge that it is the same from its having the same color and figure. From this I should conclude that I knew the wax by means of vision and not simply by the intuition of the mind; unless by chance I remember that, when looking from a window and saying I see men who pass in the street, I really do not see them, but infer that what I see is men, just as I say that I see wax. And yet what do I see from the window but hats and coats which may cover automatic machines? Yet I judge these to be men. And similarly solely by the faculty of judgment which rests in my mind, I comprehend that which I believed I saw with my eyes. . . .

READING 24

The Origin of All Our Ideas in Experience*

John Locke (1632–1704)

[REJECTION OF INNATE IDEAS AND PRINCIPLES]

1.1.1. The way shown how we come by any knowledge, sufficient to prove it not innate   It is an established opinion amongst some men, that there are in the understanding certain innate principles; some primary notions, *koinai ennoiai*, characters, as it were stamped upon the mind of man; which the soul receives in its very first being, and brings into the world with it. It would be sufficient to convince unprejudiced readers of the falseness of this supposition, if I should only show (as I hope I shall in the following parts of this Discourse) how men, barely by the use of their natural faculties, may attain to all the knowledge they have, without the help of any innate impressions; and may arrive at certainty, without any such original notions or principles. For I imagine any one will easily grant that it would be impertinent to suppose the ideas

*From John Locke, *Essay Concerning Human Understanding* (1690), Books 1 and 2.

of colors innate in a creature to whom God has given sight, and a power to receive them by the eyes from external objects: and no less unreasonable would it be to attribute several truths to the impressions of nature, and innate characters, when we may observe in ourselves faculties fit to attain as easy and certain knowledge of them as if they were originally imprinted on the mind.

1.1.15. The steps by which the mind attains several truths   The senses at first let in particular ideas, and furnish the yet empty cabinet, and the mind by degrees growing familiar with some of them, they are lodged in the memory, and names got to them. Afterwards, the mind proceeding further, abstracts them, and by degrees learns the use of general names. In this manner the mind comes to be furnished with ideas and language, the materials about which to exercise its discursive faculty. And the use of reason becomes daily more visible, as these materials that give it employment increase. But though the having of general ideas and the use of general words and reason usually grow together, yet I see not how this any way proves them innate. The knowledge of some truths, I confess, is very early in the mind but in a way that shows them not to be innate. For, if we will observe, we shall find it still to be about ideas, not innate, but acquired; it being about those first which are imprinted by external things, with which infants have earliest to do, which make the most frequent impressions on their senses. . . .

1.1.16. Assent to supposed innate truths depends on having clear and distinct ideas of what their terms mean, and not on their innateness   A child knows not that three and four are equal to seven, till he comes to be able to count seven, and has got the name and idea of equality; and then, upon explaining those words, he presently assents to, or rather perceives the truth of that proposition. But neither does he then readily assent because it is an innate truth, nor was his assent wanting till then because he wanted the use of reason; but the truth of it appears to him as soon as he has settled in his mind the clear and distinct ideas that these names stand for. And then he knows the truth of that proposition upon the same grounds and by the same means, that he knew before that a rod and a cherry are not the same thing; and upon the same grounds also that he may come to know afterwards "That it is impossible for the same thing to be and not to be." . . .

[THE ORIGIN OF ALL OUR IDEAS:
SENSATION AND REFLECTION]

2.1.2. All ideas come from sensation or reflection   Let us then suppose the mind to be, as we say, white paper, void of all characters, without any ideas: How comes it to be furnished? Whence comes it by that vast store which the busy and boundless fancy of man has painted on it with an almost endless variety? Whence has it all the materials of reason and knowledge? To this I answer, in one word, from *experience.* In that all our knowledge is founded; and from that it ultimately derives itself. Our observation employed either, about external sensible objects, or about the internal operations of our minds perceived and reflected on by ourselves, is that which supplies our understandings with all the materials of thinking. These two are the fountains of knowledge, from whence all the ideas we have, or can naturally have, do spring.

2.1.3. The objects of sensation one source of ideas   First, our Senses, conversant about particular sensible objects, do convey into the mind several distinct perceptions of things, according to those various ways wherein those objects do affect them. And thus we come by those ideas we have of yellow, white, heat, cold, soft, hard, bitter, sweet, and all those which we call sensible qualities; which when I say the senses convey into the mind, I mean, they from external objects convey into the mind what produces there those perceptions. This great source of most of the ideas we have, depending wholly upon our senses, and derived by them to the understanding, I call *sensation.*

2.1.4. The operations of our minds, the other source of them   Secondly, the other fountain from which experience furnishes the understanding with ideas is the perception of the operations of our own mind within us, as it is employed about the ideas it has got; which operations, when the soul comes to reflect on and consider, do furnish the understanding with another set of ideas, which could not be had from things without. And such are perception, thinking, doubting, believing, reasoning, knowing, willing, and all the different actings of our own minds; which we being conscious of, and observing in ourselves, do from these receive into our understandings as distinct ideas as we do from bodies affecting our senses. This source of ideas every man has wholly in himself; and though it be not sense, as having nothing to do with external objects, yet it is very like it, and might properly enough be called internal sense. But as I call the other *sensation*, so I call this *reflection*, the ideas it affords being such only as the mind gets by reflecting on its own operations within itself. By reflection then, in the following part of this discourse, I would be understood to mean, that notice which the mind takes of its own operations, and the manner of them, by reason whereof there come to be ideas of these operations in the understanding. These two, I say, viz. external material things, as the objects of *sensation,* and the operations of our own minds within, as the objects of *reflection,* are to me the only originals from whence all our ideas take their beginnings.

[SIMPLE IDEAS]

2.2.1. Uncompounded appearances   The better to understand the nature, manner, and extent of our knowledge, one thing is carefully to be observed concerning the ideas we have; and that is, that some of them are simple and some complex.

Though the qualities that affect our senses are, in the things themselves, so united and blended, that there is no separation, no distance between them, yet it is plain, the ideas they produce in the mind enter by the senses simple and un-mixed. For, though the sight and touch often take in from the same object, at the same time, different ideas—as a man sees at once motion and color; the hand feels softness and warmth in the same piece of wax. Yet, the simple ideas thus united in the same subject, are as perfectly distinct as those that come in by different senses. The coldness and hardness which a man feels in a piece of ice being as distinct ideas in the mind as the smell and whiteness of a lily; or as the taste of sugar, and smell of a rose. And there is nothing can be plainer to a man than the clear and distinct perception he has of those simple ideas; which, being each in itself uncompounded, contains in it nothing but one uniform appearance, or conception in the mind, and is not distinguishable into different ideas.

2.2.2. The mind can neither make nor destroy them These simple ideas, the materials of all our knowledge, are suggested and furnished to the mind only by those two ways above mentioned, viz. sensation and reflection. When the understanding is once stored with these simple ideas, it has the power to repeat, compare, and unite them, even to an almost infinite variety, and so can make at pleasure new complex ideas. But it is not in the power of the most exalted wit, or enlarged understanding, by any quickness or variety of thought, to invent or frame one new simple idea in the mind, not taken in by the ways before mentioned: nor can any force of the understanding destroy those that are there. The dominion of man, in this little world of his own understanding being muchwhat the same as it is in the great world of visible things; wherein his power, however managed by art and skill, reaches no farther than to compound and divide the materials that are made to his hand; but can do nothing towards the making the least particle of new matter, or destroying one atom of what is already in being. The same inability will every one find in himself, who shall go about to fashion in his understanding one simple idea, not received in by his senses from external objects, or by reflection from the operations of his own mind about them. I would have any one try to fancy any taste which had never affected his palate; or frame the idea of a scent he had never smelt: and when he can do this, I will also conclude that a blind man has ideas of colors, and a deaf man true distinct notions of sounds.

[PRIMARY AND SECONDARY QUALITIES OF BODIES]

2.8.8. Our ideas and the qualities of bodies Whatsoever the mind perceives in itself, or is the immediate object of perception, thought, or understanding, that I call idea; and the power to produce any idea in our mind, I call quality of the subject wherein that power is. Thus a snowball having the power to produce in us the ideas of white, cold, and round,—the power to produce those ideas in us, as they are in the snowball, I call qualities; and as they are sensations or perceptions in our understandings, I call them ideas; which ideas, if I speak of sometimes as in the things themselves, I would be understood to mean those qualities in the objects which produce them in us.

2.8.9. Primary qualities of bodies   Qualities thus considered in bodies are, first, such as are utterly inseparable from the body, in what state soever it be; and such as in all the alterations and changes it suffers, all the force can be used upon it, it constantly keeps; and such as sense constantly finds in every particle of matter which has bulk enough to be perceived; and the mind finds inseparable from every particle of matter, though less than to make itself singly be perceived by our senses: e.g., Take a grain of wheat, divide it into two parts; each part has still solidity, extension, figure, and mobility: divide it again, and it retains still the same qualities; and so divide it on, till the parts become insensible; they must retain still each of them all those qualities. For division (which is all that a mill, or pestle, or any other body, does upon another, in reducing it to insensible parts) can never take away either solidity, extension, figure, or mobility from any body, but only makes two or more distinct separate masses of matter, of that which was but one before; all which distinct masses, reckoned as so many distinct bodies, after division, make a certain number. These I call original or *primary qualities* of body, which I think we may observe to produce simple ideas in us, viz. solidity, extension, figure, motion or rest, and number.

2.8.10. Secondary qualities of bodies   Secondly, such qualities which in truth are nothing in the objects themselves but power to produce various sensations in us by their primary qualities, i.e., by the bulk, figure, texture, and motion of their insensible parts, as colors, sounds, tastes, etc. These I call *secondary qualities.* To these might be added a third sort, which are allowed to be barely powers; though they are as much real qualities in the subject as those which I, to comply with the common way of speaking, call qualities, but for distinction, secondary qualities. For the power in fire to produce a new color, or consistency, in wax or clay, by its primary qualities, is as much a quality in fire, as the power it has to produce in me a new idea or sensation of warmth or burning, which I felt not before, by the same primary qualities, viz. the bulk, texture, and motion of its insensible parts.

[COMPLEX IDEAS]

2.12.1. Made by the mind out of simple ones   We have hitherto considered those ideas, in the reception whereof the mind is only passive, which are those simple ones received from sensation and reflection before mentioned, whereof the mind cannot make one to itself, nor have any idea which does not wholly consist of them. But as the mind is wholly passive in the reception of all its simple ideas, so it exerts several acts of its own, whereby out of its simple ideas, as the materials and foundations of the rest, the others are framed. The acts of the mind, wherein it exerts its power over its simple ideas, are chiefly these three. (1) Combining several simple ideas into one compound one; and thus all complex ideas are made. (2) The second is bringing two ideas, whether simple or complex, together, and setting them by one another, so as to take a view of them at once, without uniting them into one; by which way it gets all its ideas of relations. (3) The third is separating them from all other ideas that accompany them in their real existence: this is called abstraction: and thus all its general ideas are made. This shows man's power, and its ways of operation, to be much the same in the material and intellectual world. For the materials in both being such as he has no power over, either to make or destroy, all that man can do is either to unite them together, or to set them by one another, or wholly separate them. I shall here begin with the first of these in the consideration of complex ideas, and come to the other two in their due places. As simple ideas are observed to exist in several combinations united together, so the mind has a power to consider several of them united together as one idea; and that not only as they are united in external objects, but as itself has joined them together. Ideas thus made up of several simple ones put together, I call complex—such as are beauty, gratitude, a man, an army, the universe; which, though complicated of various simple ideas, or complex ideas made up of simple ones, yet are, when the mind pleases, considered each by itself, as one entire thing, and signified by one name.

[THE CONCEPT OF SUBSTANCE]

2.23.1. Ideas of particular substances, how made   The mind being, as I have declared, furnished with a great number of the simple ideas, conveyed in by the senses as they are found in exterior things, or by reflection on its own operations, takes notice also that a certain number of these simple ideas go constantly together; which being presumed to belong to one thing, and words being suited to common apprehensions, and made use of for quick dispatch, are called, so united in one subject, by one name; which, by inadvertency, we are apt afterward to talk of and consider as one simple idea, which indeed is a complication of many ideas together: because, as I have said, not imagining how these simple ideas can subsist by themselves, we accustom ourselves to suppose some substratum wherein they do subsist, and from which they do result, which therefore we call substance.

2.23.2. Our obscure idea of substance in general   So that if any one will examine himself concerning his notion of pure substance in general, he will find he has no other idea of it at all, but only a supposition of he knows not what support of such qualities which are capable of producing simple ideas in us; which qualities are commonly called accidents. If any one should be asked, what is the subject wherein color or weight inheres, he would have nothing to say, but the solid extended parts; and if he were demanded, what is it that solidity and extension adhere in, he would not be in a much better case than the Indian before mentioned who, saying that the world was supported by a great elephant, was asked what the elephant rested on; to which his answer was, a great tortoise; but being again pressed to know what gave support to the broad-backed tortoise, replied, something he knew not what. And thus here, as in all other cases where we use words without having clear and distinct ideas, we talk like children: who, being questioned what such a thing is, which they know not, readily give this satisfactory answer, that it is something: which in truth signifies no more, when so used, either by children or men, but that they know not what; and that the thing they pretend to know, and talk of, is what they have no distinct idea of at all, and so are perfectly ignorant of it, and in the dark. The idea then we have, to which we give the general name substance, being nothing but the supposed, but unknown, support of those qualities we find existing, which we imagine cannot subsist *sine re substante,* without something to support them, we call that support *substantia;* which, according to the true import of the word, is, in plain English, standing under or upholding.

2.23.4. No clear or distinct idea of substance in general   Hence, when we talk or think of any particular sort of corporeal substances, as horse, stone, etc., though the idea we have of either of them be but the complication or collection of those several simple ideas of sensible qualities, which we used to find united in the thing called horse or stone; yet, because we cannot conceive how they should subsist alone, nor one in another, we suppose them existing in and supported by some common subject; which support we denote by the name substance, though it be certain we have no clear or distinct idea of that thing we suppose a support.

READING 25

Empiricism and the Limits of Knowledge[*]

David Hume (1711–1776)

[THE SOURCE OF FACTUAL REASONING]

All the objects of human reason or enquiry may naturally be divided into two kinds, to wit, *relations of ideas,* and *matters of fact.* Of the first kind are the sciences of Geometry, Algebra, and Arithmetic; and in short, every affirmation which is either intuitively or demonstratively certain. *That the square of the hypotenuse is equal to the square of the two sides,* is a proposition which expresses a relation between these figures. *That three times five is equal to the half of thirty,* expresses a relation between these numbers. Propositions of this kind are discoverable by the mere operation of thought, without dependence on what is anywhere existent in the universe. Though there never were a circle or triangle in nature, the truths demonstrated by Euclid would forever retain their certainty and evidence.

---

[*]From David Hume, *Inquiry Concerning Human Understanding,* (1748), Sections 4 and 5.

Matters of fact, which are the second objects of human reason, are not ascertained in the same manner; nor is our evidence of their truth, however great, of a like nature with the foregoing. The contrary of every matter of fact is still possible; because it can never imply a contradiction, and is conceived by the mind with the same facility and distinctness, as if ever so conformable to reality. *That the sun will not rise tomorrow* is no less intelligible a proposition, and implies no more contradiction than the affirmation, *that it will rise.* We should in vain, therefore, attempt to demonstrate its falsehood. Were it demonstratively false, it would imply a contradiction, and could never be distinctly conceived by the mind.

It may, therefore, be a subject worthy of curiosity, to enquire what is the nature of that evidence which assures us of any real existence and matter of fact, beyond the present testimony of our senses, or the records of our memory. This part of philosophy, it is observable, has been little cultivated, either by the ancients or moderns; and therefore our doubts and errors, in the prosecution of so important an enquiry, may be the more excusable; while we march through such difficult paths without any guide or direction. They may even prove useful, by exciting curiosity, and destroying that implicit faith and security, which is the bane of all reasoning and free enquiry. The discovery of defects in the common philosophy, if any such there be, will not, I presume, be a discouragement, but rather an incitement, as is usual, to attempt something more full and satisfactory than has yet been proposed to the public.

All reasonings concerning matter of fact seem to be founded on the relation of *cause and effect.* By means of that relation alone we can go beyond the evidence of our memory and senses. If you were to ask a man, why he believes any matter of fact, which is absent; for instance, that his friend is in the country, or in France; he would give you a reason; and this reason would be some other fact; as a letter received from him, or the knowledge of his former resolutions and promises. A man finding a watch or any other machine in a desert island, would conclude that there had once been men in that island. All our reasonings concerning fact are of the same nature. And here it is constantly supposed that there is a connection between the present fact and that which is inferred from it. Were there nothing to bind them together, the inference would be entirely precarious. The hearing of an articulate voice and rational discourse in the dark assures us of the presence of some person: Why? Because these are the effects of the human make and fabric, and closely connected with it. If we anatomize all the other reasonings of this nature, we shall find that they are founded on the relation of cause and effect, and that this relation is either near or remote, direct or collateral. Heat and light are collateral effects of fire, and the one effect may justly be inferred from the other.

[CAUSE AND EFFECT BASED ON EXPERIENCE]

If we would satisfy ourselves, therefore, concerning the nature of that evidence, which assures us of matters of fact, we must enquire how we arrive at the knowledge of cause and effect.

I shall venture to affirm, as a general proposition, which admits of no exception, that the knowledge of this relation is not, in any instance, attained by reasonings *a priori;* but arises entirely from experience, when we find that any particular objects are constantly conjoined with each other. Let an object be presented to a man of ever so strong natural reason and abilities; if that object be entirely new to him, he will not be able, by the most accurate examination of its sensible qualities, to discover any of its causes or effects. Adam, though his rational faculties be supposed, at the very first, entirely perfect, could not have inferred from the fluidity and transparency of water that it would suffocate him, or from the light and warmth of fire that it would consume him. No object ever discovers, by the qualities which appear to the senses, either the causes which produced it, or the effects which will arise from it; nor can our reason, unassisted by experience, ever draw any inference concerning real existence and matter of fact.

This proposition, *that causes and effects are discoverable, not by reason but by experience,* will readily be admitted with regard to such objects, as we remember to have once been altogether unknown to us; since we must be conscious of the utter inability, which we then lay under, of foretelling what would arise from them. Present two smooth pieces of marble to a man who has no tincture of natural philosophy; he will never discover that they will adhere together in such a manner as to require great force to separate them in a direct line, while they make so small a resistance to a lateral pressure. Such events, as bear little analogy to the common course of nature, are also readily confessed to be known only by experience; nor does any man imagine that the explosion of gunpowder, or the attraction of a loadstone, could ever be discovered by arguments *a priori.* In like manner, when an effect is supposed to depend upon an intricate machinery or secret structure of parts, we make no difficulty in attributing all our knowledge of it to experience. Who will assert that he can give the ultimate reason, why milk or bread is proper nourishment for a man, not for a lion or a tiger?

But the same truth may not appear, at first sight, to have the same evidence with regard to events, which have become familiar to us from our first appearance in the world, which bear a close analogy to the whole course of nature, and which are supposed to depend on the simple qualities of objects, without any secret structure of parts. We are apt to imagine that we could discover these effects by the mere operation of our reason, without experience. We fancy, that were we brought on a sudden into this world, we could at first have inferred that one Billiard-ball would communicate motion to another upon impulse; and that we needed not to have waited for the event, in order to pronounce with certainty concerning it. Such is the influence of custom, that, where it is strongest, it not only covers our natural ignorance, but even conceals itself, and seems not to take place, merely because it is found in the highest degree.

But to convince us that all the laws of nature, and all the operations of bodies without exception, are known only by experience, the following reflections may, perhaps, suffice. Were any object presented to us, and were we required to pronounce concerning the effect, which will result from it, without consulting past observation; after what manner, I beseech you, must the mind proceed in this operation? It must invent or imagine some event, which it ascribes to the object as its effect; and it is plain that this invention must be entirely arbitrary. The mind can never possibly find the effect in the supposed cause, by the most accurate scrutiny and examination. For the effect is totally different from the cause, and consequently can never be discovered in it. Motion in the second Billiard-ball is a quite distinct event from motion in the first; nor is there any thing in the one to suggest the smallest hint of the other. A stone or piece of metal raised into the air, and left without any support, immediately falls: But to consider the matter *a priori,* is there any thing we discover in this situation which can beget the idea of a downward, rather than an upward, or any other motion, in the stone or metal?

And as the first imagination or invention of a particular effect, in all natural operations, is arbitrary, where we consult not experience; so must we also esteem the supposed tie or connection between the cause and effect, which binds them together, and renders it impossible that any other effect could result from the operation of that cause. When I see, for instance, a Billiard-ball moving in a straight line towards another; even suppose motion in the second ball should by accident be suggested to me, as the result of their contact or impulse; may I not conceive, that a hundred different events might as well follow from that cause? May not both these balls remain at absolute rest? May not the first ball return in a straight line, or leap off from the second in any line or direction? All these suppositions are consistent and conceivable. Why then should we give the preference to one, which is no more consistent or conceivable than the rest? All our reasonings *a priori* will never be able to show us any foundation for this preference.

In a word, then, every effect is a distinct event from its cause. It could not, therefore, be discovered in the cause, and the first invention or conception of it, *a priori,* must be entirely arbitrary. And even after it is suggested, the conjunction of it with the cause must appear equally arbitrary; since there are always many other effects, which, to reason, must seem fully as consistent and natural. In vain, therefore, should we pretend to determine any single event, or infer any cause or effect, without the assistance of observation and experience.

Hence we may discover the reason why no philosopher, who is rational and modest, has ever pretended to assign the ultimate cause of any natural operation, or to show distinctly the action of that power, which produces any single effect in the universe. It is confessed, that the utmost effort of human reason is to reduce the principles, productive of natural phenomena, to a greater simplicity, and to resolve the many particular effects into a few general causes, by means of reasonings from analogy, experience, and observation. But as to the causes of these general causes, we should in vain attempt their discovery; nor shall we ever be able to satisfy ourselves, by any particular explication of them. These ultimate springs and principles are totally shut up from human curiosity and enquiry. Elasticity, gravity, cohesion of parts, communication of motion by impulse; these are probably the ultimate causes and principles which we shall ever discover in nature; and we may esteem ourselves sufficiently happy, if, by accurate enquiry and reasoning, we can trace up the particular phenomena to, or near to, these general principles. The most perfect philosophy of the natural kind only staves off our ignorance a little longer: As perhaps the most perfect philosophy of the moral or metaphysical kind serves only to discover larger portions of it. Thus the observation of human blindness and weakness is the result of all philosophy, and meets us at every turn, in spite of our endeavors to elude or avoid it.

Nor is geometry, when taken into the assistance of natural philosophy, ever able to remedy this defect, or lead us into the knowledge of ultimate causes, by all that accuracy of reasoning for which it is so justly celebrated. Every part of mixed mathematics proceeds upon the supposition that certain laws are established by nature in her operations; and abstract reasonings are employed, either to assist experience in the discovery of these laws, or to determine their influence in particular instances, where it depends upon any precise degree of distance and quantity. Thus, it is a law of motion, discovered by experience, that the moment or force of any body in motion is in the compound ratio or proportion of its solid contents and its velocity; and consequently, that a small force may remove the greatest obstacle or raise the greatest weight, if, by any contrivance or machinery, we can increase the velocity of that force, so as to make it an overmatch for its antagonist. Geometry assists us in the application of this law, by giving us the just dimensions of all the parts and figures which can enter into any species of machine; but still the discovery of the law itself is owing merely to experience, and all the abstract reasonings in the world could never lead us one step towards the knowledge of it. When we reason *a priori*, and consider merely any object or cause, as it appears to the mind, independent of all observation, it never could suggest to us the notion of any distinct object, such as its effect; much less, show us the inseparable and inviolable connection between them. A man must be very sagacious who could discover by reasoning that crystal is the effect of heat, and ice of cold, without being previously acquainted with the operation of these qualities.

But we have not yet attained any tolerable satisfaction with regard to the question first proposed. Each solution still gives rise to a new question as difficult as the foregoing, and leads us on to farther enquiries. When it is asked, *What is the nature of all our reasonings concerning matter of fact?* the proper answer seems to be, that they are founded on the relation of cause and effect. When again it is asked, *What is the foundation of all our reasonings and conclusions concerning that relation?* it may be replied in one word, *experience*. But if we still carry on our sifting <u>humor</u>, and ask, *What is the foundation of all conclusions from experience?* this implies a new question, which may be of more difficult solution and explication. Philosophers, that give themselves airs of superior wisdom and sufficiency, have a hard task when they encounter persons of inquisitive dispositions, who push them from every corner to which they retreat, and who are sure at last to bring them to some dangerous dilemma. The best expedient to prevent this confusion, is to be modest in our pretensions;

and even to discover the difficulty ourselves before it is objected to us. By this means, we may make a kind of merit of our very ignorance.

[THE PROBLEM OF INDUCTION]

I shall content myself, in this section, with an easy task, and shall pretend only to give a negative answer to the question here proposed. I say then, that, even after we have experience of the operations of cause and effect, our conclusions from that experience are not founded on reasoning, or any process of the understanding. This answer we must endeavor both to explain and to defend.

It must certainly be allowed, that nature has kept us at a great distance from all her secrets, and has afforded us only the knowledge of a few superficial qualities of objects; while she conceals from us those powers and principles on which the influence of those objects entirely depends. Our senses inform us of the color, weight, and consistence of bread; but neither sense nor reason can ever inform us of those qualities which fit it for the nourishment and support of a human body. Sight or feeling conveys an idea of the actual motion of bodies; but as to that wonderful force or power, which would carry on a moving body for ever in a continued change of place, and which bodies never lose but by communicating it to others; of this we cannot form the most distant conception. But notwithstanding this ignorance of natural powers and principles, we always presume, when we see like sensible qualities, that they have like secret powers, and expect that effects, similar to those which we have experienced, will follow from them. If a body of like color and consistence with that bread, which we have formerly eat, be presented to us, we make no scruple of repeating the experiment, and foresee, with certainty, like nourishment and support. Now this is a process of the mind or thought, of which I would willingly know the foundation. It is allowed on all hands that there is no known connection between the sensible qualities and the secret powers; and consequently, that the mind is not led to form such a conclusion concerning their constant and regular conjunction, by any thing which it knows of their nature. As to past *Experience,* it can be allowed to give *direct* and *certain* information of those precise objects only, and that precise period of time, which fell under its cognizance: But why this experience should be extended to future times, and to other objects, which for aught we know, may be only in appearance similar; this is the main question on which I would insist. The bread, which I formerly eat, nourished me; that is, a body of such sensible qualities was, at that time, endued with such secret powers: But does it follow, that other bread must also nourish me at another time, and that like sensible qualities must always be attended with like secret powers? The consequence seems nowise necessary. At least, it must be acknowledged that there is here a consequence drawn by the mind; that there is a certain step taken; a process of thought, and an inference, which wants to be explained. These two propositions are far from being the same, *I have found that such an object has always been attended with such an effect,* and *I foresee, that other objects, which are, in appear-*

ance, similar, will be attended with similar effects. I shall allow, if you please, that the one proposition may justly be inferred from the other: I know, in fact, that it always is inferred. But if you insist that the inference is made by a chain of reasoning, I desire you to produce that reasoning. The connection between these propositions is not intuitive. There is required a medium, which may enable the mind to draw such an inference, if indeed it be drawn by reasoning and argument. What that medium is, I must confess, passes my comprehension; and it is incumbent on those to produce it, who assert that it really exists, and is the origin of all our conclusions concerning matter of fact.

This negative argument must certainly, in process of time, become altogether convincing, if many penetrating and able philosophers shall turn their inquiries this way and no one be ever able to discover any connecting proposition or intermediate step, which supports the understanding in this conclusion. But as the question is yet new, every reader may not trust so far to his own penetration, as to conclude, because an argument escapes his inquiry, that therefore it does not really exist. For this reason it may be requisite to venture upon a more difficult task; and enumerating all the branches of human knowledge, endeavor to show that none of them can afford such an argument.

All reasonings may be divided into two kinds, namely, demonstrative reasoning, or that concerning relations of ideas, and moral reasoning, or that concerning matter of fact and existence. That there are no demonstrative arguments in the case seems evident; since it implies no contradiction that the course of nature may change, and that an object, seemingly like those which we have experienced, may be attended with different or contrary effects. May I not clearly and distinctly conceive that a body, falling from the clouds, and which, in all other respects, resembles snow, has yet the taste of salt or feeling of fire? Is there any more intelligible proposition than to affirm, that all the trees will flourish in December and January, and decay in May and June? Now whatever is intelligible, and can be distinctly conceived, implies no contradiction, and can never be proved false by any demonstrative argument or abstract reasoning *a priori.*

If we be, therefore, engaged by arguments to put trust in past experience, and make it the standard of our future judgment, these arguments must be probable only, or such as regard matter of fact and real existence according to the division above mentioned. But that there is no argument of this kind, must appear, if our explication of that species of reasoning be admitted as solid and satisfactory. We have said that all arguments concerning existence are founded on the relation of cause and effect; that our knowledge of that relation is derived entirely from experience; and that all our experimental conclusions proceed upon the supposition that the future will be conformable to the past. To endeavor, therefore, the proof of this last supposition by probable arguments, or arguments regarding existence, must be evidently going in a circle, and taking that for granted, which is the very point in question.

In reality, all arguments from experience are founded on the similarity which we discover among natural objects, and by which we are induced to expect effects similar to those which we have found to follow from such objects.

And though none but a fool or madman will ever pretend to dispute the authority of experience, or to reject that great guide of human life, it may surely be allowed a philosopher to have so much curiosity at least as to examine the principle of human nature, which gives this mighty authority to experience, and makes us draw advantage from that similarity which nature has placed among different objects. From causes which, appear *similar,* we expect similar effects. This is the sum of all our experimental conclusions. Now it seems evident that, if this conclusion were formed by reason, it would be as perfect at first, and upon one instance, as after ever so long a course of experience. But the case is far otherwise. [There is] nothing so like as eggs. Yet no one, on account of this appearing similarity, expects the same taste and relish in all of them. It is only after a long course of uniform experiments in any kind, that we attain a firm reliance and security with regard to a particular event. Now where is that process of reasoning which, from one instance, draws a conclusion so different from that which it infers from a hundred instances that are nowise different from that single one? This question I propose as much for the sake of information, as with an intention of raising difficulties. I cannot find, I cannot imagine any such reasoning. But I keep my mind still open to instruction, if any one will vouchsafe to bestow it on me.

Should it be said that, from a number of uniform experiments, we *infer* a connection between the sensible qualities and the secret powers; this, I must confess, seems the same difficulty, couched in different terms. The question still recurs, on what process of argument this *inference* is founded? Where is the medium, the interposing ideas, which join propositions so very wide of each other? It is confessed that the color, consistence, and other sensible qualities of bread appear not, of themselves, to have any connection with the secret powers of nourishment and support. For otherwise we could infer these secret powers from the first appearance of these sensible qualities, without the aid of experience; contrary to the sentiment of all philosophers, and contrary to plain matter of fact. Here, then, is our natural state of ignorance with regard to the powers and influence of all objects. How is this remedied by experience? It only shows us a number of uniform effects, resulting from certain objects, and teaches us that those particular objects, at that particular time, were endowed with such powers and forces. When a new object, endowed with similar sensible qualities, is produced, we expect similar powers and forces, and look for a like effect. From a body of like color and consistence with bread we expect like nourishment and support. But this surely is a step or progress of the mind, which wants to be explained. When a man says, *I have found, in all past instances, such sensible qualities conjoined with such secret powers:* And when he says, *similar sensible qualities will always be conjoined with similar secret powers;* he is not guilty of a tautology, (redundancy) nor are these propositions in any respect the same. You say that the one proposition is an inference from the other. But you must confess that the inference is not intuitive; neither is it demonstrative: Of what nature is it, then? To say it is experimental, is begging the question. For all inferences from experience suppose, as their foundation, that the future will resemble the past, and that similar powers will be conjoined with similar sensible qualities. If there be any suspicion that the course of nature may change, and that the past may be no rule for the future, all experience becomes useless, and can give rise to no inference or conclusion. It is impossible, therefore, that any arguments from experience can prove this resemblance of the past to the future; since all these arguments are founded on the supposition of that resemblance. Let the course of things be allowed hitherto ever so regular; that alone, without some new argument or inference, proves not that, for the future, it will continue so. In vain do you pretend to have learned the nature of bodies from your past experience. Their secret nature, and consequently all their effects and influence, may change, without any change in their sensible qualities. This happens sometimes, and with regard to some objects: Why may it not happen always, and with regard to all objects? What logic, what process or argument secures you against this supposition? My practice, you say, refutes my doubts. But you mistake the purport of my question. As an agent, I am quite satisfied in the point; but as a philosopher, who has some share of curiosity, I will not say skepticism, I want to learn the foundation of this inference. No reading, no enquiry has yet been able to remove my difficulty, or give me satisfaction in a matter of such importance. Can I do better than propose the difficulty to the public, even though, perhaps, I have small hopes of obtaining a solution? We shall at least, by this means, be sensible of our ignorance, if we do not augment our knowledge.

I must confess that a man is guilty of unpardonable arrogance who concludes, because an argument has escaped his own investigation, that therefore it does not really exist. I must also confess that, though all the learned, for several ages, should have employed themselves in fruitless search upon any subject, it may still, perhaps, be rash to conclude positively that the subject must, therefore, pass all human comprehension. Even though we examine all the sources of our knowledge, and conclude them unfit for such a subject, there may still remain a suspicion, that the enumeration is not complete, or the examination not accurate. But with regard to the present subject, there are some considerations which seem to remove all this accusation of arrogance or suspicion of mistake.

It is certain that the most ignorant and stupid peasants—nay infants, nay even brute beasts—improve by experience, and learn the qualities of natural objects, by observing the effects which result from them. When a child has felt the sensation of pain from touching the flame of a candle, he will be careful not to put his hand near any candle; but will expect a similar effect from a cause which is similar in its sensible qualities and appearance. If you assert, therefore, that the understanding of the child is led into this conclusion by any process of argument or ratiocination, I may justly require you to produce that argument; nor have you any pretence to refuse so equitable a demand. You cannot say that the argument is abstruse, and may possibly escape your enquiry; since you confess that it is obvious to the capacity of a mere infant. If you hesitate, therefore, a moment, or if, after reflection, you produce any intricate or profound argument, you, in a manner, give up the question, and confess that it is not reasoning which engages us to suppose the past resembling the future, and to expect similar effects from causes which are, to appearance, similar. This is the proposition which I intended to enforce in the present section. If I be right, I pretend not to have made any mighty discovery. And if I be wrong, I must acknowledge myself to be indeed a very backward scholar; since I cannot now discover an argument which, it seems, was perfectly familiar to me long before I was out of my cradle.

[INFERENCES FROM EXPERIENCE ARE BASED ON HABIT]

. . . Suppose a person, though endowed with the strongest faculties of reason and reflection, to be brought on a sudden into this world; he would, indeed, immediately observe a continual succession of objects, and one event following another; but he would not be able to discover any thing farther. He would not, at first, by any reasoning, be able to reach the idea of cause and effect; since the particular powers, by which all natural operations are performed, never appear to the senses; nor is it reasonable to conclude, merely because one event, in one instance, precedes another, that therefore the one is the cause, the other the effect. Their conjunction may be arbitrary and casual. There may be no reason to infer the existence of one from the appearance of the other. And in a word, such a person, without more experience, could never employ his conjecture or reasoning concerning any matter of fact, or be assured of any thing beyond what was immediately present to his memory and senses.

Suppose, again, that he has acquired more experience, and has lived so long in the world as to have observed familiar objects or events to be constantly conjoined together; what is the consequence of this experience? He immediately infers the existence of one object from the appearance of the other. Yet he has not, by all his experience, acquired any idea or knowledge of the secret power by which the one object produces the other; nor is it by any process of reasoning, he is engaged to draw this inference. But still he finds himself determined to draw it: And though he should be convinced that his understanding has no part in the operation, he would nevertheless continue in the same course of thinking. There is some other principle which determines him to form such a conclusion.

This principle is *custom* or *habit.* For wherever the repetition of any particular act or operation produces a propensity to renew the same act or operation, without being impelled by any reasoning or process of the understanding, we always say, that this propensity is the effect of *Custom.* By employing that word, we pretend not to have given the ultimate reason of such a propensity. We only point out a principle of human nature, which is universally acknowledged, and which is well known by its effects. Perhaps we can push our enquiries no farther, or pretend to give the cause of this cause; but must rest contented with it as the ultimate principle, which we can assign, of all our conclusions from experience. It is sufficient satisfaction, that we can go so far, without repining at the narrowness of our faculties because they will carry us no farther. And it is certain we here advance a very intelligible proposition at least, if not a true one, when we assert that, after the constant conjunction of two objects—heat and flame, for instance, weight and solidity—we are determined by custom alone to expect the one from the appearance of the other. This hypothesis seems even the only one which explains the difficulty, why we draw, from a thousand instances, an inference which we are not able to draw from one instance, that is, in no respect, different from them. Reason is incapable of any such variation. The conclusions which it draws from considering one circle are the same which it would form upon surveying all the circles in the universe. But no man, having seen only one body move after being impelled by another, could infer that every other body will move after a like impulse. All inferences from experience, therefore, are effects of custom, not of reasoning.

Custom, then, is the great guide of human life. It is that principle alone which renders our experience useful to us, and makes us expect, for the future, a similar train of events with those which have appeared in the past. Without the influence of custom, we should be entirely ignorant of every matter of fact beyond what is immediately present to the memory and senses. We should never know how to adjust means to ends, or to employ our natural powers in the production of any effect. There would be an end at once of all action, as well as of the chief part of speculation.

But here it may be proper to remark, that though our conclusions from experience carry us beyond our memory and senses, and assure us of matters of fact which happened in the most distant places and most remote ages, yet some fact must always be present to the senses or memory, from which we may first proceed in drawing these conclusions. A man, who should find in a desert country the remains of pompous buildings, would conclude that the country had, in ancient times, been cultivated by civilized inhabitants; but did nothing of this nature occur to him, he could never form such an inference. We learn the events of former ages from history; but then we must peruse the volumes in which this instruction is contained, and thence carry up our inferences from one testimony to another, till we arrive at the eyewitnesses and spectators of these distant events. In a word, if we proceed not upon some fact, present to the memory or senses, our reasonings would be merely hypothetical; and however the particular links might be connected with each other, the whole chain of inferences would have nothing to support it, nor could we ever, by its means, arrive at the knowledge of any real existence. If I ask why you believe any particular matter of fact, which you relate, you must tell me some reason; and this reason will be some other fact, connected with it. But as you cannot proceed after this manner, *in infinitum*, you must at last terminate in some fact, which is present to your memory or senses; or must allow that your belief is entirely without foundation. . . .

How Is Knowledge Possible*

Immanuel Kant (1724–1804)

I. OF THE DIFFERENCE BETWEEN PURE AND EMPIRICAL KNOWLEDGE

That all our knowledge begins with experience there can be no doubt. For how is it possible that the faculty of knowledge should be awakened into action otherwise than by means of objects which affect our senses, and partly of themselves produce representations, partly rouse our powers of understanding into activity, to compare to connect, or to separate these, and so to convert the raw material of our sensible impressions into a knowledge of objects, which is called experience? In respect of time, therefore, no knowledge of ours is antecedent to experience, but begins with it.

But, though all our knowledge begins with experience, it by no means follows that all arises out of experience. For, on the contrary, it is quite possible that our empirical knowledge is a compound of that which we receive through impressions, and that which the faculty of knowledge supplies from itself (sensible impressions giving merely the occasion), an addition which we cannot distinguish from the original element given by sense, till long practice has made us attentive to, and skilful in separating it.

It is, therefore, a question which requires close investigation, and not to be answered at first sight, whether there exists a knowledge altogether independent of experience, and even of all sensible impressions? Knowledge of this kind is called *a priori,* in contradistinction to empirical knowledge, which has its sources *a posteriori,* that is, in experience.

But the expression, *"a priori,"* is not as yet definite enough adequately to indicate the whole meaning of the question above started. For, in speaking of knowledge which has its sources in experience, we are wont to say, that this or that may be known *a priori,* because we do not derive this knowledge immediately from experience, but from a general rule, which, however, we have itself borrowed from experience. Thus, if a man undermined his house, we say, "he might know *a priori* that it would have fallen;" that is, he needed not to have waited for the experience that it did actually fall. But still, *a priori,* he could not know even this much. For, that bodies are heavy, and, consequently, that they fall when their supports are taken away, must have been known to him previously, by means of experience.

By the term "knowledge *a priori,*" therefore, we shall in the following understand, not such as is independent of this or that kind of experience, but

---

*From Immanuel Kant, *Critique of Pure Reason* (1781), Introduction.

such as is absolutely so of all experience. Opposed to this is empirical knowledge, or that which is possible only *a posteriori,* that is, through experience. Knowledge *a priori* is either pure or impure. Pure knowledge *a priori* is that with which no empirical element is mixed up. For example, the proposition, "Every change has a cause," is a proposition *a priori,* but impure, because change is a conception which can only be derived from experience.

II. THE HUMAN INTELLECT, EVEN IN AN UNPHILOSOPHICAL STATE, IS IN POSSESSION OF CERTAIN MODES OF KNOWLEDGE "*A PRIORI*"

The question now is as to a criterion, by which we may securely distinguish a pure from an empirical knowledge. Experience no doubt teaches us that this or that object is constituted in such and such a manner, but not that it could not possibly exist otherwise. Now, in the first place, if we have a proposition which contains the idea of necessity in its very conception, it is a if, moreover, it is not derived from any other proposition, unless from one equally involving the idea of necessity, it is absolutely priori. Secondly, an empirical judgment never exhibits strict and absolute, but only assumed and comparative universality (by induction); therefore, the most we can say is—so far as we have hitherto observed, there is no exception to this or that rule. If, on the other hand, a judgment carries with it strict and absolute universality, that is, admits of no possible exception, it is not derived from experience, but is valid absolutely *a priori.*

Empirical universality is, therefore, only an arbitrary extension of validity, from that which may be predicated of a proposition valid in most cases, to that which is asserted of a proposition which holds good in all; as, for example, in the affirmation, "All bodies are heavy." When, on the contrary, strict universality characterizes a judgment, it necessarily indicates another peculiar source of knowledge, namely, a faculty of knowledge *a priori.* Necessity and strict universality, therefore, are infallible tests for distinguishing pure from empirical knowledge, and are inseparably connected with each other. But as in the use of these criteria the empirical limitation is sometimes more easily detected than the contingency of the judgment, or the unlimited universality which we attach to a judgment is often a more convincing proof than its necessity, it may be advisable to use the criteria separately, each being by itself infallible.

Now, that in the sphere of human knowledge we have judgments which are necessary, and in the strictest sense universal, consequently pure *a priori,* it will be an easy matter to show. If we desire an example from the sciences, we need only take any proposition in mathematics. If we cast our eyes upon the commonest operations of the understanding, the proposition, "Every change must have a cause," will amply serve our purpose. In the latter case, indeed, the conception of a cause so plainly involves the conception of a necessity of connection with an effect, and of a strict universality of the law, that the very notion of a cause would entirely disappear, were we to derive it, like Hume, from a frequent association of what happens with that which precedes; and the habit thence originating of connecting representations—the necessity inherent in the judgment being therefore merely subjective. Besides, without seeking for such examples of principles existing *a priori* in knowledge, we might easily show that such principles are the indispensable basis of the possibility of experience itself, and consequently prove their existence *a priori*. For whence could our experience itself acquire certainty, if all the rules on which it depends were themselves empirical, and consequently fortuitous? No one, therefore, can admit the validity of the use of such rules as first principles. But, for the present, we may content ourselves with having established the fact, that we do possess and exercise a faculty of pure *a priori* knowledge; and, secondly, with having pointed out the proper tests of such knowledge, namely, universality and necessity.

Not only in judgments, however, but even in conceptions, is an *a priori* origin manifest. For example, if we take away by degrees from our conceptions of a body all that can be referred to mere sensible experience—color, hardness or softness, weight, even impenetrability—the body will then vanish; but the space which it occupied still remains, and this it is utterly impossible to annihilate in thought. Again, if we take away, in like manner, from our empirical conception of any object, corporeal or incorporeal, all properties which mere experience has taught us to connect with it, still we cannot think away those through which we cogitate it as substance, or adhering to substance, although our conception of substance is more determined than that of an object. Compelled, therefore, by that necessity with which the conception of substance forces itself upon us, we must confess that it has its seat in our faculty of knowledge *a priori*.

III. PHILOSOPHY STANDS IN NEED OF A SCIENCE WHICH SHALL DETERMINE THE POSSIBILITY, PRINCIPLES, AND EXTENT OF HUMAN KNOWLEDGE *"A PRIORI"*

Of far more importance than all that has been above said, is the consideration that certain modes of our knowledge rise completely above the sphere of all possible experience, and by means of conceptions, to which there exists in the whole extent of experience no corresponding object, seem to extend the range of our judgments beyond its bounds.

And just in this transcendental or supersensible sphere, where experience affords us neither instruction nor guidance, lie the investigations of reason, which, on account of their importance, we consider far preferable to, and as having a far more elevated aim than, all that the understanding can achieve within the sphere of sensible phenomena. So high a value do we set upon these investigations, that even at the risk of error, we persist in following them out, and permit neither doubt nor disregard nor indifference to restrain us from the pursuit. These unavoidable problems of mere pure reason are *God, freedom* (of will), and *immortality*. The science which, with all its preliminaries, has for its especial object the solution of these problems is named metaphysics—a science which is at the very outset dogmatical, that is, it confidently takes upon itself the execution of this task without any previous investigation of the ability or inability of reason for such an undertaking.

Now the safe ground of experience being thus abandoned, it seems nevertheless natural that we should hesitate to erect a building with the knowledge we possess, without knowing whence they come, and on the strength of principles, the origin of which is undiscovered. Instead of thus trying to build without a foundation, it is rather to be expected that we should long ago have put the question, how the understanding can arrive at this *a priori* knowledge, and what is the extent, validity, and worth which they may possess? We say, "This is natural enough," meaning by the word natural, that which is consistent with a just and reasonable way of thinking; but if we understand by the term, that, which usually happens, nothing indeed could be more natural and more comprehensible than that this investigation should be left long unattempted. For one part of our pure knowledge, the science of mathematics, has been long firmly established, and thus leads us to form flattering expectations with regard to others, though these may be of quite a different nature. Besides, when we get beyond the bounds of experience, we are of course safe from opposition in that quarter; and the charm of widening the range of our knowledge is so great that, unless we are brought to a standstill by some evident contradiction, we hurry on undoubtingly in our course. This, however, may be avoided, if we are sufficiently cautious in the construction of our fictions, which are not the less fictions on that account.

Mathematical science affords us a brilliant example, how far, independently of all experience, we may carry our *a priori* knowledge. It is true that the mathematician occupies himself with objects and knowledge only in so far as they can be represented by means of intuition. But this circumstance is easily overlooked, because the said intuition can itself be given *a priori*, and therefore is hardly to be distinguished from a mere pure conception. Deceived by such a proof of the power of reason, we can perceive no limits to the extension of our knowledge. The light dove cleaving in free flight the thin air, whose resistance it feels, might imagine that her movements would be far more free and rapid in airless space. just in the same way did Plato, abandoning the world of sense because of the narrow limits it sets to the understanding, venture upon the wings of ideas beyond it, into the void space of pure intellect. He did not reflect that he made no real progress by all his efforts; for he met with no resistance which might serve him for a support, as it were, whereon to rest, and on which he might apply his powers, in order to let the intellect acquire momentum for its progress. It is, indeed, the common fate of human reason in speculation, to finish the imposing edifice of thought as rapidly as possible, and then for the first time to begin to examine whether the foundation is a solid one or no. Arrived at this point, all sorts of excuses are sought after, in order to console us for its want of stability, or rather, indeed, to enable Us to dispense altogether with so late and dangerous an investigation. But what frees us during the process of building from all apprehension or suspicion, and flatters us into the belief of its solidity, is this. A great part, perhaps the greatest part, of the business of our reason consists in the analysis of the conceptions which we already possess of objects. By this means we gain a multitude of knowledge, which although really nothing more than elucidations or explanations of that which (though in a confused manner) was already thought in our conceptions, are, at least in respect of their form, prized as new introspections; while, so far as regards their matter or content, we have really made no addition to our conceptions, but only disinvolved them. But as this process does furnish a real priori knowledge, which has a sure progress and useful results, reason, deceived by this, slips in, without being itself aware of it, assertions of a quite different kind; in which, to given conceptions it adds others, *a priori* indeed, but entirely foreign to them, without our knowing how it arrives at these, and, indeed, without such a question ever suggesting itself. I shall therefore at once proceed to examine the difference between these two modes of knowledge.

IV. OF THE DIFFERENCE BETWEEN ANALYTIC AND SYNTHETIC JUDGMENTS

In all judgments wherein the relation of a subject to the predicate is cogitated (I mention affirmative judgments only here; the application to negative will be very easy), this relation is possible in two different ways. Either the predicate B belongs to the subject A, as somewhat which is contained (though covertly) in the conception A; or the predicate B lies completely out of the conception A, although it stands in connection with it. In the first instance, I term the judgment analytic, in the second, synthetic. Analytic judgments (affirmative) are therefore those in which the connection of the predicate with the subject is cogitated through identity; those in which this connection is cogitated without identity, are called synthetic judgments. The former may be called explicative, the latter augmentative judgments; because the former add in the predicate nothing to the conception of the subject, but only analyze it into its constituent conceptions, which were thought already in the subject, although in a confused manner; the latter add to our conceptions of the subject a predicate which was not contained in it, and which no analysis could ever have discovered therein. For example, when I say, "All bodies are extended," this is an analytic judgment. For I need not go beyond the conception of body in order to find extension connected with it, but merely analyze the conception, that is, become conscious of the manifold properties which I think in that conception, in order to discover this predicate in it: it is therefore an analytic judgment. On the other hand, when I say, "All bodies are heavy," the predicate is something totally different from that which I think in the mere conception of a body. By the addition of such a predicate, therefore, it becomes a synthetic judgment.

Judgments of experience, as such, are always synthetic. For it would be absurd to think of grounding an analytic judgment on experience, because in forming such a judgment I need not go out of the sphere of my conceptions, and therefore recourse to the testimony of experience is quite unnecessary. That "bodies are extended" is not an empirical judgment, but a proposition which stands firm *a priori*. For before addressing myself to experience, I already have in my conception all the requisite conditions for the judgment, and I have only to extract the predicate from the conception, according to the principle of contradiction, and thereby at the same time become conscious of the necessity of the judgment, a necessity which I could never learn from experience. On the other hand, though at first I do not at all include the predicate of weight in my conception of body in general, that conception still indicates an object of experience, a part of the totality of experience, to which I can still add other parts; and this I do when I recognize by observation that bodies are heavy. I can cognize beforehand by analysis the conception of body through the characteristics of extension, impenetrability, shape, etc., all which are cogitated in this conception. But now I extend my knowledge, and looking back on experience from which I had derived this conception of body, I find weight at all times connected with the above characteristics, and therefore I synthetically add to my conceptions this as a predicate, and say, "All bodies are heavy." Thus it is experience upon which rests the possibility of the synthesis of the predicate of weight with the conception of body, because both conceptions, although the one is not contained in the other, still belong to one another (only contingently, however), as parts of a whole, namely, of experience, which is itself a synthesis of intuitions.

But to synthetic judgments *a priori*, such aid is entirely wanting. If I go out of and beyond the conception A, in order to recognize another B as connected with it, what foundation have I to rest on, whereby to render the synthesis possible? I have here no longer the advantage of looking out in the sphere of experience for what I want. Let us take, for example, the proposition, "Everything that happens has a cause." In the conception of "something that happens," I indeed think an existence which a certain time antecedes, and from this I can derive analytic judgments. But the conception of a cause lies quite out of the above conception, and indicates something entirely different from "that which happens," and is consequently not contained in that conception. How then am I able to assert concerning the general conception—"that which happens"— something entirely different from that conception, and to recognize the conception of cause although not contained in it, yet as belonging to it, and even necessarily? what is here the unknown = X, upon which the understanding rests when it believes it has found, out of the conception A a foreign predicate B, which it nevertheless considers to be connected with it? It cannot be experience, because the principle adduced annexes the two representations, cause and effect, to the representation existence, not only with universality, which experience cannot give, but also with the expression of necessity, therefore completely *a priori* and from pure conceptions. Upon such synthetic, that is augmentative propositions, depends the whole aim of our speculative knowledge *a priori*; for although analytic judgments are indeed highly important and necessary, they are so, only to arrive at that clearness of conceptions which is requisite for a sure and extended synthesis, and this alone is a real acquisition.

V. IN ALL THEORETICAL SCIENCES OF REASON, SYNTHETIC JUDGMENTS *"A PRIORI"* ARE CONTAINED AS PRINCIPLES

1. *Mathematical judgments are always synthetic.* Hitherto this fact, though incontestably true and very important in its consequences, seems to have escaped the analysts of the human mind, nay, to be in complete opposition to all their conjectures. For as it was found that mathematical conclusions all proceed according to the principle of contradiction (which the nature of every apodeictic certainty requires), people became persuaded that the fundamental principles of the science also were recognized and admitted in the same way. But the notion is fallacious; for although a synthetic proposition can certainly be discerned by means of the principle of contradiction, this is possible only when another synthetic proposition precedes, from which the latter is deduced, but never in and of itself.

Before all, be it observed, that proper mathematical propositions are always judgments *a priori*, and not empirical, because they carry along with them the conception of necessity, which cannot be given by experience. If this be demurred to, it matters not; I will then limit my assertion to pure mathematics, the very conception of which implies that it consists of knowledge altogether non-empirical and *a priori*.

We might, indeed at first suppose that the proposition $7 + 5 = 12$ is a merely analytic proposition, following (according to the principle of contradiction) from the conception of a sum of seven and five. But if we regard it more narrowly, we find that our conception of the sum of seven and five contains nothing more than the uniting of both sums into one, whereby it cannot at all be cogitated what this single number is which embraces both. The conception of twelve is by no means obtained by merely cogitating the union of seven and five; and we may analyze our conception of such a possible sum as long as we will, still we shall never discover in it the notion of twelve. We must go beyond these conceptions, and have recourse to an intuition which corresponds to one of the two—our five fingers, for example, or like Segner in his Arithmetic five points, and so by degrees, add the units contained in the five given in the intuition, to the conception of seven. For I first take the number 7, and, for the conception of 5 calling in the aid of the fingers of my hand as objects of intuition, I add the units, which I before took together to make up the number 5, gradually now by means of the material image my hand, to the number 7, and by this process, I at length see the number 12 arise. That 7 should be added to 5, I have certainly cogitated in my conception of a sum $= 7 + 5$, but not that this sum was equal to 12. Arithmetical propositions are therefore always synthetic, of which we may become more clearly convinced by trying large numbers. For it will thus become quite evident that, turn and twist our conceptions as we may, it is impossible, without having recourse to intuition, to arrive at the sum total or product by means of the mere analysis of our conceptions. just as little is any principle of pure geometry analytic. "A straight line between two points is the shortest," is a synthetic proposition. For my conception of straight contains no notion of quantity, but is merely qualitative. The conception of the shortest is therefore fore wholly an addition, and by no analysis can it be extracted from our conception of a straight line. Intuition must therefore here lend its aid, by means of which, and thus only, our synthesis is possible.

Some few principles preposited by geometricians are, indeed, really analytic, and depend on the principle of contradiction. They serve, however, like identical propositions, as links in the chain of method, not as principles—for example, a = a, the whole is equal to itself, or (a + b) > a, the whole is greater than its part. And yet even these principles themselves, though they derive their validity from pure conceptions, are only admitted in mathematics because they can be presented in intuition. What causes us here commonly to believe that the predicate of such apodeictic judgments is already contained in our conception, and that the judgment is therefore analytic, is merely the equivocal nature of the expression. We must join in thought a certain predicate to a given conception, and this necessity cleaves already to the conception. But the question is, not what we must join in thought to the given conception, but what we really think therein, though only obscurely, and then it becomes manifest that the predicate pertains to these conceptions, necessarily indeed, yet not as thought in the conception itself, but by virtue of an intuition, which must be added to the conception.

2. *The science of natural philosophy (physics) contains in itself synthetic judgments* **A Priori,** as principles. I shall adduce two propositions. For instance, the proposition, "In all changes of the material world, the quantity of matter remains unchanged"; or, that, "In all communication of motion, action and reaction must always be equal." In both of these, not only is the necessity, and therefore their origin *a priori* clear, but also that they are synthetic propositions. For in the conception of matter, I do not cogitate its permanency, but merely its presence in space, which it fills. I therefore really go out of and beyond the conception of matter, in order to think on to it something *a priori,* which I did not think in it. The proposition is therefore not analytic, but synthetic, and nevertheless conceived *a priori;* and so it is with regard to the other propositions of the pure part of natural philosophy.

3. As to **metaphysics,** even if we look upon it merely as an attempted science, yet, from the nature of human reason, an indispensable one, we find that it must contain synthetic propositions *a priori.* It is not merely the duty of metaphysics to dissect, and thereby analytically to illustrate the conceptions which we form *a priori* of things; but we seek to widen the range of our *a priori* knowledge. For this purpose, we must avail ourselves of such principles as add something to the original conception— something not identical with, nor contained in it, and by means of synthetic judgments *a priori,* leave far behind us the limits of experience; for

example, in the proposition, "the world must have a beginning," and such like. Thus metaphysics, according to the proper aim of the science, consists merely of synthetic propositions *a priori.*

VI. THE UNIVERSAL PROBLEM OF PURE REASON

It is extremely advantageous to be able to bring a number of investigations under the formula of a single problem. For in this manner, we not only facilitate our own labor, inasmuch as we define it clearly to ourselves, but also render it more easy for others to decide whether we have done justice to our undertaking. The proper problem of pure reason, then, is contained in the question: "How are synthetic judgments *a priori* possible?"

That metaphysical science has hitherto remained in so vacillating a state of uncertainty and contradiction, is only to be attributed to the fact that this great problem, and perhaps even the difference between analytic and synthetic judgments, did not sooner suggest itself to philosophers. Upon the solution of this problem, or upon sufficient proof of the impossibility of synthetic knowledge *a priori,* depends the existence or downfall of the science of metaphysics. Among philosophers, David Hume came the nearest of all to this problem; yet it never acquired in his mind sufficient precision, nor did he regard the question in its universality. On the contrary, he stopped short at the synthetic proposition of the connection of an effect with its cause (*principium causalitatis*), insisting that such proposition *a priori* was impossible.

According to his conclusions, then, all that we term metaphysical science is a mere delusion, arising from the fancied insight of reason into that which is in truth borrowed from experience, and to which habit has given the appearance of necessity. Against this assertion, destructive to all pure philosophy, he would have been guarded, had he had our problem before his eyes in its universality. For he would then have perceived that, according to his own argument, there likewise could not be any pure mathematical science, which assuredly cannot exist without synthetic propositions *a priori*—an absurdity from which his good understanding must have saved him.

In the solution of the above problem is at the same time comprehended the possibility of the use of pure reason in the foundation and construction of all sciences which contain theoretical knowledge *a priori* of objects, that is to say, the answer to the following questions:

How is pure mathematical science possible?
How is pure natural science possible?

Respecting these sciences, as they do certainly exist, it may with propriety be asked, how they are possible?—for that they must be possible is shown by the fact of their really existing. But as to metaphysics, the miserable progress it has hitherto made, and the fact that of no one system yet brought forward, far as regards its true aim, can it be said that this science really exists, leaves any one at liberty to doubt with reason the very possibility of its existence.

Yet, in a certain sense, this kind of knowledge must unquestionably be looked upon as given; in other words, metaphysics must be considered as really existing, if not as a science, nevertheless as a natural disposition of the human mind (*metaphysica naturalis*). For human reason, without any instigations imputable to the mere vanity of great knowledge, unceasingly progresses, urged on by its own feeling of need, towards such questions as cannot be answered by any empirical application of reason, or principles derived therefrom; and so there has ever really existed in every man some system of metaphysics. It will always exist, so soon as reason awakes to the action of its power of speculation. And now the question arises: "How is metaphysics, as a natural disposition, possible?" In other words, how, from the nature of universal human reason, do those questions arise which pure reason proposes to itself, and which it is impelled by its own feeling of need to answer as well as it can?

But as in all the attempts hitherto made to answer the questions which reason is prompted by its very nature to propose to itself, for example, whether the world had a beginning, or has existed from eternity, it has always met with unavoidable contradictions, we must not rest satisfied with the mere natural disposition of the mind to metaphysics, that is, with the existence of the faculty of pure reason, whence, indeed, some sort of metaphysical system always arises; but it must be possible to arrive at certainty in regard to the question whether we know or do not know the things of which metaphysics treats. We must be able to arrive at a decision on the subjects of its questions, or on the ability or inability of reason to form any judgment respecting them; and therefore either to extend with confidence the bounds of our pure reason, or to set strictly defined and safe limits to its action. This last question, which arises out of the above universal problem, would properly run thus: "How is metaphysics possible as a science?"

Thus, the critique of reason leads at last, naturally and necessarily, to science; and, on the other hand, the dogmatical use of reason without criticism leads to groundless assertions, against which others equally specious can always be set, thus ending unavoidably in skepticism.

Besides, this science cannot be of great and formidable prolixity, because it has not to do with objects of reason, the variety of which is inexhaustible, but merely with Reason herself and her problems; problems which arise out of her own bosom, and are not proposed to her by the nature of outward things, but by her own nature. And when once Reason has previously become able completely to understand her own power in regard to objects which she meets with in experience, it will be easy to determine securely the extent and limits of her attempted application to objects beyond the confines of experience.

We may and must, therefore, regard the attempts hitherto made to establish metaphysical science dogmatically as non-existent. For what of analysis, that is, mere dissection of conceptions, is contained in one or other, is not the aim of, but only a preparation for metaphysics proper, which has for its object the extension, by means of synthesis, of our *a priori* knowledge. And for this purpose, mere analysis is of course useless, because it only shows what is contained in these conceptions, but not how we arrive, *a priori*, at them; and this it is her duty to show, in order to be able afterwards to determine their valid use in regard to all objects of experience, to all knowledge in general. But little self-denial, indeed, is needed to give up these pretensions, seeing the undeniable, and in the dogmatic mode of procedure, inevitable contradictions of Reason with herself, have long since ruined the reputation of every system of metaphysics that has appeared up to this time. It will require more firmness to remain undeterred by difficulty from within, and opposition from without, from endeavoring, by a method quite opposed to all those hitherto followed, to further the growth and fruitfulness of a science indispensable to human reason—a science from which every branch it has borne may be cut away, but whose roots remain indestructible.

VII. IDEA AND DIVISION OF A PARTICULAR SCIENCE, UNDER THE NAME OF A CRITIQUE OF PURE REASON

From all that has been said, there results the idea of a particular science, which may be called the Critique of Pure Reason. For reason is the faculty which furnishes us with the principles of knowledge *a priori*. Hence, pure reason is the faculty which contains the principles of cognizing anything absolutely *a priori*.

READING 27

*Pragmatism's Conception of Truth**

William James (1842–1910)

When Clerk Maxwell was a child it is written that he had a mania for having everything explained to him, and that when people put him off with vague verbal accounts of any phenomenon he would interrupt them impatiently by saying, 'Yes; but I want you to tell me the *particular* go of it!' Had his question been about truth, only a pragmatist could have told him the particular go of it. I believe that our contemporary pragmatists, especially Messrs. Schiller and Dewey, have given the only tenable account of this subject. It is a very ticklish subject, sending subtle rootlets into all kinds of crannies, and hard to treat in the sketchy way that alone befits a public lecture. But the Schiller-Dewey view of truth has been so ferociously attacked by rationalistic philosophers, and so abominably misunderstood, that here, if anywhere, is the point where a clear and simple statement should be made.

*From William James, *Pragmatism: A New Name for Some Old Ways of Thinking* (1907), Lecture 6.

I fully expect to see the pragmatist view of truth run through the classic stages of a theory's career. First, you know, a new theory is attacked as absurd; then it is admitted to be true, but obvious and insignificant; finally it is seen to be so important that its adversaries claim that they themselves discovered it. Our doctrine of truth is at present in the first of these three stages, with symptoms of the second stage having begun in certain quarters. I wish that this lecture might help it beyond the first stage in the eyes of many of you.

[CORRESPONDENCE VERSUS PRAGMATIC THEORY OF TRUTH]

Truth, as any dictionary will tell you, is a property of certain of our ideas. It means their 'agreement,' as falsity means their disagreement, with 'reality.' Pragmatists and intellectualists both accept this definition as a matter of course. They begin to quarrel only after the question is raised as to what may precisely be meant by the term 'agreement,' and what by the term 'reality,' when reality is taken as something for our ideas to agree with.

In answering these questions the pragmatists are more analytic and painstaking, the intellectualists more offhand and irreflective. The popular notion is that a true idea must copy its reality. Like other popular views, this one follows the analogy of the most usual experience. Our true ideas of sensible things do indeed copy them. Shut your eyes and think of yonder clock on the wall, and you get just such a true picture or copy of its dial. But your idea of its 'works' (unless you are a clock-maker) is much less of a copy, yet it passes muster, for it in no way clashes with the reality. Even though it should shrink to the mere word 'works,' that word still serves you truly; and when you speak of the 'time-keeping function' of the clock, or of its spring's 'elasticity,' it is hard to see exactly what your ideas can copy.

You perceive that there is a problem here. Where our ideas cannot copy definitely their object, what does agreement with that object mean? Some idealists seem to say that they are true whenever they are what God means that we ought to think about that object. Others hold the copy-view all through, and speak as if our ideas possessed truth just in proportion as they approach to being copies of the Absolute's eternal way of thinking.

These views, you see, invite pragmatistic discussion. But the great assumption of the intellectualists is that truth means essentially an inert static relation. When you've got your true idea of anything, there's an end of the matter. You're in possession; you *know;* you have fulfilled your thinking destiny. You are where you ought to be mentally; you have obeyed your categorical imperative; and nothing more need follow on that climax of your rational destiny. Epistemologically you are in stable equilibrium.

Pragmatism, on the other hand, asks its usual question. "Grant an idea or belief to be true," it says, "what concrete difference will its being true make in anyone's actual life? How will the truth be realized? What experiences will be different from those which would obtain if the belief were false? What, in short, is the truth's cash-value in experiential terms?"

The moment pragmatism asks this question, it sees the answer: *True ideas are those that we can assimilate, validate, corroborate, and verify. False ideas are those that we cannot.* That is the practical difference it makes to us to have true ideas; that, therefore, is the meaning of truth, for it is all that truth is known-as.

This thesis is what I have to defend. The truth of an idea is not a stagnant property inherent in it. Truth *happens* to an idea. It *becomes* true, is *made* true by events. Its verity *is* in fact an event, a process: the process namely of its verifying itself, its veri-*fication*. Its validity is the process of its valid-*ation*.

[THE PROCESS OF VERIFYING TRUTH]

But what do the words verification and validation themselves pragmatically mean? They again signify certain practical consequences of the verified and validated idea. It is hard to find any one phrase that characterizes these consequences better than the ordinary agreement-formula—just such consequences being what we have in mind whenever we say that our ideas 'agree' with reality. They lead us, namely, through the acts and other ideas which they instigate, into or up to, or towards, other parts of experience with which we feel all the while—such feeling being among our potentialities—that the original ideas remain in agreement. The connections and transitions come to us from point to point as being progressive, harmonious, satisfactory. This function of agreeable leading is what we mean by an idea's verification. Such an account is vague and it sounds at first quite trivial, but it has results which it will take the rest of my hour to explain.

Let me begin by reminding you of the fact that the possession of true thoughts means everywhere the possession of invaluable instruments of action; and that our duty to gain truth, so far from being a blank command from out of the blue, or a 'stunt' self-imposed by our intellect, can account for itself by excellent practical reasons.

The importance to human life of having true beliefs about matters of fact is a thing too notorious. We live in a world of realities that can be infinitely useful or infinitely harmful. Ideas that tell us which of them to expect count as the true ideas in all this primary sphere of verification, and the pursuit of such ideas is a primary human duty. The possession of truth, so far from being here an end in itself, is only a preliminary means towards other vital satisfactions. If I am lost in the woods and starved, and find what looks like a cow-path, it is of the utmost importance that I should think of a human habitation at the end of it, for if I do so and follow it, I save myself. The true thought is useful here because the house which is its object is useful. The practical value of true ideas is thus primarily derived from the practical importance of their objects to us. Their objects are, indeed, not important at all times. I may on another occasion have no use for the house; and then my idea of it, however verifiable, will be practically irrelevant, and had better remain latent. Yet since almost any object may some day become temporarily important, the advantage of having a general stock of *extra* truths, of ideas that shall be true of merely possible situations, is obvious. We store such extra truths away in our memories, and with the overflow we fill our books of reference. Whenever such an extra truth becomes practically relevant to one of our emergencies, it passes from cold-storage to do work in the world, and our belief in it grows active. You can say of it then either that 'it is useful because it is true' or that 'it is true because it is useful.' Both these phrases mean exactly the same thing, namely that here is an idea that gets fulfilled and can be verified. True is the name for whatever idea starts the verification-process, useful is the name for its completed function in experience. True ideas would never have been singled out as such, would never have acquired a class-name, least of all a name suggesting value, unless they had been useful from the outset in this way.

From this simple cue pragmatism gets her general notion of truth as something essentially bound up with the way in which one moment in our experience may lead us towards other moments which it will be worth while to have been led to. Primarily, and on the common-sense level, the truth of a state of mind means this function of *a leading that is worthwhile*. When a moment in our experience, of any kind whatever, inspires us with a thought that is true, that means that sooner or later we dip by that thought's guidance into the particulars of experience again and make advantageous connection with them. This is a vague enough statement, but I beg you to retain it, for it is essential.

Our experience meanwhile is all shot through with regularities. One bit of it can warn us to get ready for another bit, can 'Intend' or be significant of that remoter object. The object's advent is the significance's verification. Truth, in these cases, meaning nothing but eventual verification, is manifestly incompatible with waywardness on our part. Woe to him whose beliefs play fast and loose with the order which realities follow in his experience: they will lead him nowhere or else make false connections.

By 'realities' or 'objects' here, we mean either things of common sense, sensibly present, or else common-sense relations, such as dates, places, distances, kinds, activities. Following our mental image of a house along the cowpath, we actually come to see the house; we get the image's full verification. *Such simply and fully verified leadings are certainly the originals and prototypes of the truth-process.* Experience offers indeed other forms of truth-process, but they are all conceivable as being primary verifications arrested, multiplied or substituted one for another.

Take, for instance, yonder object on the wall. You and I consider it to be a 'clock,' although no one of us has seen the hidden works that make it one. We let our notion pass for true without attempting to verify. If truths mean verification-process essentially, ought we then to call such unverified truths as this abortive? No, for they form the overwhelmingly large number of the truths we live by. Indirect as well as direct verifications pass muster. Where circumstantial evidence is sufficient, we can go without eye-witnessing. Just as we here assume Japan to exist without ever having been there, because it *works* to do so, everything we know conspiring with the belief, and nothing interfering, so we assume that thing to be a clock. We *use* it as a clock, regulating the length of our lecture by it. The verification of the assumption here means its leading to no frustration or contradiction. Verifiability of wheels and weights and pendulum is as good as verification. For one truth-process completed there are a million in our lives that function in this state of nascency. They turn us *towards* direct verification; lead us into the *surroundings* of the objects they envisage; and then, if everything runs on harmoniously, we are so sure that verification is possible that we omit it, and are usually justified by all that happens.

Truth lives, in fact, for the most part on a credit system. Our thoughts and beliefs 'pass,' so long as nothing challenges them, just as bank-notes pass so long as nobody refuses them. But this all points to direct face-to-face verifications somewhere, without which the fabric of truth collapses like a financial system with no cash-basis whatever. You accept my verification of one thing, I yours of another. We trade on each other's truth. But beliefs verified concretely by *somebody* are the posts of the whole superstructure.

Another great reason—beside economy of time—for waiving complete verification in the usual business of life is that all things exist in kinds and not singly. Our world is found once for all to have that peculiarity. So that when we have once directly verified our ideas about one specimen of a kind, we consider ourselves free to apply them to other specimens without verification. A mind that habitually discerns the kind of thing before it, and acts by the law of the kind immediately, without pausing to verify, will be a 'true' mind in ninety-nine out of a hundred emergencies, proved so by its conduct fitting everything it meets, and getting no refutation.

Indirectly or only potentially verifying processes may thus be true as well as full verification processes. They work as true processes would work, give us the same advantages, and claim our recognition for the same reasons. All this on the common-sense level of matters of fact, which we are alone considering.

[VERIFYING MENTAL RELATIONS AMONG IDEAS]

But matters of fact are not our only stock in trade. *Relations among purely mental ideas* form another sphere where true and false beliefs obtain, and here the beliefs are absolute, or unconditional. When they are true they bear the name either of definitions or of principles. It is either a principle or a definition that 1 and 1 make 2, that 2 and 1 make 3, and so on; that white differs less from gray than it does from black; that when the cause begins to act the effect also commences. Such propositions hold of all possible 'ones,' of all conceivable 'whites' and 'grays' and 'causes.' The objects here are mental objects. Their relations are perceptually obvious at a glance, and no sense-verification is necessary. Moreover, once true, always true, of those same mental objects. Truth here has an 'eternal' character. If you can find a concrete thing anywhere that is 'one' or 'white' or 'gray,' or an 'effect,' then your principles will everlastingly apply to it. It is but a case of ascertaining the kind, and then applying the law of its kind to the particular object. You are sure to get truth if you can but name the kind rightly, for your mental relations hold good of everything of that kind without exception. If you then, nevertheless, failed to get truth concretely, you would say that you had classed your real objects wrongly.

In this realm of mental relations, truth again is an affair of leading. We relate one abstract idea with another, framing in the end great systems of logical and mathematical truth, under the respective terms of which the sensible facts of experience eventually arrange themselves, so that our eternal truths hold good of realities also. This marriage of fact and theory is endlessly fertile. What we say is here already true in advance of special verification, *if we have subsumed our objects rightly.* Our ready-made ideal framework for all sorts of possible objects follows from the very structure of our thinking. We can no more play fast and loose with these abstract relations than we can do so with our sense-experiences. They coerce us; we must treat them consistently, whether or not we like the results. The rules of addition apply to our debts as rigorously as to our assets. The hundredth decimal of pi the ratio of the circumference to its diameter, is predetermined ideally now, though no one may have computed it. If we should ever need the figure in our dealings with an actual circle we should need to have it given rightly, calculated by the usual rules; for it is the same kind of truth that those rules elsewhere calculate.

Between the coercions of the sensible order and those of the ideal order, our mind is thus wedged tightly. Our ideas must agree with realities, be such realities concrete or abstract, be they facts or be they principles, under penalty of endless inconsistency and frustration.

So far, intellectualists can raise no protest. They can only say that we have barely touched the skin of the matter.

Realities mean, then, either concrete facts, or abstract kinds of things and relations perceived intuitively between them. They furthermore and thirdly mean, as things that new ideas of ours must no less take account of, the whole body of other truths already in our possession. But what now does 'agreement' with such threefold realities mean?—to use again the definition that is current.

["AGREEMENT" AS USEFUL LEADING]

Here it is that pragmatism and intellectualism begin to part company. Primarily, no doubt, to agree means to copy, but we saw that the mere word 'clock' would do instead of a mental picture of its works, and that of many realities our ideas can only be symbols and not copies. 'Past time,' 'power,' 'spontaneity'—how can our mind copy such realities?

To 'agree' in the widest sense with a reality, *can only mean to be guided either straight up to it or into its surroundings, or to be put into such working touch with it as to handle either it or something connected with it better than if we disagreed.* Better either intellectually or practically! And often agreement will only mean the negative fact that nothing contradictory from the quarter of that reality comes to interfere with the way in which our ideas guide us elsewhere. To copy a reality is, indeed, one very important way of agreeing with it, but it is far from being essential. The essential thing is the process of being guided. Any idea that helps us to *deal,* whether practically or intellectually, with either the reality or its belongings, that doesn't entangle our progress in frustrations, that *fits,* in fact, and adapts our life to the reality's whole setting, will agree sufficiently to meet the requirement. It will hold true of that reality.

Thus, *names* are just as 'true' or 'false' as definite mental pictures are. They set up similar verification-processes, and lead to fully equivalent practical results.

All human thinking gets discursified; we exchange ideas; we lend and borrow verifications, get them from one another by means of social intercourse. All truth thus gets verbally built out, stored up, and made available for everyone. Hence, we must *talk* consistently just as we must *think* consistently: for both in talk and thought we deal with kinds. Names are arbitrary, but once understood they must be kept to. We mustn't now call Abel 'Cain' or Cain 'Abel.' If we do, we ungear ourselves from the whole book of Genesis, and from all its connections with the universe of speech and fact down to the present time. We throw ourselves out of whatever truth that entire system of speech and fact may embody.

The overwhelming majority of our true ideas admit of no direct or face-to-face verification—those of past history, for example, as of Cain and Abel. The stream of time can be remounted only verbally, or verified indirectly by the present prolongations or effects of what the past harbored. Yet if they agree with these verbalities and effects, we can know that our ideas of the past are true. *As true as past time itself was,* so true was Julius Caesar, so true were antediluvian monsters, all in their proper dates and settings. That past time itself was, is guaranteed by its coherence with everything that's present. True as the present *is,* the past *was* also.

Agreement thus turns out to be essentially an affair of leading—leading that is useful because it is into quarters that contain objects that are important. True ideas lead us into useful verbal and conceptual quarters as well as directly up to useful sensible termini. They lead to consistency, stability, and flowing human intercourse. They lead away from eccentricity and isolation, from foiled and barren thinking. The untrammeled flowing of the leading-process, its general freedom from clash and contradiction, passes for its indirect verification; but all roads lead to Rome, and in the end and eventually, all true processes must lead to the face of directly verifying sensible experiences *somewhere,* which somebody's ideas have copied.

Such is the large loose way in which the pragmatist interprets the word agreement. He treats it altogether practically. He lets it cover any process of conduction from a present idea to a future terminus, provided only it run prosperously. It is only thus that 'scientific' ideas, flying as they do beyond common sense, can be said to agree with their realities. It is, as I have already said, *as if* reality were made of ether, atoms or electrons, but we mustn't think so literally. The term 'energy' doesn't even pretend to stand for anything 'objective.' It is only a way of measuring the surface of phenomena so as to string their changes on a simple formula.

Yet in the choice of these man-made formulas we cannot be capricious with impunity any more than we can be capricious on the common-sense practical level. We must find a theory that will *work*; and that means something extremely difficult; for our theory must mediate between all previous truths and certain new experiences. It must derange common sense and previous belief as little as possible, and it must lead to some sensible terminus or other that can be verified exactly. To 'work' means both these things; and the squeeze is so tight that there is little loose play for any hypothesis. Our theories are wedged and controlled as nothing else is. Yet sometimes alternative theoretic formulas are equally compatible with all the truths we know, and then we choose between them for subjective reasons. We choose the kind of theory to which we are already partial; we follow 'elegance' or 'economy.' Clerk Maxwell somewhere says it would be "poor scientific taste" to choose the more complicated of two equally well-evidenced conceptions; and you will all agree with him. Truth in science is what gives us the maximum possible sum of satisfactions, taste included, but consistency both with previous truth and with novel fact is always the most imperious claimant. . . .

READING 28

Appearance and Reality[*]

Bertrand Russell (1872–1970)

Is there any knowledge in the world which is so certain that no reasonable man could doubt it? This question, which at first sight might not seem difficult, is really one of the most difficult that can be asked. When we have realized the obstacles in the way of a straightforward and confident answer, we shall be well launched on the study of philosophy—for philosophy is merely the attempt to answer such ultimate questions, not carelessly and dogmatically, as we do in ordinary life and even in the sciences, but critically after exploring all that makes such questions puzzling, and after realizing all the vagueness and confusion that underlie our ordinary ideas.

In daily life, we assume as certain many things which, on a closer scrutiny, are found to be so full of apparent contradictions that only a great amount of thought enables us to know what it is that we really may believe. In the search for certainty, it is natural to begin with our present experiences, and in some sense, no doubt, knowledge is to be derived from them. But any statement as to what it is that our immediate experiences make us know is very likely to be wrong. It seems to me that I am now sitting in a chair, at a table of a certain

*From Bertrand Russell, *The Problems of Philosophy*, Chapter 1.

shape, on which I see sheets of paper with writing or print. By turning my head I see out of the window buildings and clouds and the sun. I believe that the sun is about ninety-three million miles from the earth; that it is a hot globe many times bigger than the earth; that, owing to the earth's rotation, it rises every morning, and will continue to do so for an indefinite time in the future. I believe that, if any other normal person comes into my room, he will see the same chairs and tables and books and papers as I see, and that the table which I see is the same as the table which I feel pressing against my arm. All this seems to be so evident as to be hardly worth stating, except in answer to a man who doubts whether I know anything. Yet all this may be reasonably doubted, and all of it requires much careful discussion before we can be sure that we have stated it in a form that is wholly true.

[PROBLEMS DISCOVERING THE REAL TABLE]

To make our difficulties plain, let us concentrate attention on the table. To the eye it is oblong, brown and shiny, to the touch it is smooth and cool and hard; when I tap it, it gives out a wooden sound. Any one else who sees and feels and hears the table will agree with this description, so that it might seem as if no difficulty would arise; but as soon as we try to be more precise our troubles begin. Although I believe that the table is "really" of the same color all over, the parts that reflect the light look much brighter than the other parts, and some parts look white because of reflected light. I know that, if I move, the parts that reflect the light will be different, so that the apparent distribution of colors on the table will change. It follows that if several people are looking at the table at the same moment, no two of them will see exactly the same distribution of colors, because no two can see it from exactly the same point of view, and any change in the point of view makes some change in the way the light is reflected.

For most practical purposes these differences are unimportant, but to the painter they are all-important: the painter has to unlearn the habit of thinking that things seem to have the color which common sense says they "really" have, and to learn the habit of seeing things as they appear. Here we have already the beginning of one of the distinctions that cause most trouble in philosophy—the distinction between "appearance" and "reality," between what things seem to be and what they are. The painter wants to know what things seem to be, the practical man and the philosopher want to know what they are; but the philosopher's wish to know this is stronger than the practical man's, and is more troubled by knowledge as to the difficulties of answering the question.

To return to the table. It is evident from what we have found, that there is no color which preeminently appears to be *the* color of the table, or even of any one particular part of the table—it appears to be of different colors from different points of view, and there is no reason for regarding some of these as more really its color than others. And we know that even from a given point of view the color will seem different by artificial light, or to a color-blind man, or to a man wearing blue spectacles, while in the dark there will be no color at all, though to touch and hearing the table will be unchanged. This color is not something which is inherent in the table, but something depending upon the table and the spectator and the way the light falls on the table. When, in ordinary life, we speak of *the* color of the table, we only mean the sort of color which it will seem to have to a normal spectator from an ordinary point of view under usual conditions of light. But the other colors which appear under other conditions have just as good a right to be considered real; and therefore, to avoid favoritism, we are compelled to deny that, in itself, the table has any one particular color.

The same thing applies to the texture. With the naked eye one can see the gram, but otherwise the table looks smooth and even. If we looked at it through a microscope, we should see roughnesses and hills and valleys, and all sorts of differences that are imperceptible to the naked eye. Which of these is the "real" table? We are naturally tempted to say that what we see through the microscope is more real, but that in turn would be changed by a still more powerful microscope. If, then, we cannot trust what we see with the naked eye, why should we trust what we see through a microscope? Thus, again, the confidence in our senses with which we began deserts us.

The *shape* of the table is no better. We are all in the habit of judging as to the "real" shapes of things, and we do this so unreflectingly that we come to think we actually see the real shapes. But, in fact, as we all have to learn if we try to draw, a given thing looks different in shape from every different point of view. If our table is "really" rectangular, it will look, from almost all points of view, as if it had two acute angles and two obtuse angles. If opposite sides are parallel, they will look as if they converged to a point away from the spectator; if they are of equal length, they will look as if the nearer side were longer. All these things are not commonly noticed in looking at a table, because experience has taught us to construct the "real" shape from the apparent shape, and the "real" shape is what interests us as practical men. But the "real" shape is not what we see; it is something inferred from what we see. And what we see is constantly changing in shape as we, move about the room; so that here again the senses seem not to give us the truth about the table itself, but only about the appearance of the table.

Similar difficulties arise when we consider the sense of touch. It is true that the table always gives us a sensation of hardness, and we feel that it resists pressure. But the sensation we obtain depends upon how hard we press the table and also upon what part of the body we press with; thus the various sensations due to various pressures or various parts of the body cannot be supposed to reveal *directly* any definite property of the table, but at most to be signs of some property which perhaps *causes* all the sensations, but is not actually apparent in any of them. And the same applies still more obviously to the sounds which can be elicited by rapping the table.

Thus it becomes evident that the real table, if there is one, is not the same as what we immediately experience by sight or touch or hearing. The real table, if there is one, is not *immediately* known to us at all, but must be an inference from what is immediately known. Hence, two very difficult questions at once arise; namely, (1) Is there a real table at all? (2) If so, what sort of object can it be?

[THE IDEALIST'S SOLUTION]

It will help us in considering these questions to have a few simple terms of which the meaning is definite and clear. Let us give the name of "sense-data" to the things that are immediately known in sensation: such things as colors, sounds, smells, hardnesses, roughnesses, and so on. We shall give the name "sensation" to the experience of being immediately aware of these things. Thus, whenever we see a color, we have a sensation *of* the color, but the color itself is a sense-datum, not a sensation. The color is that *of* which we are immediately aware, and the awareness itself is the sensation. It is plain that if we are to know anything about the table, it must be by means of the sense-data—brown color, oblong shape, smoothness, etc.—which we associate with the table; but, for the reasons which have been given, we cannot say that the table is the sense-data, or even that the sense-data are directly properties of the table. Thus a problem arises as to the relation of the sense-data to the real table, supposing there is such a thing.

The real table, if it exists, we will call a "physical object". Thus we have to consider the relation of sense-data to physical objects. The collection of all physical objects is called "matter". Thus our two questions may be re-stated as follows: (1) Is there any such thing as matter? (2) If so, what is its nature?

The philosopher who first brought prominently forward the reasons for regarding the immediate objects of our senses as not existing independently of us was Bishop Berkeley (1685–1753). His *Three Dialogues between Hylas and Philonous, in Opposition to Sceptics and Atheists,* undertake to prove that there is no such thing as matter at all, and that the world consists of nothing but minds and their ideas. Hylas has hitherto believed in matter, but he is no match for Philonous, who mercilessly drives him into contradictions and paradoxes, and makes his own denial of matter seem, in the end, as if it were almost common sense. The arguments employed are of very different value: some are important and sound, others are confused or quibbling. But Berkeley retains the merit of having shown that the existence of matter is capable of being denied without absurdity, and that if there are any things that exist independently of us they cannot be the immediate objects of our sensations.

There are two different questions involved when we ask whether matter exists, and it is important to keep them clear. We commonly mean by "matter" something which is opposed to "mind," something which we think of as occupying space and as radically incapable of any sort of thought or consciousness. It is chiefly in this sense that Berkeley denies matter; that is to say, he does not deny that the sense-data which we commonly take as signs of the existence of the table are really signs of the existence of *something* independent of us, but he does deny that this something is nonmental, that it is neither mind nor ideas entertained by some mind. He admits that there must be something which continues to exist when we go out of the room or shut our eyes, and that what we call seeing the table does really give us reason for believing in something which persists even when we are not seeing it. But he thinks that this something cannot be radically different in nature from what we see, and cannot be independent of seeing altogether, though it must be independent of *our* seeing. He is thus led to regard the "real" table as an idea in the mind of God. Such an idea has the required permanence and independence of ourselves, without being—as matter would otherwise be—something quite unknowable, in the sense that we can only infer it, and can never be directly and immediately aware of it.

. . . It will be well to consider for a moment what it is that we have discovered so far. It has appeared that, if we take any common object of the sort that is supposed to be known by the senses, what the senses *immediately* tell us is not the truth about the object as it is apart from us, but only the truth about certain sense-data which, so far as we can see, depend upon the relations between us and the object. Thus what we directly see and feel is merely "appearance," which we believe to be a sign of some "reality" behind. . . .

READING 29

Common Sense Knowledge and Scientific Knowledge*

Arthur Eddington (1882–1944)

I have settled down to the task of waiting these lectures and have drawn up my chairs to my two tables. Two tables! Yes; there are duplicates of every object about me—two tables, two chairs, two pens.

This is not a very profound beginning to a course which ought to reach transcendent levels of scientific philosophy. But we cannot touch bedrock immediately; we must scratch a bit at the surface of things first. And whenever I begin to scratch; the first thing I strike is—my two tables.

One of them has been familiar to me from earliest years. It is a commonplace object of that environment which I call the world. How shall I describe it? It has extension; it is comparatively permanent; it is colored; above all it is *substantial*. By substantial I do not merely mean that it does not collapse when I lean up on it; I mean that it is constituted of "substance," and by that word I am trying to convey to you some conception of its intrinsic nature. It is a *thing;*

*Arthur Eddington, *The Nature of the Physical World*, 1928.

not like space, which is a mere negation; nor like time, which is—Heaven knows what! But that will not help you to my meaning because it is the distinctive characteristic of a "thing" to have this substantiality, and I do not think substantiality can be described better than by saying that it is the kind of nature exemplified by an ordinary table. And so we go round in circles. After all if you are a plain commonsense man, not too much worried with scientific scruples, you will be confident that you understand the nature of an ordinary table. I have even heard of plain men who had the idea that they could better understand the mystery of their own nature if scientists would discover a way of explaining it in terms of the easily comprehensible nature of a table. Table no. 2 is my scientific table. It is a more recent acquaintance and I do not feel so familiar with it. It does not belong to the world previously mentioned—that world which spontaneously appears around me when I open *my* eyes, though how much of it is objective and how much subjective I do not here consider. It is part of a world which in more devious ways has forced itself on my attention. My scientific table is mostly emptiness. Sparsely scattered in that emptiness are numerous electric charges rushing about with great speed; but their combined bulk amounts to less than a billionth of the bulk of the table itself. Notwithstanding its strange construction it turns out to be an entirely efficient table. It supports my writing paper as satisfactorily as table no. 1; for when I lay the paper on it the little electric particles with their headlong speed keep on hitting the underside, so that the paper is maintained in shuttlecock fashion at a nearly steady level. If I lean upon this table I shall not go through; or, to be strictly accurate, the chance of my scientific elbow going through my scientific table is so excessively small that it can be neglected in practical life. Reviewing their properties one by one, there seems to be nothing to choose between the two tables for ordinary purposes; but when abnormal circumstances befall, then my scientific table shows to advantage. If the house catches fire my scientific table will dissolve quite naturally into scientific smoke, whereas my familiar table undergoes a metamorphosis of its substantial nature which I can only regard as miraculous.

There is nothing *substantial* about my second table. It is nearly all empty space—space pervaded, it is true, by fields of force, but these are assigned to the category of "influences," not of "things." Even in the minute part which is not empty we must not transfer the old notion of substance. In dissecting matter into electric charges we have traveled far from that picture of it which first gave rise to the conception of substance, and the meaning of that conception—if it ever had any—has been lost by the way. The whole trend of modem scientific views is to break down the separate categories of "things," "influences," "forms," etc., and to substitute a common background of all experience. Whether we are studying a material object, a magnetic field, a geometrical figure, or a duration of time, our scientific information is summed up in measures; neither the apparatus of measurement nor the mode of using it suggests that there is anything essentially different in these problems. The measures themselves afford no ground for a classification by categories. We feel it necessary to concede some background to the measures—an external world; but the attributes of this world, except insofar as they are reflected in the measures, are outside scientific scrutiny. Science has at last revolted against attaching the exact knowledge contained in these measurements to a traditional picture—gallery of conceptions which convey no authentic information of the background and obtrude irrelevancies into the scheme of knowledge.

I will not here stress further the nonsubstantiality of electrons, since it is scarcely necessary to the present line of thought. Conceive them as substantially as you will, there is a vast difference between my scientific table with its substance (if any) thinly scattered in specks in a region mostly empty and the table of everyday conception which we regard as the type of solid reality—an incarnate protest against Berkeleian subjectivism. It makes all the difference in the world whether the paper before me is poised as it were on a swarm of flies and sustained in shuttlecock fashion by a series of tiny blows from the swarm underneath, or whether it is supported because there is substance below it, it being the intrinsic nature of substance to occupy space to the exclusion of other substance; all the difference in conception at least, but no difference to my practical task of writing on the paper.

I need not tell you that modern physics has by delicate test and remorseless logic assured me that my second scientific table is the only one which is really there—wherever "there" may be. On the other hand I need not tell you that modern physics will never succeed in exorcising that first table—strange compound of external nature, mental imagery, and inherited prejudice—which lies visible to my eyes and tangible to my grasp. We must bid goodbye to it for the present, for we are about to turn from the familiar world to the scientific world revealed by physics. This is, or is intended to be, a wholly external world.

"You speak paradoxically of two worlds. Are they not really two aspects or two interpretations of one and the same world?"

Yes, no doubt they are ultimately to be identified after some fashion. But the process by which the external world of physics is transformed into a world of familiar acquaintance in human consciousness is outside the scope of physics. And so the world studied according to the methods of physics remains detached from the world familiar to consciousness, until after the physicist has finished his labors upon it. Provisionally, therefore, we regard the table which is the subject of physical research as altogether separate from the familiar table, without prejudging the question of their ultimate identification. It is true that the whole scientific inquiry starts from the familiar world and in the end it must return to the familiar world; but the part of the journey over which the physicist has charge is in foreign territory.

Critique of Traditional Epistemology*

Richard Rorty (b. 1931)

[ASSUMPTIONS BEHIND TRADITIONAL EPISTEMOLOGY]

Philosophers usually think of their discipline as one which discusses perennial, eternal problems—problems which arise as soon as one reflects. Some of these concern the difference between human beings and other beings, and are crystallized in questions concerning the relation between the mind and the body. Other problems concern the legitimation of claims to know, and are crystallized in questions concerning the "foundations" of knowledge. To discover these foundations is to discover something about the mind, and conversely. Philosophy as a discipline thus sees itself as the attempt to underwrite or debunk claims to knowledge made by science, morality, art, or religion. It purports to do this on the basis of its special understanding of the nature of knowledge and of mind. Philosophy can be foundational in respect to the rest of culture because culture is the assemblage of claims to knowledge, and philosophy adjudicates such claims. It can do so because it understands the foundations of knowledge, and it finds these foundations in a study of man-as-knower, of the "mental processes" or the "activity of representation" which make knowledge possible. To know is to represent accurately what is outside the mind; so to understand the possibility and nature of knowledge is to understand the way in which the mind is able to construct such representations. Philosophy's central concern is to be a general theory of representation, a theory which will divide culture up into the areas which represent reality well, those which represent it less well, and those which do not represent it at all (despite their pretense of doing so).

　　We owe the notion of a "theory of knowledge" based on an understanding of "mental processes" to the seventeenth century, and especially to Locke. We owe the notion of "the mind" as a separate entity in which "processes" occur to the same period, and especially to Descartes. We owe the notion of philosophy as a tribunal of pure reason, upholding or denying the claims of the rest of culture, to the eighteenth century and especially to Kant, but this Kantian notion presupposed general assent to Lockean notions of mental processes and Cartesian notions of mental substance. In the nineteenth century, the notion of philosophy as a foundational discipline which "grounds" knowledge-claims was consolidated in the writings of the neo-Kantians. Occasional

*From Richard Rorty, *Philosophy and the Mirror of Nature*, 1979, Introduction.

protests against this conception of culture as in need of "grounding" and against the pretensions of a theory of knowledge to perform this task (in, for example, Nietzsche and William James) went largely unheard. "Philosophy" became, for the intellectuals, a substitute for religion. It was the area of culture where one touched bottom, where one found the vocabulary and the convictions which permitted one to explain and justify one's activity as an intellectual, and thus to discover the significance of one's life.

At the beginning of our century, this claim was reaffirmed by philosophers (notably Russell and Husserl) who were concerned to keep philosophy "rigorous" and "scientific." But there was a note of desperation in their voices, for by this time the triumph of the secular over the claims of religion was almost complete. Thus the philosopher could no longer see himself as in the intellectual avant-garde, or as protecting men against the forces of superstition., Further, in the course of the nineteenth century, a new form of culture had arisen—the culture of the man of letters, the intellectual who wrote poems and novels and political treatises, and criticisms of other people's poems and novels and treatises. Descartes, Locke, and Kant had written in a period in which the secularization of culture was being made possible by the success of natural science. But by the early twentieth century the scientists had become as remote from most intellectuals as had the theologians. Poets and novelists had taken the place of both preachers and philosophers as the moral teachers of the youth. The result was that the more "scientific" and "rigorous" philosophy became, the less it had to do with the rest of culture and the more absurd its traditional pretensions seemed. The attempts of both analytic philosophers and phenomenologists to "ground" this and "criticize" that were shrugged off by those whose activities were purportedly being grounded or criticized. Philosophy as a whole was shrugged off by those who wanted an ideology or a self-image.

It is against this background that we should see the work of the three most important philosophers of our century—Wittgenstein, Heidegger, and Dewey. Each tried, in his early years, to find a new way of making philosophy "foundational"—a new way of formulating an ultimate context for thought. Wittgenstein tried to construct a new theory of representation which would have nothing to do with mentalism, Heidegger to construct a new set of philosophical categories which would have nothing to do with science, epistemology, or the Cartesian quest for certainty, and Dewey to construct a naturalized version of Hegel's vision of history. Each of the three came to see his earlier effort as self-deceptive, as an attempt to retain a certain conception of philosophy after the notions needed to flesh out that conception (the seventeenth-century notions of knowledge and mind) had been discarded. Each of the three, in his later work, broke free of the Kantian conception of philosophy as foundational, and spent his time warning us against those very temptations to which he himself had once succumbed. Thus their later work is therapeutic rather than constructive, edifying rather than systematic, designed to make the reader question his own motives for philosophizing rather than to supply him with a new philosophical program.

Wittgenstein, Heidegger, and Dewey are in agreement that the notion of knowledge as accurate representation, made possible by special mental processes, and intelligible through a general theory of representation, needs to be abandoned. For all three, the notions of "foundations of knowledge" and of philosophy as revolving around the Cartesian attempt to answer the epistemological skeptic are set aside. Further, they set aside the notion of "the mind" common to Descartes, Locke, and Kant—as a special subject of study, located in inner space, containing elements or processes which make knowledge possible. This is not to say that they have alternative "theories of knowledge" or "philosophies of mind." They set aside epistemology and metaphysics as possible disciplines. I say "set aside" rather than "argue against" because their attitude toward the traditional problematic is like the attitude of seventeenth-century philosophers toward the scholastic problematic. They do not devote themselves to discovering false propositions or bad arguments in the works of their predecessors (though they occasionally do that too). Rather, they glimpse the possibility of a form of intellectual life in which the vocabulary of philosophical reflection inherited from the seventeenth century would seem as pointless as the thirteenth-century philosophical vocabulary had seemed to the Enlightenment. To assert the possibility of a post-Kantian culture, one in which there is no all-encompassing discipline which legitimizes or grounds the others, is not necessarily to argue against any particular Kantian doctrine, any more than to glimpse the possibility of a culture in which religion either did not exist, or had no connection with science or politics, was necessarily to argue against Aquinas's claim that God's existence can be proved by natural reason. Wittgenstein, Heidegger, and Dewey have brought us into a period of "revolutionary" philosophy (in the sense of Kuhn's "revolutionary" science) by introducing new maps of the terrain (viz., of the whole panorama of human activities) which simply do not include those features which previously seemed to dominate.

[KNOWLEDGE DOES NOT INVOLVE MIRRORING NATURE]

This book is a survey of some recent developments in philosophy, especially analytic philosophy, from the point of view of the anti-Cartesian and anti-Kantian revolution which I have just described. The aim of the book is to undermine the reader's confidence in "the mind" as something about which one should have a "philosophical" view, in "knowledge" as something about which there ought to be a "theory" and which has "foundations," and in "philosophy" as it has been conceived since Kant. Thus the reader in search of a new theory on any of the subjects discussed will be disappointed. Although I discuss "solutions to the mind-body problem" this is not in order to propose one but to illustrate why I do not think there is a problem. Again, although I discuss "theories of reference" I do not offer one, but offer only suggestions about why the search for such a theory is misguided. The book, like the writings of the philosophers 1 most admire, is therapeutic rather than constructive. The therapy offered is, nevertheless, parasitic upon the constructive efforts of the very analytic philosophers whose frame of reference I am trying to put in question. Thus most of the particular criticisms of the tradition which I offer are borrowed from such systematic philosophers as Sellars, Quine, Davidson, Ryle, Malcolm, Kuhn, and Putnam.

I am as much indebted to these philosophers for the means I employ as I am to Wittgenstein, Heidegger, and Dewey for the ends to which these means are put. I hope to convince the reader that the dialectic within analytic philosophy, which has carried philosophy of mind from Broad to Smart, philosophy of language from Frege to Davidson, epistemology from Russell to Sellars, and philosophy of science from Carnap to Kuhn, needs to be carried a few steps further. These additional steps will, I think, put us in a position to criticize the very notion of "analytic philosophy," and indeed of "philosophy" itself as it has been understood since the time of Kant.

From the standpoint I am adopting, indeed, the difference between "analytic" and other sorts of philosophy is relatively unimportant—a matter of style and tradition rather than a difference of "method" or of first principles. The reason why the book is largely written in the vocabulary of contemporary analytic philosophers, and with reference to problems discussed in the analytic literature, is merely autobiographical. They are the vocabulary and the literature with which I am most familiar, and to which I owe what grasp I have of philosophical issues. Had I been equally familiar with other contemporary modes of writing philosophy, this would have been a better and more useful book, although an even longer one. As I see it, the kind of philosophy which stems from Russell and Frege is, like classical Husserlian phenomenology, simply one more attempt to put philosophy in the position which Kant wished it to have—that of judging other areas of culture on the basis of its special knowledge of the "foundations" of these areas. "Analytic" philosophy is one more variant of Kantian philosophy, a variant marked principally by thinking of representation as linguistic rather than mental, and of philosophy of language rather than "transcendental critique," or psychology, as the discipline which exhibits the "foundations of knowledge." This emphasis on language, I shall be arguing in chapters four and six, does not essentially change the Cartesian-Kantian problematic, and thus does not really give philosophy a new self-image. For analytic philosophy is still committed to the construction of a permanent, neutral framework for inquiry, and thus for all of culture.

It is the notion that human activity (and inquiry, the search for knowledge, in particular) takes place within a framework which can be isolated prior to the conclusion of inquiry—a set of presuppositions discoverable a priori—which links contemporary philosophy to the Descartes-Locke-Kant tradition. For the notion that there is such a framework only makes sense if we think of this framework as imposed by the nature of the knowing subject, by the nature of his faculties or by the nature of the medium within which he works. The very idea of "philosophy" as something distinct from "science" would make little sense without the Cartesian claim that by turning inward we could find ineluctable truth, and the Kantian claim that this truth imposes limits on the possible results of empirical inquiry. The notion that there could be such a thing as "foundations of knowledge" (all knowledge—in every field, past, present, and future) or a "theory of representation" (all representation, in familiar vocabularies and those not yet dreamed of) depends on the assumption that there is some such a priori constraint. If we have a Deweyan conception of knowledge, as what we are justified in believing, then we will not imagine that there are enduring constraints on what can count as knowledge, since we will see "justification" as a social phenomenon rather than a transaction between "the knowing subject" and "reality." If we have a Wittgensteinian notion of language as tool rather than mirror, we will not look for necessary conditions of the possibility of linguistic representation. If we have a Heideggerian conception of philosophy, we will see the attempt to make the nature of the knowing subject a source of necessary truths as one more self-deceptive attempt to substitute a "technical" and determinate question for that openness to strangeness which initially tempted us to begin thinking. . . .

I hope that what I have been saying has made clear why I chose "Philosophy and the Mirror of Nature" as a title. It is pictures rather than propositions, metaphors rather than statements, which determine most of our philosophical convictions. The picture which holds traditional philosophy captive is that of the mind as a great mirror, containing various representations—some accurate, some not—and capable of being studied by pure, nonempirical methods. Without the notion of the mind as mirror, the notion of knowledge as accuracy of representation would not have suggested itself. Without this latter notion, the strategy common to Descartes and Kant—getting more accurate representations by inspecting, repairing, and polishing the mirror, so to speak—would not have made sense. Without this strategy in mind, recent claims that philosophy could consist of "conceptual analysis" or "phenomenological analysis" or "explication of meanings" or examination of "the logic of our language" or of "the structure of the constituting activity of consciousness" would not have made sense. It was such claims as these which Wittgenstein mocked in the *Philosophical Investigations,* and it is by following Wittgenstein's lead that analytic philosophy has progressed toward the "post-positivistic" stance it presently occupies. But Wittgenstein's flair for deconstructing captivating pictures needs to be supplemented by historical awareness—awareness of the source of all this mirror imagery—and that seems to me Heidegger's greatest contribution. Heidegger's way of recounting history of philosophy lets us see the beginnings of the Cartesian imagery in the Greeks and the metamorphoses of this imagery during the last three centuries. He thus lets us "distance" ourselves from the tradition. Yet neither Heidegger nor Wittgenstein lets us see the historical phenomenon of mirror-imagery, the story of the domination of the mind of the West by ocular metaphors, within a social perspective. Both men are concerned with the rarely favored individual rather than with society—with the chances of keeping oneself apart from the banal self-deception typical of the latter days of a decaying tradition. Dewey, on the other hand, though he had neither

Wittgenstein's dialectical acuity nor Heidegger's historical learning, wrote his polemics against traditional mirror-imagery out of a vision of a new kind of society. In his ideal society, culture is no longer dominated by the ideal of objective cognition but by that of aesthetic enhancement. In that culture, as he said, the arts and the sciences would be "the unforced flowers of life." I would hope that we are now in a position to see the charges of "relativism" and "irrationalism" once leveled against Dewey as merely the mindless defensive reflexes of the philosophical tradition which he attacked. Such charges have no weight if one takes seriously the criticisms of mirror-imagery which he, Wittgenstein, and Heidegger make. This book has little to add to these criticisms, but I hope that it presents some of them in a way which will help pierce through that crust of philosophical convention which Dewey vainly hoped to shatter.

PART FIVE

Free Will and Determinism

*F*rom the earliest philosophers to present-day thinkers, one question continues to raise a perplexing problem, namely: Is the human will free? Why should this be a problem? Our commonsense intuitions tell us that we constantly face choices, or that we make mistakes, or that we are undecided about some matter and are still thinking about it. We are, thus, deliberating. To face a choice implies that the will is free to move in different directions. To say that you made a mistake means not only that you *should* have but that you *could* have behaved in a different way. The act of taking your time to think out your course of action, the act of deliberation, implies not only that you are situated in a physical sense in a particular place with physical forces at work in your being or personality but also that you are situated in a special condition of freedom, as if there were a limit to the power of, or an insulation from, the various forces upon you, giving you a chance to choose your direction of behavior.

However, the problem is not all that simple. There are many things about you that you are not free to choose. You did not choose to be born, to have brown eyes, to be six feet tall, to have blond hair, or even to have a particular disease. All this has been determined genetically—a rather obvious point. Even many ways of thinking or of accepting certain moral values have been programmed by your family and culture. Beyond that there are some behaviors that we do not consider to be free, as when the driver of an automobile hits another automobile while driving under the influence of drugs or alcohol. What all this suggests is that much of our life and behavior is determined and could be no other way. The question is, how much is determined?

The determinist argues that everything—that is, every event and every aspect of nature—is determined and could be no other way. For example, in his *System of Values* (1770) French philosopher Baron d'Holbach wrote that a person is born without his consent; his organization does in nowise depend upon himself; his ideas come to him involuntarily; his habits are in the power of those who cause him to contract them; he is unceasingly modified by causes whether visible or concealed, over which he has no control, which necessarily regulate his mode of existence, give the hue to his way of thinking and determine his manner of acting. He is good or bad, happy or miserable, wise or foolish, reasonable or irrational, without his will being for anything in these various states. Nevertheless, in spite of the shackles by which he is bound, it is pretended he is a free agent or that independent of these causes by which he moved, he determines his own will, and regulates his own condition. Determinists, such as d'Holbach, are mostly influenced by the notion that every event has a *cause,* that scientific laws of nature define how all things work and are interrelated. For the determinist, all of reality, including human nature, functions as a machine. Consider the engine of any automobile: All of its parts are connected to one another. The generator causes the spark plug to ignite the gasoline in the cylinder; the impact of the explosion pushes down the piston, which, being connected to the cam shaft, causes the next piston to move up; all this is connected to the drive shaft, which in turn is connected to the gears that finally make the wheels turn. For the determinist, all of human existence can be explained according to this mechanical model.

We are faced, then, with two opposite points of view regarding the human will. The *determinist* argues that in no way is the will free, and the *indeterminist* argues that human experience is incomprehensible without the assumption that the will is free. Some philosophers attempt to take a middle position between these two views—a position often called *soft determinism* or *compatiblism.* On this view, depending on how we define "free will" and "determinism," there may be some way to consistently espouse both of these positions at the same time.

Stoic philosophers from ancient Greece were among the first to offer a deterministic view of human action. According to Stoics, all events that take place in the universe are determined by a larger cosmic force, which they variously referred to as fate, destiny, God, or the *logos.* As a component of the larger scheme of things, human behavior is similarly determined by fate. Even though we may *feel* that we have choices, free will is really an illusion—and a determined illusion at that. The Stoic philosopher Epictetus (c. 50–c. 120) makes this point in his *Handbook.* All of human unhappiness, Epictetus believes, owes to our vain attempts to control things beyond our power; if we have any hopes at being happy in life then we must resign ourselves to fate. Epictetus recognizes that it is a difficult task for any of us to abandon notions of human freedom. To psychologically help us accept our respective fates, he offers a series of potent and sometimes shocking metaphors.

Epictetus does not actually *argue* for determinism but simply presumes it to be true. One of the first systematic defenses of determinism was offered by Scottish philosopher David Hume (1711–1776) in his *Enquiry Concerning Human Understanding.* Hume argues that all human action is causally determined by prior motivations, and no act of our human will can override those prior motivations. Hume makes his argument in two steps—based on two possible ways of defining the notion of "causality." First, specific motives are constantly conjoined with specific actions, and, second, the presence of specific motives will prompt us to make an immediate mental inference regarding a specific human action. For Hume, then, if free will (or "liberty" as he terms it) means an ability to act contrary to our motives, then we simply have no free will. However, Hume offers a more watered-down notion of free will, namely, the ability to act in accord with our motivations. In this sense, free will is compatible with his rigid view of determinism.

Shortly after Hume, fellow Scottish philosopher Thomas Reid (1710–1796) attacked Hume's determinism in defense of a more meaningful notion of free will. In his *Essays on the Active Powers of Man* (1788), he argues that we are free to the extent that we have a power over the motivations of our will. All people, according to Reid, have a natural commonsense conviction regarding the freedom of our wills, which we assume in any number of daily activities. Many defenses of free will after Reid make a similar point: If we abandon the notion of free will, then we sacrifice the notion of moral responsibility. In *The Dilemma of Determinism* (1884), American philosopher William James (1842–1919) asks how it is possible to explain our judgments of regret if we could never have behaved differently. This problem, he believes, should prompt us to reject determinism.

In recent years a better understanding of physics and human brain functions has taken the free will and determinism debate in different direction. According to American philosopher John Searle (b. 1932) in *Minds, Brains and Science* (1984), there is no room for free will in the contemporary scientific view of things. The issue rests on what he calls "bottom-up" causation. That is, "Since all of the surface features of the world are entirely caused by and realized in systems of micro-elements, the behavior of micro-elements is sufficient to determine everything that happens." In spite of such bottom-up determinism, Searle believes that we still must explain how our conviction of human freedom arose and why we cannot give up that conviction.

Resigning Oneself to Fate*

Epictetus (c. 50–c. 120)

1. Some things are in our control and others not. Things in our control are opinion, pursuit, desire, aversion, and, in a word, whatever are our own actions. Things not in our control are body, property, reputation, command, and, in one word, whatever are not our own actions.

   The things in our control are by nature free, unrestrained, unhindered; but those not in our control are weak, slavish, restrained, belonging to others. Remember, then, that if you suppose that things which are slavish by nature are also free, and that what belongs to others is your own, then you will be hindered. You will lament, you will be disturbed, and you will find fault both with gods and men. But if you suppose that only to be your own which *is* your own, and what belongs to others such as it really is, then no one will ever compel you or restrain you. Further, you will find fault with no one or accuse no one. You will do nothing against your will. No one will hurt you, you will have no enemies, and you will not be harmed.

   Aiming therefore at such great things, remember that you must not allow yourself to be carried, even with a slight tendency, towards the attainment of lesser things. Instead, you must entirely quit some things and for the present postpone the rest. But if you would both have these great things, along with power and riches, then you will not gain even the latter, because you aim at the former too: but you will absolutely fail of the former, by which alone happiness and freedom are achieved.

   Work, therefore to be able to say to every harsh appearance, "You are but an appearance, and not absolutely the thing you appear to be."

*From Epictetus *The Enchiridion* (c. 135 C.E.), Sects. 1–15.

And then examine it by those rules which you have, and first, and chiefly, by this: whether it concerns the things which are in our own control, or those which are not; and, if it concerns anything not in our control, be prepared to say that it is nothing to you.

2. Remember that following desire promises the attainment of that of which you are desirous; and aversion promises the avoiding that to which you are averse. However, he who fails to obtain the object of his desire is disappointed, and he who incurs the object of his aversion wretched. If, then, you confine your aversion to those objects only which are contrary to the natural use of your faculties, which you have in your own control, you will never incur anything to which you are averse. But if you are averse to sickness, or death, or poverty, you will be wretched. Remove aversion, then, from all things that are not in our control, and transfer it to things contrary to the nature of what is in our control. But, for the present, totally suppress desire: for, if you desire any of the things which are not in your own control, you must necessarily be disappointed; and of those which are, and which it would be laudable to desire, nothing is yet in your possession. Use only the appropriate actions of pursuit and avoidance; and even these lightly, and with gentleness and reservation.

3. With regard to whatever objects give you delight, are useful, or are deeply loved, remember to tell yourself of *what general nature they are,* beginning from the most insignificant things. If, for example, you are fond of a specific ceramic cup, remind yourself that it is only ceramic cups in general of which you are fond. Then, if it breaks, you will not be disturbed. If you kiss your child, or your wife, say that you only kiss things which are human, and thus you will not be disturbed if either of them dies.

4. When you are going about any action, remind yourself what nature the action is. If you are going to bathe, picture to yourself the things which usually happen in the bath: some people splash the water, some push, some use abusive language, and others steal. Thus you will more safely go about this action if you say to yourself, "I will now go bathe, and keep my own mind in a state conformable to nature." And in the same manner with regard to every other action. For thus, if any hindrance arises in bathing, you will have it ready to say, "It was not only to bathe that I desired, but to keep my mind in a state conformable to nature; and I will not keep it if I am bothered at things that happen."

5. Men are disturbed, not by things, but by the principles and notions which they form concerning things. Death, for instance, is not terrible, else it would have appeared so to Socrates. But the terror consists in our notion of death that it is terrible. When therefore we are hindered, or disturbed, or grieved, let us never attribute it to others, but to ourselves; that is, to our own principles. An uninstructed person will lay the fault of his own bad condition upon others. Someone just starting instruction will lay the fault on himself. Some who is perfectly instructed will place blame neither on others nor on himself.

6. Don't be prideful with any excellence that is not your own. If a horse should be prideful and say, " I am handsome," it would be supportable. But when you are prideful, and say, "I have a handsome horse," know that you are proud of what is, in fact, only the good of the horse. What, then, is your own? Only your reaction to the appearances of things. Thus, when you behave conformably to nature in reaction to how things appear, you will be proud with reason; for you will take pride in some good of your own.

7. Consider when, on a voyage, your ship is anchored; if you go on shore to get water you may along the way amuse yourself with picking up a shellish, or an onion. However, your thoughts and continual attention ought to be bent towards the ship, waiting for the captain to call on board; you must then immediately leave all these things, otherwise you will be thrown into the ship, bound neck and feet like a sheep. So it is with life. If, instead of an onion or a shellfish, you are given a wife or child, that is fine. But if the captain calls, you must run to the ship, leaving them, and regarding none of them. But if you are old, never go far from the ship: lest, when you are called, you should be unable to come in time.

8. Don't demand that things happen as you wish, but wish that they happen as they *do* happen, and you will go on well.

9. Sickness is a hindrance to the body, but not to your ability to choose, unless that is your choice. Lameness is a hindrance to the leg, but not to your ability to choose. Say this to yourself with regard to everything that happens, then you will see such obstacles as hindrances to something else, but not to yourself.

10. With every accident, ask yourself what abilities you have for making a proper use of it. If you see an attractive person, you will find that self-restraint is the ability you have against your desire. If you are in pain, you will find fortitude. If you hear unpleasant language, you will find patience. And thus habituated, the appearances of things will not hurry you away along with them.

11. Never say of anything, "I have lost it"; but, "I have returned it." Is your child dead? It is returned. Is your wife dead? She is returned. Is your estate taken away? Well, and is not that likewise returned? "But he who took it away is a bad man." What difference is it to you who the giver assigns to take it back? While he gives it to you to possess, take care of it; but don't view it as your own, just as travelers view a hotel.

12. If you want to improve, reject such reasonings as these: "If I neglect my affairs, I'll have no income; if I don't correct my servant, he will be bad." For it is better to die with hunger, exempt from grief and fear, than to live in affluence with perturbation; and it is better your servant should be bad, than you unhappy.

Begin therefore from little things. Is a little oil spilt? A little wine stolen? Say to yourself, "This is the price paid for being without passion, for tranquillity, and nothing is to be had for nothing." When you call your servant, it is possible that he may not come; or, if he does, he may not do what you want. But he is by no means of such importance that it should be in his power to give you any disturbance.

13. If you want to improve, be content to be thought foolish and stupid with regard to external things. Don't wish to be thought to know anything; and even if you appear to be somebody important to others, distrust yourself. For, it is difficult to both keep your faculty of choice in a state conformable to nature, and at the same time acquire external things. But while you are careful about the one, you must of necessity neglect the other.

14. If you wish your children, and your wife, and your friends to live for ever, you are stupid; for you wish to be in control of things which you cannot, you wish for things that belong to others to be your own. So likewise, if you wish your servant to be without fault, you are a fool; for you wish vice not to be vice," but something else. But, if you wish to have your desires undisappointed, this is in your own control. Exercise, therefore, what is in your control. He is the master of every other person who is able to confer or remove whatever that person wishes either to have or to avoid. Whoever, then, would be free, let him wish nothing, let him decline nothing, which depends on others else he must necessarily be a slave.

15. Remember that you must behave in life as at a dinner party. Is anything brought around to you? Put out your hand and take your share with moderation. Does it pass by you? Don't stop it. Is it not yet come? Don't stretch your desire towards it, but wait till it reaches you. Do this with regard to children, to a wife, to public posts, to riches, and you will eventually be a worthy partner of the feasts of the gods. And if you don't even take the things which are set before you, but are able even to reject them, then you will not only be a partner at the feasts of the gods, but also of their empire. For, by doing this, Diogenes, Heraclitus and others like them, deservedly became, and were called, divine.

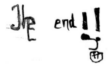

READING 32

The Argument for Determinism[*]

David Hume (1711–1776)

. . . It is universally allowed that matter, in all its operations, is actuated by a necessary force, and that every natural effect is so precisely determined by the energy of its cause that no other effect, in such particular circumstances, could possibly have resulted from it. The degree and direction of every motion is, by the laws of nature, prescribed with such exactness that a living creature may

---

[*]From David Hume, *Enquiry Concerning Human Understanding,* (1748), Section 7.1.

as soon arise from the shock of two bodies as motion in any other degree or direction than what is actually produced by it. Would we, therefore, form a just and precise idea of *necessity*, we must consider whence that idea arises when we apply it to the operation of bodies.

It seems evident that, if all the scenes of nature were continually shifted in such a manner that no two events bore any resemblance to each other, but every object was entirely new, without any similitude to whatever had been seen before, we should never, in that case, have attained the least idea of necessity, or of a connection among these objects. We might say, upon such a supposition, that one object or event has followed another; not that one was produced by the other. The relation of cause and effect must be utterly unknown to mankind. Inference and reasoning concerning the operations of nature would, from that moment, be at an end; and the memory and senses remain the only canals, by which the knowledge of any real existence could possibly have access to the mind. Our idea, therefore, of necessity and causation arises entirely from the uniformity observable in the operations of nature, where (1) similar objects are constantly conjoined together, and (2) the mind is determined by custom to infer the one from the appearance of the other. These two circumstances form the whole of that necessity, which we ascribe to matter. Beyond the constant *conjunction* of similar objects, and the consequent *inference* from one to the other, we have no notion of any necessity or connection.

If it appear, therefore, that all mankind have ever allowed, without any doubt or hesitation, that these two circumstances take place in the voluntary actions of men, and in the operations of mind; it must follow, that all mankind have ever agreed in the doctrine of necessity, and that they have hitherto disputed, merely for not understanding each other.

[CONSTANT CONJUNCTION BETWEEN MOTIVES AND ACTIONS]

As to the first circumstance, the constant and regular conjunction of similar events, we may possibly satisfy ourselves by the following considerations: It is universally acknowledged that there is a great uniformity among the actions of men, in all nations and ages, and that human nature remains still the same, in its principles and operations. The same motives always produce the same actions: The same events follow from the same causes. Ambition, avarice, self-love, vanity, friendship, generosity, public spirit: These passions, mixed in various degrees, and distributed through society, have been, from the beginning of the world, and still are, the source of all the actions and enterprises, which have ever been observed among mankind. Would you know the sentiments, inclinations, and course of life of the Greeks and Romans? Study well the temper and actions of the French and English: You cannot be much mistaken in transferring to the former *most* of the observations which you have made with regard to the latter. Mankind are so much the same, in all times and places, that history informs us of nothing new or strange in this

particular. Its chief use is only to discover the constant and universal principles of human nature, by showing men in all varieties of circumstances and
situations, and furnishing us with materials from which we may form our observations and become acquainted with the regular springs of human action
and behavior. These records of wars, intrigues, factions, and revolutions, are
so many collections of experiments, by which the politician or moral philosopher fixes the principles of his science, in the same manner as the physician
or natural philosopher becomes acquainted with the nature of plants, miner-
als, and other external objects, by the experiments which he forms concerning
them. Nor are the earth, water, and other elements, examined by Aristotle,
and Hippocrates, more like to those which at present lie under our observation than the men described by Polybius and Tacitus are to those who now
govern the world.

Should a traveler, returning from a far country, bring us an account of
men, wholly different from any with whom we were ever acquainted; men,
who were entirely divested of avarice, ambition, or revenge; who knew no
pleasure but friendship, generosity, and public spirit; we should immediately,
from these circumstances, detect the falsehood, and prove him a liar, with the
same certainty as if he had stuffed his narration with stories of centaurs and
dragons, miracles and prodigies. And if we would explode any forgery in history, we cannot make use of a more convincing argument, than to prove, that
the actions ascribed to any person are directly contrary to the course of nature,
and that no human motives, in such circumstances, could ever induce him to
such a conduct. The veracity of Quintus Curtius is as much to be suspected,
when he describes the supernatural courage of Alexander, by which he was
hurried on singly to attack multitudes, as when he describes his supernatural
force and activity, by which he was able to resist them. So readily and universally do we acknowledge a uniformity in human motives and actions as well
as in the operations of body.

Hence likewise the benefit of that experience, acquired by long life and a
variety of business and company, in order to instruct us in the principles of
human nature, and regulate our future conduct, as well as speculation. By
means of this guide, we mount up to the knowledge of men's inclinations and
motives, from their actions, expressions, and even gestures; and again descend
to the interpretation of their actions from our knowledge of their motives and
inclinations. The general observations treasured up by a course of experience,
give us the clue of human nature, and teach us to unravel all its intricacies.
Pretexts and appearances no longer deceive us. Public declarations pass for
the specious coloring of a cause. And though virtue and honor be allowed
their proper weight and authority, that perfect disinterestedness, so often pretended to, is never expected in multitudes and parties; seldom in their leaders;
and scarcely even in individuals of any rank or station. But were there no uniformity in human actions, and were every experiment which we could form of
this kind irregular and anomalous, it were impossible to collect any general
observations concerning mankind; and no experience, however accurately di-
gested by reflection, would ever serve to any purpose. Why is the aged

husbandman more skilful in his calling than the young beginner but because there is a certain uniformity in the operation of the sun, rain, and earth towards the production of vegetables; and experience teaches the old practitioner the rules by which this operation is governed and directed.

We must not, however, expect that this uniformity of human actions should be carried to such a length as that all men, in the same circumstances, will always act precisely in the same manner, without making any allowance for the diversity of characters, prejudices, and opinions. Such a uniformity in every particular, is found in no part of nature. On the contrary, from observing the variety of conduct in different men, we are enabled to form a greater variety of maxims, which still suppose a degree of uniformity and regularity.

Are the manners of men different in different ages and countries? We learn thence the great force of custom and education, which mould the human mind from its infancy and form it into a fixed and established character. Is the behavior and conduct of the one sex very unlike that of the other? Is it thence we become acquainted with the different characters which nature has impressed upon the sexes, and which she preserves with constancy and regularity? Are the actions of the same person much diversified in the different periods of his life, from infancy to old age? This affords room for many general observations concerning the gradual change of our sentiments and inclinations, and the different maxims which prevail in the different ages of human creatures. Even the characters, which are peculiar to each individual, have a uniformity in their influence; otherwise our acquaintance with the persons and our observation of their conduct could never teach us their dispositions, or serve to direct our behavior with regard to them.

I grant it possible to find some actions, which seem to have no regular connection with any known motives, and are exceptions to all the measures of conduct which have ever been established for the government of men. But if we would willingly know what judgment should be formed of such irregular and extraordinary actions, we may consider the sentiments commonly entertained with regard to those irregular events which appear in the course of nature, and the operations of external objects. All causes are not conjoined to their usual effects with like uniformity. An artificer, who handles only dead matter, may be disappointed of his aim, as well as the politician, who directs the conduct of sensible and intelligent agents. *there are always surprises*

The vulgar, who take things according to their first appearance, attribute the uncertainty of events to such an uncertainty in the causes as makes the latter often fail of their usual influence; though they meet with no impediment in their operation. But philosophers, observing that, almost in every part of nature, there is contained a vast variety of springs and principles, which are hid, by reason of their minuteness or remoteness, find, that it is at least possible the contrariety of events may not proceed from any contingency in the cause, but from the secret operation of contrary causes. This possibility is converted into certainty by farther observation, when they remark that, upon an exact scrutiny, a contrariety of effects always betrays a contrariety of causes, and proceeds from their mutual opposition. A peasant can give no better reason for the stopping of any clock or watch than to say that it does not commonly go right: But an artist easily perceives that the same force in the spring or pendulum has always the same influence on the wheels; but fails of its usual effects, perhaps by reason of a grain of dust, which puts a stop to the whole movement. From the observation of several parallel instances, philosophers form a maxim that the connection between all causes and effects is equally necessary, and that its seeming uncertainty in some instances proceeds from the secret opposition of contrary causes.

Thus, for instance, in the human body, when the usual symptoms of health or sickness disappoint our expectation; when medicines operate not with their wonted powers; when irregular events follow from any particular cause; the philosopher and physician are not surprised at the matter, nor are ever tempted to deny, in general, the necessity and uniformity of those principles by which the animal economy is conducted. They know that a human body is a mighty complicated machine: That many secret powers lurk in it, which are altogether beyond our comprehension: That to us it must often appear very uncertain in its operations: And that therefore the irregular events, which outwardly discover themselves, can be no proof that the laws of nature are not observed with the greatest regularity in its internal operations and government.

The philosopher, if he be consistent, must apply the same reasoning to the actions and volitions of intelligent agents. The most irregular and unexpected resolutions of men may frequently be accounted for by those who know every particular circumstance of their character and situation. A person of an obliging disposition gives a peevish answer: But he has the toothache, or has not dined. A stupid fellow discovers an uncommon alacrity in his carriage: But he has met with a sudden piece of good fortune. Or even when an action, as sometimes happens, cannot be particularly accounted for, either by the person himself or by others; we know, in general, that the characters of men are, to a certain degree, inconstant and irregular. This is, in a manner, the constant character of human nature; though it be applicable, in a more particular manner, to some persons who have no fixed rule for their conduct, but proceed in a continued course of caprice and inconstancy. The internal principles and motives may operate in a uniform manner, notwithstanding these seeming irregularities; in the same manner as the winds, rain, cloud, and other variations of the weather are supposed to be governed by steady principles; though not easily discoverable by human sagacity and enquiry.

[INFERRING ACTIONS FROM MOTIVES]

Thus it appears, not only that the conjunction between motives and voluntary actions is as regular and uniform as that between the cause and effect in any part of nature; but also that this regular conjunction has been universally acknowledged among mankind, and has never been the subject of dispute, either in philosophy or common life. Now, as it is from past experience that we draw all *inferences* concerning the future, and as we conclude that objects will always be conjoined together which we find to have always been conjoined; it may seem superfluous to prove that this experienced uniformity in human actions is a source whence we draw inferences concerning them. But in order to throw the argument into a greater variety of lights we shall also insist, though briefly, on this latter topic.

The mutual dependence of men is so great in all societies that scarce any human action is entirely complete in itself, or is performed without some reference to the actions of others, which are requisite to make it answer fully the intention of the agent. The poorest artificer, who labors alone, expects at least the protection of the magistrate, to ensure him the enjoyment of the fruits of his labor. He also expects that, when he carries his goods to market, and offers them at a reasonable price, he shall find purchasers, and shall be able, by the money he acquires, to engage others to supply him with those commodities which are requisite for his subsistence. In proportion as men extend their dealings, and render their intercourse with others more complicated, they always comprehend, in their schemes of life, a greater variety of voluntary actions, which they expect, from the proper motives, to cooperate with their own. In all these conclusions they take their measures from past experience, in the same manner as in their reasonings concerning external objects; and firmly believe that men, as well as all the elements, are to continue, in their operations, the same that they have ever found them. A manufacturer reckons upon the labor of his servants for the execution of any work as much as upon the tools which he employs, and would be equally surprised were his expectations disappointed. In short, this experimental inference and reasoning concerning the actions of others enters so much into human life that no man, while awake, is ever a moment without employing it. Have we not reason, therefore, to affirm that all mankind have always agreed in the doctrine of necessity according to the foregoing definition and explication of it?

Nor have philosophers even entertained a different opinion from the people in this particular. For, not to mention that almost every action of their life supposes that opinion, there are even few of the speculative parts of learning to which it is not essential. What would become of *history*, had we not a dependence on the veracity of the historian according to the experience which we have had of mankind? How could _politics_ be a science, if laws and forms of government had not a uniform influence upon society? Where would be the foundation of _morals_, if particular characters had no certain or determinate power to produce particular sentiments, and if these sentiments had no constant operation on actions? And with what pretence could we employ our *criticism* upon any poet or polite author, if we could not pronounce the conduct and sentiments of his actors either natural or unnatural to such characters, and in such circumstances? It seems almost impossible, therefore, to engage either in science or action of any kind without acknowledging the doctrine of necessity, and this *inference* from motive to voluntary actions, from characters to conduct.

And indeed, when we consider how aptly *natural* and *moral* evidence link together, and form only one chain of argument, we shall make no scruple to allow that they are of the same nature, and derived from the same principles. A prisoner who has neither money nor interest, discovers the impossibility of his escape, as well when he considers the obstinacy of the gaoler, as the walls and bars with which he is surrounded; and, in all attempts for his freedom, chooses rather to work upon the stone and iron of the one, than upon the inflexible nature of the other. The same prisoner, when conducted to the scaffold, foresees his death as certainly from the constancy and fidelity of his guards, as from the operation of the axe or wheel. His mind runs along a certain train of ideas: The refusal of the soldiers to consent to his escape; the action of the executioner; the separation of the head and body; bleeding, convulsive motions, and death. Here is a connected chain of natural causes and voluntary actions; but the mind feels no difference between them in passing from one link to another: Nor is it less certain of the future event than if it were connected with the objects present to the memory or senses, by a train of causes, cemented together by what we are pleased to call a *physical* necessity. The same experienced union has the same effect on the mind, whether the united objects be motives, volition, and actions; or figure and motion. We may change the name of things; but their nature and their operation on the understanding never change.

Were a man, whom I know to be honest and opulent, and with whom I live in intimate friendship, to come into my house, where I am surrounded with my servants, I rest assured that he is not to stab me before he leaves it in order to rob me of my silver standish; and I no more suspect this event than the falling of the house itself, which is new, and solidly built and founded.— *But he may have been seized with a sudden and unknown frenzy.*—So may a sudden earthquake arise, and shake and tumble my house about my ears. I shall therefore change the suppositions. I shall say that I know with certainty that he is not to put his hand into the fire and hold it there till it be consumed: And this event, I think I can foretell with the same assurance, as that, if he throw himself out at the window, and meet with no obstruction, he will not remain a moment suspended in the air. No suspicion of an unknown frenzy can give the least possibility to the former event, which is so contrary to all the known principles of human nature. A man who at noon leaves his purse full of gold on the pavement at Charing-Cross, may as well expect that it will fly away like a feather, as that he will find it untouched an hour after. Above one half of human reasonings contain inferences of a similar nature, attended with more or less degrees of certainty proportioned to our experience of the usual conduct of mankind in such particular situations.

[WHY PEOPLE OPPOSE NECESSITY]

I have frequently considered, what could possibly be the reason why all mankind, though they have ever, without hesitation, acknowledged the doctrine of necessity in their whole practice and reasoning, have yet discovered such a reluctance to acknowledge it in words, and have rather shown a

propensity, in all ages, to profess the contrary opinion. The matter, I think, may be accounted for after the following manner. If we examine the operations of body, and the production of effects from their causes, we shall find that all our faculties can never carry us farther in our knowledge of this relation than barely to observe that particular objects are *constantly conjoined* together, and that the mind is carried, by a *customary transition,* from the appearance of one to the belief of the other. But though this conclusion concerning human ignorance be the result of the strictest scrutiny of this subject, men still entertain a strong propensity to believe that they penetrate farther into the powers of nature, and perceive something like a necessary connection between the cause and the effect. When again they turn their reflections towards the operations of their own minds, and *feel* no such connection of the motive and the action; they are thence apt to suppose, that there is a difference between the effects which result from material force, and those which arise from thought and intelligence. But being once convinced that we know nothing farther of causation of any kind than merely the *constant conjunction* of objects, and the consequent *inference* of the mind from one to another, and finding that these two circumstances are universally allowed to have place in voluntary actions; we may be more easily led to own the same necessity common to all causes. And though this reasoning may contradict the systems of many philosophers, in ascribing necessity to the determinations of the will, we shall find, upon reflection, that they dissent from it in words only, not in their real sentiment. Necessity, according to the sense in which it is here taken, has never yet been rejected, nor can ever, I think, be rejected by any philosopher. It may only, perhaps, be pretended that the mind can perceive, in the operations of matter, some farther connection between the cause and effect; and connection that has no place in voluntary actions of intelligent beings. Now whether it be so or not, can only appear upon examination; and it is incumbent on these philosophers to make good their assertion, by defining or describing that necessity, and pointing it out to us in the operations of material causes.

It would seem, indeed, that men begin at the wrong end of this question concerning liberty and necessity, when they enter upon it by examining the faculties of the soul, the influence of the understanding, and the operations of the will. Let them first discuss a more simple question, namely, the operations of body and of brute unintelligent matter; and try whether they can there form any idea of causation and necessity, except that of a constant conjunction of objects, and subsequent inference of the mind from one to another. If these circumstances form, in reality, the whole of that necessity, which we conceive in matter, and if these circumstances be also universally acknowledged to take place in the operations of the mind, the dispute is at an end; at least, must be owned to be thenceforth merely verbal. But as long as we will rashly suppose, that we have some farther idea of necessity and causation in the operations of external objects; at the same time, that we can find nothing farther in the voluntary actions of the mind; there is no possibility of bringing the question to any determinate issue, while we proceed upon so erroneous a supposition. The only method of undeceiving us is to mount up higher; to examine the narrow extent of science when applied to material causes; and to convince ourselves that all we know of them is the constant conjunction and inference above mentioned. We may, perhaps, find that it is with difficulty we are induced to fix such narrow limits to human understanding: But we can afterwards find no difficulty when we come to apply this doctrine to the actions of the will. For as it is evident that these have a regular conjunction with motives and circumstances and characters, and as we always draw inferences from one to the other, we must be obliged to acknowledge in words that necessity, which we have already avowed, in every deliberation of our lives, and in every step of our conduct and behavior.

[THE NOTION OF LIBERTY]

But to proceed in this reconciling project with regard to the question of liberty and necessity; the most contentious question of metaphysics, the most contentious science; it will not require many words to prove, that all mankind have ever agreed in the doctrine of liberty as well as in that of necessity; and that the whole dispute, in this respect also, has been hitherto merely verbal. For what is meant by liberty, when applied to voluntary actions? We cannot surely mean that actions have so little connection with motives, inclinations, and circumstances, that one does not follow with a certain degree of uniformity from the other, and that one affords no inference by which we can conclude the existence of the other. For these are plain and acknowledged matters of fact. By liberty, then, we can only mean *a power of acting or not acting, according to the determinations of the will;* this is, if we choose to remain at rest, we may; if we choose to move, we also may. Now this hypothetical liberty is universally allowed to belong to every one who is not a prisoner and in chains. Here, then, is no subject of dispute.

Whatever definition we may give of liberty, we should be careful to observe two requisite circumstances; *first,* that it be consistent with plain matter of fact; *secondly,* that it be consistent with itself. If we observe these circumstances, and render our definition intelligible, I am persuaded that all mankind will be found of one opinion with regard to it.

It is universally allowed that nothing exists without a cause of its existence, and that chance, when strictly examined, is a mere negative word, and means not any real power which has anywhere a being in nature. But it is pretended that some causes are necessary, some not necessary. Here then is the advantage of definitions. Let any one *define* a cause, without comprehending, as a part of the definition, a *necessary connection* with its effect; and let him show distinctly the origin of the idea, expressed by the definition; and I shall readily give up the whole controversy. But if the foregoing explication of the matter be received, this must be absolutely impracticable. Had not objects a regular conjunction with each other, we should never have entertained any notion of cause and effect; and this regular conjunction produces that inference of the understanding, which is the only connection, that we can have any comprehension of. Whoever attempts a definition of cause, exclusive of these circumstances, will be obliged either to employ unintelligible terms or such as are synonymous to the term which he endeavors to define. And if the definition above mentioned be admitted; liberty, when opposed to necessity, not to constraint, is the same thing with chance; which is universally allowed to have no existence.

READING 33

An Argument for Free Will from Common Sense Convictions*

Thomas Reid (1710–1796)

[FIVE ARGUMENTS IN DEFENSE OF FREE WILL]

We have, by our constitution, a natural conviction or belief that we act freely. A conviction so early, so universal, and so necessary in most of our rational operations, that it must be the result of our constitution, and the work of Him that made us.

Some of the most strenuous advocates for the doctrine of necessity acknowledge, that it is impossible to act upon it. They say that we have a natural sense or conviction that we act freely, but that this is a fallacious sense.

This doctrine is dishonorable to our maker, and lays a foundation for universal skepticism. It supposes the Author of our being to have given us one faculty on purpose to deceive us, and another by which we may detect the fallacy, and find that be imposed upon us.

If any one of our natural faculties be fallacious, there can be no reason to trust to any of them; for he that made one made all.

The genuine dictate of our natural faculties is the voice of God, no less than what he reveals from heaven; and to say that it is fallacious, is to impute a lie to the God of truth.

If candor and veracity be not an essential part of moral excellence, there is no such thing as moral excellence, nor any reason to rely on the declarations and promises of the Almighty. A man may be tempted to lie, but not without being conscious of guilt and of meanness. Shall we impute to the Almighty what we cannot impute to a man without a heinous affront?

Passing this opinion, therefore, as shocking to an ingenuous minds and, in its consequences, subversive of all religion, all morals, and all knowledge, let us proceed to consider the evidence of our having a natural conviction that we have some degree of active power.

*From Thomas Reid, *Essays on the Active Powers of the Human Mind* (1788), Essay 4, Chap. 6, First Argument.

free will

The very conception or idea of <u>active power</u> must be derived from something in our own constitution. It is impossible to account for it otherwise. We see events, but we see not the power that produces them. We perceive one event to follow another, but we perceive not the chain that binds them together. The notion of power and causation, therefore, cannot be got from external objects.

Yet the notion of causes, and the belief that every event must have a cause which had power to produce it, is found in every human mind so firmly established, that it cannot be rooted out.

This notion and this belief must have its origin from something in our constitution; and that it is natural to man, appears from the following observations.

First, we are conscious of many voluntary exertions, some easy, others more difficult, some requiring a great effort. These are exertions of power. And though a man may be unconscious of his power when he does not exert it, he must have both the conception and the belief of it when he knowingly and willingly exerts it, with intention to produce some effect.

Secondly, deliberation about an action of moment, whether we shall do it or not, implies a conviction that it is in our power. To deliberate about an end, we must be convinced that the means are in our power; and to deliberate about the means, we must be convinced that we have power to choose the most proper.

Thirdly, suppose our deliberation brought to an issue, and that we resolved to do what appeared proper, can we form such a resolution or purpose, without any conviction of power to execute it? No; it is impossible. A man cannot resolve to pay out a sum of money, which he neither has, nor hopes ever to have.

Fourthly, again, when I plight my faith in any promise or contract, I must believe that I shall have power to perform what I promise. Without this persuasion, a promise would be downright fraud.

There is a condition implied in every promise, *if we live,* and *if God continue with its the power which he has given us.* Our conviction, therefore, of this power derogates not in the least from our dependence upon God. The rudest savage is taught by nature to admit this condition in all promises, whether it be expressed or not. For it is a dictate of common sense, that we can be under no obligation to do what it is impossible for us to do.

If we act upon the system of necessity, there must be another condition implied in all deliberation, in every resolution, and in every promise; and that is, *if we shall be willing.* But the will not being in our power, we cannot engage for it.

If this condition be understood, as it must be understood if we act upon the system of necessity, there can be no deliberation or resolution, nor any obligation in a promise. A man might as well deliberate resolved and promise, upon the actions of other men as upon his own.

It is no less evident, that we have a conviction of power in other men, when we advise, or persuade, or command, or conceive them to be under obligation by their promises.

✦ Fifthly, is it possible for any man to blame himself for yielding to necessity? Then he may blame himself for dying, or for being a man. Blame supposes a wrong use of power; and when a man does as well as it was possible for him to do, wherein is he to be blamed? Therefore all conviction of wrong conduct, all remorse, and self-condemnation, imply a conviction of our power to have done better. Take away this conviction, and there may be a sense of misery, or a dread of evil to come, but there can be no sense of guilt, or resolution to do better.

[THE COMMON SENSE BELIEF IN FREE WILL]

Many who hold the doctrine of necessity, disown these consequences of it, and think to evade them. To such they ought not to be imputed; but their inseparable connection with that doctrine appears self-evident; and therefore some late patrons of it have had the boldness to avow them. "They cannot accuse themselves of having done any thing wrong in the ultimate sense of the words. In a strict sense, they have nothing to do with repentance, confession, and pardon, these being adapted to a fallacious view of things."

Those who can adopt these sentiments, may indeed celebrate, with high encomiums, *the great and glorious doctrine of necessity.* It restores them, in their own conceit, to the state of innocence. It delivers them from all the pangs of guilt and remorse, and from all fear about their future conduct, though not about their fate. They may be as secure that they shall do nothing wrong, as those who have finished their course. A doctrine so flattering to the mind of a sinner, is very apt to give strength to weak arguments.

After all, it is acknowledged by those who boast or this glorious doctrine, "That every man, let him use what efforts he can, will necessarily feel the sentiments of shame, remorse, and repentance, and, oppressed with a sense of guilt, will have recourse to that mercy of which he stands in need."

The meaning of this seems to me to be, that although the doctrine of necessity be supported by invincibly arguments, and though it be the most consolatory doctrine in the world; yet no man in his most serious moments, when he sits himself before the throne of his maker, can possibly believe it, but must then necessarily lay aside this glorious doctrine, and all its flattering consequences, and return to the humiliating conviction of his having made a bad use of the power which God had given him.

If the belief of our having active power be necessarily implied in those rational operations we have mentioned, it must be coeval with our reason; it must be as universal among men, and as necessary in the conduct of life, as those operations are.

We cannot recollect by memory when it began. It cannot be a prejudice of education, or of false philosophy. It must be a part of our constitution, or the necessary result of our constitution, and therefore the work or God.

It resembles, in this respect, our belief of the existence of a material world; our belief that those we converse with are living and intelligent beings; our belief that those things did really happen which we distinctly remember, and our belief that we continue the same identical persons.

We find difficulty in accounting for our belief of these things; and some philosophers think, that they have discovered good reasons for throwing it off. But it sticks fast, and the greatest skeptic finds, that he must yield to it in his practice, while he wages war with it in speculation.

[RESPONSES TO POSSIBLE OBJECTIONS]

If it be objected to this argument, that the belief of our acting freely cannot be implied in the operations we have mentioned, because those operations are performed by them who believe that we are, in all our actions, governed by necessity; the answer to this objection is, that men in their practice may be governed by a belief which in speculation they reject.

However strange and unaccountable this may appears, there are many well-known instances of it.

I knew a man who was as much convinced as any man of the folly of the popular belief of apparitions in the dark, yet he could not sleep in a room alone, nor go alone into a room in the dark. Can it be said, that his fear did not imply a belief of danger? This is impossible. Yet his philosophy convinced him, that he was in no more danger in the dark when alone, than with company.

Here an unreasonable belief, which was merely a prejudice of the nursery, stuck so fast as to govern his conduct, in opposition to his speculative belief as a philosopher, and a man of sense.

There are few persons who can look down from the battlement of a very high tower without fear, while their reason convinces them that they are in no more danger than when standing upon the ground.

There have been persons who professed to believe that there is no distinction between virtue and vice, yet in their practice, they resented injuries, and esteemed noble and virtuous actions.

There have been skeptics who professed to disbelieve their senses, and every human faculty; but no skeptic was ever known, who did not, in practice, pay a regard to his senses and to his other faculties.

There are some points of belief so necessary, that, without them, a man would not he the being which God made him. These may be opposed in speculation, but it is impossible to root them out. In a speculative hour they seem to vanish, but in practice they resume their authority. This seems to be the case of those who hold the doctrine of necessity, and yet act as if they were free.

This natural conviction of some degree of power in ourselves and in other men, respects voluntary actions only. For as all our power is directed by our will, we can form no conception of power, properly so called, that is; not under the direction of will. And therefore our exertions, our deliberations, our purposes, our promises, are only in things that depend upon our will. Our advices, exhortations, and commands, are only in things that depend upon the will or those to whom they are addressed. We impute no guilt to ourselves, nor to others; in things where the will is not concerned.

But it deserves our notice, that we do not conceive everything, without exception to be in a man's power which depends upon his will. There are many exceptions to this general rule. The most obvious of these I shall mention, because they both serve to illustrate the rule, and are or importance in the question concerning the liberty of man.

In the rage of madness, men are absolutely deprived of the power of self-government. They act voluntarily, but their will is driven as by a tempest, which, in lucid intervals, they resolve to oppose with all their might, but are overcome when the fit of madness returns.

Idiots are like men walking in the dark, who cannot be said to have the power of choosing their may, because they cannot distinguish the good road from the bad. Having no light in their understanding, they must either sit still, or be carried on by some blind impulse.

Between the darkness of infancy, which is equal to that of idiots, and the maturity of reason, there is a long twilight which, by <u>insensible</u> degrees, advances to the perfect day.

In this period of life, man has but little of the power of self-government. His actions, by nature, as well as by the laws of society, are in the power of others more than in his own. His folly and indiscretion, his levity and inconstancy, are considered as the fault of youth, rather than of the man. We consider him as half a man and half a child, and expect that each by turns should play its part. He would be thought a severe and unequitable censor of manners, who required the same cool deliberation, the same steady conduct, and the same mastery over himself in a boy of thirteen, as in a man of thirty.

It is an old adage, that violent anger is a short fit of madness. If this be literally true in any case, a man in such a fit of passion, cannot be said to have the command of himself. If real madness could be proved, it must have the effect of madness while it lasts, whether it be for an hour or for life. But the madness of a short fit of passion, if it be really madness, is incapable of proof; and therefore is not admitted in human tribunals as an exculpation. And, I believe, <u>there is no case where a man can satisfy his own mind that his passion,</u> ⟨no excuses⟩ <u>both in its beginning and in its progress, was irresistible.</u> The Searcher of hearts alone knows infallibly what allowance is due in cases of this kind.

But a violent passion, though it may not be irresistible, is difficult to be resisted: and a man, surely, has not the same power over himself in passion, as when he is cool. On this account it is allowed by all men to alleviate, when it cannot exculpate; and has its weight in criminal courts, as well as in private judgment.

It ought likewise to be observed, that he who has accustomed himself to restrain his passions, enlarges by habit his power over them, and consequently over himself. When we consider that a Canadian savage can acquire the power of defying death, in its most dreadful forms, and of braving the most exquisite torment for many long hours, without losing the command of himself; we may learn from this, that, in the constitution of human natures there is ample scope for the enlargement of that power of self-command, without which there can be no virtue nor magnanimity.

There are cases, however, in which a man's voluntary actions are thought to be very little, if at all, in his power, on account of the violence of the motive that impels him. The magnanimity of a hero, or of a martyr, is not expected in every man, and on all occasions.

If a man trusted by the government with a secret, which it is high treason to disclose, be prevailed upon by a bribe, we have no mercy for him, and hardly allow the greatest bribe to be any alleviation of his crime.

But, on the other hand, if the secret be extorted by the rack, or by the dread of present death, we pity him more than we blame him, and would think it severe and unequitable to condemn him as a traitor.

What is the reason that all men agree in condemning this man as a traitor in the first case, and in the last, either exculpate him, or think his fault greatly alleviated? If he acted necessarily in both cases, compelled by an irresistible motive, I can see no reason why we should not pass the same judgment on both.

But the reason of these different judgments is evidently this, that the love of money, and of what is called a man's interest, is a cool motive, which leaves to a man the entire power over himself: but the torment of the rack, or the dread of present death, are so violent motives, that men who have not uncommon strength of mind, are not masters of themselves in such a situation, and therefore what they do is not imputed, or is thought less criminal.

If a man resist such motives, we admire his fortitude, and think his conduct heroical rather than human. If he yields, we impute it to human frailty, and think him rather to be pitied than severely censured.

Inveterate habits are acknowledged to diminish very considerably the power a man has over himself. Although we may think him highly blamable in acquiring them, yet when they are confirmed to a certain degree, we consider him as no longer master or himself, and hardly reclaimable without a miracle.

Thus we see, that the power which we are led by common sense to ascribe to man, respects his voluntary actions only, and that it has various limitations even with regard to them. Some actions that depend upon our will are easy, others very difficult, and some, perhaps, beyond our power. In different men, the power of self-government is different, and in the same man at different times. It may be diminished, or perhaps lost, by bad habits; it may be greatly increased by good habits.

These are facts attested by experience, and supported by the common judgment of mankind. Upon the system of liberty, they are perfectly intelligible; but, I think, irreconcilable to that of necessity; for, how can there be an easy and a difficult in actions equally subject to necessity? or, how can power be greater or less, increased or diminished, in those who have no power?

This natural conviction of our acting freely, which is acknowledged by many who hold the doctrine of necessity, ought to throw the whole burden of proof upon that side: for, by this, the side of liberty has what lawyers call *jus quæsitum,* or a right of ancient possession, which ought to stand good till it be overturned. If it cannot be proved that we always act from necessity, there is no need of arguments on the other side, to convince us that we are free agents.

To illustrate this by a similar case: if a philosopher would persuade me, that my fellow men with whom I converse, are not thinking intelligent beings, but mere machines; though I might be at a loss to find arguments against this strange opinion, I should think it reasonable to hold the belief which nature gave me before I was capable of weighing evidence, until convincing proof is brought against it.

READING 34

How Can We Explain Judgments of Regret?*

William James (1842–1910)

[THE DISPUTE BETWEEN DETERMINISM AND INDETERMINISM]

What does determinism profess?

It professes that those parts of the universe already laid down absolutely appoint and decree what the other parts shall be. The future has no ambiguous possibilities hidden in its womb: the part we call the present is compatible with only one totality. Any other future complement than the one fixed from eternity is impossible. The whole is in each and every part, and welds it with the rest into an absolute unity, an iron block, in which there can be no equivocation or shadow of turning.

> With earth's first clay they did the last man knead,
>
> And there of the last harvest sowed the seed.
>
> And the first morning of creation wrote
>
> What the last dawn of reckoning shall read.

Indeterminism, on the contrary, says that the parts have a certain amount of loose play on one another, so that the laying down of one of them does not necessarily determine what the others shall be. It admits that possibilities may be in excess of actualities, and that things not yet revealed to our knowledge may really in themselves be ambiguous.•Of two alternative futures which we conceive, both may now be really possible; and the one become impossible only at the very moment when the other excludes it by becoming real itself. •

*From William James, "The Dilemma of Determinism," in *Unitarian Review,* September 1884.

Indeterminism thus denies the world to be one unbending unit of fact. It says there is a certain ultimate pluralism in it; and, so saying, it corroborates our ordinary unsophisticated view of things. To that view, actualities seem to float in a wider sea of possibilities from out of which they are chosen; and, *somewhere,* indeterminism says, such possibilities exist, and form a part of truth.

Determinism, on the contrary, says they exist *nowhere,* and that necessity on the one hand and impossibility on the other are the sole categories of the real. Possibilities that fail to get realized are, for determinism, pure illusions: they never were possibilities at all. There is nothing inchoate, it says, about this universe of ours, all that was or is or shall be actual in it having been from eternity virtually there. The cloud of alternatives our minds escort this mass of actuality withal is a cloud of sheer deceptions, to which "impossibilities" is the only name that rightfully belongs.

The issue, it will be seen, is a perfectly sharp one, which no eulogistic terminology can smear over or wipe out. The truth *must* lie with one side or the other, and its lying with one side makes the other false.

The question relates solely to the existence of possibilities, in the strict sense of the term, as things that may, but need not, be. Both sides admit that a volition, for instance, has occurred. The indeterminists say another volition might have occurred in its place: the determinists swear that nothing could possibly have occurred in its place. Now, can science be called in to tell us which of these two point-blank contradicters of each other is right? Science professes to draw no conclusions but such as are based on matters of fact, things that have actually happened; but how can any amount of assurance that something actually happened give us the least grain of information as to whether another thing might or might not have happened in its place? Only facts can be proved by other facts. With things that are possibilities and not facts, facts have no concern. If we have no other evidence than the evidence of existing facts, the possibility-question must remain a mystery never to be cleared up.

And the truth is that facts practically have hardly anything to do with making us either determinists or indeterminists. Sure enough, we make a flourish of quoting facts this way or that; and if we are determinists, we talk about the infallibility with which we can predict one another's conduct; while if we are indeterminists, we lay great stress on the fact that it is just because we cannot foretell one another's conduct, either in war or statecraft or in any of the great and small intrigues and businesses of men, that life is so intensely anxious and hazardous a game. But who does not see the wretched insufficiency of this so-called objective testimony on both sides? What fills up the gaps in our minds is something not objective, not external. What divides us into *possibility* men and *anti-possibility* men is different faiths or postulates—postulates of rationality. To this man the world seems more rational with possibilities in it—to that man more rational with possibilities excluded; and talk as we will about having to yield to evidence, what makes us monists or pluralists, determinists or indeterminists, is at bottom always some sentiment like this.

The stronghold of the deterministic sentiment is the antipathy to the idea of chance. As soon as we begin to talk indeterminism to our friends, number of them shaking their heads. This notion of alternative possibility, they say, this admission that any one of several things may come to pass, is, after all, only a round-about name for chance; and chance is something the notion of which no sane mind can for an instant tolerate in the world. What is it, they ask, but barefaced crazy unreason, the negation of intelligibility and law? And if the slightest particle of it exist anywhere, what is to prevent the whole fabric from failing together, the stars from going out, and chaos from recommencing her topsy-turvy reign?

Remarks of this sort about chance will put an end to discussion as quickly as anything one can find. I have already told you that "chance" was a word I wished to keep and use. Let us then examine exactly what it means, and see whether it ought to be such a terrible bugbear to us. I fancy that squeezing the thistle boldly will rob it of its sting.   *   the end

The sting of the word "chance" seems to lie in the assumption that it means something positive, and that if anything happens by chance, it must needs be something of an intrinsically irrational and preposterous sort. Now, chance means nothing of the kind. It is a purely negative and relative term, giving us no information about that of which it is predicated, except that it happens to be disconnected with something else—not controlled, secured, or necessitated by other things in advance of its own actual presence.

As this point is the most subtle one of the whole lecture, and at the same time the point on which all the rest hinges, I beg you to pay particular attention to it. What I say is that it tells us nothing about what a thing may be in itself to call it "chance." It may be a bad thing, it may be a good thing. It may be lucidity, transparency, fitness incarnate, matching the whole system of other things, when it has once befallen, in an unimaginably perfect way. All you mean by calling it "chance" is that this is not guaranteed, that it may also fall out otherwise. For the system of other things has no positive hold on the chance-thing. Its origin is in a certain fashion negative: it escapes, and says, Hands off! coming, when it comes, as a free gift, or not at all. . . .

Nevertheless, many persons talk as if the minutest dose of disconnectedness of one part with another, the smallest modicum of independence, the faintest tremor of ambiguity about the future, for example, would ruin everything, and turn this goodly universe into a sort of insane sand-heap or nulli-verse—no universe at all. Since future human volitions are as a matter of fact the only ambiguous things we are tempted to believe in, let us stop for a moment to make ourselves sure whether their independent and accidental character need be fraught with such direful consequences to the universe as these.

What is meant by saying that my choice of which way to walk home after the lecture is ambiguous and matter of chance as far as the present moment is concerned? It means that both Divinity Avenue and Oxford Street are called; but that only one, and that one *either* one, shall be chosen. Now, I ask you seriously to suppose that this ambiguity of my choice is real; and then to make the impossible hypothesis that the choice is made twice over,

→ 2 possibilities here↑, one or the other

and each time falls on a different street. In other words, imagine that I first walk through Divinity Avenue, and then imagine that the powers governing the universe annihilate ten minutes of time with all that it contained, and set me back at the door of this hall just as I was before the choice was made. Imagine then that, everything else being the same, I now make a different choice and traverse Oxford Street. You, as passive spectators, look on and see the two alternative universes—one of them with me walking through Divinity Avenue in it, the other with the same me walking through Oxford Street. Now, if you are determinists you believe one of these universes to have been from eternity impossible: you believe it to have been impossible because of the intrinsic irrationality or accidentality somewhere involved in it. But looking outwardly at these universes, can you say which is the impossible and accidental one, and which the rational and necessary one? I doubt if the most iron-clad determinist among you could have the slightest glimmer of light on this point. In other words, either universe *after the fact* and once there would, to our means of observation and understanding, appear just as rational as the other. . . .

We have seen what determinism means: we have seen that indeterminism is rightly described as meaning chance; and we have seen that chance, the very name of which we are urged to shrink from as from a metaphysical pestilence, means only the negative fact that no part of the world, however big, can claim to control absolutely the destinies of the whole. But although, in discussing the word "chance," I may at moments have seemed to be arguing for its real existence, I have not meant to do so yet. We have not yet ascertained whether this be a world of chance or no; at most, we have agreed that it seems so. And I now repeat what I said at the outset, that, from any strict theoretical point of view, the question is insoluble. To deepen our theoretic sense of the *difference* between a world with chances in it and a deterministic world is the most I can hope to do; and this I may now at last begin upon, after all our tedious clearing of the way.

[IMPLICATIONS OF A DETERMINISTIC WORLD]

I wish first of all to show you just what the notion that this is a deterministic world implies. The implications I call your attention to are all bound up with the fact that it is a world in which we constantly have to make what I shall, with your permission, call judgments of regret. Hardly an hour passes in which we do not wish that something might be otherwise. . . . Even from the point of view of our own ends, we should probably make a botch of remodeling the universe. How much more then from the point of view of ends we cannot see! Wise men therefore regret as little as they can. But still some regrets are pretty obstinate and hard to stifle—regrets for acts of wanton cruelty or treachery, for example, whether performed by others or by ourselves. Hardly any one can remain *entirely* optimistic after reading the confession of the murderer at Brockton the other day: how, to get rid of the wife whose continued existence bored him, he inveigled her into a desert spot, shot her four times, and then, as she lay on the ground and said to him, "You didn't do it on purpose, did you, dear?" replied, "No, I didn't do it on purpose," as he raised a rock and smashed her skull. Such an occurrence, with the mild sentence and self-satisfaction of the prisoner, is a field for a crop of regrets, which one need not take up in detail. We feel that, although a perfect mechanical fit to the rest of the universe, it is a bad moral fit, and that something else would really have been better in its place.

But for the deterministic philosophy the murder, the sentence, and the prisoner's optimism were all necessary from eternity; and nothing else for a moment had a ghost of a chance of being put into their place. To admit such a chance, the determinists tell us, would be to make a suicide of reason; so we must steel our hearts against the thought. And here our plot thickens, for we see the first of all those difficult implications of determinism and monism which it is my purpose to make you feel. If this Brockton murder was called for by the rest of the universe, if it had to come at its pre-appointed hour, and if nothing else would have been consistent with the sense of the whole, what are we to think of the universe? Are we stubbornly to stick to our judgment of regret, and say, though it *couldn't* be, yet it *would* have been a better universe with something different from this Brockton murder in it? That, of course, seems the natural and spontaneous thing for us to do; and yet it is nothing short of deliberately espousing a kind of pessimism. The judgment of regret calls the murder bad. Calling a thing bad means, if it mean anything at all, that the thing ought not to be, that something else ought to be in its stead. Determinism, in denying that anything else can be in its stead, virtually defines the universe as a place in which what ought to be is impossible—in other words, as an organism whose constitution is afflicted with an incurable taint, an irremediable flaw. The pessimism of a Schopenhauer says no more than this—that the murder is a symptom; and that it is a vicious symptom because it belongs to a vicious whole, which can express its nature no otherwise than by bringing forth just such a symptom as that at this particular spot. Regret for the murder must transform itself, if we are determinists and wise, into a larger regret. It is absurd to regret the murder alone. Other things being what they are, *it* could not be different. What we should regret is that whole frame of things of which the murder is one member. I see no escape whatever from this pessimistic conclusion if, being determinists, our judgment of regret is to be allowed to stand at all.

The only deterministic escape from pessimism is everywhere to abandon the judgment of regret. That this can be done, history shows to be not impossible. The devil, *quoad existentiam,* may be good. That is, although he be a *principle* of evil, yet the universe, with such a principle in it, may practically be a better universe than it could have been without. On every hand, in a small way, we find that a certain amount of evil is a condition by which a higher form of good is brought. There is nothing to prevent anybody from generalizing this view, and trusting that if we could but see things in the largest of all ways, even such matters as this Brockton murder would appear to be paid for by the uses that follow in their train. An optimism *quand meme,* a systematic and infatuated optimism like that ridiculed by Voltaire in his *Candide,* is one of the possible ideal ways in which a man may train himself to look on life. Bereft of dogmatic hardness and lit up with the expression of a tender and pathetic hope, such an optimism has been the grace of some of the most religious characters that ever lived.

> Throb thine with Nature's throbbing breast,
>
> And all is clear from east to west.

Even cruelty and treachery may be among the absolutely blessed fruits of time, and to quarrel with any of their details may be blasphemy. The only real blasphemy, in short, may be that pessimistic temper of the soul which lets it give way to such things as regrets, remorse, and grief.

Thus, our deterministic pessimism may become a deterministic optimism at the price of extinguishing our judgments of regret.

But does not this immediately bring us into a curious logical predicament? Our determinism leads us to call our judgments of regret wrong, because they are pessimistic in implying that what is impossible yet ought to be. But how then about the judgments of regret themselves? If they are wrong, other judgments, judgments of approval presumably, ought to be in their place. But as they are necessitated, nothing else *can* be in their place; and the universe is just what it was before—namely, a place in which what ought to be appears impossible. We have got one foot out of the pessimistic bog, but the other one sinks all the deeper. We have rescued our actions from the bonds of evil, but our judgments are now held fast. When murders and treacheries cease to be sins, regrets are theoretic absurdities and errors. The theoretic and the active life thus play a kind of see-saw with each other on the ground of evil. The rise of either sends the other down. Murder and treachery cannot be good without regret being bad: regret cannot be good without treachery and murder being bad. Both, however, are supposed to have been foredoomed; so something must be fatally unreasonable, absurd, and wrong in the world. It must be a place of which either sin or error forms a necessary part. From this dilemma there seems at first sight no escape. Are we then so soon to fall back into the pessimism from which we thought we had emerged? And is there no possible way by which we may, with good intellectual consciences, call the cruelties and the treacheries, the reluctances and the regrets, all good together? . . .

The only consistent way of representing a pluralism and a world whose parts may affect one another through their conduct being either good or bad is the indeterministic way. What interest, zest, or excitement can there be in achieving the right way, unless we are enabled to feel that the wrong way is also a possible and a natural way—nay, more, a menacing and an imminent way? And what sense can there be in condemning ourselves for taking the wrong way, unless we need have done nothing of the sort, unless the right way was open to us as well? I cannot understand the willingness to act, no matter how we feel, without the belief that acts are really good and bad. I cannot understand the belief that an act is bad, without regret at its happening. I cannot understand regret without the admission of real, genuine possibilities in the world. Only *then* is it other than a mockery to feel, after we have failed to do our best, that an irreparable opportunity is gone from the universe, the loss of which it must forever after mourn. . . .

READING 35

The Freedom of the Will[*]

John Searle (b. 1932)

[THE TRADITIONAL PROBLEM OF FREE WILL AND DETERMINISM]

In these pages, I have tried to answer what to me are some of the most worrisome questions about how we as human beings fit into the rest of the universe. Our conception of ourselves as free agents is fundamental to our overall self-conception. Now, ideally, I would like to be able to keep both my commonsense conceptions and my scientific beliefs. In the case of the relation between mind and body, for example, I was able to do that. But when it comes to the question of freedom and determinism, I am—like a lot of other philosophers—unable to reconcile the two.

One would think that after over 2000 years of worrying about it, the problem of the freedom of the will would by now have been finally solved. Well, actually most philosophers think it has been solved. They think it was solved by Thomas Hobbes and David Hume and various other empirically-minded philosophers whose solutions have been repeated and improved right into the twentieth century. I think it has not been solved. In this lecture I want to give you an account of what the problem is, and why the contemporary solution is not a solution, and then conclude by trying to explain why the problem is likely to stay with us.

On the one hand we are inclined to say that since nature consists of particles and their relations with each other, and since everything can be accounted for in terms of those particles and their relations, there is simply no room for freedom of the will. As far as human freedom is concerned, it doesn't matter whether physics is deterministic, as Newtonian physics was, or whether it allows for an indeterminacy at the level of particle physics, as contemporary quantum mechanics does. Indeterminism at the level of particles in physics is

---

[*]From John Searle, "Freedom of the Will," in *Minds, Brains and Science* (1984).

really no support at all to any doctrine of the freedom of the will; because first, the statistical indeterminacy at the level of particles does not show any indeterminacy at the level of the objects that matter to us—human bodies, for example. And secondly, even if there is an element of indeterminacy in the behavior of physical particles—even if they are only statistically predictable—still, that by itself gives no scope for human freedom of the will; because it doesn't follow from the fact that particles are only statistically determined that the human mind can force the statistically—determined particles to swerve from their paths. Indeterminism is no evidence that there is or could be some mental energy of human freedom that can move molecules in directions that they were not otherwise going to move. So it really does look as if everything we know about physics forces us to some form of denial of human freedom.

The strongest image for conveying this conception of determinism is still that formulated by Laplace: If an ideal observer knew the positions of all the particles at a given instant and knew all the laws governing their movements, he could predict and retrodict the entire history of the universe. Some of the predictions of a contemporary quantum-mechanical Laplace might be statistical, but they would still allow no room for freedom of the will.

So much for the appeal of determinism. Now let's turn to the argument for the freedom of the will. As many philosophers have pointed out, if there is any fact of experience that we are all familiar with, it's the simple fact that our own choices, decisions, reasonings, and cogitations seem to make a difference to our actual behavior. There are all sorts of experiences that we have in life where it seems just a fact of our experience that though we did one thing, we feel we know perfectly well that we could have done something else. We know we could have done something else, because we chose one thing for certain reasons. But we were aware that there were also reasons for choosing something else, and indeed, we might have acted on those reasons and chosen that something else. Another way to put this point is to say: it is just a plain empirical fact about our behavior that it isn't predictable in the way that the behavior of objects rolling down an inclined plane is predictable. And the reason it isn't predictable in that way is that we could often have done otherwise than we in fact did. Human freedom is just a fact of experience. If we want some empirical proof of this fact, we can simply point to the further fact that it is always up to us to falsify any predictions anybody might care to make about our behavior. If somebody predicts that I am going to do something, I might just damn well do something else. Now, that sort of option is simply not open to glaciers moving down mountainsides or balls rolling down inclined planes or the planets moving in their elliptical orbits.

This is a characteristic philosophical conundrum. On the one hand, a set of very powerful arguments force us to the conclusion that free will has no place in the universe. On the other hand, a series of powerful arguments based on facts of our own experience inclines us to the conclusion that there must be some freedom of the will because we all experience it all the time.

[THE COMPATIBILISM SOLUTION]

There is a standard solution to this philosophical conundrum. According to this solution, free will and determinism are perfectly compatible with each other. Of course, everything in the world is determined, but some human actions are nonetheless free. To say that they are free is not to deny that they are determined; it is just to say that they are not constrained. We are not forced to do them. So, for example, if a man is forced to do something at gunpoint, or if he is suffering from some psychological compulsion, then his behavior is genuinely unfree. But if on the other hand he freely acts, if he acts, as we say, of his own free will, then his behavior is free. Of course it is also completely determined, since every aspect of his behavior is determined by the physical forces operating on the particles that compose his body, as they operate on all of the bodies in the universe. So, free behavior exists, but it is just a small corner of the determined world—it is that corner of determined human behavior where certain kinds of force and compulsions are absent.

Now, because this view asserts the compatibility of free will and determinism, it is usually called simply "compatibilism." I think it is inadequate as a solution to the problem, and here is why. The problem about the freedom of the will is not about whether or not there are inner psychological reasons that cause us to do things as well as external physical causes and inner compulsions. Rather, it is about whether or not the causes of our behavior, whatever they are, are sufficient to *determine* the behavior so that things *have to* happen the way they do happen.

There's another way to put this problem. Is it ever true to say of a person that he could have done otherwise, all other conditions remaining the same? For example, given that a person chose to vote for the Tories, could he have chosen to vote for one of the other parties, all other conditions remaining the same? Now compatibilism doesn't really answer that question in a way that allows any scope for the ordinary notion of the freedom of the will. What it says is that all behavior is determined in such a way that it couldn't have occurred otherwise, all other conditions remaining the same. Everything that happened was indeed determined. It's just that some things were determined by certain sorts of inner psychological causes (those which we call our "reasons for acting") and not by external forces or psychological compulsions. So, we are still left with a problem. Is it ever true to say of a human being that he could have done otherwise?

The problem about compatibilism, then, is that it doesn't answer the question, "Could we have done otherwise, all other conditions remaining the same?" in a way that is consistent with our belief in our own free will. Compatibilism, in short, denies the substance of free will while maintaining its verbal shell.

[OTHER POSSIBLE SOLUTIONS]

Let us try, then, to make a fresh start. I said that we have a conviction of our own free will simply based on the facts of human experience. But how reliable are those experiences? As I mentioned earlier, the typical case, often described by philosophers, which inclines us to believe in our free will is a case where we confront a bunch of choices, reason about what is the best thing to do, make up our minds, and then do the thing we have decided to do.

But perhaps our belief that such experiences support the doctrine of human freedom is illusory. Consider this sort of example. A typical hypnosis experiment has the following form. Under hypnosis the patient is given a posthypnotic suggestion. You can tell him, for example, to do some fairly trivial, harmless thing, such as, let's say, crawl around on the floor. After the patient comes out of hypnosis, he might be engaging in conversation, sitting, drinking coffee, when suddenly he says something like, "What a fascinating floor in this room!" or "I want to check out this rug" or "I'm thinking of investing in floor coverings and I'd like to investigate this floor." He then proceeds to crawl around on the floor. Now the interest of these cases is that the patient always gives some more or less adequate reason for doing what he does. That is, he seems to himself to be behaving freely. We, on the other hand, have good reasons to believe that his behavior isn't free at all, that the reasons he gives for his apparent decision to crawl around on the floor are irrelevant, that his behavior was determined in advance, that in fact he is in the grip of a posthypnotic suggestion. Anybody who knew the facts about him could have predicted his behavior in advance. Now, one way to pose the problem of determinism, or at least one aspect of the problem of determinism, is: "Is all human behavior like that?" Is all human behavior like the man operating under a post-hypnotic suggestion?

But now if we take the example seriously, it looks as if it proves to be an argument for the freedom of the will and not against it. The agent thought he was acting freely, though in fact his behavior was determined. But it seems empirically very unlikely that all human behavior is like that. Sometimes people are suffering from the effects of hypnosis, and sometimes we know that they are in the grip of unconscious urges which they cannot control. But are they always like that? Is all behavior determined by such *psychological* compulsions? If we try to treat psychological determinism as a factual claim about our behavior, then it seems to be just plain false. The thesis of psychological determinism is that prior psychological causes determine all of our behavior in the way that they determine the behavior of the hypnosis subject or the heroin addict. On this view, all behavior, in one way or another, is psychologically compulsive. But the available evidence suggests that such a thesis is false. We do indeed normally act on the basis of our intentional states—our beliefs, hopes, fears, desires, etc.—and in that sense our mental states function causally. But this form of cause and effect is not deterministic. We might have had exactly those mental states and still not have done what we did. As far as psychological causes are concerned, we could have done otherwise. Instances of hypnosis and psychologically compulsive behavior on the other hand are usually pathological and easily distinguishable from normal free action. So, psychologically speaking, there is scope for human freedom.

But is this solution really an advance on compatibilism? Aren't we just saying, once again, that yes, all behavior is determined, but what we call free behavior is the sort determined by rational thought processes? Sometimes the conscious, rational thought processes don't make any difference, as in the hypnosis case, and sometimes they do, as in the normal case. Normal cases are those where we say the agent is really free. But of course those normal rational thought processes are as much determined as anything else. So once again, don't we have the result that everything we do was entirely written in the book of history billions of years before we were born, and therefore, nothing we do is free in any philosophically interesting sense? If we choose to call our behavior free, that is just a matter of adopting a traditional terminology. Just as we continue to speak of "sunsets" even though we know the sun doesn't literally set; so we continue to speak of "acting of our own free will" even though there is no such phenomenon.

One way to examine a philosophical thesis, or any other kind of a thesis for that matter, is to ask, "What difference would it make? How would the world be any different if that thesis were true as opposed to how the world would be if that thesis were false?" Part of the appeal of determinism, I believe, is that it seems to be consistent with the way the world in fact proceeds, at least as far as we know anything about it from physics. That is, if determinism were true, then the world would proceed pretty much the way it does proceed, the only difference being that certain of our beliefs about its proceedings would be false. Those beliefs are important to us because they have to do with the belief that we could have done things differently from the way we did in fact do them. And this belief in turn connects with beliefs about moral responsibility and our own nature as persons. But if libertarianism, which is the thesis of free will, were true, it appears we would have to make some really radical changes in our beliefs about the world. In order for us to have radical freedom, it looks as if we would have to postulate that inside each of us was a self that was capable of interfering with the causal order of nature. That is, it looks as if we would have to contain some entity that was capable of making molecules swerve from their paths. I don't know if such a view is even intelligible, but it's certainly not consistent with what we know about how the world works from physics. And there is not the slightest evidence to suppose that we should abandon physical theory in favor of such a view.

So far, then, we seem to be getting exactly nowhere in our effort to resolve the conflict between determinism and the belief in the freedom of the will. Science allows no place for the freedom of the will, and indeterminism in physics offers no support for it. On the other hand, we are unable to give up the belief in the freedom of the will. Let us investigate both of these points a bit further.

[BOTTOM-UP CAUSATION]

Why exactly is there no room for the freedom of the will on the contemporary scientific view? Our basic explanatory mechanisms in physics work

from the bottom up. That is to say, we explain the behavior of surface features of a phenomenon such as the transparency of glass or the liquidity of
water, in terms of the behavior of microparticles such as molecules. And the
relation of the mind to the brain is an example of such a relation.
Mental features are caused by, and realized in neurophysiological
phenomena. . . . But we get causation from the mind to the body, that is
we get top-down causation over a passage of time: and we get top-down
causation over time because the top level and the bottom level go together.
So, for example, suppose I wish to cause the release of the neurotransmitter
acetylcholine at the axon end-plates of my motorneurons, I can do it by simply deciding to raise my arm and then raising it. Here, the mental event, the
intention to raise my arm, causes the physical event, the release of
acetylcholine—a case of top-down causation if ever there was one. But the
top-down causation works only because the mental events are grounded in
the neurophysiology to start with. So, corresponding to the description of
the causal relations that go from the top to the bottom, there is another description of the same series of events where the causal relations bounce entirely along the bottom, that is, they are entirely a matter of neurons and
neuron firings at synapses, etc. As long as we accept this conception of how
nature works, then it doesn't seem that there is any scope for the freedom of
the will because on this conception the mind can only affect nature in so far
as it is a part of nature. But if so, then like the rest of nature, its features are
determined at the basic micro-levels of physics.

This is an absolutely fundamental point in this chapter, so let me repeat
it. The form of determinism that is ultimately worrisome is not psychological determinism. The idea that our states of mind are sufficient to determine
everything we do is probably just false. The worrisome form of determinism is more basic and fundamental. Since all of the surface features of the
world are entirely caused by and realized in systems of micro-elements,
the behavior of micro-elements is sufficient to determine everything that
happens. Such a "bottom up" picture of the world allows for top-down causation (our minds, for example, can affect our bodies). But top-down causation only works because the top level is already caused by and realized in
the bottom levels.

Well then, let's turn to the next obvious question. What is it about our experience that makes it impossible for us to abandon the belief in the freedom
of the will? If freedom is an illusion, why is it an illusion we seem unable to
abandon? The first thing to notice about our conception of human freedom is
that it is essentially tied to consciousness. We only attribute freedom to conscious beings. If, for example, somebody built a robot which we believed to be
totally unconscious, we would never feel any inclination to call it free. Even if
we found its behavior random and unpredictable, we would not say that it
was acting freely in the sense that we think of ourselves as acting freely. If on
the other hand somebody built a robot that we became convinced had consciousness, in the same sense that we do, then it would at least be an open
question whether or not that robot had freedom of the will.

[OUR CONVICTION OF HUMAN FREEDOM]

The second point to note is that it is not just any state of the consciousness that gives us the conviction of human freedom. If life consisted entirely of the reception of passive perceptions, then it seems to me we would never so much as form the idea of human freedom. If you imagine yourself totally immobile, totally unable to move, and unable even to determine the course of your own thoughts, but still receiving stimuli, for example, periodic mildly painful sensations, there would not be the slightest inclination to conclude that you have freedom of the will.

I said earlier that most philosophers think that the conviction of human freedom is somehow essentially tied to the process of rational decision-making. But I think that is only partially true. In fact, weighing up reasons is only a very special case of the experience that gives us the conviction of freedom. The characteristic experience that gives us the conviction of human freedom, and it is an experience from which we are unable to strip away the conviction of freedom, is the experience of engaging in voluntary, intentional human actions. In our discussion of intentionality we concentrated on that form of intentionality which consisted in conscious intentions in action, intentionality which is causal in the way that I described, and whose conditions of satisfaction are that certain bodily movements occur, and that they occur as caused by that very intention in action. It is this experience which is the foundation stone of our belief in the freedom of the will. Why? Reflect very carefully on the character of the experiences you have as you engage in normal, everyday ordinary human actions. You will sense the possibility of alternative courses of action built into these experiences. Raise your arm or walk across the room or take a drink of water, and you will see that at any point in the experience you have a sense of alternative courses of action open to you.

If one tried to express it in words, the difference between the experience of perceiving and the experience of acting is that in perceiving one has the sense: "This is happening to me," and in acting one has the sense: "I am making this happen." But the sense that "I am making this happen" carries with it the sense that "I could be doing something else." In normal behavior, each thing we do carries the conviction, valid or invalid, that we could be doing something else right here and now, that is, all other conditions remaining the same. This, I submit, is the source of our unshakable conviction of our own free will. It is perhaps important to emphasize that I am discussing normal human action. If one is in the grip of a great passion, if one is in a great rage, for example, one loses this sense of freedom and one can even be surprised to discover what one is doing.

Once we notice this feature of the experience of acting, a great many of the puzzling phenomena I mentioned earlier are easily explained. Why for example do we feel that the man in the case of post-hypnotic suggestion is not acting freely in the sense in which we are, even though he might think that he is acting freely? The reason is that in an important sense he doesn't know what he is doing. His actual intention-in-action is totally unconscious. The options that he sees as available to him are irrelevant to the actual motivation of this action. . . . . If somebody tells me to do something at gunpoint, even in such a case I have an experience which has the sense of alternative courses of action built into it. If, for example, I am instructed to walk across the room at gunpoint, still part of the experience is that I sense that it is literally open to *me* at any step to do something else. The experience of freedom is thus an essential component of any case of acting with an intention.

Again, you can see this if you contrast the normal case of action with the Penfield cases [i.e., causing bodily motions through electric stimulation of the brain], where stimulation of the motor cortex produces an involuntary movement of the arm or leg. In such a case the patient experiences the movement passively, as he would experience a sound or a sensation of pain. Unlike intentional actions, there are no options built into the experience. To see this point clearly, try to imagine that a portion of your life was like the Penfield experiments on a grand scale. Instead of walking across the room you simply find that your body is moving across the room; instead of speaking you simply hear and feel words coming out of your mouth. Imagine your experiences are those of a purely passive but conscious puppet and you will have imagined away the experience of freedom. But in the typical case of intentional action, there is no way we can carve off the experience of freedom. It is an essential part of the experience of acting.

This also explains, I believe, why we cannot give up our conviction of freedom. We find it easy to give up the conviction that the earth is flat as soon as we understand the evidence for the heliocentric theory of the solar system. Similarly when we look at a sunset, in spite of appearances we do not feel compelled to believe that the sun is setting behind the earth, we believe that the appearance of the sun setting is simply an illusion created by the rotation of the earth. In each case it is possible to give up a commonsense conviction because the hypothesis that replaces it both accounts for the experiences that led to that conviction in the first place as well as explaining a whole lot of other facts that the commonsense view is unable to account for. That is why we gave up the belief in a flat earth and literal "sunsets" in favor of the Copernican conception of the solar system. But we can't similarly give up the conviction of freedom because that conviction is built into every normal, conscious intentional action. And we use this conviction in identifying and explaining actions. This sense of freedom is not just a feature of deliberation, but is part of any action, whether premeditated or spontaneous. The point has nothing essentially to do with deliberation; deliberation is simply a special case.

We don't navigate the earth on the assumption of a flat earth, even though the earth looks flat, but we do act on the assumption of freedom. In fact we can't act otherwise than on the assumption of freedom, no matter how much we learn about how the world works as a determined physical system.

We can now draw the conclusions that are implicit in this discussion. First, if the worry about determinism is a worry that all of our behavior is in fact psychologically compulsive, then it appears that the worry is unwarranted. Insofar as psychological determinism is an empirical hypothesis like any other, then the evidence we presently have available to us suggests it is false. Thus, this does give us a modified form of compatibilism. It gives us the view that psychological libertarianism is compatible with physical determinism.

Secondly, it even gives us a sense of "could have" in which people's behavior, though determined, is such that in that sense they could have done otherwise: The sense is simply that as far as the *psychological* factors were concerned, they could have done otherwise. The notions of ability, of what we are able to do and what we could have done, are often relative to some such set of criteria. For example, I could have voted for Carter in the 1980 American election, even if I did not; but I could not have voted for George Washington. He was not a candidate. So there is a sense of "could have," in which there were a range of choices available to me, and in that sense there were a lot of things I could have done, all other things being equal, which I did not do. Similarly, because the psychological factors operating on me do not always, or even in general, compel me to behave in a particular fashion, I often, psychologically speaking, could have done something different from what I did in fact do.

But third, this form of compatibilism still does not give us anything like the resolution of the conflict between freedom and determinism that our urge to radical libertarianism really demands. As long as we accept the bottom-up conception of physical explanation, and it is a conception on which the past three hundred years of science are based, then psychological facts about ourselves, like any other higher level facts, are entirely causally explicable in terms of and entirely realized in systems of elements at the fundamental microphysical level. Our conception of physical reality simply does not allow for radical freedom.

Fourth, and finally, for reasons I don't really understand, evolution has given us a form of experience of voluntary action where the experience of freedom, that is to say, the experience of the sense of alternative possibilities, is built into the very structure of conscious, voluntary, intentional human behavior. For that reason, I believe, neither this discussion nor any other will ever convince us that our behavior is unfree.

PART SIX

Ethics

*I*n countless ways, virtually every day we are all faced with the simple ethical question "What should I do?" Though this question is a simple one, the answer is not so simple. If, for example, the question takes the form "Should I tell the truth?" even the most rigorous moral philosopher might say yes but agree that there could be exceptional cases. To distinguish when one should and should not tell the truth involves further analysis of what really constitutes an ethical or moral situation, and what our obligations might be in such situations. Philosophical discussions of ethics focus largely on two issues. The first, which is *metaethical* in nature, involves discovering the source of our moral obligation. Is morality grounded in human instinct, social convention, the will of God, or the rational order of the universe itself? The second issue, which is *normative* in nature, involves discovering a method for determining whether a given act is right or wrong. Do we judge the rightness of an action based on selfish considerations, the best interests of society, an intuitive list of moral duties, or an ideal conception of moral good character traits?

An initial metaethical question was raised by several Chinese philosophers more than 2,000 years ago. Are human beings inherently good or inherently evil? Confucian philosopher Mencius (390–305 B.C.E.) argued that people are indeed good by nature, but we may become evil when social forces distort our true nature. By contrast, Confucian philosopher Hsun-tzu (298–238 B.C.E.) believed that we are inherently evil and must rely on education and social convention to suppress our selfishness and mold us into beings that care about others. In his dialog *Euthyphro*, Greek philosopher Plato (427–347 B.C.E.) discusses the metaethical question concerning the relation between morality and the will of the gods. The dialog is an investigation of various definitions of piety, and, in the process of the investigation, the character Socrates raises the famous dilemma: "whether the pious or holy is beloved by the gods because it is holy, or holy because it is beloved of the gods."

When ancient Greek philosophers considered questions of normative ethics, they often thought in terms of morally good character traits or *virtues* that people should acquire. The most important thing about moral behavior is that it should be habitual and arise spontaneously from good qualities that we've acquired. Aristotle (384–322 B.C.E.) took this approach in his *Nicomachean Ethics.* The starting point of his theory is the element of purpose or function. Everything in nature, he says, has a function, including, for example, every organ of the human body. A thing is good if it fulfills its unique function, as when we say a good hand, a good heart, or a good eye. Aristotle asks, if every organ has a purpose or function, what about the total person—does a person, as person, have a unique function? Aristotle finds this unique function in human reason, so that the good person is one who behaves in accordance with reason. And, when we follow our reason, we will develop virtuous character traits. He discusses a range of virtues, including courage, temperance, generosity, self-respect, good temper, and modesty. Each of these, he argues, occupies a middle ground between two extreme vices. Courage, for example, rests somewhere in between the vice of cowardice (too little courage) and rashness (too much fearlessness).

Shortly after Aristotle, Greek philosopher Epicurus (341–271 B.C.E.) took a different view of normative ethics—a view that has been echoed by a variety of moral philosophers down through the centuries to the present. According to Epicurus, the standard of right and wrong conduct is pleasure and the absence of pain. In his words, "we recognize pleasure as the first and fitting good, for from it proceeds all choice and avoidance, and we return to it as the feeling-standard by which we judge every good."

Near the close of the eighteenth century, German philosopher Immanuel Kant (1724–1804) objected to both the virtue theory of Aristotle and the pleasure-seeking theory of Epicurus. Like Aristotle, Kant believes that reason should be our guide in moral matters. However, in his *Fundamental Principles of the Metaphysics of Morals* (1785), he argues that human reason supplies us with a fundamental law of moral duty. The ethics of duty is sometimes called *deontological,* based on the word *deon,* "that which is obligatory." He calls this law of duty the categorical imperative: "Act only on that maxim whereby you can at the same time will that it should become a universal law."

Partly in response to Kant, British philosopher John Stuart Mill (1818–1883) championed the pleasure-seeking theory of Epicurus. Instead of a dutiful obedience to formal rules of conduct, Mill argues in his *Utilitarianism* (1861) that a good act is one whose consequence is general happiness or pleasure and the avoidance of pain. The term *utilitarian* derives from the view that the morality of an action is based on *utility*—that is, useful consequences. Because of its emphasis on consequences, Mill's theory is sometimes called *consequentialist.*

Reacting against the entire tradition of Western moral theories, German philosopher Friederich Nietzsche (1844–1900) expresses the view that there are no preexisting rules of good and evil. His philosophy calls for a person's fullest expression of all intrinsic vital powers and passions, although he urges a balance between the Dionysian (passionate) element in human nature and the Apollonian (rational) element. In recent years, another challenge has been made against traditional moral theories, this time by women philosophers, who contend that much of Western moral theory has a distinct male bias against women. In her essay "In a Different Voice" (1977), Carol Gilligan (b. 1936) addresses this issue and suggests that, from a woman's perspective, morality should focus primarily on an injunction to care for others. The male perspective, by contrast, emphasizes strict adherence to moral rules.

In the final essay of this section, from *Moral Philosophy through the Ages* (2001), James Fieser (b. 1958) investigates the moral theory of cultural relativism—the view that moral values are creations of society. Fieser defends this theory, which has been associated with a variety of skeptical philosophers over the centuries, and argues for a version called *nonvariable cultural relativism*.

Is Human Nature Inherently Good or Evil?*

Mencius (390–305 B.C.E.) and Hsun-tzu (298–238 B.C.E.)

[MENCIUS: PEOPLE ARE INHERENTLY GOOD]

KAO: Human nature is like a tree, and righteousness *(i)* is like a wooden cup or a bowl. The fashioning of benevolence and righteousness out of a person's nature is like the making of cups and bowls from the tree.

MENCIUS: Without touching the nature of the tree, can you make it into cups and bowls? You must do violence and injury to the tree before you can make cups and bowls with it. If you must do violence and injury to the tree in order to make cups and bowls with it, on your principles you must in the same way do violence and injury to humanity in order to fashion from it benevolence and righteousness. Thus, your words would certainly lead all people on to consider benevolence and righteousness to be calamities.

KAO: Human nature is like water whirling around in a corner. Open a passage for it to the east, and it will flow to the east. Open a passage for it to the west, and it will flow to the west. Human nature is indifferent to good and evil, just as water is indifferent to the east and west.

MENCIUS: Water indeed will flow indifferently to the east or west, but will it flow indifferently up or down? The tendency of human nature to do good is like the tendency of water to flow downwards. All people have this tendency to good, just as all water flows downwards. Now, by striking water and causing it to leap up, you may make it go over your forehead, and, by

*From *The Mencius*, Book 6, and *The Hsun-tzu*, Chapter 17.

damming and leading it, you may force it up a hill. But are such
movements according to the nature of water? It is the force applied which
causes them. When people are made to do what is not good, their nature is
dealt with in this way.

KUNG-TU: The philosopher Kao says that human nature is neither good nor
bad. Some say that human nature may be made to practice good and it
may be made to practice evil . . . Others say that the nature of some is
good, and the nature of others is bad. . . . And now you say that human
nature is good. Are all those other views, then, wrong?

MENCIUS: From the feelings proper to it, human nature is constituted for the
practice of what is good. This is what I mean in saying human nature is
good. If people do what is not good, the blame cannot be placed to their
natural powers. The feeling of commiseration belongs to all people. So do
that of shame and dislike, and that of reverence and respect, and that of
approving and disproving. The feeling of commiseration implies the principle of humanity *(jen)*. The feelings of shame and dislike imply the principle of righteousness *(i)*. The feelings of reverence and respect imply the
principle of social custom *(li)*. The feelings of approving and disapproving
imply the principle of knowledge *(chih)*. Humanity, righteousness, social
custom, and knowledge are not infused into us from outside factors. We
are certainly furnished with them. Any different view simply owes to an
absence of reflection. Hence it is said, "Look and you will find them. Neglect and you will lose them." People differ from one another in regard to
them: some have twice as much as others, some five times as much, and
some to an incalculable amount. This is because they cannot fully carry
out their natural powers. The *Book of Poetry* states that "In producing hu-
mankind, heaven gave people their various faculties and relations with
their specific laws. These are the invariable rules of nature for everyone to
hold; all love this admirable virtue." Confucius said, "The writer of this
ode indeed knows the principle of our nature." We may thus see that
every faculty and relation must have its law, and since there are invariable
rules for all to hold, they consequently love this admirable virtue.

[HSUN-TZU: PEOPLE ARE INHERENTLY EVIL]

Human nature is evil and the good that we show is artificial. Even at birth
human nature includes the love of gain. Since we act according to our desires, conflict and robberies emerge. We will not find self-denial and altruism. Human nature includes envy and dislike, and as actions are in accordance with these, violence and injuries spring up, whereas loyalty and faith
do not. Human nature includes the desires of the ears and the eyes, leading
to the love of sounds and beauty. And as the actions are in accordance with
these, lewdness and disorder spring up, whereas righteousness and social
custom, with their various orderly displays, do not. It thus appears that

following human nature and yielding to its feelings will surely create strife and theft. It will lead to violation of everyone's duties and disruption of all order, until we are in a state of savagery. We must have the influence of teachers and laws, and the guidance of social custom and righteousness. For, from these we get self-denial, altruism, and an observance of the well-ordered regulations of conduct, which results in a state of good government. From all this it is plain that human nature is evil; the good which it shows is artificial.

Consider some illustrations. A crooked stick must be submitted to the pressing-frame to soften and bond it, and then it becomes straight. A blunt knife must be submitted to the grindstone and whetstone, and then it becomes sharp. Similarly, human nature, being evil, must be submitted to teachers and laws, and then it becomes correct. It must be submitted to social custom and righteousness, and then it is capable of being governed. If people were without teachers and laws, our condition would be one of deviation and insecurity, and would be entirely wrong. If we were without social custom and righteousness, our condition would be one of rebellious disorder and we would reject all government. The sage kings of old understood that human nature was evil, in a state of hazardous deviation, improper, rebellious, disorderly, and resistant to governance. Accordingly, they set up the principles of righteousness and social custom, and framed laws and regulations. These efforts served to straighten and embellish our natural feelings. They correct them, tame them, change them and guide them. By this means we might proceed on a path of moral governance which is in agreement with reason. Now, the superior person is the one who is transformed by teachers and laws. He takes on the distinction of learning, and follows the path of social custom and righteousness. The inferior person is the one who follows his nature and its feelings, indulges its resentments, and walks contrary to social custom and righteousness. Looking at the subject in this way, we see clearly that human nature is evil, and the good that it shows is artificial.

Mencius said, "Man has only to learn, and his nature appears to be good;" but I reply, It is not so. To say so shows that he had not attained to the knowledge of human nature, nor examined into the difference between what is natural in people and what is artificial. The natural is what the constitution spontaneously moves to: it does not need to be learned, it does not need to be followed hard after; propriety and righteousness are what the sages have given birth to: it is by learning that men become capable of them, it is by hard practice that they achieve them. That which is in people—not needing to be learned and striven after—is what I call natural. That in people which is attained to by learning, and achieved by hard striving, is what I call artificial. This is the distinction between those two. By human nature, eyes are capable of seeing and ears are capable of hearing. But the power of seeing is inseparable from the eyes, and the power of hearing is inseparable from the ears. It is plain that the faculties of seeing and hearing do not need to be learned.

Mencius says, "The nature of man is good, but all lose and ruin their nature, and therefore it becomes bad." But I say that this representation is erroneous. People being born with their nature, when they thereafter depart from its simple constituent elements, must lose it. From this consideration we may see clearly that human nature is evil. What might be called the nature's being good, would be if there were no departing from its simplicity to beautify it, no departing from its elementary dispositions to sharpen it. Suppose that those simple elements no more needed beautifying, and the mind's thoughts no more needed to be turned to good, than the power of vision which is inseparable from the eyes, and the power of hearing which is inseparable from the ears, need to be learned. Then we might say that human nature is good, just as we say that eyes see and ears hear. It is human nature, when hungry, to desire to be filled; when cold, to desire to be warmed; when tired, to desire rest. These are the feelings and nature of people.

Imagine, for example, that a person is hungry in the presence of an elder, but does not dare to sit before him. He instead yields to that elder; tired with labor, he nevertheless does not dare to ask for rest. Imagine similarly a son's yielding to his father and a younger brother to his elder; or, a son's laboring for his father and a younger brother for his elder. These examples illustrate conduct that is contrary to nature and against one's feelings. However, these actions are in accord with the course laid down for a filial son, and to the refined distinctions of propriety and righteousness. It appears, then, that if feelings and nature were in accord with each other, there would be no self-denial and yielding to others. Self-denial and yielding to others are simply contrary to the feelings and the nature. In this way we come to see how clear it is that human nature is evil, and the good which it shows is artificial.

One might ask, "If human nature is evil, what is the source of social custom and righteousness?" I reply, all social custom and righteousness are the artificial productions of the sages, and should not be thought of as growing out of human nature. It is just as when a potter makes a vessel from the clay. The vessel is the product of the workman's art, and should not be thought of as growing out of human nature. Or it is as when another workman cuts and hews a vessel out of wood; it is the product of his art, and is not to be considered as growing out of human nature. The sages pondered long in thought and gave themselves to practice, and so they succeeded in producing social custom and righteousness, and setting up laws and regulations. In this way social custom and righteousness, laws and regulations, are artificial products of the sages, and should not be seen as growing properly from human nature.

READING 37

Does God Create Morality?*

Plato (427–347 B.C.E.)

[EUTHYPHRO PROSECUTING HIS FATHER]

EUTHYPHRO: Why have you left the Lyceum, Socrates? and what are you doing in the Porch of the King Archon? Surely you cannot be concerned in a suit before the King, like myself?

SOCRATES: Not in a suit, Euthyphro; impeachment is the word which the Athenians use.

EUTHYPHRO: What! I suppose that some one has been prosecuting you, for I cannot believe that you are the prosecutor of another.

SOCRATES: Certainly not.

EUTHYPHRO: Then some one else has been prosecuting you?

SOCRATES: Yes.

EUTHYPHRO: And who is he?

SOCRATES: A young man who is little known, Euthyphro; and I hardly know him: his name is Meletus, and he is of the deme of Pitthis. Perhaps you may remember his appearance; he has a beak, and long straight hair, and a beard which is ill grown.

EUTHYPHRO: No, I do not remember him, Socrates. But what is the charge which he brings against you?

SOCRATES: What is the charge? Well, a very serious charge, which shows a good deal of character in the young man, and for which he is certainly not to be despised. He says he knows how the youth are corrupted and who are their corruptors. I fancy that he must be a wise man, and seeing that I am the reverse of a wise man, he has found me out, and is going to accuse me of corrupting his young friends. And of this our mother the state is to be the judge. Of all our political men he is the only one who seems to me to begin in the right way, with the cultivation of virtue in youth; like a good husbandman, he makes the young shoots his first care, and clears away us who are the destroyers of them. This is only the first step; he will afterwards attend to the elder branches; and if he goes on as he has begun, he will be a very great public benefactor.

EUTHYPHRO: I hope that he may; but I rather fear, Socrates, that the opposite will turn out to be the truth. My opinion is that in attacking you he is simply aiming a blow at the foundation of the state. But in what way does he say that you corrupt the young?

SOCRATES: He brings a wonderful accusation against me, which at first hearing excites surprise: he says that I am a poet or maker of gods, and that I

*From Plato, "Euthyphro."

invent new gods and deny the existence of old ones; this is the ground of his indictment.

EUTHYPHRO: I understand, Socrates; he means to attack you about the familiar sign which occasionally, as you say, comes to you. He thinks that you are a neologian, and he is going to have you up before the court for this. He knows that such a charge is readily received by the world, as I myself know too well; for when I speak in the assembly about divine things, and foretell the future to them, they laugh at me and think me a madman. Yet every word that I say is true. But they are jealous of us all; and we must be brave and go at them.

SOCRATES: Their laughter, friend Euthyphro, is not a matter of much consequence. For a man may be thought wise; but the Athenians, I suspect, do not much trouble themselves about him until he begins to impart his wisdom to others, and then for some reason or other, perhaps, as you say, from jealousy, they are angry.

EUTHYPHRO: I am never likely to try their temper in this way.

SOCRATES: I dare say not, for you are reserved in your behavior, and seldom impart your wisdom. But I have a benevolent habit of pouring out myself to everybody, and would even pay for a listener, and I am afraid that the Athenians may think me too talkative. Now if, as I was saying, they would only laugh at me, as you say that they laugh at you, the time might pass gaily enough in the court; but perhaps they may be in earnest, and then what the end will be you soothsayers only can predict.

EUTHYPHRO: I dare say that the affair will end in nothing, Socrates, and that you will win your cause; and I think that I shall win my own.

SOCRATES: And what is your suit, Euthyphro? are you the pursuer or the defendant?

EUTHYPHRO: I am the pursuer.

SOCRATES: Of whom?

EUTHYPHRO: You will think me mad when I tell you.

SOCRATES: Why, has the fugitive wings?

EUTHYPHRO: Nay, he is not very volatile at his time of life.

SOCRATES: Who is he?

EUTHYPHRO: My father.

SOCRATES: Your father! my good man?

EUTHYPHRO: Yes.

SOCRATES: And of what is he accused?

EUTHYPHRO: Of murder, Socrates.

SOCRATES: By the powers, Euthyphro! how little does the common herd know of the nature of right and truth. A man must be an extraordinary man, and have made great strides in wisdom, before he could have seen his way to bring such an action.

EUTHYPHRO: Indeed, Socrates, he must.

SOCRATES: I suppose that the man whom your father murdered was one of your relatives—clearly he was; for if he had been a stranger you would never have thought of prosecuting him.

EUTHYPHRO: I am amused, Socrates, at your making a distinction between one who is a relation and one who is not a relation; for surely the pollution is the same in either case, if you knowingly associate with the murderer when you ought to clear yourself and him by proceeding against him. The real question is whether the murdered man has been justly slain. If justly, then your duty is to let the matter alone; but if unjustly, then even if the murderer lives under the same roof with you and eats at the same table, proceed against him. Now the man who is dead was a poor dependant of mine who worked for us as a field laborer on our farm in Naxos, and one day in a fit of drunken passion he got into a quarrel with one of our domestic servants and slew him. My father bound him hand and foot and threw him into a ditch, and then sent to Athens to ask of a diviner what he should do with him. Meanwhile he never attended to him and took no care about him, for he regarded him as a murderer; and thought that no great harm would be done even if he did die. Now this was just what happened. For such was the effect of cold and hunger and chains upon him, that before the messenger returned from the diviner, he was dead. And my father and family are angry with me for taking the part of the murderer and prosecuting my father. They say that he did not kill him, and that if he did, the dead man was but a murderer, and I ought not to take any notice, for that a son is impious who prosecutes a father. Which shows, Socrates, how little they know what the gods think about piety and impiety.

SOCRATES: Good heavens, Euthyphro! and is your knowledge of religion and of things pious and impious so very exact, that, supposing the circumstances to be as you state them, you are not afraid lest you too may be doing an impious thing in bringing an action against your father?

EUTHYPHRO: The best of Euthyphro, and that which distinguishes him, Socrates, from other men, is his exact knowledge of all such matters. What should I be good for without it?

SOCRATES: Rare friend! I think that I cannot do better than be your disciple. Then before the trial with Meletus comes on I shall challenge him, and say that I have always had a great interest in religious questions, and now, as he charges me with rash imaginations and innovations in religion, I have become your disciple. You, Meletus, as I shall say to him, acknowledge Euthyphro to be a great theologian, and sound in his opinions; and if you approve of him you ought to approve of me, and not have me into court; but if you disapprove, you should begin by indicting him who is my teacher, and who will be the ruin, not of the young, but of the old; that is to say, of myself whom he instructs, and of his old father whom he admonishes and chastises. And if Meletus refuses to listen to me, but will go on, and will not shift the indictment from me to you, I cannot do better than repeat this challenge in the court.

EUTHYPHRO: Yes, indeed, Socrates; and if he attempts to indict me I am mistaken if I do not find a flaw in him; the court shall have a great deal more to say to him than to me.

SOCRATES: And I, my dear friend, knowing this, am desirous of becoming your
disciple. For I observe that no one appears to notice you—not even this
Meletus; but his sharp eyes have found me out at once, and he has indicted me for impiety. And therefore, I adjure you to tell me the nature of
piety and impiety, which you said that you knew so well, and of murder,
and of other offences against the gods. What are they? Is not piety in every
action always the same? and impiety, again—is it not always the opposite
of piety, and also the same with itself, having, as impiety, one notion
which includes whatever is impious?

EUTHYPHRO: To be sure, Socrates.

[EUTHYPHRO'S FIRST DEFINITION OF PIETY]

SOCRATES: And what is piety, and what is impiety?

EUTHYPHRO: Piety is doing as I am doing; that is to say, prosecuting any one
who is guilty of murder, sacrilege, or of any similar crime—whether he
be your father or mother, or whoever he may be—that makes no difference; and not to prosecute them is impiety. And please to consider,
Socrates, what a notable proof I will give you of the truth of my words, a
proof which I have already given to others:—of the principle, I mean,
that the impious, whoever he may be, ought not to go unpunished. For
do not men regard Zeus as the best and most righteous of the gods?—
and yet they admit that he bound his father (Cronos) because he
wickedly devoured his sons, and that he too had punished his own father (Uranus) for a similar reason, in a nameless manner. And yet when I
proceed against my father, they are angry with me. So inconsistent are
they in their way of talking when the gods are concerned, and when I
am concerned.

SOCRATES: May not this be the reason, Euthyphro, why I am charged with
impiety—that I cannot away with these stories about the gods? and therefore I suppose that people think me wrong. But, as you who are well informed about them approve of them, I cannot do better than assent to
your superior wisdom. What else can I say, confessing as I do, that I know
nothing about them? Tell me, for the love of Zeus, whether you really believe that they are true.

EUTHYPHRO: Yes, Socrates; and things more wonderful still, of which the world
is in ignorance.

SOCRATES: And do you really believe that the gods fought with one another,
and had dire quarrels, battles, and the like, as the poets say, and as you
may see represented in the works of great artists? The temples are full of
them; and notably the robe of Athene, which is carried up to the Acropolis
at the great Panathenaea, is embroidered with them. Are all these tales of
the gods true, Euthyphro?

EUTHYPHRO: Yes, Socrates; and, as I was saying, I can tell you, if you would like to
hear them, many other things about the gods which would quite amaze you.

SOCRATES: I dare say; and you shall tell me them at some other time when I have leisure. But just at present I would rather hear from you a more precise answer, which you have not as yet given, my friend, to the question, What is "piety"? When asked, you only replied, Doing as you do, charging your father with murder.

EUTHYPHRO: And what I said was true, Socrates.

SOCRATES: No doubt, Euthyphro; but you would admit that there are many other pious acts?

EUTHYPHRO: There are.

SOCRATES: Remember that I did not ask you to give me two or three examples of piety, but to explain the general idea which makes all pious things to be pious. Do you not recollect that there was one idea which made the impious impious, and the pious pious?

EUTHYPHRO: I remember.

SOCRATES: Tell me what is the nature of this idea, and then I shall have a standard to which I may look, and by which I may measure actions, whether yours or those of any one else, and then I shall be able to say that such and such an action is pious, such another impious.

EUTHYPHRO: I will tell you, if you like.

SOCRATES: I should very much like.

[EUTHYPHRO'S SECOND DEFINITION: PIETY IS THAT WHICH IS DEAR TO THE GODS]

EUTHYPHRO: Piety, then, is that which is dear to the gods, and impiety is that which is not dear to them.

SOCRATES: Very good, Euthyphro; you have now given me the sort of answer which I wanted. But whether what you say is true or not I cannot as yet tell, although I make no doubt that you will prove the truth of your words.

EUTHYPHRO: Of course.

SOCRATES: Come, then, and let us examine what we are saying. That thing or person which is dear to the gods is pious, and that thing or person which is hateful to the gods is impious, these two being the extreme opposites of one another. Was not that said?

EUTHYPHRO: It was.

SOCRATES: And well said?

EUTHYPHRO: Yes, Socrates, I thought so; it was certainly said.

SOCRATES: And further, Euthyphro, the gods were admitted to have enmities and hatreds and differences?

EUTHYPHRO: Yes, that was also said.

SOCRATES: And what sort of difference creates enmity and anger? Suppose for example that you and I, my good friend, differ about a number; do differences of this sort make us enemies and set us at variance with one another? Do we not go at once to arithmetic, and put an end to them by a sum?

EUTHYPHRO: True.

SOCRATES: Or suppose that we differ about magnitudes, do we not quickly end the differences by measuring?

EUTHYPHRO: Very true.

SOCRATES: And we end a controversy about heavy and light by resorting to a weighing machine?

EUTHYPHRO: To be sure.

SOCRATES: But what differences are there which cannot be thus decided, and which therefore make us angry and set us at enmity with one another? I dare say the answer does not occur to you at the moment, and therefore I will suggest that these enmities arise when the matters of difference are the just and unjust, good and evil, honorable and dishonorable. Are not these the points about which men differ, and about which when we are unable satisfactorily to decide our differences, you and I and all of us quarrel, when we do quarrel?

EUTHYPHRO: Yes, Socrates, the nature of the differences about which we quarrel is such as you describe.

SOCRATES: And the quarrels of the gods, noble Euthyphro, when they occur, are of a like nature?

EUTHYPHRO: Certainly they are.

SOCRATES: They have differences of opinion, as you say, about good and evil, just and unjust, honorable and dishonorable: there would have been no quarrels among them, if there had been no such differences—would there now?

EUTHYPHRO: You are quite right.

SOCRATES: Does not every man love that which he deems noble and just and good, and hate the opposite of them?

EUTHYPHRO: Very true.

SOCRATES: But, as you say, people regard the same things, some as just and others as unjust,—about these they dispute; and so there arise wars and fightings among them.

EUTHYPHRO: Very true.

SOCRATES: Then the same things are hated by the gods and loved by the gods, and are both hateful and dear to them?

EUTHYPHRO: True.

SOCRATES: And upon this view the same things, Euthyphro, will be pious and also impious?

EUTHYPHRO: So I should suppose.

SOCRATES: Then, my friend, I remark with surprise that you have not answered the question which I asked. For I certainly did not ask you to tell me what action is both pious and impious: but now it would seem that what is loved by the gods is also hated by them. And therefore, Euthyphro, in thus chastising your father you may very likely be doing what is agreeable to Zeus but disagreeable to Cronos or Uranus, and what is acceptable to Hephaestus but unacceptable to Hera, and there may be other gods who have similar differences of opinion.

EUTHYPHRO: But I believe, Socrates, that all the gods would be agreed as to the propriety of punishing a murderer: there would be no difference of opinion about that.

SOCRATES: Well, but speaking of men, Euthyphro, did you ever hear any one arguing that a murderer or any sort of evil-doer ought to be let off?

EUTHYPHRO: I should rather say that these are the questions which they are always arguing, especially in courts of law: they commit all sorts of crimes, and there is nothing which they will not do or say in their own defense.

SOCRATES: But do they admit their guilt, Euthyphro, and yet say that they ought not to be punished?

EUTHYPHRO: No; they do not.

SOCRATES: ·Then there are some things which they do not venture to say and do: for they do not venture to argue that the guilty are to be unpunished, but they deny their guilt, do they not?

EUTHYPHRO: Yes.

SOCRATES: Then they do not argue that the evil-doer should not be punished, but they argue about the fact of who the evil-doer is, and what he did and when?

EUTHYPHRO: True.

SOCRATES: And the gods are in the same case, if as you assert they quarrel about just and unjust, and some of them say while others deny that injustice is done among them. For surely neither God nor man will ever venture to say that the doer of injustice is not to be punished?

EUTHYPHRO: That is true, Socrates, in the main.

SOCRATES: But they join issue about the particulars—gods and men alike; and, if they dispute at all, they dispute about some act which is called in question, and which by some is affirmed to be just, by others to be unjust. Is not that true?

EUTHYPHRO: Quite true.

SOCRATES: Well then, my dear friend Euthyphro, do tell me, for my better instruction and information, what proof have you that in the opinion of all the gods a servant who is guilty of murder, and is put in chains by the master of the dead man, and dies because he is put in chains before he who bound him can learn from the interpreters of the gods what he ought to do with him, dies unjustly; and that on behalf of such a one a son ought to proceed against his father and accuse him of murder. How would you show that all the gods absolutely agree in approving of his act? Prove to me that they do, and I will applaud your wisdom as long as I live.

EUTHYPHRO: It will be a difficult task; but I could make the matter very clear indeed to you.

SOCRATES: I understand; you mean to say that I am not so quick of apprehension as the judges: for to them you will be sure to prove that the act is unjust, and hateful to the gods.

EUTHYPHRO: Yes indeed, Socrates; at least if they will listen to me.

[SOCRATES AMENDS AND CRITICIZES
EUTHYPHRO'S DEFINITION]

SOCRATES: But they will be sure to listen if they find that you are a good speaker. There was a notion that came into my mind while you were speaking; I said to myself: "Well, and what if Euthyphro does prove to me that all the gods regarded the death of the serf as unjust, how do I know anything more of the nature of piety and impiety? for granting that this action may be hateful to the gods, still piety and impiety are not adequately defined by these distinctions, for that which is hateful to the gods has been shown to be also pleasing and dear to them." And therefore, Euthyphro, I do not ask you to prove this; I will suppose, if you like, that all the gods condemn and abominate such an action. But I will amend the definition so far as to say that what all the gods hate is impious, and what they love pious or holy; and what some of them love and others hate is both or neither. Shall this be our definition of piety and impiety?

EUTHYPHRO: Why not, Socrates?

SOCRATES: Why not! certainly, as far as I am concerned, Euthyphro, there is no reason why not. But whether this admission will greatly assist you in the task of instructing me as you promised, is a matter for you to consider.

EUTHYPHRO: Yes, I should say that what all the gods love is pious and holy, and the opposite which they all hate, impious.

SOCRATES: Ought we to enquire into the truth of this, Euthyphro, or simply to accept the mere statement on our own authority and that of others? What do you say?

EUTHYPHRO: We should enquire; and I believe that the statement will stand the test of enquiry.

SOCRATES: We shall know better, my good friend, in a little while. The point which I should first wish to understand is whether the pious or holy is beloved by the gods because it is holy, or holy because it is beloved of the gods.

EUTHYPHRO: I do not understand your meaning, Socrates.

SOCRATES: I will endeavor to explain: we speak of carrying and we speak of being carried, of leading and being led, seeing and being seen. You know that in all such cases there is a difference, and you know also in what the difference lies?

EUTHYPHRO: I think that I understand.

SOCRATES: And is not that which is beloved distinct from that which loves?

EUTHYPHRO: Certainly.

SOCRATES: Well; and now tell me, is that which is carried in this state of carrying because it is carried, or for some other reason?

EUTHYPHRO: No; that is the reason.

SOCRATES: And the same is true of what is led and of what is seen?

EUTHYPHRO: True.

SOCRATES: And a thing is not seen because it is visible, but conversely, visible because it is seen; nor is a thing led because it is in the state of being led, or carried because it is in the state of being carried, but the converse of this. And now I think, Euthyphro, that my meaning will be intelligible; and my meaning is, that any state of action or passion implies previous action or passion. It does not become because it is becoming, but it is in a state of becoming because it becomes; neither does it suffer because it is in a state of suffering, but it is in a state of suffering because it suffers. Do you not agree?

EUTHYPHRO: Yes.

SOCRATES: Is not that which is loved in some state either of becoming or suffering?

EUTHYPHRO: Yes.

SOCRATES: And the same holds as in the previous instances; the state of being loved follows the act of being loved, and not the act the state.

EUTHYPHRO: Certainly.

SOCRATES: And what do you say of piety, Euthyphro: is not piety, according to your definition, loved by all the gods?

EUTHYPHRO: Yes.

SOCRATES: Because it is pious or holy, or for some other reason?

EUTHYPHRO: No, that is the reason.

SOCRATES: It is loved because it is holy, not holy because it is loved?

EUTHYPHRO: Yes.

SOCRATES: And that which is dear to the gods is loved by them, and is in a state to be loved of them because it is loved of them?

EUTHYPHRO: Certainly.

SOCRATES: Then that which is dear to the gods, Euthyphro, is not holy, nor is that which is holy loved of God, as you affirm; but they are two different things.

EUTHYPHRO: How do you mean, Socrates?

SOCRATES: I mean to say that the holy has been acknowledged by us to be loved of God because it is holy, not to be holy because it is loved.

EUTHYPHRO: Yes.

SOCRATES: But that which is dear to the gods is dear to them because it is loved by them, not loved by them because it is dear to them.

EUTHYPHRO: True.

SOCRATES: But, friend Euthyphro, if that which is holy is the same with that which is dear to God, and is loved because it is holy, then that which is dear to God would have been loved as being dear to God; but if that which is dear to God is dear to him because loved by him, then that which is holy would have been holy because loved by him. But now you see that the reverse is the case, and that they are quite different from one another. For one (theophiles) is of a kind to be loved cause it is loved, and the other (osion) is loved because it is of a kind to be loved. Thus you appear to me, Euthyphro, when I ask you what is the essence of holiness, to offer an attribute only, and not the essence—the attribute of being loved by all the gods. But you still refuse to explain to me the nature of holiness. And therefore, if you please, I will ask you not to hide your treasure, but to tell

me once more what holiness or piety really is, whether dear to the gods or
not (for that is a matter about which we will not quarrel); and what is
impiety?

EUTHYPHRO: I really do not know, Socrates, how to express what I mean. For
somehow or other our arguments, on whatever ground we rest them,
seem to turn round and walk away from us.

SOCRATES: Your words, Euthyphro, are like the handiwork of my ancestor
Daedalus; and if I were the sayer or propounder of them, you might say
that my arguments walk away and will not remain fixed where they are
placed because I am a descendant of his. But now, since these notions are
your own, you must find some other gibe, for they certainly, as you yourself allow, show an inclination to be on the move.

EUTHYPHRO: Nay, Socrates, I shall still say that you are the Daedalus who sets
arguments in motion; not I, certainly, but you make them move or go
round, for they would never have stirred, as far as I am concerned.

SOCRATES: Then I must be a greater than Daedalus: for whereas he only made
his own inventions to move, I move those of other people as well. And the
beauty of it is, that I would rather not. For I would give the wisdom of
Daedalus, and the wealth of Tantalus, to be able to detain them and keep
them fixed. But enough of this. As I perceive that you are lazy, I will myself endeavor to show you how you might instruct me in the nature of
piety; and I hope that you will not grudge your labor. Tell me, then—Is
not that which is pious necessarily just?

EUTHYPHRO: Yes.

SOCRATES: And is, then, all which is just pious? or, is that which is pious all
just, but that which is just, only in part and not all, pious?

EUTHYPHRO: I do not understand you, Socrates.

SOCRATES: And yet I know that you are as much wiser than I am, as you are
younger. But, as I was saying, revered friend, the abundance of your wisdom makes you lazy. Please to exert yourself, for there is no real difficulty
in understanding me. What I mean I may explain by an illustration of
what I do not mean. The poet (Stasinus) sings—

"Of Zeus, the author and creator of all these things,

You will not tell: for where there is fear there is also reverence."

Now I disagree with this poet. Shall I tell you in what respect?

EUTHYPHRO: By all means.

SOCRATES: I should not say that where there is fear there is also reverence; for I
am sure that many persons fear poverty and disease, and the like evils,
but I do not perceive that they reverence the objects of their fear.

EUTHYPHRO: Very true.

SOCRATES: But where reverence is, there is fear; for he who has a feeling of reverence and shame about the commission of any action, fears and is afraid
of an ill reputation.

EUTHYPHRO: No doubt.

SOCRATES: Then we are wrong in saying that where there is fear there is also reverence; and we should say, where there is reverence there is also fear. But there is not always reverence where there is fear; for fear is a more extended notion, and reverence is a part of fear, just as the odd is a part of number, and number is a more extended notion than the odd. I suppose that you follow me now?

EUTHYPHRO: Quite well.

SOCRATES: That was the sort of question which I meant to raise when I asked whether the just is always the pious, or the pious always the just; and whether there may not be justice where there is not piety; for justice is the more extended notion of which piety is only a part. Do you dissent?

EUTHYPHRO: No, I think that you are quite right.

[A THIRD DEFINITION: PIETY IS PART OF JUSTICE]

SOCRATES: Then, if piety is a part of justice, I suppose that we should enquire what part? If you had pursued the enquiry in the previous cases; for instance, if you had asked me what is an even number, and what part of number the even is, I should have had no difficulty in replying, a number which represents a figure having two equal sides. Do you not agree?

EUTHYPHRO: Yes, I quite agree.

SOCRATES: In like manner, I want you to tell me what part of justice is piety or holiness, that I may be able to tell Meletus not to do me injustice, or indict me for impiety, as I am now adequately instructed by you in the nature of piety or holiness, and their opposites.

EUTHYPHRO: Piety or holiness, Socrates, appears to me to be that part of justice which attends to the gods, as there is the other part of justice which attends to men.

SOCRATES: That is good, Euthyphro; yet still there is a little point about which I should like to have further information, What is the meaning of "attention"? For attention can hardly be used in the same sense when applied to the gods as when applied to other things. For instance, horses are said to require attention, and not every person is able to attend to them, but only a person skilled in horsemanship. Is it not so?

EUTHYPHRO: Certainly.

SOCRATES: I should suppose that the art of horsemanship is the art of attending to horses?

EUTHYPHRO: Yes.

SOCRATES: Nor is every one qualified to attend to dogs, but only the huntsman?

EUTHYPHRO: True.

SOCRATES: And I should also conceive that the art of the huntsman is the art of attending to dogs?

EUTHYPHRO: Yes.

SOCRATES: As the art of the oxherd is the art of attending to oxen?

EUTHYPHRO: Very true.

SOCRATES: In like manner holiness or piety is the art of attending to the gods?—that would be your meaning, Euthyphro?

EUTHYPHRO: Yes.

SOCRATES: And is not attention always designed for the good or benefit of that to which the attention is given? As in the case of horses, you may observe that when attended to by the horseman's art they are benefited and improved, are they not?

EUTHYPHRO: True.

SOCRATES: As the dogs are benefited by the huntsman's art, and the oxen by the art of the oxherd, and all other things are tended or attended for their good and not for their hurt?

EUTHYPHRO: Certainly, not for their hurt.

SOCRATES: But for their good?

EUTHYPHRO: Of course.

SOCRATES: And does piety or holiness, which has been defined to be the art of attending to the gods, benefit or improve them? Would you say that when you do a holy act you make any of the gods better?

EUTHYPHRO: No, no; that was certainly not what I meant.

SOCRATES: And I, Euthyphro, never supposed that you did. I asked you the question about the nature of the attention, because I thought that you did not.

EUTHYPHRO: You do me justice, Socrates; that is not the sort of attention which I mean.

SOCRATES: Good: but I must still ask what is this attention to the gods which is called piety?

EUTHYPHRO: It is such, Socrates, as servants show to their masters.

SOCRATES: I understand—a sort of ministration to the gods.

EUTHYPHRO: Exactly.

SOCRATES: Medicine is also a sort of ministration or service, having in view the attainment of some object—would you not say of health?

EUTHYPHRO: I should.

SOCRATES: Again, there is an art which ministers to the ship-builder with a view to the attainment of some result?

EUTHYPHRO: Yes, Socrates, with a view to the building of a ship.

SOCRATES: As there is an art which ministers to the house-builder with a view to the building of a house?

EUTHYPHRO: Yes.

SOCRATES: And now tell me, my good friend, about the art which ministers to the gods: what work does that help to accomplish? For you must surely know if, as you say, you are of all men living the one who is best instructed in religion.

EUTHYPHRO: And I speak the truth, Socrates.

SOCRATES: Tell me then, oh tell me—what is that fair work which the gods do by the help of our ministrations?

EUTHYPHRO: Many and fair, Socrates, are the works which they do.

SOCRATES: Why, my friend, and so are those of a general. But the chief of them is easily told. Would you not say that victory in war is the chief of them?

EUTHYPHRO: Certainly.

SOCRATES: Many and fair, too, are the works of the husbandman, if I am not mistaken; but his chief work is the production of food from the earth?

EUTHYPHRO: Exactly.

SOCRATES: And of the many and fair things done by the gods, which is the chief or principal one?

EUTHYPHRO: I have told you already, Socrates, that to learn all these things accurately will be very tiresome. Let me simply say that piety or holiness is learning how to please the gods in word and deed, by prayers and sacrifices. Such piety is the salvation of families and states, just as the impious, which is unpleasing to the gods, is their ruin and destruction.

SOCRATES: I think that you could have answered in much fewer words the chief question which I asked, Euthyphro, if you had chosen. But I see plainly that you are not disposed to instruct me—clearly not: else why, when we reached the point, did you turn aside? Had you only answered me I should have truly learned of you by this time the nature of piety. Now, as the asker of a question is necessarily dependent on the answerer, whither he leads I must follow; and can only ask again, what is the pious, and what is piety? Do you mean that they are a sort of science of praying and sacrificing?

EUTHYPHRO: Yes, I do.

SOCRATES: And sacrificing is giving to the gods, and prayer is asking of the gods?

EUTHYPHRO: Yes, Socrates.

SOCRATES: Upon this view, then, piety is a science of asking and giving?

EUTHYPHRO: You understand me capitally, Socrates.

SOCRATES: Yes, my friend; the reason is that I am a votary of your science, and give my mind to it, and therefore nothing which you say will be thrown away upon me. Please then to tell me, what is the nature of this service to the gods? Do you mean that we prefer requests and give gifts to them?

EUTHYPHRO: Yes, I do.

SOCRATES: Is not the right way of asking to ask of them what we want?

EUTHYPHRO: Certainly.

SOCRATES: And the right way of giving is to give to them in return what they want of us. There would be no meaning in an art which gives to any one that which he does not want.

EUTHYPHRO: Very true, Socrates.

SOCRATES: Then piety, Euthyphro, is an art which gods and men have of doing business with one another?

EUTHYPHRO: That is an expression which you may use, if you like.

SOCRATES: But I have no particular liking for anything but the truth. I wish, however, that you would tell me what benefit accrues to the gods from our gifts. There is no doubt about what they give to us; for there is no good thing which they do not give; but how we can give any good thing to them in return is far from being equally clear. If they give everything and we give nothing, that must be an affair of business in which we have very greatly the advantage of them.

EUTHYPHRO: And do you imagine, Socrates, that any benefit accrues to the gods from our gifts?

SOCRATES: But if not, Euthyphro, what is the meaning of gifts which are conferred by us upon the gods?

EUTHYPHRO: What else, but tributes of honor; and, as I was just now saying, what pleases them?

SOCRATES: Piety, then, is pleasing to the gods, but not beneficial or dear to them?

EUTHYPHRO: I should say that nothing could be dearer.

SOCRATES: Then once more the assertion is repeated that piety is dear to the gods?

EUTHYPHRO: Certainly.

SOCRATES: And when you say this, can you wonder at your words not standing firm, but walking away? Will you accuse me of being the Daedalus who makes them walk away, not perceiving that there is another and far greater artist than Daedalus who makes them go round in a circle, and he is yourself; for the argument, as you will perceive, comes round to the same point. Were we not saying that the holy or pious was not the same with that which is loved of the gods? Have you forgotten?

EUTHYPHRO: I quite remember.

SOCRATES: And are you not saying that what is loved of the gods is holy; and is not this the same as what is dear to them—do you see?

EUTHYPHRO: True.

SOCRATES: Then either we were wrong in our former assertion; or, if we were right then, we are wrong now.

EUTHYPHRO: One of the two must be true.

SOCRATES: Then we must begin again and ask, What is piety? That is an inquiry which I shall never be weary of pursuing as far as in me lies; and I entreat you not to scorn me, but to apply your mind to the utmost, and tell me the truth. For, if any man knows, you are he; and therefore I must detain you, like Proteus, until you tell. If you had not certainly known the nature of piety and impiety, I am confident that you would never, on behalf of a serf, have charged your aged father with murder. You would not have run such a risk of doing wrong in the sight of the gods, and you would have had too much respect for the opinions of men. I am sure, therefore, that you know the nature of piety and impiety. Speak out then, my dear Euthyphro, and do not hide your knowledge.

EUTHYPHRO: Another time, Socrates; for I am in a hurry, and must go now.

SOCRATES: Alas! my companion, and will you leave me in despair? I was hoping that you would instruct me in the nature of piety and impiety; and then I might have cleared myself of Meletus and his indictment. I would have told him that I had been enlightened by Euthyphro, and had given up rash innovations and speculations, in which I indulged only through ignorance, and that now I am about to lead a better life.

READING 38

Morality and Virtue*

Aristotle (384–322 B.C.E.)

Happiness is something which is both precious and final. This seems to be so because it is a first principle or ultimate starting point. For, it is for the sake of happiness that we do everything else, and we regard the cause of all good things to be precious and divine. Moreover, since happiness is an activity of the soul in accordance with complete or perfect virtue, it is necessary to consider virtue, as this will be the best way of studying happiness.

[GENERAL FEATURES OF MORAL VIRTUES]

It appears that virtue is the object upon which the true statesman has expended the largest amount of trouble, as it is his wish to make the citizens virtuous and obedient to the laws. We have instances of such statesmen in the legislators of Crete and Lacedaemon and such other legislators as have resembled them. But if this inquiry is proper to political science, it will clearly accord with our original purpose to pursue it. But it is clear that it is human virtue which we have to consider; for the good of which we are in search is, as we said, human good, and the happiness, human happiness. By human virtue or excellence we mean not that of the body, but that of the soul, and by happiness we mean an activity of the soul.

If this is so, it is clearly necessary for statesmen to have some knowledge of the nature of the soul in the same way as it is necessary for one who is to treat the eye or any part of the body, to have some knowledge of it, and all the more as political science is better and more honorable than medical science. Clever doctors take a great deal of trouble to understand the body, and similarly the statesman must make a study of the soul. But he must study it with a view to his particular object and so far only as his object requires; for to elaborate the study of it further would, I think, be to aggravate unduly the labor of our present undertaking.

[Virtue and the Divisions of the Soul]

There are some facts concerning the soul which are adequately stated in the popular or exoterical discourses, and these we may rightly adopt. It is stated e.g. that the soul has two parts, one irrational and the other possessing reason. But whether these parts are distinguished like the parts of the body and like everything that is itself divisible, or whether they are theoretically distinct, but

*From Aristotle, *Nicomachean Ethics*, Books 1 and 2.

in fact inseparable, as convex and concave in the circumference of a circle, is of no importance to the present inquiry.

Again, it seems that of the irrational part of the soul one part is common, *i.e., shared by man with all living things,* and vegetative; I mean the part which is the cause of nutrition and increase. For we may assume such a faculty of the soul to exist in all things that receive nutrition, even in embryos, and the same faculty to exist in things that are full grown, as it is more reasonable to suppose that it is the same faculty than that it is different. It is clear then that the virtue or excellence of this faculty is not distinctively human but is shared by man with all living things; for it seems that this part and this faculty are especially active in sleep, whereas good and bad people are never so little distinguishable as in sleep—from which we get the saying that there is no difference between the happy and the miserable during half their lifetime. And this is only natural; for sleep is an inactivity of the soul in respect of its virtue or vice, except in so far as certain impulses affect it to a slight extent, and make the visions of the virtuous better than those of ordinary people. But enough has been said on this point, and we must now leave the principle of nutrition, as it possesses no natural share in human virtue.

It seems that there is another natural principle of the soul which is irrational and yet in a sense partakes of reason. For in a continent or incontinent person we praise the reason, and that part of the soul which possesses reason, as it exhorts men rightly and exhorts them to the best conduct. But it is clear that there is in them another principle which is naturally different from reason and fights and contends against reason. For just as the paralyzed parts of the body, when we intend to move them to the right, are drawn away in a contrary direction to the left, so it is with the soul; the impulses of incontinent people run counter to reason. But there is this difference, however, that while in the body we see the part which is drawn astray, in the soul we do not see it. But it is probably right to suppose with equal certainty that there is in the soul too something different from reason, which opposes and thwarts it, although the sense in which it is distinct from reason is immaterial. But it appears that this part too partakes of reason, as we said; at all events in a continent person it obeys reason, while in a temperate or courageous person it is probably still more obedient, as being absolutely harmonious with reason.

It appears then that the irrational part of the soul is itself twofold; for the vegetative faculty does not participate at all in reason, but the faculty of desire or general concupiscence participates in it more or less, in so far as it is submissive and obedient to reason. But *it is obedient* in the sense in which we speak of "paying attention to a father" or "to friends," but not in the sense in which we speak of "paying attention to mathematics." All correction, rebuke and exhortation is a witness that the irrational part of the soul is in a sense subject to the influence of reason. But if we are to say that this part too possesses reason, then the part which possesses reason will have two divisions, one possessing reason absolutely and in itself, the other listening to it as a child listens to its father.

Virtue or excellence again, admits of a distinction which depends on this difference. For we speak of some virtues as intellectual and of others as moral, wisdom, intelligence and prudence, being intellectual, liberality and temperance being moral, virtues. For when we describe a person's character, we do not say that he is wise or intelligent but that he is gentle or temperate. Yet we praise a wise man too in respect of his mental state, and such mental states as deserve to be praised we call virtuous.

[Virtues are Acquired]

Virtue or excellence being twofold, partly intellectual and partly moral, intellectual virtue is both originated and fostered mainly by teaching; it therefore demands experience and time. Moral virtue on the other hand is the outcome of habit, and accordingly its name is derived by a slight deflection of habit. From this fact it is clear that no moral virtue is implanted in us by nature; a law of nature cannot be altered by habituation. Thus, a stone naturally tends to fall downwards, and it cannot be habituated or trained to rise upwards, even if we were to habituate it by throwing it upwards ten thousand times; nor again can fire be trained to sink downwards, not anything else that follows one natural law be habituated or trained to follow another. It is neither by nature then nor in defiance of nature that virtues are implanted in us. Nature gives us the capacity of receiving them, and that capacity is perfected by habit.

Again, if we take the various natural powers which belong to us, we first acquire the proper faculties and afterwards display the activities. It is clearly so with the senses. It was not by seeing frequently or hearing frequently that we acquired the senses of seeing or hearing; on the contrary it was because we possessed the senses that we made use of them, not by making use of them that we obtained them. But the virtues we acquire by first exercising them, as is the case with all the arts, for it is by doing what we ought to do when we have learnt the arts that we learn the arts themselves; we become e.g. builders by building and harpists by playing the harp. Similarly it is by doing just acts that we become just, by doing temperate acts that we become temperate, by doing courageous acts that we become courageous. The experience of states is a witness to this truth, for it is by training the habits that legislators make the citizens good. This is the object which all legislators have at heart; if a legislator does not succeed in it, he fails of his purpose, and it constitutes the distinction between a good polity and a bad one.

Again, the causes and means by which any virtue is produced and by which it is destroyed are the same; and it is equally so with any art; for it is by playing the harp that both good and bad harpists are produced and the case of builders and all other artisans is similar, as it is by building well that they will be good builders and by building badly that they will be bad builders. If it were not so, there would be no need of anybody to teach them; they would all be born good or bad in their several trades. The case of the virtues is the same.

It is by acting in such transactions as take place between man and man that we become either just or unjust. It is by acting in the face of danger and by habituating ourselves to fear or courage that we become either cowardly or courageous. It is much the same with our desires and angry passions. Some people become temperate and gentle, others become licentious and passionate according as they conduct themselves in one way or another way in particular circumstances. In a word character traits are the results of activities corresponding to the character traits themselves. It is our duty therefore to give a certain character to the activities, as the character traits depend upon the differences of the activities. Accordingly the difference between one training of the habits and another from early days is not a light matter, but is serious or rather all-important.

[The Study of Virtue]

Our present study is not, like other studies, purely speculative in its intention; for the object of our inquiry is not to know the nature of virtue but to become ourselves virtuous, as that is the sole benefit which it conveys. It is necessary therefore to consider the right way of performing actions, for it is actions as we have said that determine the character of the resulting character traits.

That we should act in accordance with right reason is a common general principle, which may here be taken for granted. The nature of right reason, and its relation to the virtues generally, will be subjects of discussion hereafter. But it must be admitted at the outset that all reasoning upon practical matters must be like a sketch in outline, it cannot be scientifically exact. We began by laying down the principle that the kind of reasoning demanded in any subject must be such as the subject matter itself allows; and questions of practice and expediency no more admit of invariable rules than questions of health.

But if this is true of general reasoning upon ethics, still more true is it that scientific exactitude is impossible in reasoning upon particular ethical cases. They do not fall under any art or any law, but the agents themselves are always bound to pay regard to the circumstances of the moment as much as in medicine or navigation.

Still, although such is the nature of the present argument, we must try to make the best of it.

The first point to be observed then is that in such matters as we are considering deficiency and excess are equally fatal. It is so, as we observe, in regard to health and strength; for we must judge of what we cannot see by the evidence of what we do see. Excess or deficiency of gymnastic exercise is fatal to strength. Similarly an excess or deficiency of meat and drink is fatal to health, whereas a suitable amount produces, augments and sustains it. It is the same then with temperance, courage, and the other virtues. A person who avoids and is afraid of everything and faces nothing becomes a coward; a person who is not afraid of anything but is ready to face everything becomes foolhardy. Similarly, he who enjoys every pleasure and never abstains from any pleasure is licentious; he who eschews all pleasures like a boor is an insensible sort of person. For temperance and courage are destroyed by excess and deficiency but preserved by the mean state.

Again, not only are the causes and the agencies of production, increase and destruction in the character traits the same, but the sphere of their activity will be proved to be the same also. It is so in other instances which are more conspicuous, e.g. in strength; for strength is produced by taking a great deal of food and undergoing a great deal of labor, and it is the strong man who is able to take most food and to undergo most labor. The same is the case with the virtues. It is by abstinence from pleasures that we become temperate, and, when we have become temperate, we are best able to abstain from them. So too with courage; it is by habituating ourselves to despise and face alarms that we become courageous, and, when we have become courteous, we shall be best able to face them.

[Virtues are Character Traits]

We have next to consider the nature of virtue.

Now, as the qualities of the soul are three, viz. emotions, faculties and character traits, it follows that virtue must be one of the three. By the emotions I mean desire, anger, fear, courage, envy, joy, love, hatred, regret, emulation, pity, in a word whatever is attended by pleasure or pain. I call those faculties in respect of which we are said to be capable of experiencing these emotions, e.g. capable of getting angry or being pained or feeling pity. And I call those character traits in respect of which we are well or ill disposed towards the emotions, ill-disposed e.g. towards the passion of anger, if our anger be too violent or too feeble, and well-disposed, if it be duly moderated, and similarly towards the other emotions.

Now neither the virtues nor the vices are emotions; for we are not called good or evil in respect of our emotions but in respect of our virtues or vices. Again, we are not praised or blamed in respect of our emotions; a person is not praised for being angry in an absolute sense, but only for being angry in a certain way; but we are praised or blamed in respect of our virtues or vices. Again, whereas we are angry or afraid without deliberate purpose, the virtues are in some sense deliberate purposes, or do not exist in the absence of deliberate purpose. It may be added that while we are said to be moved in respect of our emotions, in respect of our virtues or vices we are not said to be moved but to have a certain disposition.

These reasons also prove that the virtues are not faculties. For we are not called either good or bad, nor are we praised or blamed, as having an abstract capacity for emotion. Also while Nature gives us our faculties, it is not Nature that makes us good or bad, but this is a point which we have already discussed. If then the virtues are neither emotions nor faculties, it remains that they must be moral states.

The nature of virtue has been now generically described. But it is not enough to state merely that virtue is a moral state, we must also describe the character of that moral state.

It must be laid down then that every virtue or excellence has the effect of producing a good condition of that of which it is a virtue or excellence, and of enabling it to perform its function well. Thus the excellence of the eye makes the eye good and its function good, as it is by the excellence of the eye that we see well. Similarly, the excellence of the horse makes a horse excellent and good at racing, at carrying its rider and at facing the enemy.

If then this is universally true, the virtue or excellence of man will be such a moral state as makes a man good and able to perform his proper function well. We have already explained how this will be the case, but another way of making it clear will be to study the nature or character of this virtue.

[THE VIRTUOUS MEAN BETWEEN EXTREMES]

[Doctrine of the Mean]

Now in everything, whether it be continuous or discrete, it is possible to take a greater, a smaller, or ail equal amount, and this either absolutely or in relation to ourselves, the equal being a mean between excess and deficiency. By the mean in respect of the thing itself, or the absolute mean, I understand that which is equally distinct from both extremes and this is one and the same thing for everybody. By the mean considered relatively to ourselves I understand that which is neither too much nor too little; but this is not one thing, nor is it the same for everybody. Thus if 10 be too much and 2 too little we take 6 as a mean in respect of the thing itself; for 6 is as much greater than 2 as it is less than 10, and this is a mean in arithmetical proportion. But the mean considered relatively to ourselves must not be ascertained in this way. It does not follow that if 10 pounds *of meat* be too much and 2 be too little for a man to eat, a trainer will order him 6 pounds, as this may itself be too much or too little for the person who is to take it; it will be too little e.g. for Milo, but too much for a beginner in gymnastics. It will be the same with running and wrestling; *the right amount will vary with the individual.* This being so, everybody who understands his business avoids alike excess and deficiency; he seeks and chooses the mean, not the absolute mean, but the mean considered relatively to ourselves.

Every science then performs its function well, if it regards the mean and refers the works which it produces to the mean. This is the reason why it is usually said of successful works that it is impossible to take anything from them or to add anything to them, which implies that excess or deficiency is fatal to excellence but that the mean state ensures it. Good artists too, as we say, have an eye to the mean in their works. But virtue, like Nature herself, is more accurate and better than any art; virtue therefore will aim at the mean; I speak of moral virtue, as it is moral virtue which is concerned with emotions and actions, and it is these which admit of excess and deficiency and the mean. Thus it is possible to go too far, or not to go far enough, in respect of fear, courage, desire, anger, pity, and pleasure and pain generally, and the excess and the deficiency are alike wrong; but to experience these emotions at the right times and on the right occasions and towards the right persons and for the right causes and in the right manner is the mean or the supreme good, which is characteristic of virtue. Similarly there may be excess, deficiency, or the mean, in regard to actions. But virtue is concerned with emotions and actions, and here excess is an error and deficiency a fault, whereas the mean is successful and laudable, and success and merit are both characteristics of virtue.

It appears then that virtue is a mean state, so far at least as it aims at the mean.

Again, there are many different ways of going wrong; for evil is in its nature infinite, to use the Pythagorean figure, but good is finite. But there is only one possible way of going right. Accordingly the former is easy and the latter difficult; it is easy to miss the mark but difficult to hit it. This again is a reason why excess and deficiency are characteristics of vice and the mean state a characteristic of virtue: "For good is simple, evil manifold." Virtue then is a state of deliberate moral purpose consisting in a mean that is relative to ourselves, the mean being determined by reason, or as a prudent man would determine it.

It is a mean state *firstly as lying* between two vices, the vice of excess on the one hand, and the vice of deficiency on the other, and secondly because, whereas the vices either fall short of or go beyond what is proper in the emotions and actions, virtue not only discovers but embraces the mean.

Accordingly, virtue, if regarded in its essence or theoretical conception, is a mean state, but, if regarded from the point of view of the highest good, or of excellence, it is an extreme.

But it is not every action or every emotion that admits of a mean state. There are some whose very name implies wickedness, as e.g. malice, shamelessness, and envy, among emotions, or adultery, theft, and murder, among actions. All these, and others like them, are censured as being intrinsically wicked, not merely the excesses or deficiencies of them. It is never possible then to be right in respect of them; they are always sinful. Right or wrong in such actions as adultery does not depend on our committing therewith the right person, at the right time or in the right manner; on the contrary it is sinful to do anything of the kind at all. It would be equally wrong then to suppose that there can be a mean state or an excess or deficiency in unjust, cowardly or licentious conduct; for, if it were so, there would be a mean state of an excess or of a deficiency, an excess of an excess and a deficiency of a deficiency. But as in temperance and courage there can be no excess or deficiency because the mean is, in a sense, an extreme, so too in these cases there cannot be a mean or an excess or deficiency, but, however the acts may be done, they are wrong. For it is a general rule that an excess or deficiency does not admit of a mean state, nor a mean state of an excess or deficiency.

But it is not enough to lay down this as a general rule; it is necessary to apply it to particular cases, as in reasonings upon actions general statements, although they are broader, are less exact than particular statements. For all action refers to particulars, and it is essential that our theories should harmonize with the particular cases to which they apply.

[Examples of Virtues and Vices]

We must take particular virtues then from the catalogue of virtues. In regard to feelings of fear and confidence courage is a mean state. On the side of excess, he whose fearlessness is excessive has no name, as often happens, but he whose confidence is excessive is foolhardy, while he whose timidity is excessive and whose confidence is deficient is a coward.

In respect of pleasures and pains, although not indeed of all pleasures and pains, and to a less extent in respect of pains than of pleasures, the mean state is temperance, the excess is licentiousness. We never find people who are deficient in regard to pleasures; accordingly such people again have not received a name, but we may call them insensible.

As regards the giving and taking of money, the mean state is liberality, the excess and deficiency are prodigality and illiberality. Here the excess and deficiency take opposite forms; for while the prodigal man is excessive in spending and deficient in taking, the illiberal man is excessive in taking and deficient in spending.

In respect of money there are other dispositions as well. There is the mean state which is magnificence; for the magnificent man, as having to do with large sums of money, differs from the liberal man who has to do only with small sums; and the excess *corresponding to it* is bad taste or vulgarity, the deficiency is meanness. These are different from the excess and deficiency of liberality; what the difference is will be explained hereafter.

In respect of honor and dishonor the mean state is highmindedness, the excess is what is called vanity, the deficiency littlemindedness. Corresponding to liberality, which, as we said, differs from magnificence as having to do not with great but with small sums of money, there is a moral state which has to do with petty honor and is related to highmindedness which has to do with great honor; for it is possible to aspire to honor in the right way, or in a way which is excessive or insufficient, and if a person's aspirations are excessive, he is called ambitious, if they are deficient, he is called unambitious, while if they are between the two, he has no name. The dispositions too are nameless, except that the disposition of the ambitious person is called ambition. The consequence is that the extremes lay claim to the mean or intermediate place. We ourselves speak of one who observes the mean sometimes as ambitious, and at other times as unambitious; we sometimes praise an ambitious, and at other times an unambitious person. The reason for our doing so will be stated in due course, but let us now discuss the other virtues in accordance with the method which we have followed hitherto.

Anger, like other emotions, has its excess, its deficiency, and its mean state. It may be said that they have no names, but as we call one who observes the mean gentle, we will call the mean state gentleness. Among the extremes, if a person errs on the side of excess, he may be called passionate and his vice passionateness, if on that of deficiency, he may be called impassive and his deficiency impassivity.

There are also three other mean states with a certain resemblance to each other, and yet with a difference. For while they are all concerned with intercourse in speech and action, they are different in that one of them is concerned with truth in such intercourse, and the others with pleasantness, one with pleasantness in amusement and the other with pleasantness in the various circumstances of life. We must therefore discuss these states in order to make it clear that in all cases it is the mean state which is an object of praise, and the extremes are neither right nor laudable but censurable. It is true that these mean and extreme states are generally nameless, but we must do our best here as elsewhere to give them a name, so that our argument may be clear and easy to follow.

In the matter of truth then, he who observes the mean may be called truthful, and the mean state truthfulness. Pretence, if it takes the form of exaggeration, is boastfulness, and one who is guilty of pretence is a boaster; but if it takes the form of depreciation it is irony, and he who is guilty of it is ironical.

As regards pleasantness in amusement, he who observes the mean is witty, and his disposition wittiness; the excess is buffoonery, and he who is guilty of it a buffoon, whereas he who is deficient in wit may be called a boor and his moral state boorishness.

As to the other kind of pleasantness, viz. pleasantness in life, he who is pleasant in a proper way is friendly, and his mean state friendliness; but he who goes too far, if he has no ulterior object in view, is obsequious, while if his object is self interest, he is a flatterer, and he who does not go far enough and always makes himself unpleasant is a quarrelsome and morose sort of person.

There are also mean states in the emotions and in the expression of the emotions. For although modesty is not a virtue, yet a modest person is praised as if he were virtuous; for here too one person is said to observe the mean and another to exceed it, as e.g. the bashful man who is never anything but modest, whereas a person who has insufficient modesty or no modesty at all is called shameless, and one who observes the mean modest.

Righteous indignation, again, is a mean state between envy and malice. They are all concerned with the pain and pleasure which we feel at the fortunes of our neighbors. A person who is righteously indignant is pained at the prosperity of the undeserving; but the envious person goes further and is pained at anybody's prosperity, and the malicious person is so far from being pained that he actually rejoices at misfortunes.

[THE DIFFICULTY OF THE VIRTUOUS LIFE]

It has now been sufficiently shown that moral virtue is a mean state, and in what sense it is a mean state; it is a mean state as lying between two vices, a vice of excess on the one side and a vice of deficiency on the other, and as aiming at the mean in the emotions and actions.

That is the reason why it is so hard to be virtuous; for it is always hard work to find the mean in anything, e.g. it is not everybody, but only a man of science, who can find the mean or center of a circle. So too anybody can get angry—that is an easy matter—and anybody can give or spend money, but to give it to the right persons, to give the right amount of it and to give it at the right time and for the right cause and in the right way, this is not what anybody can do, nor is it easy. That is the reason why it is rare and laudable and noble to do well. Accordingly one who aims at the mean must begin by departing from that extreme which is the more contrary to the mean; he must act in the spirit of Calypso's advice, "Far from this smoke and swell you keep your bark," for of the two extremes one is more sinful than the other. As it is difficult then to hit the mean exactly, we must take the second best course, as the saying is, and choose the lesser of two evils, and this we shall best do in the way that we have described, i.e. by steering clear of the evil which is further from the mean. We must also observe the things to which we are ourselves particularly prone, as different natures have different inclinations, and we may ascertain what these are by a consideration of our feelings of pleasure and pain. And then we must drag ourselves in the direction opposite to them; for it is by removing ourselves as far as possible from what is wrong that we shall arrive at the mean, as we do, when we pull a crooked stick straight.

But in all cases we must especially be on our guard against what is pleasant and against pleasure, as we are not impartial judges of pleasure. Hence our attitude towards pleasure must be like that of the elders of the people in the Iliad towards Helen, and we must never be afraid of applying the words they use; for if we dismiss pleasure as they dismissed Helen, we shall be less likely to go wrong. It is by action of this kind, to put it summarily, that we shall best succeed in hitting the mean.

It may be admitted that this is a difficult task, especially in particular cases. It is not easy to determine e.g. the right manner, objects, occasions, and duration of anger. There are times when we ourselves praise people who are deficient in anger, and call them gentle, and there are other times when we speak of people who exhibit a savage temper as spirited. It is not however one who deviates a little from what is right, but one who deviates a great deal, whether on the side of excess or of deficiency, that is censured; for he is sure to be found out. Again, it is not easy to decide theoretically how far and to what extent a man may go before he becomes censurable, but neither is it easy to define theoretically anything else within the region of perception; such things fall under the head of particulars, and our judgment of them depends upon our perception.

So much then is plain, that the mean state is everywhere laudable, but that we ought to incline at one time towards the excess and at another towards the deficiency; for this will be our easiest manner of hitting the mean, or in other words of attaining excellence.

READING 39

Pleasure and Life's Aim[*]

Epicurus (341–271 B.C.E.)

—believed pleasure is purpose of life (enjoys food + drink)

[DO NOT FEAR THE GODS OR DEATH]

Epicurus to Menoeceus: greetings!

The young should not put off philosophizing, nor the old grow weary in it. For no one can come to health of soul either too early or too late. He who says the season for philosophy has not arrived or has gone by is like someone who says that the time for *eudaimonia* *(happiness)* has not yet arrived or is past. One should philosophize while young and while old, so that while growing old one might be young in good things through gratitude for things past, and likewise in youth one might be old through fearlessness respecting the things to come. Consequently it is necessary to exercise oneself in the things making for *eudaimonia,* for when it is present we have everything, but when it is absent we do everything to acquire it.

Do and practice those things to which I constantly exhort you, embracing them as the very principles of the good life. First, reckoning in accordance with the idea of God engraved on the common mind, namely that God is immortal and blessed, attribute to him neither what is alien to his immortality nor removed from his blessedness. Believe about him all that preserves his immortality and blessedness. Gods exist, for the knowledge of them is by distinct intellectual perception. But they are not as the vulgar crowd, which is unable to maintain a consistent conception of them, supposes. The impious person is not the one who denies the gods of the crowd, but rather the one who saddles the Gods with the opinions of the crowd. For the declarations of the crowd concerning the gods are not divinely infused concepts but false opinions, [such as the idea that] it is from the Gods that the worst misfortunes fall upon the evil, and profits upon [the good]. For since they are always accustomed to their own character traits, they endorse those similar to their own [that is, they attribute them to the gods], but consider all others alien.

Accustom yourself to the thought that death is nothing to us. For all good and evil reside in sensation, but death is the removal of all sensation. Therefore the correct understanding, that death is nothing to us, makes the mortality of life enjoyable not by adding infinite time, but by removing the yearning for immortality. Nothing is terrible in life to one who has truly grasped that nothing terrible belongs to not living. So that one is foolish who says that he fears death not because it will be painful when it arrives but is painful because

—believes we're on our own, no god is looking after us

*From Epicurus, "Letter to Menoeceus," in Diogenes Laertius's *Lives of Eminent Philosophers.*

of its inevitable approach. For that which is no trouble when it arrives is, in expectation, an empty pain. Death, the most chilling of evils, is nothing to us, since really when we are, death is not, and on the other hand when death arrives, we are not. It is nothing either to the living or the dead since for the former it is not, and the latter are no longer.

But at one moment the crowd flees from death as the greatest of evils, at another moment longs for it as repose from the evils of life. But the wise person neither deprecates life nor fears its cessation. Life neither offends him nor does he believe cessation of life to be any evil. Just as he does not seek the greatest quantity of food, but rather the most pleasing food, so also he plucks the sweetest fruits of time, not the longest span of time.

He who exhorts the young to live beautifully but the old to make a fine end is simple minded, not only because of the desirability of life but because the practice of living well and dying well are the same. But that one is much worse who says it would be better not to be born,

'Once born most swiftly to pass right through Hades' gates.'

For if he says this from conviction why does he not depart from life? For such a course of action is available, had he firmly wished it. But if he is joking, it amounts to idle chatter among folks who ignore him.

We should keep bearing in mind that the future is neither wholly ours nor wholly not ours, so that we neither entirely expect its sure occurrence, nor give up hope as though it were entirely beyond reach.

[THE NATURE OF PLEASURE]

We must consider that some desires are inborn, some vain, and of those inborn some are necessary and others inborn only. Of those which are necessary some are necessary for *eudaimonia,* some for bodily repose, others for life itself. Now undisturbed contemplation of these matters enables us to bring back all choice and avoidance into the service of bodily health and *ataraxia* [mental repose], for such is the goal of the blessed life. Thanks to these we perform all our actions, so as to feel neither distress nor fright. Once this is the case for us, the tempest of the soul is dispersed so that the living being does not have to proceed as though lacking something nor seek something different by which he might fulfill the good of body and soul. For we have need of pleasure when we feel distress at its absence, but when we are not distressed we are no longer addicted to pleasure. Accordingly we count pleasure as the originating principle and the goal of the blessed life. For we recognize pleasure as the first and fitting good, for from it proceeds all choice and avoidance, and we return to it as the feeling-standard by which we judge every good.

But since pleasure is the first and natural good, for this very reason we do not choose every pleasure, but pass over many where great discomfort for us follows from them. And we consider many pains to be better than pleasure, since a greater pleasure comes to us after enduring distress for a long time. Every pleasure is good by natural kinship to us, yet not all are to be chosen, even as all distress is bad, yet not all is of such a nature as to be avoided. By calculating the advantages and disadvantages one will look to make a judgment on all these things. For sometimes we treat the good as bad, and conversely the bad as good. Therefore habituation to plain things rather than luxuries produces complete health, and makes a person fit for the exigencies of life and disposes us better when approaching luxuries after long intervals [without them], and prepares us to be without fear in the face of contingency.

We consider self sufficiency a great good not because we always prefer having few things, but so that, where we lack plenty, we may use what little we have in the genuine conviction that those enjoy the sweetest luxuries who need them least, and that all that is natural is easily obtained, while vain things are difficult to attain. So, when all the pain of need is removed, plain flavors bring us pleasure equal to that of gourmet dining. Bread and water give the highest pleasure when set before one who needs them.

When therefore we declare pleasure to be the goal, we do not refer to the pleasures of profligates and those at ease in enjoyments, as some think who are ignorant and disagree or scarcely get the point, but rather we refer to the absence of bodily pain and mental disturbance. For it is not continuous drinking and reveling or indulgences in boys and women, nor fish and all the rest born by a rich table, which produce a pleasant life, but rather sober reasoning, searching out the grounds of all choice and avoidance, and extirpating opinion, from which the greatest disturbance of the soul proceeds.

The origin and greatest good of all these things is prudence. Hence prudence is more prized than philosophy, for from it spring all the rest of the virtues, and prudence teaches us that it is not possible to live pleasantly without living prudently, finely and justly, nor to live prudently, finely and justly without pleasure. For the virtues are by nature bound up with living pleasantly; it is inseparable from them. For that reason you think no one better than that one who believes piously about the Gods, maintains a fearless attitude towards death, has by reasoned determined the naturally ordained end, and understands the (properly) delimited goods to be easily fulfilled and attained (whereas the course of distress is short), and who laughs at the allotments of fate, whom some have brought in as mistress of all. [Such a prudent one thinks that the chief power in determining events lies with us] for on the one hand some things happen by necessity, on the other some are by chance, and some are within our control. For while necessity cannot be persuaded from its course, and he sees chance to be unstable, that which is within out control is without a master, and blame and its opposite naturally attach to it. So it is better to follow the myths about the Gods than to be enslaved to the fated dealings posited by the determinists. For the former suggests a possibility of placating the Gods by worship, but the latter suggests implacable necessity. The prudent one does not entertain the idea that, as the crowd supposes, chance is a God (for God's acts are fixed) or an uncertain cause. He does not think good or evil are given to people by chance for blessed living, but that opportunities for great good or evil are supplied by it. He considers it better to incur bad luck while acting rationally than to be lucky while acting irrationally. For it is better to fail in well chosen actions than to succeed in badly chosen actions through luck.

Therefore, practice these and related matters on your own, day and night, and do the same with one like yourself, and, whether awake or asleep you will never be disturbed but will live as a God among men. For one living among immortal blessings is not like a mortal being.

READING 40

The Categorical Imperative*

Immanuel Kant (1724–1804)

[THE CHIEF GOOD IS A GOOD WILL]

Nothing can possibly be conceived in the world, or even out of it, which can be called good, without qualification, except a *good will*. Intelligence, wit, judgment, and the other *talents* of the mind, however they may be named, or courage, resolution, perseverance, as qualities of temperament, are undoubtedly good and desirable in many respects; but these gifts of nature may also become extremely bad and mischievous if the will which is to make use of them, and which, therefore, constitutes what is called *character*, is not good. It is the same with the *gifts of fortune.* Power, riches, honor, even health, and the general well-being and contentment with one's condition which is called *happiness,* inspire pride, and often presumption, if there is not a good will to correct the influence of these on the mind, and with this also to rectify the whole principle of acting and adapt it to its end. The sight of a being who is not adorned with a single feature of a pure and good will, enjoying unbroken prosperity, can never give pleasure to an impartial rational spectator. Thus a good will appears to constitute the indispensable condition even of being worthy of happiness.

There are even some qualities which are of service to this good will itself and may facilitate its action, yet which have no intrinsic unconditional value, but always presuppose a good will, and this qualifies the esteem that we justly have for them and does not permit us to regard them as absolutely good. Moderation in the affections and passions, self-control, and calm deliberation are not only good in many respects, but even seem to constitute part of the intrinsic worth of the person; but they are far from deserving to be called good

*From Immanuel Kant, *Fundamental Principles of the Metaphysics of Morals,* (1785), Sections 1 and 2.

without qualification, although they have been so unconditionally praised by the ancients. For without the principles of a good will, they may become extremely bad, and the coolness of a villain not only makes him far more dangerous, but also directly makes him more abominable in our eyes than he would have been without it.

[THE GOODNESS OF THE WILL
INDEPENDENT OF CONSEQUENCES]

A good will is good not because of what it performs or effects, not by its aptness for the attainment of some proposed end, but simply by virtue of the volition; that is, it is good in itself, and considered by itself is to be esteemed much higher than all that can be brought about by it in favour of any inclination, nay even of the sum total of all inclinations. Even if it should happen that, owing to special disfavor of fortune, or the stingy provision of a step-motherly nature, this will should wholly lack power to accomplish its purpose, if with its greatest efforts it should yet achieve nothing, and there should remain only the good will (not, to be sure, a mere wish, but the summoning of all means in our power), then, like a jewel, it would still shine by its own light, as a thing which has its whole value in itself. Its usefulness or fruitfulness can neither add nor take away anything from this value. It would be, as it were, only the setting to enable us to handle it the more conveniently in common commerce, or to attract to it the attention of those who are not yet connoisseurs, but not to recommend it to true connoisseurs, or to determine its value. . . .

[FIRST PROPOSITION: TO HAVE MORAL WORTH,
AN ACTION MUST BE DONE FROM DUTY]

. . . We can readily distinguish whether the action which agrees with duty is done *from duty,* or from a selfish view. It is much harder to make this distinction when the action accords with duty and the subject has besides a *direct* inclination to it. For example, it is always a matter of duty that a dealer should not over charge an inexperienced purchaser; and wherever there is much commerce the prudent tradesman does not overcharge, but keeps a fixed price for everyone, so that a child buys of him as well as any other. Men are thus honestly served; but this is not enough to make us believe that the tradesman has so acted from duty and from principles of honesty: his own advantage required it; it is out of the question in this case to suppose that he might besides have a direct inclination in favour of the buyers, so that, as it were, from love he should give no advantage to one over another. Accordingly the action was done neither from duty nor from direct inclination, but merely with a selfish view.

On the other hand, it is a duty to maintain one's life; and, in addition, everyone has also a direct inclination to do so. But on this account the of anxious care which most men take for it has no intrinsic worth, and their maxim has no moral import. They preserve their life *as duty requires,* no doubt, but not *because duty requires.* On the other hand, if adversity and hopeless sorrow have completely taken away the relish for life; if the unfortunate one, strong in mind, indignant at his fate rather than desponding or dejected, wishes for death, and yet preserves his life without loving it—not from inclination or fear, but from duty—then his maxim has a moral worth.

[EXAMPLE OF THE PHILANTHROPIST]

To be beneficent when we can is a duty; and besides this, there are many minds so sympathetically constituted that, without any other motive of vanity or self-interest, they find a pleasure in spreading joy around them and can take delight in the satisfaction of others so far as it is their own work. But I maintain that in such a case an action of this kind, however proper, however amiable it may be, has nevertheless no true moral worth, but is on a level with other inclinations, e.g., the inclination to honor, which, if it is happily directed to that which is in fact of public utility and accordant with duty and consequently honorable, deserves praise and encouragement, but not esteem. For the maxim lacks the moral import, namely, that such actions be done *from duty,* not from inclination. Put the case that the mind of that philanthropist were clouded by sorrow of his own, extinguishing all sympathy with the lot of others, and that, while he still has the power to benefit others in distress, he is not touched by their trouble because he is absorbed with his own; and now suppose that he tears himself out of this dead insensibility, and performs the action without any inclination to it, but simply from duty, then first has his action its genuine moral worth. . . .

[SECOND PROPOSITION: MORAL WORTH OF AN ACTION DERIVES NOT FROM RESULTS BUT BECAUSE IT WAS BASED ON PRINCIPLE]

The second proposition is: That an action done from duty derives its moral worth, *not from the purpose* which is to be attained by it, but from the maxim by which it is determined, and therefore does not depend on the realization of the object of the action, but merely on the principle of volition by which the action has taken place, without regard to any object of desire. It is clear from what precedes that the purposes which we may have in view in our actions, or their effects regarded as ends and springs of the will, cannot give to actions any unconditional or moral worth. In what, then, can their worth lie, if it is not to consist in the will and in reference to its expected effect? It cannot lie anywhere but in the *principle of the will* without regard to the ends which can be attained by the action. For the will stands between its a priori principle, which is formal, and its a posteriori spring, which is material, as between two roads, and as it must be determined by something, in that it must be determined by the formal principle of volition when an action is done from duty, in which case every material principle has been withdrawn from it.

[THIRD PROPOSITION: DUTY IS THE NECESSITY
OF ACTING FROM RESPECT OF THE MORAL LAW]

The third proposition, which is a consequence of the two preceding, I would express thus *Duty is the necessity of acting from respect for the law.* I may have inclination for an object as the effect of my proposed action, but I cannot have respect for it, just for this reason, that it is an effect and not an energy of will. Similarly I cannot have respect for inclination, whether my own or another's; I can at most, if my own, approve it; if another's, sometimes even love it; i.e., look on it as favorable to my own interest. It is only what is connected with my will as a principle, by no means as an effect—what does not subserve my inclination, but overpowers it, or at least in case of choice excludes it from its calculation—in other words, simply the law of itself, which can be an object of respect, and hence a command. Now an action done from duty must wholly exclude the influence of inclination and with it every object of the will, so that nothing remains which can determine the will except objectively the *law*, and subjectively *pure respect* for this practical law, and consequently the maxim that I should follow this law even to the thwarting of all my inclinations.

Thus the moral worth of an action does not lie in the effect expected from it, nor in any principle of action which requires to borrow its motive from this expected effect. For all these effects—agreeableness of one's condition and even the promotion of the happiness of others—could have been also brought about by other causes, so that for this there would have been no need of the will of a rational being; whereas it is in this alone that the supreme and unconditional good can be found. The pre-eminent good which we call moral can therefore consist in nothing else than *the conception of law* in itself, *which certainly is only possible in a rational being,* in so far as this conception, and not the expected effect, determines the will. This is a good which is already present in the person who acts accordingly, and we have not to wait for it to appear first in the result.

[PROMISE: AN EXAMPLE OF MORAL LAW]

But what sort of law can that be, the conception of which must determine the will, even without paying any regard to the effect expected from it, in order that this will may be called good absolutely and without qualification? As I have deprived the will of every impulse which could arise to it from obedience to any law, there remains nothing but the universal conformity of its actions to law in general, which alone is to serve the will as a principle, i.e., I am never to act otherwise than *so that I could also will that my maxim should become a universal law.* Here, now, it is the simple conformity to law in general, without assuming any particular law applicable to certain actions, that serves the will as its principle and must so serve it, if duty is not to be a vain delusion and a chimerical notion. The common reason of men in its practical judgments perfectly coincides with this and always has in view the principle here suggested. Let the question be, for example: May I when in distress make a promise with the intention not to keep it? I readily distinguish here between the two significations which the question may have: Whether it is prudent, or whether it is right, to make a false promise? The former may undoubtedly of be the case. I see clearly indeed that it is not enough to extricate myself from a present difficulty by means of this subterfuge, but it must be well considered whether there may not hereafter spring from this lie much greater inconvenience than that from which I now free myself, and as, with all my supposed *cunning,* the consequences cannot be so easily foreseen but that credit once lost may be much more injurious to me than any mischief which I seek to avoid at present, it should be considered whether it would not be more *prudent* to act herein according to a universal maxim and to make it a habit to promise nothing except with the intention of keeping it. But it is soon clear to me that such a maxim will still only be based on the fear of consequences. Now it is a wholly different thing to be truthful from duty and to be so from apprehension of injurious consequences. In the first case, the very notion of the action already implies a law for me; in the second case, I must first look about elsewhere to see what results may be combined with it which would affect myself. For to deviate from the principle of duty is beyond all doubt wicked; but to be unfaithful to my maxim of prudence may often be very advantageous to me, although to abide by it is certainly safer. The shortest way, however, and an unerring one, to discover the answer to this question whether a lying promise is consistent with duty, is to ask myself, Should I be content that my maxim (to extricate myself from difficulty by a false promise) should hold good as a universal law, for myself as well as for others? and should I be able to say to myself, "Every one may make a deceitful promise when he finds himself in a difficulty from which he cannot otherwise extricate himself?" Then I presently become aware that while I can will the lie, I can by no means will that lying should be a universal law. For with such a law there would be no promises at all, since it would be in vain to allege my intention in regard to my future actions to those who would not believe this allegation, or if they over hastily did so would pay me back in my own coin. Hence my maxim, as soon as it should be made a universal law, would necessarily destroy itself.

[IMPERATIVES: HYPOTHETICAL AND CATEGORICAL]

Everything in nature works according to laws. Rational beings alone have the faculty of acting according to *the conception* of laws, that is according to principles, i.e., have a will. . . .

Now all imperatives command either *hypothetically* or *categorically.* The former represent the practical necessity of a possible action as means to *something else* that is willed (or at least which one might possibly will). The categorical imperative would be that which represented an action as necessary of itself without reference to another end, i.e., as objectively necessary.

Since every practical law represents a possible action as good and, on this account, for a subject who is practically determinable by reason, necessary, all imperatives are formula determining an action which is necessary according to the principle of a will good in some respects. If now the action is good only as a means to something else, then the imperative is *hypothetical*; if it is conceived as good *in itself* and consequently as being necessarily the principle of a will which of itself conforms to reason, then it is *categorical*. . . .

There is therefore but one categorical imperative, namely, this: *Act only on that maxim whereby you can at the same time will that it should become a universal law*. . . .

[THE FORMULA OF THE LAW OF NATURE]

Since the universality of the law according to which effects are produced constitutes what is properly called nature in the most general sense (as to form), that is the existence of things so far as it is determined by general laws, the imperative of duty may be expressed thus: *Act as if the maxim of your action were to become by your will a universal law of nature.*

We will now enumerate a few duties, adopting the usual division of them into duties to ourselves and to others, and into perfect and imperfect duties.

1. A man reduced to despair by a series of misfortunes feels wearied of life, but is still so far in possession of his reason that he can ask himself whether it would not be contrary to his duty to himself to take his own life. Now he inquires whether the maxim of his action could become a universal law of nature. His maxim is: "From self-love I adopt it as a principle to shorten my life when its longer duration is likely to bring more evil than satisfaction." It is asked then simply whether this principle founded on self-love can become a universal law of nature. Now we see at once that a system of nature of which it should be a law to destroy life by means of the very feeling whose special nature it is to impel to the improvement of life would contradict itself and, therefore, could not exist as a system of nature; hence that maxim cannot possibly exist as a universal law of nature and, consequently, would be wholly inconsistent with the supreme principle of all duty.

2. Another finds himself forced by necessity to borrow money. He knows that he will not be able to repay it, but sees also that nothing will be lent to him unless he promises stoutly to repay it in a definite time. He desires to make this promise, but he has still so much conscience as to ask himself: "Is it not unlawful and inconsistent with duty to get out of a difficulty in this way?" Suppose however that he resolves to do so: then the maxim of his action would be expressed thus: "When I think myself in want of money, I will borrow money and promise to repay it, although I know that I never can do so." Now this principle of self-love or of one's own advantage may perhaps be consistent with my whole future welfare; but the question now is, "Is it right?" I change then the suggestion of self-love into a universal law, and state the question thus: "How would it be if my maxim were a universal

law?" Then I see at once that it could never hold as a universal law of nature, but would necessarily contradict itself. For supposing it to be a universal law that everyone when he thinks himself in a difficulty should be able
to promise whatever he pleases, with the purpose of not keeping his promise, the promise itself would become impossible, as well as the end that one
might have in view in it, since no one would consider that anything was
promised to him, but would ridicule all such statements as vain pretences.

3. A third finds in himself a talent which with the help of some culture might
   make him a useful man in many respects. But he finds himself in comfortable circumstances and prefers to indulge in pleasure rather than to take
   pains in enlarging and improving his happy natural capacities. He asks,
   however, whether his maxim of neglect of his natural gifts, besides agreeing with his inclination to indulgence, agrees also with what is called
   duty. He sees then that a system of nature could indeed subsist with such
   a universal law although men (like the South Sea islanders) should let
   their talents rest and resolve to devote their lives merely to idleness,
   amusement, and propagation of their species—in a word, to enjoyment;
   but he cannot possibly *will* that this should be a universal law of nature, or
   be implanted in us as such by a natural instinct. For, as a rational being, he
   necessarily wills that his faculties be developed, since they serve him and
   have been given him, for all sorts of possible purposes.

4. A fourth, who is in prosperity, while he sees that others have to contend
   with great wretchedness and that he could help them, thinks: "What concern is it of mine? Let everyone be as happy as Heaven pleases, or as he
   can make himself; I will take nothing from him nor even envy him, only I
   do not wish to contribute anything to his welfare or to his assistance in
   distress!" Now no doubt if such a mode of thinking were a universal law,
   the human race might very well subsist and doubtless even better than in
   a state in which everyone talks of sympathy and good-will, or even takes
   care occasionally to put it into practice, but, on the other side, also cheats
   when he can, betrays the rights of men, or otherwise violates them. But although it is possible that a universal law of nature might exist in accordance with that maxim, it is impossible to *will* that such a principle should
   have the universal validity of a law of nature. For a will which resolved
   this would contradict itself, inasmuch as many cases might occur in which
   one would have need of the love and sympathy of others, and in which,
   by such a law of nature, sprung from his own will, he would deprive himself of all hope of the aid he desires. . . .

[THE FORMULA OF THE END ITSELF]

Supposing, however, that there were something *whose existence* has *in itself* an
absolute worth, something which, being *an end in itself,* could be a source of
definite laws; then in this and this alone would lie the source of a possible categorical imperative, i.e., a practical law.

Now I say: man and generally any rational being *exists* as an end in himself, *not merely as a means* to be arbitrarily used by this or that will, but in all his actions, whether they concern himself or other rational beings, must be always regarded at the same time as an end. All objects of the inclinations have only a conditional worth, for if the inclinations and the wants founded on them did not exist, then their object would be without value. But the inclinations, themselves being sources of want, are so far from having an absolute worth for which they should be desired that on the contrary it must be the universal wish of every rational being to be wholly free from them. Thus the worth of any object which is *to be acquired* by our action is always conditional. Beings whose existence depends not on our will but on nature's, have nevertheless, if they are irrational beings, only a relative value as means, and are therefore called *things;* rational beings, on the contrary, are called *persons,* because their very nature points them out as ends in themselves, that is as something which must not be used merely as means, and so far therefore restricts freedom of action (and is an object of respect). These, therefore, are not merely subjective ends whose existence has a worth *for us* as an effect of our action, but *objective ends,* that is, things whose existence is an end in itself; an end moreover for which no other can be substituted, which they should subserve *merely* as means, for otherwise nothing whatever would possess *absolute worth;* but if all worth were conditioned and therefore contingent, then there would be no supreme practical principle of reason whatever.

If then there is a supreme practical principle or, in respect of the human will, a categorical imperative, it must be one which, being drawn from the conception of that which is necessarily an end for everyone because it is *an end in itself,* constitutes an *objective* principle of will, and can therefore serve as a universal practical law. The foundation of this principle is: rational nature exists as an end in itself. Man necessarily conceives his own existence as being so; so far then this is a *subjective* principle of human actions. But every other rational being regards its existence similarly, just on the same rational principle that holds for me: so that it is at the same time an objective principle, from which as a supreme practical law all laws of the will must be capable of being deduced. Accordingly the practical imperative will be as follows: *So act as to treat humanity, whether in your own person or in that of any other, in every case as an end withal, never as means only.* . . .

Utilitarianism: Basing Morality on Consequences*

John Stuart Mill (1818–1883)

[PLEASURE AND THE GREATEST HAPPINESS PRINCIPLE]

The creed which accepts as the foundation of morals, Utility, or the Greatest Happiness Principle, holds that actions are right in proportion as they tend to promote happiness, wrong as they tend to produce the reverse of happiness. By happiness is intended pleasure, and the absence of pain; by unhappiness, pain, and the privation of pleasure. To give a clear view of the moral standard set up by the theory, much more requires to be said; in particular, what things it includes in the ideas of pain and pleasure; and to what extent this is left an open question. But these supplementary explanations do not affect the theory of life on which this theory of morality is grounded—namely, that pleasure, and freedom from pain, are the only things desirable as ends; and that all desirable things (which are as numerous in the utilitarian as in any other scheme) are desirable either for the pleasure inherent in themselves, or as means to the promotion of pleasure and the prevention of pain.

Now, such a theory of life excites in many minds, and among them in some of the most estimable in feeling and purpose, inveterate dislike. To suppose that life has (as they express it) no higher end than pleasure—no better and nobler object of desire and pursuit—they designate as utterly mean and grovelling; as a doctrine worthy only of swine, to whom the followers of Epicurus were, at a very early period, contemptuously likened; and modern holders of the doctrine are occasionally made the subject of equally polite comparisons by its German, French, and English assailants.

When thus attacked, the Epicureans have always answered, that it is not they, but their accusers, who represent human nature in a degrading light; since the accusation supposes human beings to be capable of no pleasures except those of which swine are capable. If this supposition were true, the charge could not be gainsaid, but would then be no longer an imputation; for if the sources of pleasure were precisely the same to human beings and to swine, the rule of life which is good enough for the one would be good enough for the other. The comparison of the Epicurean life to that of beasts is felt as degrading, precisely because a beast's pleasures do not satisfy a human being's conceptions of happiness. Human beings have faculties more elevated than the animal appetites, and when once made conscious of them, do not regard anything as

*From J. S. Mill, *Utilitarianism* (1861), Chapters 2 and 3.

happiness which does not include their gratification. I do not, indeed, consider the Epicureans to have been by any means faultless in drawing out their scheme of consequences from the utilitarian principle. To do this in any sufficient manner, many Stoic, as well as Christian elements require to be included. But there is no known Epicurean theory of life which does not assign to the pleasures of the intellect, of the feelings and imagination, and of the moral sentiments, a much higher value as pleasures than to those of mere sensation. It must be admitted, however, that utilitarian writers in general have placed the superiority of mental over bodily pleasures chiefly in the greater permanency, safety, uncostliness, etc., of the former—that is, in their circumstantial advantages rather than in their intrinsic nature. And on all these points utilitarians have fully proved their case; but they might have taken the other, and, as it may be called, higher ground, with entire consistency. It is quite compatible with the principle of utility to recognize the fact, that some kinds of pleasure are more desirable and more valuable than others. It would be absurd that while, in estimating all other things, quality is considered as well as quantity, the estimation of pleasures should be supposed to depend on quantity alone.

[SOME PLEASURES QUALITATIVELY BETTER THAN OTHERS]

If I am asked, what I mean by difference of quality in pleasures, or what makes one pleasure more valuable than another, merely as a pleasure, except its being greater in amount, there is but one possible answer. Of two pleasures, if there be one to which all or almost all who have experience of both give a decided preference, irrespective of any feeling of moral obligation to prefer it, that is the more desirable pleasure. If one of the two is, by those who are competently acquainted with both, placed so far above the other that they prefer it, even though knowing it to be attended with a greater amount of discontent, and would not resign it for any quantity of the other pleasure which their nature is capable of, we are justified in ascribing to the preferred enjoyment a superiority in quality, so far outweighing quantity as to render it, in comparison, of small account.

Now it is an unquestionable fact that those who are equally acquainted with, and equally capable of appreciating and enjoying, both, do give a most marked preference to the manner of existence which employs their higher faculties. Few human creatures would consent to be changed into any of the lower animals, for a promise of the fullest allowance of a beast's pleasures; no intelligent human being would consent to be a fool, no instructed person would be an ignoramus, no person of feeling and conscience would be selfish and base, even though they should be persuaded that the fool, the dunce, or the rascal is better satisfied with his lot than they are with theirs. They would not resign what they possess more than he for the most complete satisfaction of all the desires which they have in common with him. If they ever fancy they would, it is only in cases of unhappiness so extreme, that to escape from it they would exchange their lot for almost any other, however undesirable in their own eyes. A being of higher faculties requires more to make him happy, is capable probably of more acute suffering, and certainly accessible to it at more points, than one of an inferior type; but in spite of these liabilities, he can never really wish to sink into what he feels to be a lower grade of existence. We may give what explanation we please of this unwillingness; we may attribute it to pride, a name which is given indiscriminately to some of the most and to some of the least estimable feelings of which mankind are capable: we may refer it to the love of liberty and personal independence, an appeal to which was with the Stoics one of the most effective means for the inculcation of it; to the love of power, or to the love of excitement, both of which do really enter into and contribute to it: but its most appropriate appellation is a sense of dignity, which all human beings possess in one form or other, and in some, though by no means in exact, proportion to their higher faculties, and which is so essential a part of the happiness of those in whom it is strong, that nothing which conflicts with it could be, otherwise than momentarily, an object of desire to them.

Whoever supposes that this preference takes place at a sacrifice of happiness—that the superior being, in anything like equal circumstances, is not happier than the inferior—confounds the two very different ideas, of happiness, and content. It is indisputable that the being whose capacities of enjoyment are low, has the greatest chance of having them fully satisfied; and a highly endowed being will always feel that any happiness which he can look for, as the world is constituted, is imperfect. But he can learn to bear its imperfections, if they are at all bearable; and they will not make him envy the being who is indeed unconscious of the imperfections, but only because he feels not at all the good which those imperfections qualify. It is better to be a human being dissatisfied than a pig satisfied; better to be Socrates dissatisfied than a fool satisfied. And if the fool, or the pig, are a different opinion, it is because they only know their own side of the question. The other party to the comparison knows both sides.

[PREFERRING HIGHER PLEASURES
TO LOWER PLEASURES]

It may be objected, that many who are capable of the higher pleasures, occasionally, under the influence of temptation, postpone them to the lower. But this is quite compatible with a full appreciation of the intrinsic superiority of the higher. Men often, from infirmity of character, make their election for the nearer good, though they know it to be the less valuable; and this no less when the choice is between two bodily pleasures, than when it is between bodily and mental. They pursue sensual indulgences to the injury of health, though perfectly aware that health is the greater good.

It may be further objected, that many who begin with youthful enthusiasm for everything noble, as they advance in years sink into indolence and selfishness. But I do not believe that those who undergo this very common change, voluntarily choose the lower description of pleasures in preference to the higher. I believe that before they devote themselves exclusively to the one, they have already become incapable of the other. Capacity for the nobler feelings is in most natures a very tender plant, easily killed, not only by hostile influences, but by mere want of sustenance; and in the majority of young persons it speedily dies away if the occupations to which their position in life has devoted them, and the society into which it has thrown them, are not favourable to keeping that higher capacity in exercise. Men lose their high aspirations as they lose their intellectual tastes, because they have not time or opportunity for indulging them; and they addict themselves to inferior pleasures, not because they deliberately prefer them, but because they are either the only ones to which they have access, or the only ones which they are any longer capable of enjoying. It may be questioned whether any one who has remained equally susceptible to both classes of pleasures, ever knowingly and calmly preferred the lower; though many, in all ages, have broken down in an ineffectual attempt to combine both.

From this verdict of the only competent judges, I apprehend there can be no appeal. On a question which is the best worth having of two pleasures, or which of two modes of existence is the most grateful to the feelings, apart from its moral attributes and from its consequences, the judgment of those who are qualified by knowledge of both, or, if they differ, that of the majority among them, must be admitted as final. And there needs be the less hesitation to accept this judgment respecting the quality of pleasures, since there is no other tribunal to be referred to even on the question of quantity. What means are there of determining which is the acutest of two pains, or the intensest of two pleasurable sensations, except the general suffrage of those who are familiar with both? Neither pains nor pleasures are homogeneous, and pain is always heterogeneous with pleasure. What is there to decide whether a particular pleasure is worth purchasing at the cost of a particular pain, except the feelings and judgment of the experienced? When, therefore, those feelings and judgment declare the pleasures derived from the higher faculties to be preferable in kind, apart from the question of intensity, to those of which the animal nature, disjoined from the higher faculties, is suspectible, they are entitled on this subject to the same regard.

According to the Greatest Happiness Principle, as above explained, the ultimate end, with reference to and for the sake of which all other things are desirable (whether we are considering our own good or that of other people), is an existence exempt as far as possible from pain, and as rich as possible in enjoyments, both in point of quantity and quality; the test of quality, and the rule for measuring it against quantity, being the preference felt by those who in their opportunities of experience, to which must be added their habits of self-consciousness and self-observation, are best furnished with the means of comparison. This, being, according to the utilitarian opinion, the end of human action, is necessarily also the standard of morality; which may accordingly be defined, the rules and precepts for human conduct, by the observance of which an existence such as has been described might be, to the greatest extent possible, secured to all mankind; and not to them only, but, so far as the nature of things admits, to the whole sentient creation.

[PLEASURE AND SELF-SACRIFICE]

. . . The utilitarian morality does recognize in human beings the power of sacrificing their own greatest good for the good of others. It only refuses to admit that the sacrifice is itself a good. A sacrifice which does not increase, or tend to increase, the sum total of happiness, it considers as wasted. The only self-renunciation which it applauds, is devotion to the happiness, or to some of the means of happiness, of others; either of mankind collectively, or of individuals within the limits imposed by the collective interests of mankind.

I must again repeat, what the assailants of utilitarianism seldom have the justice to acknowledge, that the happiness which forms the utilitarian standard of what is right in conduct, is not the agent's own happiness, but that of all concerned. As between his own happiness and that of others, utilitarianism requires him to be as strictly impartial as a disinterested and benevolent spectator. In the golden rule of Jesus of Nazareth, we read the complete spirit of the ethics of utility. To do as you would be done by, and to love your neighbor as yourself, constitute the ideal perfection of utilitarian morality. . . .

[WHETHER THERE IS ENOUGH TIME
TO CALCULATE THE EFFECTS OF OUR CONDUCT]

Again, defenders of utility often find themselves called upon to reply to such objections as this—that there is not time, previous to action, for calculating and weighing the effects of any line of conduct on the general happiness. This is exactly as if any one were to say that it is impossible to guide our conduct by Christianity, because there is not time, on every occasion on which anything has to be done, to read through the Old and New Testaments. The answer to the objection is, that there has been ample time, namely, the whole past duration of the human species. During all that time, mankind have been learning by experience the tendencies of actions; on which experience all the prudence, as well as all the morality of life, are dependent. People talk as if the commencement of this course of experience had hitherto been put off, and as if, at the moment when some man feels tempted to meddle with the property or life of another, he had to begin considering for the first time whether murder and theft are injurious to human happiness. . . .

[WHETHER WE ARE BORN
WITH THE FEELING OF MORAL DUTY]

It is not necessary, for the present purpose, to decide whether the feeling of duty is innate or implanted. Assuming it to be innate, it is an open question to what objects it naturally attaches itself; for the philosophic supporters of that theory are now agreed that the intuitive perception is of principles of morality and not of the details. If there be anything innate in the matter, I see no reason why the feeling which is innate should not be that of regard to the pleasures and pains of others. If there is any principle of morals which is intuitively obligatory, I should say it must be that. If so, the intuitive ethics would coincide with the utilitarian, and there would be no further quarrel between them. Even as it is, the intuitive moralists, though they believe that there are other intuitive moral obligations, do already believe this to one; for they unanimously hold that a large portion of morality turns upon the consideration due to the interests of our fellow-creatures. Therefore, if the belief in the transcendental origin of moral obligation gives any additional efficacy to the internal sanction, it appears to me that the utilitarian principle has already the benefit of it.

On the other hand, if, as is my own belief, the moral feelings are not innate, but acquired, they are not for that reason the less natural. It is natural to man to speak, to reason, to build cities, to cultivate the ground, though these are acquired faculties. The moral feelings are not indeed a part of our nature, in the sense of being in any perceptible degree present in all of us; but this, unhappily, is a fact admitted by those who believe the most strenuously in their transcendental origin. Like the other acquired capacities above referred to, the moral faculty, if not a part of our nature, is a natural outgrowth from it; capable, like them, in a certain small degree, of springing up spontaneously; and susceptible of being brought by cultivation to a high degree of development. Unhappily it is also susceptible, by a sufficient use of the external sanctions and of the force of early impressions, of being cultivated in almost any direction: so that there is hardly anything so absurd or so mischievous that it may not, by means of these influences, be made to act on the human mind with all the authority of conscience. To doubt that the same potency might be given by the same means to the principle of utility, even if it had no foundation in human nature, would be flying in the face of all experience.

READING 42

*Turning Values Upside Down**

Friederich Nietzsche (1818–1883)

BEYOND GOOD AND EVIL

I hope to be forgiven for discovering that all moral philosophy hitherto has been tedious and has belonged to the soporific appliances—and that "virtue," in my opinion, has been more injured by the *tediousness* of its

---

*From Friedrich Nietzsche, *Beyond Good and Evil* (1886), *The Twilight of the Idols* (1888), and *The Will to Power*, (1906).

advocates than by anything else; at the same time, however, I would not wish to overlook their general usefulness. It is desirable that as few people as possible should reflect upon morals, and consequently it is *very* desirable that morals should not some day become interesting! But let us not be afraid! Things still remain today as they have always been: I see no one in Europe who has (or discloses) an idea of the fact that philosophizing concerning morals might be conducted in a dangerous, captious, and ensnaring manner—that *calamity* might be involved therein. Observe, for example, the indefatigable, inevitable English utilitarians: how ponderously and respectably they stalk on, stalk along (a Homeric metaphor expresses it better) in the footsteps of Bentham, just as he had already stalked in the footsteps of the respectable Helvétius! (no, he was not a dangerous man, Helvétius, *ce senateur Pococurante,* to use an expression of Galiani). No new thought, nothing of the nature of a finer turning or better expression of an old thought, not even a proper history of what has been previously thought on the subject: an *impossible* literature, taking it all in all unless one knows how to leaven it with some mischief. In effect, the old English vice called cant, which is *moral Tartuffism,* has insinuated itself also into these moralists (whom one must certainly read with an eye to their motives if one *must* read them), concealed this time under the new form of the scientific spirit; moreover, there is not absent from them a secret struggle with the pangs of conscience, from which a race of former Puritans must naturally suffer, in all their scientific tinkering with morals. (Is not a moralist the opposite of a Puritan? That is to say, as a thinker who regards morality as questionable, as worthy of interrogation, in short, as a problem? Is moralizing not—immoral?) In the end, they all want English morality to be recognized as authoritative, inasmuch as mankind, or the "general utility," or "the happiness of the greatest number,"—no! the happiness of *England,* will be best served thereby. They would like, by all means, to convince themselves that the striving after *English* happiness, I mean after *comfort and fashion* (and in the highest instance, a seat in Parliament), is at the same time the true path of virtue; in fact, that in so far as there has been virtue in the world hitherto, it has just consisted in such striving. Not one of those ponderous, conscience-stricken herding-animals (who undertake to advocate the cause of egoism as conducive to the general welfare) wants to have any knowledge or inkling of the facts that the "general welfare" is no ideal, no goal, no notion that can be at all grasped, but is only a nostrum,—that what is fair to one *may not* at all be fair to another, that the requirement of one morality for all is really a detriment to higher men, in short, that there is a *distinction of* rank between man and man, and consequently between morality and morality. They are an unassuming and fundamentally mediocre species of men, these utilitarian Englishmen, and, as already remarked, in so far as they are tedious, one cannot think highly enough of their utility. One ought even to *encourage* them, as has been partially attempted in the following rhymes:

> Hail, ye worthies, barrow-wheeling,
>
> "Longer—better," aye revealing,
>
> Stiffer aye in head and knee;
>
> Unenraptured, never jesting,
>
> Mediocre everlasting,
>
> *Sans genie et sans esprit!*

Every elevation of the type "man," has hitherto been the work of an aristo-cratic society—and so will it always be—a society believing in a long scale of gradations of rank and differences of worth among human beings, and requir-ing slavery in some form or other. Without the *pathos of distance,* such as grows out of the incarnated difference of classes, out of the constant out-looking and down-looking of the ruling caste on subordinates and instruments, and out of their equally constant practice of obeying and commanding, of keeping down and keeping at a distance—that other more mysterious pathos could never have arisen, the longing for an ever new widening of distance within the soul itself, the formation of ever higher, rarer, further, more extended, more com-prehensive states, in short, just the elevation of the type "man," the continued "self-surmounting of man," to use a moral formula in a super-moral sense. To be sure, one must not resign oneself to any humanitarian illusions about the history of the origin of an aristocratic society (that is to say, of the preliminary condition for the elevation of the type "man"): the truth is hard. Let us ac-knowledge unprejudicedly how every higher civilization hitherto has *origi-nated!* Men with a still natural nature, barbarians in every terrible sense of the word, men of prey, still in possession of unbroken strength of will and desire for power, threw themselves upon weaker, more moral, more peaceful races (perhaps trading or cattle-rearing communities), or upon old mellow civiliza-tions in which the final vital force was flickering out in brilliant fireworks of wit and depravity. At the commencement, the noble caste was always the bar-barian caste: their superiority did not consist first of all in their physical, but in their Psychical power—they were more *complete* men (which at every point also implies the same as "more complete beasts").

To refrain mutually from injury, from violence, from exploitation, and put one's will on a par with that of others: this may result in a certain rough sense in good conduct among individuals when the necessary conditions are given (namely, the actual similarity of the individuals in amount of force and degree of worth, and their co-relation within one Organization). As soon, however, as one wished to take this principle more generally, and if possible even as *the fundamental principle of society,* it would immediately disclose what it really is—namely, a Will to the *denial* of life, a principle of dissolution and decay. Here one must think profoundly to the very basis and resist all senti-mental weakness: life itself is essentially appropriation, injury, conquest of the strange and weak, suppression, severity, obtrusion of peculiar forms, incorporation, and at the least, putting it mildest, exploitation;—but why should one for ever use precisely these words on which for ages a disparaging purpose has been stamped? Even the Organization within which, as was previously supposed, the individuals treat each other as equal—it takes place in every healthy aristocracy—must itself, if it be a living and not a dying Organization, do all that towards other bodies, which the individuals within it refrain from doing to each other: it will have to be the incarnated Will to Power, it will endeavor to grow, to gain ground, attract to itself and acquire ascendency—not owing to any morality or immorality, but because it *lives,* and because life is precisely Will to Power. On no point, however, is the ordinary consciousness of Europeans more unwilling to be corrected than on this matter; people now rave everywhere, even under the guise of science, about coming conditions of society in which "the exploiting character" is to be absent:—that sounds to my ears as if they promised to invent a mode of life which should refrain from all organic functions. "Exploitation" does not belong to a depraved, or imperfect and primitive society: it belongs to the *nature* of the living being as a primary organic function; it is a consequence of the intrinsic Will to Power, which is precisely the Will to Life.—Granting that as a theory this is a novelty—as a reality it is the *fundamental fact* of all history: let us be so far honest towards ourselves!

In a tour through the many finer and coarser moralities which have hitherto prevailed or still prevail on the earth, I found certain traits recurring regularly together and connected with one another, until finally two primary types revealed themselves to me, and a radical distinction was brought to light. There is *master*-morality and *slave*-morality;—I would at once add, however, that in all higher and mixed civilizations, there are also attempts at the reconciliation of the two moralities; but one finds still oftener the confusion and mutual misunderstanding of them, indeed, sometimes their close juxtaposition—even in the same man, within one soul. The distinctions of moral values have either originated in a ruling caste, pleasantly conscious of being different from the ruled—or among the ruled class, the slaves and dependents of all sorts. In the first case, when it is the rulers who determine the conception "good," it is the exalted, proud disposition which is regarded as the distinguishing feature, and that which determines the order of rank. The noble type of man separates from himself the beings in whom the opposite of this exalted, proud disposition displays itself: he despises them. Let it at once be noted that in this first kind of morality the antithesis "good" and "bad" means practically the same as "noble" and "despicable";—the antithesis "good" and "*evil*" is of a different origin. The cowardly, the timid, the insignificant, and those thinking merely of narrow utility are despised; moreover, also, the distrustful, with their constrained glances, the self-abasing, the dog-like kind of men who let themselves be abused, the mendicant flatterers, and above all the liars:—it is a fundamental belief of all aristocrats that the common people are untruthful. "We truthful ones"—the nobility in ancient Greece called themselves. It is obvious that everywhere the designations of moral value were at first applied to *men,* and were only derivatively and at a later period applied to *actions*; it is a gross mistake, therefore, when historians of morals start with questions like,

"Why have sympathetic actions been praised?" The noble type of man regards himself as a determiner of values; he does not require to be approved of; he passes the judgment: "What is injurious to me is injurious in itself"; he knows that it is he himself only who confers honor on things; he is a creator of values. He honors whatever he recognizes in himself: such morality is self-glorification. In the foreground there is the feeling of plenitude, of power, which seeks to over-flow, the happiness of high tension, the consciousness of a wealth which would fain give and bestow:—the noble man also helps the unfortunate, but not—or scarcely—out of pity, but rather from an impulse generated by the superabun-dance of power. The noble man honors in himself the powerful one, him also who has power over himself, who knows how to speak and how to keep silence, who takes pleasure in subjecting himself to severity and hardness, and has rever-ence for all that is severe and hard. "Wotan placed a hard heart in my breast," says an old Scandinavian Saga: it is thus rightly expressed from the soul of a proud Viking. Such a type of man is even proud of *not* being made for sympathy; the hero of the Saga therefore adds warningly: "He who has not a hard heart when young, will never have one." The noble and brave who think thus are the furthest removed from the morality which sees precisely in sympathy, or in act-ing for the good of others, or in *désintéressement,* the characteristic of the moral; faith in oneself, pride in oneself, a radical enmity and irony towards "selfless-ness," belong as definitely to noble morality, as do a careless scorn and precau-tion in presence of sympathy and the "warm heart."—It is the powerful who *know* how to honor, it is their art, their domain for invention. The profound rev-erence for age and for tradition—all law rests on this double reverence,—the be-lief and prejudice in favor of ancestors and unfavorable to newcomers, is typical in the morality of the powerful; and if, reversely, men of "modern ideas" believe almost instinctively in "progress" and the "future," and are more and more lack-ing in respect for old age, the ignoble origin of these "ideas" has complacently betrayed itself thereby. A morality of the ruling class, however, is more especially foreign and irritating to present-day taste in the sternness of its principle that one has duties only to one's equals; that one may act towards beings of a lower rank, towards all that is foreign, just as seems good to one, or "as the heart desires," and in any case "beyond good and evil": it is here that sympathy and similar sen-timents can have a place. The ability and obligation to exercise prolonged grati-tude and prolonged revenge—both only within the circle of equals,—artfulness in retaliation, *raffinement* of the idea in friendship, a certain necessity to have ene-mies (as outlets for the emotions of envy, quarrelsomeness, arrogance—in fact, in order to be a good *friend):* all these are typical characteristics of the noble moral-ity, which, as has been pointed out, is not the morality of "modern ideas," and is therefore at present difficult to realize, and also to unearth and disclose.—It is otherwise with the second type of morality, *slave-morality.* Supposing that the abused, the oppressed, the suffering, the unemancipated, the weary, and those uncertain of themselves, should moralize, what will be the common element in their moral estimates? Probably a pessimistic suspicion with regard to the entire situation of man will find expression, perhaps a condemnation of man, together with his situation. The slave has an unfavorable eye for the virtues of the powerful; he has a skepticism and distrust, a *refinement* of distrust of everything "good" that is there honored—he would fain persuade himself that the very happiness there is not genuine. On the other hand, *those* qualities which serve to alleviate the existence of sufferers are brought into prominence and flooded with light; it is here that sympathy, the kind, helping hand, the warm heart, patience, diligence, humility, and friendliness attain to honor; for here these are the most useful qualities, and almost the only means of supporting the burden of existence. Slave-morality is essentially the morality of utility. Here is the seat of the origin of the famous antithesis "good" and "evil":—power and dangerousness are assumed to reside in the evil, a certain dreadfulness, subtlety, and strength, which do not admit of being despised. According to slave-morality, therefore, the "evil" man arouses fear: according to master-morality, it is precisely the "good" man who arouses fear and seeks to arouse it, while the bad man is regarded as the despicable being. The contrast attains its maximum when, in accordance with the logical consequences of slave-morality, a shade of depreciation—it may be slight and well-intentioned—at last attaches itself even to the "good" man of this morality; because, according to the servile mode of thought, the good man must in any case be the *safe* man: he is good-natured, easily deceived, perhaps a little stupid, *un bonhomme.* Everywhere that slave-morality gains the ascendency, language shows a tendency to approximate the significations of the words "good" and "stupid."—A last fundamental difference: the desire for *freedom*, the instinct for happiness and the refinements of the feeling of liberty belong as necessarily to slave-morals and morality, as artifice and enthusiasm in reverence and devotion are the regular symptoms of an aristocratic mode of thinking and estimating.—Hence we can understand without further detail why love as *a passion*—it is our European speciality—must absolutely be of noble origin; as is well known, its invention is due to the Provencal poet-cavaliers, those brilliant ingenious men of the "gai saber," to whom Europe owes so much, and almost owes itself.

THE TWILIGHT OF THE IDOLS

What then, alone, can our teaching be?—That no one gives man his qualities, either God, society, his parents, his ancestors, nor himself (this nonsensical idea, which is at last refuted here, was taught as "intelligible freedom" Kant, and perhaps even as early as Plato himself). No one is responsible for the fact that he exists at all, that he is constituted as he is, and that he happens to be in certain circumstances and in a particular environment. The fatality of his being cannot be divorced from the fatality of all that which has been and will be. This is not the result of an individual attention, of a will, of an aim, there is no attempt at attaining to any "ideal man," or "ideal happiness" or "ideal morality" with him—it is absurd to wish him to be careering towards some sort of purpose. We invented the concept "purpose"; in reality purpose is altogether lacking. One is necessary, one is a piece of fate, one belongs to the whole, one is in the whole—there is nothing that could judge, measure, compare, and condemn our existence, for that would mean judging, measuring, comparing and condemning the whole. *But there is nothing outside the whole!* The fact that no one shall any longer be made responsible, that the nature of existence may not be traced to a *causa prima*, that the world is an entity neither as a sensorium nor as a spirit—this alone is the great deliverance—*thus alone is the innocence of Becoming restored.* . . . The concept "God" has been the greatest objection to existence hitherto. . . . We deny God, we deny responsibility in God: thus alone do we save the world.

THE WILL TO POWER

I regard Christianity as the most fatal and seductive lie that has ever existed— as the greatest and most *impious* lie: I can discern the last sprouts branches of its ideal beneath every form of disguise, I decline to enter into compromise or false position in reference to it—I urge people to declare open war with it.

The morality of paltry people as the measure of all things: this is the most repugnant kind of degeneracy that civilization has ever yet brought into existence. And this *kind of ideal* is hanging still, under the name of "God," over men's heads!!

However modest one's demands may be concerning intellectual cleanliness, when one touches the New Testament one cannot help experiencing a sort of inexpressible feeling of discomfort; for the unbounded cheek with which the least qualified people will have their say in its pages, in regard to the greatest problems of existence, and claim to sit in judgment on such matters, exceeds all limits. The impudent levity with which the most unwieldy problems are spoken of here (life, the world, God, the purpose of life), as if they were not problems at all, but the most simple things which these little bigots *know all about!!!*

This was the most fatal form of insanity that has ever yet existed on earth:—when these little lying abortions of bigotry begin laying claim to the words "God," "last judgment," "truth," "love," "wisdom," "Holy Spirit," and thereby distinguishing themselves from the rest of the world; when such men begin to transvalue values to suit themselves, as though they were the sense, the salt, the standard, and the measure of all things; then all that one should do is this: build lunatic asylums for their incarceration. To *persecute* them was an egregious act of antique folly: this was taking them too seriously; it was making them serious.

The whole fatality was made possible by the fact that a similar form of megalomania was already *in existence,* the *Jewish* form (once the gulf separating the Jews from the Christian-Jews was bridged, the Christian-Jews were *compelled* to employ those self-preservative measures afresh which were discovered by the Jewish instinct, for their own self-preservation, after having accentuated them); and again through the fact that Greek moral philosophy had done everything that could be done to prepare the way for moral-fanaticism, even among Greeks and Romans, and to render it palatable. . . . Plato, the great importer of corruption, who was the first who refused to see Nature in morality, and who had already deprived the Greek gods of all their worth by his notion "*good,*" was already tainted with *Jewish bigotry* (in Egypt?). . . .

The *law,* which is the fundamentally realistic formula of certain self-preservative measures of a community, forbids certain actions that have a definite tendency to jeopardize the welfare of that community: it does *not* forbid the attitude of mind which gives rise to these actions—for in the pursuit of other ends the community requires these forbidden actions, namely, when it is a matter of opposing its *enemies.* The moral idealist now steps forward and says: "God sees into men's hearts: the action itself counts for nothing; the reprehensible attitude of mind from which it proceeds must be extirpated. . . . " In normal conditions men laugh at such things; it is only in exceptional cases, when a community lives *quite* beyond the need of waging war in order to maintain itself, that an ear is lent to such things. Any attitude of mind is abandoned, the utility of which cannot be conceived.

This was the case, for example, when Buddha appeared among a people that was both peaceable and afflicted with great intellectual weariness.

This was also the case in regard to the first Christian community (as also the Jewish), the primary condition of which was the absolutely *unpolitical* Jewish society. Christianity could grow only upon the soil of Judaism—that is to say, among a people that had already renounced the political life, and which led a sort of parasitic existence within the Roman sphere of government. Christianity goes a step *farther;* it allows men to "emasculate" themselves even more; the circumstances actually favor their doing so.—*Nature* is *expelled* from morality when it is said, "Love ye your enemies": for *Nature's* injunction, "Ye shall *love* your neighbor and *hate* your enemy," has now become senseless in the law (in instinct); now, even *the love a man feels for his neighbor* must first be based upon something (*a sort of love of God*). *God* is introduced everywhere, and *utility* is withdrawn; the natural *origin* of morality is denied everywhere: the *veneration of Nature,* which lies in *acknowledging a natural morality,* is destroyed to the roots. . . .

Whence comes the *seductive charm* of this emasculate ideal of man? Why are we not *disgusted* by it, just as we are disgusted at the thought of a eunuch? . . . The answer is obvious: it is not the voice of the eunuch that revolts us, despite the cruel mutilation of which it is the result; for, as a matter of fact, it has grown sweeter. . . . And owing to the very fact that the "male organ" has been amputated from virtue, its voice now has a feminine ring, which, formerly, was not to be discerned.

On the other hand, we have only to think of the terrible hardness, dangers, and accidents to which a life of manly virtues leads—the life of a Corsican, even at the present day, or that of a heathen Arab (which resembles the Corsican's life even to the smallest detail: the Arab's songs might have been written by Corsicans)—in order to perceive how the most robust type of man was fascinated and moved by the voluptuous ring of this "goodness" and "purity. . . . A pastoral melody . . . an idyll . . . the "good man": such things have most effect in ages when tragedy is abroad.

The Astuteness of moral castration.—How is war waged against the virile passions and valuations? No violent physical means are available; the war must therefore be one of ruses, spells, and lies—in short, a "spiritual war."

First recipe: One appropriates virtue in general, and makes it the main feature of one's ideal; the older ideal is denied and declared to be *the reverse of all ideals.* Slander has to be carried to a fine art for this purpose.

Second recipe: One's own type is set up as a general *standard;* and this is projected into all things, behind all things, and behind the destiny of all things—as God.

Third recipe: The opponents of one's ideal are declared to be the opponents of God; one arrogates to oneself a *right* to great pathos, to power, and a right to curse and to bless.

Fourth recipe: All suffering, all gruesome, terrible, and fatal things are declared to be the results of opposition to *one's* ideal—all suffering is *punishment* even in the case of one's adherents (except it be a trial, etc.).

Fifth recipe: One goes so far as to regard Nature as the reverse of one's ideal, and the lengthy sojourn amid natural conditions is considered a great trial of patience—a sort of martyrdom; one studies contempt, both in one's attitudes and one's looks towards all "natural things."

Sixth recipe: The triumph of anti-naturalism and ideal castration, the triumph of the world of the pure, good, sinless, and blessed, is projected into the future as the consummation, the finale, the great hope, and the "Coming of the Kingdom of God."

I hope that one may still be allowed to laugh at this artificial hoisting up of a small species of man to the position of an absolute standard of all things?

To what extent psychologists have been corrupted by the moral idiosyncrasy!—Not one of the ancient philosophers had the courage to advance the theory of the non-free will (that is to say, the theory that denies morality);—not one had the courage to identify the typical feature of happiness, of every kind of happiness ("pleasure"), with the will to power: for the pleasure of power was considered immoral;—not one had the courage to regard virtue as a *result of immorality* (as a result of a will to power) in the service of a species (or of a race, or of a *polis);* for the will to power was considered immoral.

In the whole of moral evolution, there is no sign of truth: all the conceptual elements which come into play are fictions; all the psychological tenets are false; all the forms of logic employed in this department of prevarication are sophisms. The chief feature of all moral philosophers is their total lack of intellectual cleanliness and self-control: they regard "fine feelings" as arguments: their heaving breasts seem to them the bellows of godliness. . . . Moral philosophy is the most suspicious period in the history of the human intellect.

The first great example: in the name of morality and under its patronage, a great wrong was committed, which as a matter of fact was in every respect an act of decadence. Sufficient stress cannot be laid upon this fact, that the great Greek philosophers not only represented the decadence of *every kind of Greek ability*, but also made it *contagious.* . . . This "virtue" made wholly abstract was the highest form of seduction; to make oneself abstract means to *turn one's back on the world.*

The moment is a very remarkable one: the Sophists are within sight of the first *criticism* of morality, the first *knowledge* of morality:—they classify the majority of moral valuations (in view of their dependence upon local conditions) together;—they lead one to understand that every form of morality is capable of being upheld dialectically: that is to say, they guessed that all the fundamental principles of a morality must be *sophistical*—a proposition which was afterwards proved in the grandest possible style by the ancient philosophers from Plato onwards (up to Kant);—they postulate the primary truth that there is no such thing as a "moral *per se,*" a "good *per se,*" and that it is madness to talk of "truth" in this respect.

Wherever was *intellectual uprightness* to be found in those days?

The Greek culture of the Sophists had grown out of all the Greek instincts; it belongs to the culture of the age of Pericles as necessarily as Plato does not: it has its predecessors in Heraclitus, Democritus, and in the scientific types of the old philosophy; it finds expression in the elevated culture of Thucydides, for instance. And—it has ultimately shown itself to be right: every step in the science of epistemology and morality has *confirmed the attitude of* the Sophists. . . . Our modern attitude of mind is, to a great extent, Heraclitean, Democritean, and Protagorean. . . to say that it is *Protagorean* is even sufficient: because Protagoras was in himself a synthesis of the two men Heraclitus and Democritus.

(*Plato: a great Cagliostro,*—let us think of how Epicurus judged him; how Timon, Pyrrho's friend, judged him—Is Plato's integrity by any chance beyond question? . . . But we at least know what he wished to have *taught as* absolute truth—namely, things which were to him not even relative truths: the separate and immortal life of "souls.")

READING 43

Is There a Characteristically Feminine Voice Defining Morality?*

Carol Gilligan (b. 1936)

The men whose theories have largely informed [the] understanding of [human] development have all been plagued by the same problem, the problem of women, whose sexuality remains more diffuse, whose perception of self is so much more tenaciously embedded in relationships with others and whose moral dilemmas hold them in a mode of judgment that is insistently

*From Carol Gilligan, "In a Different Voice: Women's Conception of Self and of Morality," *Harvard Educational Review,* 1977, Vol. 47, pp. 481–517.

contextual. The solution has been to consider women either as deviant or deficient in their development.

That there is a discrepancy between concepts of womanhood and adulthood is nowhere more clearly evident than in the series of studies on sex-role stereotypes. . . . The repeated finding of these studies is that the qualities deemed necessary for adulthood—the capacity for autonomous thinking, clear decision making, and responsible action—are those associated with masculinity but, considered undesirable as attributes of the feminine self. The stereotypes suggest a splitting of love and work that relegates the expressive capacities requisite for the former to women while the instrumental abilities necessary for the latter reside in the masculine domain. Yet, looked at from a different perspective, these stereotypes reflect a conception of adulthood that is itself out of balance, favoring the separateness of the individual self over its connection to others and leaning more toward an autonomous life of work than toward the interdependence of love and care. . . .

The revolutionary contribution of Piaget's work is the experimental confirmation and refinement of Kant's assertion that knowledge is actively constructed rather than passively received. Time, space, self, and other, as well as the categories of developmental theory, all arise out of the active interchange between the individual and the physical and social world in which he lives and of which he strives to make sense. . . .

Kohlberg (1969), in his extension of the early work of Piaget, discovered six stages of moral judgment, which he claimed formed an invariant sequence, each successive stage representing a more adequate construction of the moral problem, which in turn provides the basis for its more just resolution. The stages divide into three levels, each of which denotes a significant expansion of the moral point of view from an egocentric through a societal to a universal ethical conception. With this expansion in perspective comes the capacity to free moral judgment from the individual needs and social conventions with which it had earlier been confused and anchor it instead in principles of justice that are universal in application. These principles provide criteria upon which both individual and societal claims can be impartially assessed. In Kohlberg's view, at the highest stages of development morality is freed from both psychological and historical constraints, and the individual can judge independently of his own particular needs and of the values of those around him.

That the moral sensibility of women differs from that of men was noted by Freud (1925/1961) in the following by now well-quoted statement:

> I cannot evade the notion (though I hesitate to give it expression) that for women the level of what is ethically normal is different from what it is in man. Their superego is never so inexorable, so impersonal, so independent of its emotional origins as we require it to be in men. Character-traits which critics of every epoch have brought up against women—that they show less sense of justice than men, that they are less ready to submit to the great exigencies of life, that they are more often influenced in their judgments by feelings of af-

fection or hostility—all these would be amply accounted for by the modification in the formation of their superego.

While Freud's explanation lies in the deviation of female from male development around the construction and resolution of the Oedipal problem, the
same observations about the nature of morality in women emerge from the
work of Piaget and Kohlberg. Piaget (1932/1965), in his study of the rules of
children's games, observed that, in the games they played, girls were "less ex-
plicit about agreement [than boys] and less concerned with legal elaboration."
In contrast to the boys' interest in the codification of rules, the girls adopted a
more pragmatic attitude, regarding "a rule as good so long as the game repays
it." As a result, in comparison to boys, girls were found to be more tolerant
and more easily reconciled to innovations.

Kohlberg (1971) also identifies a strong interpersonal bias in the moral
judgments of women, which leads them to be considered as typically at the
third of his six-stage developmental sequence. At that stage, the good is identified with "what pleases or helps others and is approved of by them." This
mode of judgment is conventional in its conformity to generally held notions
of the good but also psychological in its concern with intention and consequences as the basis for judging the morality of action.

That women fall largely into this level of moral-judgment is hardly surprising when we read from the Broverman et al. (1972) list that prominent
among the twelve attributes considered to be desirable for women are tact,
gentleness, awareness of the feelings of others, strong need for security, and
easy expression of tender feelings. And yet, herein lies the paradox, for the
very traits that have traditionally defined the "goodness" of women, their care
for and sensitivity to the needs of others, are those that mark them as deficient
in moral development. The infusion of feeling into their judgments keeps
them from developing a more independent and abstract ethical conception in
which concern for others derives from principles of justice rather than from
compassion and care. Kohlberg, however, is less pessimistic than Freud in his
assessment, for he sees the development of women as extending beyond the
interpersonal level, following the same path toward independent, principled
judgment that he discovered in the research on men from which his stages
were derived. In Kohlberg's view, women's development will proceed beyond
Stage Three when they are challenged to solve moral problems that require
them to see beyond the relationships that have in the past generally bound
their moral experience.

What then do women say when asked to construct the moral domain; how
do we identify the characteristically "feminine" voice? A Radcliffe undergraduate, responding to the question, "If you had to say what morality meant to
you, how would you sum it up," replies:

> When I think of the word morality, I think of obligations. I usually think of it
> as conflicts between personal desires and social things, social considerations,
> or personal desires of yourself versus personal desires of another person or
> people or whatever. Morality is that whole realm of how you decide these

conflicts. A moral person is one who would decide, like by placing themselves more often than not as equals, a truly moral person would always consider another person as their equal . . . in a situation of social interaction, something is morally wrong where the individual ends up screwing a lot of people. And it is morally right when everyone comes out better off.

Yet when asked if she can think of someone whom she would consider a genuinely moral person, she replies, "Well, immediately I think of Albert Schweitzer because he has obviously given his life to help others." Obligation and sacrifice override the ideal of equality, setting up a basic contradiction in her thinking.

Another undergraduate responds to the question, "What does it mean to say something is morally right or wrong?," by also speaking first of responsibilities and obligations:

Just what it has to do with responsibilities and obligations and values, mainly values. . . . In my life situation I relate morality and interpersonal relationships that have to do with respect for the other person and myself. [Why respect other people?] Because they have a consciousness or feelings that can be hurt, an awareness that can be hurt.

The concern about hurting others persists as a major theme in the responses of two other Radcliffe students:

[Why be moral?] Millions of people have to live together peacefully. I personally don't want to hurt other people. That's a real criterion, a main criterion for me. It underlies my sense of justice. It isn't nice to inflict pain. I empathize with anyone in pain. Not hurting others is important in my own private morals. Years ago, I would have jumped out of a window not to hurt my boyfriend. That was pathological. Even today though, I want approval and love and I don't want enemies. Maybe that's why there is morality—so people can win approval, love and friendship.

My main moral principle is not hurting other people as long as you aren't going against your own conscience and as long as you remain true to yourself. . . . There are many moral issues such as abortion, the draft, killing, stealing, monogamy, etc. If something is a controversial issue like these, then I always say it is up to the individual. The individual has to decide and then follow his own conscience. There are no moral absolutes. . . . Laws are pragmatic instruments, but they are not absolutes. A viable society can't make exceptions all the time, but I would personally. . . . I'm afraid I'm heading for some big crisis with my boyfriend someday, and someone will get hurt, and he'll get more hurt than I will. I feel an obligation to not hurt him, but also an obligation to not lie. I don't know if it is possible to not lie and not hurt.

The common thread that runs through these statements, the wish not to hurt others and the hope that in morality lies a way of solving conflicts so that no one will get hurt, is striking in that it is independently introduced by each of the four women as the most specific item in their response to a most general question. The moral person is one who helps others; goodness is service, meeting one's obligations and responsibilities to others, if possible, without sacrificing oneself. While the first of the four women ends by denying the conflict she initially introduced, the last woman anticipates a conflict between remaining true to herself and adhering to her principle of not hurting others. The dilemma that would test the limits of this judgment would be one where helping others is seen to be at the price of hurting the self.

The reticence about taking stands on "controversial issues," the willingness to "make exceptions all the time" expressed in the final example above, is echoed repeatedly by other Radcliffe students, as in the following two examples:

> I never feel that I can condemn anyone else. I have a very relativistic position. The basic idea that I cling to is the sanctity of human life. I am inhibited about impressing my beliefs on others.

> I could never argue that my belief on a moral question is anything that another person should accept. I don't believe in absolutes. . . . If there is an absolute for moral decisions, it is human life . . .

When women feel excluded from direct participation in society, they see themselves as subject to a consensus or judgment made and enforced by the men on whose protection and support they depend and by whose names they are known. A divorced middle-aged woman, mother of adolescent daughters, resident of a sophisticated university community, tells the story as follows:

> As a woman, I feel I never understood that I was a person, that I can make decisions and I have a right to make decisions. I always felt that that belonged to my father or my husband in some way or church which was always represented by a male clergyman. They were the three men in my life: father, husband, and clergyman, and they had much more to say about what I should or shouldn't do. They were really authority figures which I accepted. I didn't rebel against that. It only has lately occurred to me that I never even rebelled against it, and my girls are much more conscious of this, not in the militant sense, but just in the recognizing sense. . . . I still let things happen to me rather than make them happen, than to make choices, although I know all about choices. I know the procedures and the steps and all. [Do you have any clues about why this might be true?] Well, I think in one sense, there is less responsibility involved. Because if you make a dumb decision, you have to take the rap. If it happens to you, well, you can complain about it. I think that if you don't grow up feeling that you ever had any choices, you don't either have the sense that you have emotional responsibility. With this sense of choice comes this sense of responsibility.

The essence of the moral decision is the exercise of choice and the willingness to accept responsibility for that choice. To the extent that women perceive themselves as having no choice, they correspondingly excuse themselves from the responsibility that decision entails. Childlike in the vulnerability of their dependence and consequent fear of abandonment, they claim to wish only to please but in return for their goodness they expect to be loved and cared for. This, then, is an "altruism" always at risk, for it presupposes an innocence constantly in danger of being compromised by an awareness of the trade-off that has been made. Asked to describe herself, a Radcliffe senior responds:

> I have heard of the onion skin theory. I see myself as an onion, as a block of different layers, the external layers for people that I don't know that well, the agreeable, the social, and as you go inward there are more sides for people I know that I show. I am not sure about the innermost, whether there is a core, or whether I have just picked up everything as I was growing up, these different influences. I think I have a neutral attitude towards myself, but I do think in terms of good and bad. Good—I try to be considerate and thoughtful of other people and I try to be fair in situations and be tolerant. I use the words but I try and work them out practically. Bad things—I am not sure if they are bad, if they are altruistic or I am doing them basically for approval of other people. [Which things are these?] The values I have when I try to act them out. They deal mostly with interpersonal type relations. If I were doing it for approval, it would be a very tenuous thing. If I didn't get the right feedback, there might go all my values.

. . . Women have traditionally deferred to the judgment of men, although often while intimating a sensibility of their own which is at variance with that judgment. Maggie Tulliver, in *The Hill on the Floss* (Eliot, 1860/1965), responds to the accusations that ensue from the discovery of her secretly continued relationship with Phillip Wakeham by acceding to her brother's moral judgment while at the same time asserting a different set of standards by which she attests her own superiority:

> I don't want to defend myself. . . . I know I've been wrong—often continually. But yet, sometimes when I have done wrong, it has been because I have feelings that you would be the better for if you had them. If *you* were in fault ever, if you had done anything very wrong, I should be sorry for the pain it brought you; I should not want punishment to be heaped on you.

The morality of responsibility which women describe stands apart from the morality of rights which underlies Kohlberg's conception of the highest stages of moral judgment. Kohlberg . . . sees the progression toward these stages as resulting from the generalization of the self-centered adolescent rejection of societal morality into a principled conception of individual natural rights. To illustrate this progression, he cites an example . . . of a male college senior whose moral judgment also was scored by Kohlberg as at Stage Five or Six:

> [Morality] is a prescription, it is a thing to follow, and the idea of having a concept of morality is to try to figure out what it is that people can do in order to make life with each other livable, make for a kind of balance, a kind of equilibrium, a harmony in which everybody feels he has a place and an equal share in things, and it's doing that—doing that is kind of contributing to a state of affairs that go beyond the individual in the absence of which, the individual has no chance for self-fulfillment of any kind. Fairness; morality is kind of essential, it seems to me, for creating the kind of environment, interaction between people, that is prerequisite to this fulfillment of most individual goals and so on. If you want other people to not interfere with your pursuit of whatever you are into, you have to play the game.

In contrast, a woman in her late twenties responds to a similar question by defining a morality not of rights but of responsibility:

[What makes something a moral issue?] Some sense of trying to uncover a right path in which to live, and always in my mind is that the world is full of real and recognizable trouble, and is it heading for some sort of doom and is it right to bring children into this world when we currently have an overpopulation problem, and is it right to spend money on a pair of shoes when I have a pair of shoes and other people are shoeless. . . . It is part of a self-critical view, part of saying, how am I spending my time and in what sense am I working? I think I have a real drive to, I have a real maternal drive to take care of someone. To take care of my mother, to take care of children, to take care of other people's children, to take care of my own children, to take care of the world. I think that goes back to your other question, and when I am dealing with moral issues, I am sort of saying to myself constantly, are you taking care of all the things that you think are important and in what ways are you wasting yourself and wasting those issues?

. . . From another perspective, however, this judgment represents a different moral conception, disentangled from societal conventions and raised to the principled level. In this conception, moral judgment is oriented toward issues of responsibility. The way in which the responsibility orientation guides moral decision at the post-conventional level is described by the following woman in her thirties:

[Is there a right way to make moral decisions?] The only way I know is to try to be as awake as possible, to try to know the range of what you feel, to try to consider all that's involved, to be as aware as you can be to what's going on, as conscious as you can of where you're walking. [Are there principles that guide you?] The principle would have something to do with responsibility, responsibility and caring about yourself and others. . . . But it's not that on the one hand you choose to be responsible and on the other hand you choose to be irresponsible—both ways you can be responsible. That's why there's not just a principle that once you take hold of you settle—the principle put into practice here is still going to leave you with conflict.

The moral imperative that emerges repeatedly in the women's interviews is an injunction to care, a responsibility to discern and alleviate the "real and recognizable trouble" of this world. For the men Kohlberg studied, the moral imperative appeared rather as an injunction to respect the rights of others and thus to protect from interference the right to life and self-fulfillment. Women's insistence on care is at first self-critical rather than self-protective, while men initially conceive obligation to others negatively in terms of noninterference. Development for both sexes then would seem to entail an integration of rights and responsibilities through the discovery of the complementarity of these disparate views. For the women I have studied, this integration between rights and responsibilities appears to take place through a principled understanding of equity and reciprocity. This understanding tempers the self-destructive potential of a self-critical morality by asserting the equal right of all persons to care.

READING 44

Cultural Relativism*

James Fieser (b. 1958)

. . . For centuries, moral philosophers have reflected on the philosophical problems raised by clashing social values. The key question is whether moral values exist independently of human social creations. Cultural relativism is the view that societies create their own traditions, pass them along from one generation to another, and continually reinforce them through rewards and punishments. In this view, morality is a distinctly human invention, so it makes no sense to look for a foundation of morality outside of human social approval. This isn't simply an issue of anthropological curiosity concerning how different people and cultures view morality. Instead, it is an issue of whether *my* and *your* specific moral obligations are grounded in nothing other than cultural approval.

Cultural relativism is a component of a broader moral theory called moral relativism, which holds more generally that moral values are *human* inventions. This broader theory includes both (1) individual relativism—namely, that each person creates his or her own moral standards—and (2) cultural relativism—namely, that social cultures create moral standards. We will focus here on the theory of cultural relativism, looking at its historical development and the key arguments against it.

CLASSIC CULTURAL RELATIVISM

The issue of cultural relativism was one of the first hotly debated issues in Western moral philosophy, and the views of early cultural relativists remain even today largely unchanged.

Xenophanes and the Greek Skeptics

One of the earliest accounts of cultural relativism was offered by the ancient Greek philosopher Xenophanes (570–475 B.C.E.). Although his writings are lost to us, enough quotations from his works survive that we can gain a general view of his position. Xenophanes focuses specifically on the culturally relative nature of *religious* beliefs, rather than ethical beliefs per se. In two fragments, he explains how different ethnic groups depict their deities differently:

> Ethiopians say that their gods are flat-nosed and dark, Thracians that theirs are blue-eyed and red-haired.

*From James Fieser, *Moral Philosophy Through the Ages* (2001), Chapter 1.

> If oxen and horses and lions had hands and were able to draw with their
> hands and do the same things as men, horses would draw the shapes of gods
> to look like horses and oxen to look like ox, and each would make the gods'
> bodies have the same shape as they themselves had.

In the first of these passages, Xenophanes notes that different ethnic groups portray the gods with physical attributes that are unique to their own people. In the second passage, he speculates that if animals could draw they would make the gods look like animals. Xenophanes' point is that our own cultural experiences shape the things that we say about the gods, and our religious views aren't really objective descriptions of the gods themselves.

Although Xenophanes' comments are confined to views of gods, it isn't much of a stretch to extend this reasoning to ethical issues and see that morality is also culturally relative. Greek historians after Xenophanes fueled the discussion of cultural relativism in both religion and ethics by providing graphic examples of differing cultural practices in various civilizations of the day. After surveying the traditions of different regions, the Greek historian Heroditus (484–425 B.C.E.) concluded, "Everyone without exception believes his own native customs, and the religion he was brought up in, to be the best." Heroditus's point is that, not only do we all adopt the religious and ethical value systems of our respective cultures, but we typically go a step further and denounce foreign value systems as inferior to our own.

The next big step in the development of cultural relativism was made by ancient Greek philosophers of the skeptical tradition, who were directly influenced by Xenophanes. Once again, we only have sketchy information about the earliest philosophers in this tradition. The founder was a charismatic and original moral philosopher named Pyrrho (c. 365–275 B.C.E.), who had several loyal followers but who wrote nothing himself. In one of his few surviving statements, Pyrrho argues that in moral matters we cannot determine whether anything is truly good or bad, and so we must suspend judgment.

As the skeptical tradition continued, followers of Pyrrho developed this line of reasoning, and eventually the views of the skeptics were systematically written down by Greek philosopher Sextus Empiricus (fl. 200 C.E.). Sextus presents the definitive statement of cultural relativism. Drawing on anthropological data compiled by earlier Greek historians, Sextus gives example after example of moral standards that differ from one society or culture to another. These include attitudes about homosexuality, incest, cannibalism, human sacrifice, the killing of the elderly, infanticide, theft, and consumption of animal flesh.

Sextus believes that this social diversity in and of itself is a good reason to adopt cultural relativism. The differing cultural attitudes are quite extreme, and Sextus clearly wants to shock us into thinking seriously about this diversity. Here is his account of differing attitudes concerning the treatment of corpses:

> Some wrap the dead up completely and then cover them with earth, thinking
> that it is impious to expose them to the sun; but the Egyptians take out their

entrails and embalm them and keep them above ground with themselves. The fish-eating tribes of the Ethiopians cast them into the lakes, there to be devoured by the fish; the Hyrcanians expose them as prey to dogs, and some of the Indians to vultures. And they say that some of the Troglodytes take the corpse to a hill, and then after tying its head to its feet cast stones upon it amidst laughter, and when they have made a heap of stones over it they leave it there. And some of the barbarians stay and eat those who are over sixty years old, but bury in the earth those who die young. Some burn the dead; and of these some recover and preserve their bones, while others show no care but leave them scattered about. And they say that the Persians impale their dead and embalm them with niter, after which they wrap them round in bandages. (*Outlines of Pyrrhonism*, 3.24)

Sextus concludes that "the skeptic, seeing so great a diversity of usages, suspends judgment as to the natural existence of anything good or bad or (in general) fit or unfit to be done." That is, we should doubt the existence of an independent and universal standard of morality, and instead regard moral values as the result of cultural preferences.

Sextus and other Pyrrhonian skeptics have a particular goal in mind in advancing cultural relativism. That goal is personal tranquility. Suppose I believe that there exists a fixed and objective standard of truth; suppose further that this standard guides all my actions. Since I see myself on the side of moral truth, I become morally outraged by those who don't follow these moral standards. Ultimately, I make myself miserable through my extreme convictions. However, once I seriously reflect on the wide diversity of cultural practices that Sextus describes, I will be more inclined to see that my own cultural practices are rooted in social customs. I will then get off my moral high horse and be content to accept the moral diversity that I see in other cultures.

Later Defenders of Cultural Relativism.

Christian philosophers of the Middle Ages harshly rejected the skepticism and cultural relativism of their Greek predecessors. According to most medieval Christian philosophers, moral values are eternal principles, mandated by God and binding on all humans. Although some "heathen" cultures might consistently engage in bizarre customs, such as ceremonial prostitution, medieval philosophers argued that these practices are immoral no matter how widespread they are. This Christian view of morals was finally challenged by skeptically minded Enlightenment philosophers, who were inspired by Sextus Empiricus's writings.

French philosopher Michel Eyquem de Montaigne (1533–1592) was among the first to resurrect the skeptical views of Sextus. Montaigne wholeheartedly endorsed Sextus's cultural relativism, which he articulates in an essay entitled "Of Custom, and That we should not Easily Change a Law Received" (1580). In this essay, Montaigne describes dozens of strange cultural practices from foreign countries, focusing especially on sexually-related practices. In one culture, unmarried women "may prostitute themselves to as many as they please," and when they get pregnant, they can lawfully abort their fetuses "in the sight of everyone." In another culture, male guests at weddings are invited to sleep with the bride even before the groom does, "and the greater number of them there is, the greater is her honor and the opinion of her ability and strength." Montaigne describes one culture in which gender roles are strangely reversed: Houses of prostitution contain young men "for the pleasure of women," and "wives go to war as well as the husbands."

In addition to sexually related practices, Montaigne lists others from almost every aspect of life:

> [There are societies] where they boil the bodies of their dead, and afterwards pound them to a pulp, which they mix with their wine, and drink it; where the most coveted burial is to be eaten by dogs . . . where they live in that rare and unsociable opinion of the mortality of the soul; . . . where women urinate standing and men squatting; where they send their blood in a token of friendship . . . where the children nurse for four years, and often twelve; . . . where they circumcise the women; . . . in another it is reputed a holy duty for a man to kill his father at a certain age; . . . where children of seven years old endured being whipped to death, without changing expression . . . (*Essays* "Of Custom")

Montaigne concludes that custom has the power to shape every possible kind of cultural practice. Although we pretend that morality is a fixed feature of nature, morality, too, is formed through custom: "The laws of conscience, which we pretend to be derived from nature, proceed from custom." Montaigne argues further that peer pressure is so strong that we automatically approve of our society's customs: "As everyone has an inward veneration for the opinions and manners approved of and received among his own people, no one can, without very great reluctance, depart from them, or apply himself to them without approval."

Almost two centuries later, Scottish philosopher David Hume (1711–1776) reiterated Sextus's skeptical view of cultural relativism. Hume presents a fictitious dialog in which the leading character argues that many moral practices are accepted by some cultures, but condemned by others; these include homosexual pedophilia, adultery, infanticide, and euthanasia. The leading character in Hume's dialog boldly concludes that "fashion, vogue, custom, and law [are] the chief foundation of all moral determinations."

Cultural relativism received another boost from sociologists of the late nineteenth and early twentieth centuries. Perhaps the best example is American sociologist William Graham Sumner (1840–1910). In his classic work *Folkways* (1906), Sumner argues that the morality of a given society simply amounts to the folkways or traditions of that society. For Sumner, theories that try to ground morality in some absolute standard are misguided:

> In the folkways, whatever is, is right. . . . When we come to the folkways we are at the end of our analysis. . . . Therefore rights can never be "natural" or

"God-given," or absolute in any sense. The morality of a group at a time is the sum of the taboos and prescriptions in the folkways by which right conduct is defined. (*Folkways,* 1.31)

Sumner argues that there are no exceptions to this: A society's values concerning slavery, abortion, killing of the elderly, and cannibalism only reflect that society's traditional taboos and prescriptions.

One of the most articulate philosophical defenders of cultural relativism in recent years was Australian philosopher J. L. Mackie (1917–1981). Like his skeptical predecessors, Mackie believes that moral values vary from culture to culture. Also like his predecessors, he believes that there simply are no objective moral values, a view that he calls moral skepticism. For Mackie, this means that morality is something that we invent: "Morality is not to be discovered but to be made: we have to decide what moral views to adopt, what moral stands to take." From Xenophanes on through Mackie, the key points associated with the tradition of cultural relativism are these:

- *Cultural relativism:* Moral values are created by society.
- *Social diversity:* Moral values vary from culture to culture.
- *Moral skepticism:* There is no objective moral truth.

THE ARGUMENT FROM SOCIAL DIVERSITY

A running theme among cultural relativists is that values differ from society to society, and the best explanation for such variation is that societies simply create their own values. We can express this intuition more formally in the argument here:

1. Morally significant values differ from society to society.
2. These differing moral values are grounded either in objective moral standards or only in social custom.
3. It is difficult to explain how these differing moral values are grounded in objective moral standards.
4. Therefore, it is more reasonable to believe that these differing moral values are grounded in social custom.

To understand this argument we need to consider it premise by premise. Premise 1 advocates the view of social diversity, that is, the view that different cultures in fact have different moral values. Defenders of this claim—from Sextus to Mackie—believe that this is a matter of factual observation. We can directly see differences in values among various cultures. For example, Sumner argues that our observations will clearly reveal that even taboos against incest are "by no means universal or uniform, or attended by the same intensity of repugnance." Similarly, in our own day, we directly observe that many East African cultures favor the practice of female genital mutilation; by contrast, in North America, we plainly abhor the practice. If we make accurate observations, then we must accept the fact of social diversity for at least some morally significant values.

If we grant premise 1, we can next consider the other two premises of this argument. Premise 2 maintains that there are two contending ways of understanding where moral values come from. Values are grounded in either (1) an objective standard that is independent of human society or (2) social custom. Over the centuries, moral objectivists have proposed a variety of objective standards of morality. For example, some objectivists hold that moral standards are grounded in eternal truths, or in laws of nature, or in God's commands—in some more stable level of reality beyond mere human social custom. Premise 2 then, is at least a plausible way of seeing the possible foundations of moral standards: Either they are grounded in a more stable level of reality *beyond* social custom, or they are grounded *in* social custom.

Finally, premise 3 states that it is hard to see how moral standards are grounded in an objective reality if they change from culture to culture. Moral objectivists believe that our objectively grounded moral beliefs should shape our cultural practices. For example, we condemn stealing in our culture because some objective standard tells us that stealing is wrong. However, when we consider the wide variety of conflicting moral values in societies around the world, it does not seem reasonable that these all are grounded in a universal and objective standard. On face value, then, premise 3 also seems credible.

The conclusion that we draw, then, is that moral values are grounded in social custom, which—compared to moral objectivism—more reasonably explains the moral diversity that we see. Suppose, for example, that I believe that polygamy is immoral while my friend from Saudi Arabia believes that polygamy is morally permissible. The more reasonable explanation is that our respective cultures influence our individual beliefs, rather than the objectivist alternative that objectively informed beliefs influence our cultures. Cultural relativism, then, is the most reasonable explanation for why our moral beliefs mimic our culture. Although this argument seems plausible at face value, critics have pointed out some flaws. We will look at two criticisms.

Balfour's Criticism: Many Customs Are Simply Depraved

Over the centuries, critics of cultural relativism have attacked the argument from social diversity on several grounds. One response is to challenge premise 3, which states that "it is difficult to explain how these differing moral values are grounded in objective moral standards." The entire argument from social diversity will topple if we can offer a cogent explanation as to how differing cultural values might be grounded in an objective reality.

In responding to Hume's statement of cultural relativism, eighteenth-century Scottish philosopher James Balfour (1705–1795) argued that, even if customs do vary over time and from place to place, there is still an underlying ideal moral standard that these cultures simply ignore. The whole batch of these cultures are simply corrupt, and these corrupt values only highlight true morality all the more.

Such an opinion leads to this unavoidable consequence, that whatever any set of men, or even any individual person, may think fit to do, however criminal in itself, must yet be deemed a virtue; because it is immediately agreeable to those who practice it.

But let us suppose that a whole nation should universally countenance a bad practice, this never would alter the nature of things, nor give sanction to vice. . . .

But so far are the depraved customs of the multitude, or even the practices of the great from being the just standard of morality, that virtue shines forth with the greater lustre from amidst bad practices; and even an universal corruption renders it the more conspicuous. (*Delineation*, 5)

Part of Balfour's attack is plausible—namely, his contention that the customs of the multitude may be depraved. Perhaps there exists an objective standard of morality, and our particular moral beliefs become distorted as we try to perceive objective standards through our diverse cultures. So, if I believe polygamy is immoral and my friend from Saudi Arabia believes it is moral, then at least one of us, and perhaps both of us, might have a distorted understanding of objective morality.

Even if this is so, we need to know *how to determine* which of our practices are depraved and which reflect true morality. Balfour's solution is that the true standard of morality "shines forth with the greater luster from amid bad practices." For Balfour, the contrast between depraved practices and true morality is so pronounced that we all can intuitively see the difference. Unfortunately, Balfour's solution does not work. Certainly, Balfour genuinely believed that some moral values "shine forth" as more legitimate than others. But it probably never occurred to Balfour that the strength of his moral convictions might have been shaped by his eighteenth-century Scottish moral tradition, which was heavily influenced by Calvinistic religious beliefs. In a different culture, other moral values might "shine forth" to those people as more legitimate than those that Balfour holds to be true. In short, since our internal intuitions themselves may be products of our respective cultures, we can't safely appeal to these intuitions to determine which of our practices are depraved and which reflect true morality.

Objectivist moral philosophers have offered a variety of more stringent litmus tests to help distinguish between true morality and depraved values; these proposed tests include rationality, natural law, religious scripture, and human nature. Although these appear to be more rigorous than Balfour's test, they nevertheless all fall prey to the same problem that Balfour's did. That is, they all may be products of their respective cultures. A chemical test to determine the pH level of swimming pools will work the same around the world. A mathematical test to determine the structural integrity of bridge designs will also work the same around the world. But notions of rationality, natural law, scripture, and human nature are matters of debate and do not represent uniform standards. Ultimately, if we can't offer a uniform test to distinguish true morality from depraved values, then we should accept premise 3 in the argument from social diversity.

Rachels's Criticism: Some Key Values Do Not Vary

A second approach to attacking the argument from social diversity is to challenge premise 1, which holds that "many morally significant values differ from culture to culture." Some critics of relativism argue that there is less variation than relativists claim. Although many values do vary from culture to culture, they say, a large number of these so-called values are not truly moral in nature and would be better classified as "rules of prudence." That is, they involve personal lifestyle choices that, in spite of their strangeness, don't warrant moral condemnation by anyone. Many of the culturally relative practices noted by Sextus Empiricus fall into the prudence category, including men wearing "dresses":

> No man here would dress himself in a flowered robe reaching to the feet, although this dress, which with us is thought shameful, is held to be highly respectable by the Persians. And when, at the court of Dionysis the tyrant of Sicily, a dress of this description was offered to the philosophers Plato and Aristippus, Plato sent it away with the words "A man am I, and never could I don a woman's garb." . . . (*Outlines of Pyrrhonism,* 3.24)

Even Sextus's discussion of the differing cultural rituals surrounding corpses involves issues of prudence rather than morality. The same goes for many social customs that Montaigne lists. Distinguishing between true morality and prudence takes away some of the force from premise 1 in the argument from social diversity. But some critics of relativism argue even further that, if we look hard enough, we will actually find basic moral values that are *the same* in all cultures. In Hume's "Dialogue" on cultural relativism, one character in the conversation who opposes relativism argues just this point:

> It appears, that there never was any quality recommended by any one, as a virtue or moral excellence, but on account of its being useful, or agreeable to a man himself, or to others. For what other reason can ever be assigned for praise or approbation? Or where would be the sense of extolling a good character or action, which, at the same time, is allowed to be good for nothing? All the differences, therefore, in morals, may be reduced to this one general foundation, and may be accounted for by the different views, which people take of these circumstances. ("A Dialogue")

In other words, although there might be some diversity with regard to *specific* types of conduct, there is one general moral standard that we find in all societies. This uniform moral standard involves the usefulness of right conduct and the pleasure that we immediately experience from such conduct. Consequently, underlying general moral standards don't vary from culture to culture.

In recent years, James Rachels has made a similar argument for three core common values: (1) caring for children, (2) truth telling, and (3) prohibitions against murder. For Rachels, these are all necessary conditions for the survival of a society since, if a society consistently violated any one of these, it would disintegrate. As to caring for children, all societies need to replenish their supply of educated and productive citizens; otherwise, in only a few generations, that society would die out. As to truth telling, the successful operation of industries, businesses, schools, and governments rests on the individuals involved trusting each other's word. For example, I would not buy groceries at my local store if I couldn't trust that the grocer would let me take home what I paid for. As to prohibitions against murder, if society allowed us to randomly kill other humans for sport or at whim, then everyone would head for the hills and stay as far from society as possible.

The list of common values doesn't need to stop with the three that Rachels mentions. Society would fall apart if there were no prohibition against stealing either privately held or publicly held property. Imagine what would happen, for example, if, to expand my garden, I simply annexed my neighbor's backyard or the street in front of my house. Society also must commit itself to enforcing its core values; otherwise, the values themselves would be empty words.

So, by distinguishing between issues of morality and prudence, and by identifying common social values, the critic of relativism successfully raises serious questions about the truth of premise 1. What at first seems to be an obvious truth for relativists—that moral values differ from culture to culture—now seems more like a hasty generalization. The critic's victory may not be absolute, though, especially when we consider sexual values such as those concerning pedophilia, incest, homosexuality, adultery, and polygamy. Most of us don't see these as issues of mere prudence; indeed, attitudes about these practices vary so widely that we can't link them with a core value. Nevertheless, enough damage is done to premise 1 that the sweeping conclusion of the argument from social diversity no longer follows. That is, it isn't necessarily more reasonable to believe that differing moral values are grounded in social customs.

COMMON ARGUMENTS
AGAINST CULTURAL RELATIVISM

Even if the argument from social diversity falls as a proof for cultural relativism, this isn't a decisive loss for the cultural relativist. The issue of cultural variability is not necessarily the central issue behind the cultural relativism/objectivism dispute. Even if all cultures throughout time consistently endorsed a particular value, such as that murder is wrong, cultural relativists could still argue that this value is grounded in societal traditions, not in objective standards. There may be common factors that prompt *all* societies to create and endorse similar values, such as a prohibition against murder. But this doesn't make these values any less social creations; moral values would still be grounded in social approval. So, we may distinguish between two ways of viewing cultural relativism:

Variable cultural relativism: Moral values are grounded in social approval, and these values vary in different cultures.
Nonvariable cultural relativism: Moral values are grounded in social approval, and these values do not necessarily vary in different cultures.

Nonvariable cultural relativism is a more modest approach to relativism since it grants in principle that moral values might be the same in different cultures. Although this sidesteps the objection that Rachels offered, even this more modest relativism has its critics. We will consider three objections.

Whether Cultural Relativists Deny All Moral Values

Critics of cultural relativism sometimes argue that denying an objective basis of morality amounts to rejecting all moral values. But this criticism confuses the cultural relativist's position with that of the moral nihilist, who holds that there are no moral values at all, but simply repressive social conventions that a truly free person will reject. The cultural relativist, by contrast, recognizes society's moral values, and even endorses them; he or she denies only that they are grounded in an objective realm.

To clarify the relativist's point, it is helpful to distinguish between issues of metaethics and issues of normative ethics. Metaethics investigates where morality comes from, and one of the key issues of metaethics concerns whether moral values exist in an objective realm that is external to human society. The relativist denies that moral values exist in a realm outside of human society. Normative ethics, by contrast, involves a quest for the best values and guiding principles of human conduct. Some leading normative values are the Ten Commandments of Judaism, the Confucian principle of reciprocity that we should avoid treating others in ways we wouldn't want to be treated ourselves, and the Utilitarian position that we should pursue the greatest happiness for the greatest number of people. The cultural relativist will acknowledge the binding nature of some set of moral values such as these. Like everyone else, the relativist lives in a society, raises children, is appalled by crime, and hopes for a better future. There are many practical and emotional reasons to adopt and perpetuate normative moral standards. In short, it is only the more abstract metaethical issue of objectively existing values that the relativist questions. The relativist would argue that it is the normative that really matters in life, that makes us good citizens.

Whether Cultural Relativism Leads to Horrible Values

Critics of cultural relativism argue that, without the objective grounding of moral principles, societies would create many arbitrary and perhaps horrible values and simply give them the rubber stamp of "morality." But if societies ground values in fixed objective principles, these values will be good ones. The cultural relativist has three replies to this charge. First, even if we grant that there are objective moral principles, objectivists simply assume that these principles are fixed, unchanging, and essentially good. However, this is a position that must be argued for rather than merely assumed. The nineteenth-century German idealist philosopher G. W. F. Hegel (1770–1831) believed that the universe is a giant, continually evolving spirit. As this absolute spirit evolves over time, so, too, do human social values evolve on earth: They started out a bit rough but over time became better. Hegel may not have gotten the story of the universe right, but the cultural relativist will argue that, even if moral principles are objective, they are not necessarily unchanging, non-arbitrary, or even good.

Second, for the sake of argument, let's grant that there are objective moral principles that are unchanging. However, if we have no clear litmus test for recognizing them, then, in practice, we may create our value system independently of them. So, the mere existence of objective moral principles alone doesn't *guarantee* that we will formulate our social value systems in a certain way. The objectivist needs to bolster his or her views with additional theories about how we recognize these unchanging moral truths and how we *are motivated* to follow them. In our discussion of Balfour's criticism, we noted that this is difficult to do.

Third, cultural relativists don't necessarily hold that moral values are completely arbitrary creations of human society. Some aspects of human nature might influence the kinds of customs that we approve of. Sextus Empiricus and most other traditional philosophers argued that humans and animals alike are biologically programmed to find some things pleasing and other things painful. Skeptical philosophers also point to other factors in human nature that might influence how we develop social conventions, such as our natural sense of selfpreservation, fear of death, and desire to live in peace. Even Mackie argues that we "create" morality in response to our natural drive to improve our well-being as active social creatures. Cultural relativists would still deny that moral values are permanently *fixed* through our natural drives; however, relativists don't typically deny altogether the influence of human nature.

Whether Cultural Relativism rules out Universal Judgments

Perhaps the strongest resistance to cultural relativism comes from our negative reactions to what we see as barbaric customs such as female genital mutilation. Regardless of how defenders of such practices view them in their homelands, we feel strongly that they are wrong. It isn't simply that they are wrong here in the United States; they are wrong *everywhere*, even in the cultures in which they are practiced the most. The cultural relativist doesn't seem justified in making this universal pronouncement if he or she denies the existence of an independent and objective moral realm.

In response, imagine that morality is a game we play that involves following specific rules created by society. Some of the rules have us arrive at a normative list of dos and don'ts; other rules involve punishments and rewards for those who break or abide by these dos and don'ts; still others govern the vocabulary we use when playing the morality game. For example, I'm allowed to call you a "good person" if you consistently perform the "dos." I am allowed to call you a "bad person" if you consistently violate the "don'ts." The rules also allow me to make universal pronouncements, such as "Female genital mutilation is wrong everywhere." Not only can I say this, but, according to the rules, I can also *mean* it, *argue* for it, feel anger toward those who perform this practice, and stipulate that defenders of this practice are simply wrong. All of these rules are consistent with the cultural relativist's view that morality is grounded in a combination of human nature and social convention.

The moral objectivist won't be satisfied with this game-based notion of universal pronouncement. Instead, objectivists such as Balfour will still argue that we need objective moral principles to give full force to universal pronouncements. The relativist can agree that there is in fact a greater metaethical strength to the objectivist's notion of universal pronouncement. However, the relativist will argue that nothing is gained with objectivism from the standpoint of universal pronouncements. The rules of the morality game remain the same for both the objectivist and the cultural relativist, and both are entitled to make universal pronouncements according to the rules.

PART SEVEN

Political Philosophy

One of the most complicated problems facing modern society is how to bring into harmony the elements of authority, human rights, and freedom. The concept of authority, in particular, has been a matter of constant perplexity. Who has the authority to tell another person what he may or may not do in society? Does the government have the right to override the wishes of a citizen? Is a law, as a command of the government, just or right simply because that law has been officially promulgated? Or must a law, in order to be just, conform to some higher standard of justice? And finally, what should a person do if he concludes that a law is unjust: Should he obey it, or does he have a right to disobey it? Answering these questions is the task of political philosophy. One of oldest and greatest works of political philosophy, which addresses several of these questions, is the *Crito* by Plato (427–347 B.C.E.). The dialog is set in the aftermath of Plato's *Apology*. Socrates was found guilty of atheism and corrupting the youth and sentenced to death by an Athenian jury. Socrates is in his final hours before his execution, and his young friend and student Crito makes one last attempt to get Socrates to escape and save his life. Crito offers a string of reasons for why Socrates should disobey the jury's decision. However, Socrates insists that he should abide by their decision, regardless of the fatal consequences. Socrates feels that he must obey the laws of Athens both because he owes his government a debt of gratitude and also because he sees himself contractually bound to the Athenian government.

Philosophers after Plato addressed the issues of society and governmental authority in different ways, depending on what concept they thought was most important to emphasize. In his *Politics* Aristotle (384–322 B.C.E.) set forth the idea that the state "is a creation of nature" and that "man is by nature a political animal." Thomas Aquinas (1224–1274), in his *Summa Theologica*, emphasizes the moral dimension of law. For him, law is more than an expression of power or an arbitrary command. Law, he said, is a dictate of reason. Indeed, Aquinas linked the law of government to the moral law within in human reason, which, in turn, was linked to the eternal law which, according to Aquinas, is identical with God's reason. It follows in Aquinas's theory, therefore, that if a law of a government is contrary to the natural law known by human reason, then such a civil law does not even have the character of law and presumably does not have to be obeyed. Although the question of obedience to law is involved here, that was not Aquinas's chief concern. He appears to be more interested in clarifying what a law is and how necessary it is for a law, to be a law, to conform to natural morality. Here, as in other aspects of his thought, Aquinas was influenced by the philosophy of Aristotle.

In the seventeenth century, discussions of political philosophy focused heavily on the issue of the source of governmental authority. In *De Cive* (1651) British philosopher Thomas Hobbes (1588–1678) offers what reads like a grammar of obedience. He emphasizes obedience to the law primarily because of his horror at the prospect of anarchy. He describes what it would be like if each person were completely free to decide what it would take to preserve his own life. Under these circumstances, each person would have a right to do anything and everything he considered necessary for this end. Because people frequently want the same thing although only one can have it, and because we have inconsistent ideas of what is just and right or even what religion requires, life becomes a continuous struggle and conflict, or a "war of all against all." In order, then, to overcome this anarchy, it is necessary for people to agree upon one lawgiver, the sovereign, whose laws everyone must obey. Thus, obedience to the laws is what creates and preserves a civil society. The alternative, says Hobbes, is for us to retain our former freedom in the state of nature to decide by ourselves what justice is and what our conduct should be.

During the seventeenth and eighteenth centuries, political philosophers and political revolutionaries alike frequently emphasized the notion of *natural rights,* that is, rights that we are all born with and that are uncreated by governments. These writers frequently described these rights as the rights of *man.* Although many writers used the term "man" in the gender neutral sense of "human being," others believed that men were morally and intellectually superior to women, and, thus, the notion of the "rights of man" applied primarily to men. In her *Vindication of the Rights of Woman,* British philosopher Mary Wollstonecraft (1759–1797) harshly attacks sexist philosophers of her day and defends the notion of women's rights.

Political philosophy took a dramatic turn in the nineteenth century with German philosopher Karl Marx (1818–1883) and his *Manifesto of the Communist Party.* In this work, Marx denounces economic systems in which the ruling middle class (the bourgeoisie)—exploit the working class (the proletariat). The solution to this class conflict, according to Marx, is an all-out revolution of the working class, by which they would take control of the country's economic system. Around the same time, in his book *On Liberty,* British philosopher John Stuart Mill (1818–1883) defended the notion of individual freedom. As long as others are not harmed by our conduct, then, according to Mill, we should be free to engage in almost any activity we please, without governmental interference.

One of the most important theories of political philosophy in recent years is that by American philosopher John Rawls (b. 1921). In his essay "Justice as Fairness," Rawls fashioned a provocative theory of justice that contains a novel relationship between freedom and equality. Whereas justice requires political equality for all, economic *inequality* is consistent with justice, says Rawls, provided that as a result of the unequal distribution of economic resources all people, especially the disadvantaged, are better off as a result of that unequal distribution.

Obedience to the State*

Plato (427–347 B.C.E.)

[WHETHER SOCRATES SHOULD ESCAPE]

SOCRATES: Why have you come at this hour, Crito? it must be quite early.

CRITO: Yes, certainly.

SOCRATES: What is the exact time?

CRITO: The dawn is breaking.

SOCRATES: I wonder that the keeper of the prison would let you in.

CRITO: He knows me because I often come, Socrates; moreover. I have done him a kindness.

SOCRATES: And are you only just arrived?

CRITO: No, I came some time ago.

SOCRATES: Then why did you sit and say nothing, instead of at once awakening me?

CRITO: I should not have liked myself, Socrates, to be in such great trouble and unrest as you are—indeed I should not: I have been watching with amazement your peaceful slumbers; and for that reason I did not awake you, because I wished to minimize the pain. I have always thought you to be of a happy disposition; but never did I see anything like the easy, tranquil manner in which you bear this calamity.

SOCRATES: Why, Crito, when a man has reached my age he ought not to be repining at the approach of death.

CRITO: And yet other old men find themselves in similar misfortunes, and age does not prevent them from repining.

*From Plato, *Crito*.

SOCRATES: That is true. But you have not told me why you come at this early hour.

CRITO: I come to bring you a message which is sad and painful; not, as I believe, to yourself, but to all of us who are your friends, and saddest of all to me.

SOCRATES: What? Has the ship come from Delos, on the arrival of which I am to die?

CRITO: No, the ship has not actually arrived, but she will probably be here to-day, as persons who have come from Sunium tell me that they have left her there; and therefore to-morrow, Socrates, will be the last day of your life.

SOCRATES: Very well, Crito; if such is the will of God, I am willing; but my belief is that there will be a delay of a day.

CRITO: Why do you think so?

SOCRATES: I will tell you. I am to die on the day after the arrival of the ship?

CRITO: Yes; that is what the authorities say.

SOCRATES: But I do not think that the ship will be here until to-morrow; this I infer from a vision which I had last night, or rather only just now, when you fortunately allowed me to sleep.

CRITO: And what was the nature of the vision?

SOCRATES: There appeared to me the likeness of a woman, fair and comely, clothed in bright raiment, who called to me and said: O Socrates, "The third day hence to fertile Phthia shalt thou go." (Homer, Il.)

CRITO: What a singular dream, Socrates!

SOCRATES: There can be no doubt about the meaning, Crito, I think.

CRITO: Yes; the meaning is only too clear. But, oh! my beloved Socrates, let me entreat you once more to take my advice and escape. For if you die I shall not only lose a friend who can never be replaced, but there is another evil: people who do not know you and me will believe that I might have saved you if I had been willing to give money, but that I did not care. Now, can there be a worse disgrace than this—that I should be thought to value money more than the life of a friend? For the many will not be persuaded that I wanted you to escape, and that you refused.

SOCRATES: But why, my dear Crito, should we care about the opinion of the many? Good men, and they are the only persons who are worth considering, will think of these things truly as they occurred.

CRITO: But you see, Socrates, that the opinion of the many must be regarded, for what is now happening shows that they can do the greatest evil to any one who has lost their good opinion.

SOCRATES: I only wish it were so, Crito; and that the many could do the greatest evil; for then they would also be able to do the greatest good—and what a fine thing this would be! But in reality they can do neither; for they cannot make a man either wise or foolish; and whatever they do is the result of chance.

CRITO: Well, I will not dispute with you; but please to tell me, Socrates, whether you are not acting out of regard to me and your other friends:

are you not afraid that if you escape from prison we may get into trouble with the informers for having stolen you away, and lose either the whole or a great part of our property; or that even a worse evil may happen to us? Now, if you fear on our account, be at ease; for in order to save you, we ought surely to run this, or even a greater risk; be persuaded, then, and do as I say.

SOCRATES: Yes, Crito, that is one fear which you mention, but by no means the only one.

CRITO: Fear not—there are persons who are willing to get you out of prison at no great cost; and as for the informers they are far from being exorbitant in their demands—a little money will satisfy them. My means, which are certainly ample, are at your service, and if you have a scruple about spending all mine, here are strangers who will give you the use of theirs; and one of them, Simmias the Theban, has brought a large sum of money for this very purpose; and Cebes and many others are prepared to spend their money in helping you to escape. I say, therefore, do not hesitate on our account, and do not say, as you did in the court, that you will have a difficulty in knowing what to do with yourself anywhere else. For men will love you in other places to which you may go, and not in Athens only; there are friends of mine in Thessaly, if you like to go to them, who will value and protect you, and no Thessalian will give you any trouble. Nor can I think that you are at all justified, Socrates, in betraying your own life when you might be saved; in acting thus you are playing into the hands of your enemies, who are hurrying on your destruction. And further I should say that you are deserting your own children; for you might bring them up and educate them; instead of which you go away and leave them, and they will have to take their chance; and if they do not meet with the usual fate of orphans, there will be small thanks to you. No man should bring children into the world who is unwilling to persevere to the end in their nurture and education. But you appear to be choosing the easier part, not the better and manlier, which would have been more becoming in one who professes to care for virtue in all his actions, like yourself. And indeed, I am ashamed not only of you, but of us who are your friends, when I reflect that the whole business will be attributed entirely to our want of courage. The trial need never have come on, or might have been managed differently; and this last act, or crowning folly, will seem to have occurred through our negligence and cowardice, who might have saved you, if we had been good for anything; and you might have saved yourself, for there was no difficulty at all. See now, Socrates, how sad and discreditable are the consequences, both to us and you. Make up your mind then, or rather have your mind already made up, for the time of deliberation is over, and there is only one thing to be done, which must be done this very night, and if we delay at all will be no longer practicable or possible; I beseech you therefore, Socrates, be persuaded by me, and do as I say.

[ONLY THE GOOD AND JUST LIFE IS WORTH HAVING]

SOCRATES: Dear Crito, your zeal is invaluable, if a right one; but if wrong, the greater the zeal the greater the danger; and therefore we ought to consider whether I shall or shall not do as you say. For I am and always have been one of those natures who must be guided by reason, whatever the reason may be which upon reflection appears to me to be the best; and now that this chance has befallen me, I cannot repudiate my own words: the principles which I have hitherto honored and revered I still honor, and unless we can at once find other and better principles, I am certain not to agree with you; no, not even if the power of the multitude could inflict many more imprisonments, confiscations, deaths, frightening us like children with hobgoblin terrors. What will be the fairest way of considering the question? Shall I return to your old argument about the opinions of men?—we were saying that some of them are to be regarded, and others not. Now were we right in maintaining this before I was condemned? And has the argument which was once good now proved to be talk for the sake of talking—mere childish nonsense? That is what I want to consider with your help, Crito:—whether, under my present circumstances, the argument appears to be in any way different or not; and is to be allowed by me or disallowed. That argument, which, as I believe, is maintained by many persons of authority, was to the effect, as I was saying, that the opinions of some men are to be regarded, and of other men not to be regarded. Now you, Crito, are not going to die tomorrow—at least, there is no human probability of this, and therefore you are disinterested and not liable to be deceived by the circumstances in which you are placed. Tell me then, whether I am right in saying that some opinions, and the opinions of some men only, are to be valued, and that other opinions, and the opinions of other men, are not to be valued. I ask you whether I was right in maintaining this?

CRITO: Certainly.

SOCRATES: The good are to be regarded, and not the bad?

CRITO: Yes.

SOCRATES: And the opinions of the wise are good, and the opinions of the unwise are evil?

CRITO: Certainly.

SOCRATES: And what was said about another matter? Is the pupil who devotes himself to the practice of gymnastics supposed to attend to the praise and blame and opinion of every man, or of one man only—his physician or trainer, whoever he may be?

CRITO: Of one man only.

SOCRATES: And he ought to fear the censure and welcome the praise of that one only, and not of the many?

CRITO: Clearly so.

SOCRATES: And he ought to act and train, and eat and drink in the way which seems good to his single master who has understanding, rather than according to the opinion of all other men put together?

CRITO: True.

SOCRATES: And if he disobeys and disregards the opinion and approval of the one, and regards the opinion of the many who have no understanding, will he not suffer evil?

CRITO: Certainly he will.

SOCRATES: And what will the evil be, whither tending and what affecting, in the disobedient person?

CRITO: Clearly, affecting the body; that is what is destroyed by the evil.

SOCRATES: Very good; and is not this true, Crito, of other things which we need not separately enumerate? In questions of just and unjust, fair and foul, good and evil, which are the subjects of our present consultation, ought we to follow the opinion of the many and to fear them; or the opinion of the one man who has understanding? ought we not to fear and reverence him more than all the rest of the world: and if we desert him shall we not destroy and injure that principle in us which may be assumed to be improved by justice and deteriorated by injustice;—there is such a principle?

CRITO: Certainly there is, Socrates.

SOCRATES: Take a parallel instance:—if, acting under the advice of those who have no understanding, we destroy that which is improved by health and is deteriorated by disease, would life be worth having? And that which has been destroyed is—the body?

CRITO: Yes.

SOCRATES: Could we live, having an evil and corrupted body?

CRITO: Certainly not.

SOCRATES: And will life be worth having, if that higher part of man be destroyed, which is improved by justice and depraved by injustice? Do we suppose that principle, whatever it may be in man, which has to do with justice and injustice, to be inferior to the body?

CRITO: Certainly not.

SOCRATES: More honorable than the body?

CRITO: Far more.

SOCRATES: Then, my friend, we must not regard what the many say of us: but what he, the one man who has understanding of just and unjust, will say, and what the truth will say. And therefore you begin in error when you advise that we should regard the opinion of the many about just and unjust, good and evil, honorable and dishonorable.—"Well," some one will say, "but the many can kill us."

CRITO: Yes, Socrates; that will clearly be the answer.

SOCRATES: And it is true; but still I find with surprise that the old argument is unshaken as ever. And I should like to know whether I may say the same of another proposition—that not life, but a good life, is to be chiefly valued?

CRITO: Yes, that also remains unshaken.

SOCRATES: And a good life is equivalent to a just and honorable one—that holds also?

CRITO: Yes, it does.

SOCRATES: From these premises I proceed to argue the question whether I ought or ought not to try and escape without the consent of the Athenians: and if I am clearly right in escaping, then I will make the attempt; but if not, I will abstain. The other considerations which you mention, of money and loss of character and the duty of educating one's children, are, I fear, only the doctrines of the multitude, who would be as ready to restore people to life, if they were able, as they are to put them to death—and with as little reason. But now, since the argument has thus far prevailed, the only question which remains to be considered is, whether we shall do rightly either in escaping or in suffering others to aid in our escape and paying them in money and thanks, or whether in reality we shall not do rightly; and if the latter, then death or any other calamity which may ensue on my remaining here must not be allowed to enter into the calculation.

CRITO: I think that you are right, Socrates; how then shall we proceed?

SOCRATES: Let us consider the matter together, and do you either refute me if you can, and I will be convinced; or else cease, my dear friend, from repeating to me that I ought to escape against the wishes of the Athenians: for I highly value your attempts to persuade me to do so, but I may not be persuaded against my own better judgment. And now please to consider my first position, and try how you can best answer me.

CRITO: I will.

SOCRATES: Are we to say that we are never intentionally to do wrong, or that in one way we ought and in another way we ought not to do wrong, or is doing wrong always evil and dishonorable, as I was just now saying, and as has been already acknowledged by us? Are all our former admissions which were made within a few days to be thrown away? And have we, at our age, been earnestly discoursing with one another all our life long only to discover that we are no better than children? Or, in spite of the opinion of the many, and in spite of consequences whether better or worse, shall we insist on the truth of what was then said, that injustice is always an evil and dishonor to him who acts unjustly? Shall we say so or not?

CRITO: Yes.

SOCRATES: Then we must do no wrong?

CRITO: Certainly not.

SOCRATES: Nor when injured injure in return, as the many imagine; for we must injure no one at all? (E.g. compare Rep.)

CRITO: Clearly not.

SOCRATES: Again, Crito, may we do evil?

CRITO: Surely not, Socrates.

SOCRATES: And what of doing evil in return for evil, which is the morality of the many—is that just or not?

CRITO: Not just.

SOCRATES: For doing evil to another is the same as injuring him?

CRITO: Very true.

SOCRATES: Then we ought not to retaliate or render evil for evil to any one, whatever evil we may have suffered from him. But I would have you consider, Crito, whether you really mean what you are saying. For this opinion has never been held, and never will be held, by any considerable number of persons; and those who are agreed and those who are not agreed upon this point have no common ground, and can only despise one another when they see how widely they differ. Tell me, then, whether you agree with and assent to my first principle, that neither injury nor retaliation nor warding off evil by evil is ever right. And shall that be the premise of our argument? Or do you decline and dissent from this? For so I have ever thought, and continue to think; but, if you are of another opinion, let me hear what you have to say. If, however, you remain of the same mind as formerly, I will proceed to the next step.

CRITO: You may proceed, for I have not changed my mind.

SOCRATES: Then I will go on to the next point, which may be put in the form of a question:—Ought a man to do what he admits to be right, or ought he to betray the right?

CRITO: He ought to do what he thinks right.

SOCRATES: But if this is true, what is the application? In leaving the prison against the will of the Athenians, do I wrong any? or rather do I not wrong those whom I ought least to wrong? Do I not desert the principles which were acknowledged by us to be just—what do you say?

CRITO: I cannot tell, Socrates, for I do not know.

[GRATITUDE AND CIVIL OBEDIENCE]

SOCRATES: Then consider the matter in this way:—Imagine that I am about to play truant (you may call the proceeding by any name which you like), and the laws and the government come and interrogate me: "Tell us, Socrates," they say; "what are you about? are you not going by an act of yours to overturn us—the laws, and the whole state, as far as in you lies? Do you imagine that a state can subsist and not be overthrown, in which the decisions of law have no power, but are set aside and trampled upon by individuals?" What will be our answer, Crito, to these and the like words? Any one, and especially a rhetorician, will have a good deal to say on behalf of the law which requires a sentence to be carried out. He will argue that this law should not be set aside; and shall we reply, "Yes; but the state has injured us and given an unjust sentence." Suppose I say that?

CRITO: Very good, Socrates.

SOCRATES: "And was that our agreement with you?" the law would answer; "or were you to abide by the sentence of the state?" And if I were to express my astonishment at their words, the law would probably add: "Answer, Socrates, instead of opening your eyes—you are in the habit of asking and answering questions. Tell us,—What complaint have you to make against us which justifies you in attempting to destroy us and the state? In the first place did we not bring you into existence? Your father married your mother by our aid and begat you. Say whether you

have any objection to urge against those of us who regulate marriage?"
None, I should reply. "Or against those of us who after birth regulate
the nurture and education of children, in which you also were trained?
Were not the laws, which have the charge of education, right in commanding your father to train you in music and gymnastic?" Right, I
should reply. "Well then, since you were brought into the world and
nurtured and educated by us, can you deny in the first place that you
are our child and slave, as your fathers were before you? And if this is
true you are not on equal terms with us; nor can you think that you
have a right to do to us what we are doing to you. Would you have any
right to strike or revile or do any other evil to your father or your master, if you had one, because you have been struck or reviled by him, or
received some other evil at his hands?—you would not say this? And
because we think right to destroy you, do you think that you have any
right to destroy us in return, and your country as far as in you lies? Will
you, O professor of true virtue, pretend that you are justified in this?
Has a philosopher like you failed to discover that our country is more to
be valued and higher and holier far than mother or father or any ancestor, and more to be regarded in the eyes of the gods and of men of understanding? also to be soothed, and gently and reverently entreated
when angry, even more than a father, and either to be persuaded, or if
not persuaded, to be obeyed? And when we are punished by her,
whether with imprisonment or stripes, the punishment is to be endured
in silence; and if she lead us to wounds or death in battle, thither we follow as is right; neither may any one yield or retreat or leave his rank,
but whether in battle or in a court of law, or in any other place, he must
do what his city and his country order him; or he must change their
view of what is just: and if he may do no violence to his father or
mother, much less may he do violence to his country." What answer
shall we make to this, Crito? Do the laws speak truly, or do they not?
CRITO: I think that they do.

[THE SOCIAL CONTRACT AND CIVIL OBEDIENCE]

SOCRATES: Then the laws will say: "Consider, Socrates, if we are speaking
truly that in your present attempt you are going to do us an injury. For,
having brought you into the world, and nurtured and educated you, and
given you and every other citizen a share in every good which we had to
give, we further proclaim to any Athenian by the liberty which we allow
him, that if he does not like us when he has become of age and has seen
the ways of the city, and made our acquaintance, he may go where he
pleases and take his goods with him. None of us laws will forbid him or
interfere with him. Any one who does not like us and the city, and who
wants to emigrate to a colony or to any other city, may go where he likes,
retaining his property. But he who has experience of the manner in which

we order justice and administer the state, and still remains, has entered into an implied contract that he will do as we command him. And he who disobeys us is, as we maintain, thrice wrong: first, because in disobeying us he is disobeying his parents; secondly, because we are the authors of his education; thirdly, because he has made an agreement with us that he will duly obey our commands; and he neither obeys them nor convinces us that our commands are unjust; and we do not rudely impose them, but give him the alternative of obeying or convincing us;—that is what we offer, and he does neither.

"These are the sort of accusations to which, as we were saying, you, Socrates, will be exposed if you accomplish your intentions; you, above all other Athenians." Suppose now I ask, why I rather than anybody else? they will justly retort upon me that I above all other men have acknowledged the agreement. "There is clear proof," they will say, "Socrates, that we and the city were not displeasing to you. Of all Athenians you have been the most constant resident in the city, which, as you never leave, you may be supposed to love. For you never went out of the city either to see the games, except once when you went to the Isthmus, or to any other place unless when you were on military service; nor did you travel as other men do. Nor had you any curiosity to know other states or their laws: your affections did not go beyond us and our state; we were your especial favorites, and you acquiesced in our government of you; and here in this city you begat your children, which is a proof of your satisfaction. Moreover, you might in the course of the trial, if you had liked, have fixed the penalty at banishment; the state which refuses to let you go now would have let you go then. But you pretended that you preferred death to exile, and that you were not unwilling to die. And now you have forgotten these fine sentiments, and pay no respect to us the laws, of whom you are the destroyer; and are doing what only a miserable slave would do, running away and turning your back upon the compacts and agreements which you made as a citizen. And first of all answer this very question: Are we right in saying that you agreed to be governed according to us in deed, and not in word only? Is that true or not?" How shall we answer, Crito? Must we not assent?

CRITO: We cannot help it, Socrates.

SOCRATES: Then will they not say: "You, Socrates, are breaking the covenants and agreements which you made with us at your leisure, not in any haste or under any compulsion or deception, but after you have had seventy years to think of them, during which time you were at liberty to leave the city, if we were not to your mind, or if our covenants appeared to you to be unfair. You had your choice, and might have gone either to Lacedaemon or Crete, both which states are often praised by you for their good government, or to some other Hellenic or foreign state. Whereas you, above all other Athenians, seemed to be so fond of the state, or, in other words, of us her laws (and who would care about a state which has no laws?), that you never stirred out of her; the halt, the blind, the maimed, were not more stationary in her than you were. And now you run away and forsake your agreements. Not so, Socrates, if you will take our advice; do not make yourself ridiculous by escaping out of the city.

"For just consider, if you transgress and err in this sort of way, what good will you do either to yourself or to your friends? That your friends will be driven into exile and deprived of citizenship, or will lose their property, is tolerably certain; and you yourself, if you fly to one of the neighboring cities, as, for example, Thebes or Megara, both of which are well governed, will come to them as an enemy, Socrates, and their government will be against you, and all patriotic citizens will cast an evil eye upon you as a subverter of the laws, and you will confirm in the minds of the judges the justice of their own condemnation of you. For he who is a corrupter of the laws is more than likely to be a corrupter of the young and foolish portion of mankind. Will you then flee from well-ordered cities and virtuous men? and is existence worth having on these terms? Or will you go to them without shame, and talk to them, Socrates? And what will you say to them? What you say here about virtue and justice and institutions and laws being the best things among men? Would that be decent of you? Surely not. But if you go away from well-governed states to Crito's friends in Thessaly, where there is great disorder and license, they will be charmed to hear the tale of your escape from prison, set off with ludicrous particulars of the manner in which you were wrapped in a goatskin or some other disguise, and metamorphosed as the manner is of runaways; but will there be no one to remind you that in your old age you were not ashamed to violate the most sacred laws from a miserable desire of a little more life? Perhaps not, if you keep them in a good temper; but if they are out of temper you will hear many degrading things; you will live, but how?—as the flatterer of all men, and the servant of all men; and doing what?—eating and drinking in Thessaly, having gone abroad in order that you may get a dinner. And where will be your fine sentiments about justice and virtue? Say that you wish to live for the sake of your children—you want to bring them up and educate them—will you take them into Thessaly and deprive them of Athenian citizenship? Is this the benefit which you will confer upon them? Or are you under the impression that they will be better cared for and educated here if you are still alive, although absent from them; for your friends will take care of them? Do you fancy that if you are an inhabitant of Thessaly they will take care of them, and if you are an inhabitant of the other world that they will not take care of them? Nay; but if they who call themselves friends are good for anything, they will—to be sure they will.

"Listen, then, Socrates, to us who have brought you up. Think not of life and children first, and of justice afterwards, but of justice first, that you may be justified before the princes of the world below. For neither will you nor any that belong to you be happier or holier or juster in this life, or happier in another, if you do as Crito bids. Now you depart in innocence, a sufferer and not a doer of evil; a victim, not of the laws, but of men. But if you go forth, returning evil for evil, and injury for injury, breaking the covenants and agreements which you have made with us, and wronging those whom you ought least of all to wrong, that is to say, yourself, your friends, your country, and us, we shall be angry with you while you live, and our brethren, the laws in the world below, will receive you as an enemy; for they will know that you have done your best to destroy us. Listen, then, to us and not to Crito."

This, dear Crito, is the voice which I seem to hear murmuring in my ears, like the sound of the flute in the ears of the mystic; that voice, I say, is humming in my ears, and prevents me from hearing any other. And I know that anything more which you may say will be vain. Yet speak, if you have anything to say.

CRITO: I have nothing to say, Socrates.

SOCRATES: Leave me then, Crito, to fulfill the will of God, and to follow whither he leads.

READING 46

The Natural Basis of Society*

Aristotle
(384–322 B.C.E.)

BOOK ONE

[Definition and Structure of the State]

1. Every state is a community of some kind, and every community is established with a view to some good; for mankind always act in order to obtain that which they think good. But, if all communities aim at some good, the state or political community, which is the highest of all, and which embraces all the rest, aims at good in a greater degree than any other, and at the highest good.

    Some people think that the qualifications of a statesman, king, householder, and master are the same, and that they differ, not in kind, but only in the number of their subjects. For example, the ruler over a few is called a master; over more, the manager of a household; over a still larger number, a statesman or king, as if there were no difference between a great household and a small state. The distinction which is made between the king and the statesman is as follows: When the

---

*From Aristotle, *Politics*, Books 1, 3, and 7.

government is personal, the ruler is a king; when, according to the rules of the political science, the citizens rule and are ruled in turn, then he is called a statesman.

But all this is a mistake; for governments differ in kind, as will be evident to any one who considers the matter according to the method which has hitherto guided us. As in other departments of science, so in politics, the compound should always be resolved into the simple elements or least parts of the whole. We must therefore look at the elements of which the state is composed, in order that we may see in what the different kinds of rule differ from one another, and whether any scientific result can be attained about each one of them.

2. He who thus considers things in their first growth and origin, whether a state or anything else, will obtain the clearest view of them. In the first place there must be a union of those who cannot exist without each other; namely, of male and female, that the race may continue (and this is a union which is formed, not of deliberate purpose, but because, in common with other animals and with plants, mankind have a natural desire to leave behind them an image of themselves), and of natural ruler and subject, that both may be preserved. For that which can foresee by the exercise of mind is by nature intended to be lord and master, and that which can with its body give effect to such foresight is a subject, and by nature a slave; hence master and slave have the same interest. Now nature has distinguished between the female and the slave. For she is not niggardly, like the smith who fashions the Delphian knife for many uses; she makes each thing for a single use, and every instrument is best made when intended for one and not for many uses. But among barbarians no distinction is made between women and slaves, because there is no natural ruler among them: they are a community of slaves, male and female. Wherefore the poets say, "It is meet that Hellenes should rule over barbarians;—as if they thought that the barbarian and the slave were by nature one." Out of these two relationships between man and woman, master and slave, the first thing to arise is the family, and Hesiod is right when he says, "First house and wife and an ox for the plough," for the ox is the poor man's slave. The family is the association established by nature for the supply of men's everyday wants, and the members of it are called by Charondas "companions of the cupboard," and by Epimenides the Cretan, "companions of the manger." But when several families are united, and the association aims at something more than the supply of daily needs, the first society to be formed is the village. And the most natural form of the village appears to be that of a colony from the family, composed of the children and grandchildren, who are said to be suckled "with the same milk." And this is the reason why Hellenic states were originally governed by kings; because the Hellenes were under royal rule before they came together, as the barbarians still are. Every family is ruled by the eldest, and therefore in the colonies of the family the kingly form of government prevailed because they were of the same blood. As Homer says: "Each one gives law to his

children and to his wives." For they lived dispersedly, as was the manner in ancient times. Wherefore men say that the Gods have a king, because they themselves either are or were in ancient times under the rule of a king. For they imagine, not only the forms of the Gods, but their ways of life to be like their own.

When several villages are united in a single complete community, large enough to be nearly or quite self-sufficing, the state comes into existence, originating in the bare needs of life, and continuing in existence for the sake of a good life. And therefore, if the earlier forms of society are natural, so is the state, for it is the end of them, and the nature of a thing is its end. For what each thing is when fully developed, we call its nature, whether we are speaking of a man, a horse, or a family. Besides, the final cause and end of a thing is the best, and to be self-sufficing is the end and the best.

Hence it is evident that the state is a creation of nature, and that man is by nature a political animal. And he who by nature and not by mere accident is without a state, is either a bad man or above humanity; he is like the "Tribeless, lawless, heartless one," whom Homer denounces—the natural outcast is forthwith a lover of war; he may be compared to an isolated piece at draughts.

Now, that man is more of a political animal than bees or any other gregarious animals is evident. Nature, as we often say, makes nothing in vain, and man is the only animal whom she has endowed with the gift of speech. And whereas mere voice is but an indication of pleasure or pain, and is therefore found in other animals (for their nature attains to the perception of pleasure and pain and the intimation of them to one another, and no further), the power of speech is intended to set forth the expedient and inexpedient, and therefore likewise the just and the unjust. And it is a characteristic of man that he alone has any sense of good and evil, of just and unjust, and the like, and the association of living beings who have this sense makes a family and a state.

Further, the state is by nature clearly prior to the family and to the individual, since the whole is of necessity prior to the part; for example, if the whole body be destroyed, there will be no foot or hand, except in an equivocal sense, as we might speak of a stone hand; for when destroyed the hand will be no better than that. But things are defined by their working and power; and we ought not to say that they are the same when they no longer have their proper quality, but only that they have the same name. The proof that the state is a creation of nature and prior to the individual is that the individual, when isolated, is not self-sufficing; and therefore he is like a part in relation to the whole. But he who is unable to live in society, or who has no need because he is sufficient for himself, must be either a beast or a god: he is no part of a state. A social instinct is implanted in all men by nature, and yet he who first founded the state was the greatest of benefactors. For man, when perfected, is the best of animals, but, when separated from law and justice, he is the worst of all; since armed injustice is the more dangerous, and he is equipped at birth with arms, meant to be used by intelligence and virtue, which he may use for the worst ends. Wherefore, if he have not virtue, he is the most unholy and the most savage of animals, and the most full of lust and gluttony. But justice is the bond of men in states, for the administration of justice, which is the determination of what is just, is the principle of order in political society. . . .

BOOK THREE

[The Good Citizen]

1. He who would inquire into the essence and attributes of various kinds of governments must first of all determine "What is a state?" At present this is a disputed question. Some say that the state has done a certain act; others, no, not the state, but the oligarchy or the tyrant. And the legislator or statesman is concerned entirely with the state; a constitution or government being an arrangement of the inhabitants of a state. But a state is composite, like any other whole made up of many parts; these are the citizens, who compose it. It is evident, therefore, that we must begin by asking, Who is the citizen, and what is the meaning of the term? For here again there may be a difference of opinion. He who is a citizen in a democracy will often not be a citizen in an oligarchy. Leaving out of consideration those who have been made citizens, or who have obtained the name of citizen any other accidental manner, we may say, first, that a citizen is not a citizen because he lives in a certain place, for resident aliens and slaves share in the place; nor is he a citizen who has no legal right except that of suing and being sued; for this right may be enjoyed under the provisions of a treaty. Nay, resident aliens in many places do not possess even such rights completely, for they are obliged to have a patron, so that they do but imperfectly participate in citizenship, and we call them citizens only in a qualified sense, as we might apply the term to children who are too young to be on the register, or to old men who have been relieved from state duties. Of these we do not say quite simply that they are citizens, but add in the one case that they are not of age, and in the other, that they are past the age, or something of that sort; the precise expression is immaterial, for our meaning is clear. Similar difficulties to those which I have mentioned may be raised and answered about deprived citizens and about exiles. But the citizen whom we are seeking to define is a citizen in the strictest sense, against whom no such exception can be taken, and his special characteristic is that he shares in the administration of justice, and in offices. Now of offices some are discontinuous, and the same persons are not allowed to hold them twice, or can only hold them after a fixed interval; others have no limit of time—for example, the office of a dicast or ecclesiast. It may, indeed, be argued that these are not magistrates at all,

and that their functions give them no share in the government. But surely it is ridiculous to say that those who have the power do not govern. Let us not dwell further upon this, which is a purely verbal question; what we want is a common term including both dicast and ecclesiast. Let us, for the sake of distinction, call it "indefinite office," and we will assume that those who share in such office are citizens. This is the most comprehensive definition of a citizen, and best suits all those who are generally so called. . . .

4. There is a point nearly allied to the preceding: Whether the virtue of a good man and a good citizen is the same or not. But, before entering on this discussion, we must certainly first obtain some general notion of the virtue of the citizen. Like the sailor, the citizen is a member of a community. Now, sailors have different functions, for one of them is a rower, another a pilot, and a third a look-out man, a fourth is described by some similar term; and while the precise definition of each individual's virtue applies exclusively to him, there is, at the same time, a common definition applicable to them all. For they have all of them a common object, which is safety in navigation. Similarly, one citizen differs from another, but the salvation of the community is the common business of them all. This community is the constitution; the virtue of the citizen must therefore be relative to the constitution of which he is a member. If, then, there are many forms of government, it is evident that there is not one single virtue of the good citizen which is perfect virtue. But we say that the good man is he who has one single virtue which is perfect virtue. Hence it is evident that the good citizen need not of necessity possess the virtue which makes a good man.

The same question may also be approached by another road, from a consideration of the best constitution. If the state cannot be entirely composed of good men, and yet each citizen is expected to do his own business well, and must therefore have virtue, still inasmuch as all the citizens cannot be alike, the virtue of the citizen and of the good man cannot coincide. All must have the virtue of the good citizen—thus, and thus only, can the state be perfect; but they will not have the virtue of a good man, unless we assume that in the good state all the citizens must be good.

Again, the state, as composed of unlikes, may be compared to the living being: as the first elements into which a living being is resolved are soul and body, as soul is made up of rational principle and appetite, the family of husband and wife, property of master and slave, so of all these, as well as other dissimilar elements, the state is composed; and, therefore, the virtue of all the citizens cannot possibly be the same, any more than the excellence of the leader of a chorus is the same as that of the performer who stands by his side. I have said enough to show why the two kinds of virtue cannot be absolutely and always the same.

But will there then be no case in which the virtue of the good citizen and the virtue of the good man coincide? To this we answer that the good ruler is a good and wise man, and that he who would be a statesman must be a wise man. And some persons say that even the education of the ruler should be of a special kind; for are not the children of kings instructed in riding and military exercises? As Euripides says: "No subtle arts for me, but what the state requires." As though there were a special education needed by a ruler. If then the virtue of a good ruler is the same as that of a good man, and we assume further that the subject is a citizen as well as the ruler, the virtue of the good citizen and the virtue of the good man cannot be absolutely the same, although in some cases they may; for the virtue of a ruler differs from that of a citizen. It was the sense of this difference which made Jason say that "he felt hungry when he was not a tyrant," meaning that he could not endure to live in a private station. But, on the other hand, it may be argued that men are praised for knowing both how to rule and how to obey, and he is said to be a citizen of approved virtue who is able to do both. Now if we suppose the virtue of a good man to be that which rules, and the virtue of the citizen to include ruling and obeying, it cannot be said that they are equally worthy of praise. Since, then, it is sometimes thought that the ruler and the ruled must learn different things and not the same, but that the citizen must know and share in them both, the inference is obvious. There is, indeed, the rule of a master, which is concerned with menial offices—the master need not know how to perform these, but may employ others in the execution of them: the other would be degrading; and by the other I mean the power actually to do menial duties, which vary much in character and are executed by various classes of slaves, such, for example, as handicraftsmen, who, as their name signifies, live by the labor of their hands: under these the mechanic is included. Hence in ancient times, and among some nations, the working classes had no share in the government—a privilege which they only acquired under the extreme democracy. Certainly the good man and the statesman and the good citizen ought not to learn the crafts of inferiors except for their own occasional use; if they habitually practice them, there will cease to be a distinction between master and slave.

This is not the rule of which we are speaking; but there is a rule of another kind, which is exercised over freemen and equals by birth—a constitutional rule, which the ruler must learn by obeying, as he would learn the duties of a general of cavalry by being under the orders of a general of cavalry, or the duties of a general of infantry by being under the orders of a general of infantry, and by having had the command of a regiment and of a company. It has been well said that "he who has never learned to obey cannot be a good commander." The two are not the same, but the good citizen ought to be capable of both; he should know how to govern like a freeman, and how to obey like a freeman—these are the virtues of a citizen. And, although the temperance and justice of a ruler are distinct from those of a subject, the virtue of a good man will include both; for the virtue of the good man who is free and also a subject, e.g., his justice, will not be one but will comprise distinct kinds, the one qualifying him to rule, the other to obey, and differing as the temperance and courage of men and women differ. For a man would be thought a coward if he had no more courage than a courageous woman, and a woman would be thought loquacious if she imposed no more restraint on her conversation than the good man; and indeed their part in the management of the household is different, for the duty of the one is to acquire, and of the other to preserve. Practical wisdom only is characteristic of the ruler: it would seem that all other virtues must equally belong to ruler and subject. The virtue of the subject is certainly not wisdom, but only true opinion; he may be compared to the maker of the flute, while his master is like the flute-player or user of the flute.

From these considerations may be gathered the answer to the question, whether the virtue of the good man is the same as that of the good citizen, or different, and how far the same, and how far different. . . .

[The True Aim of the State is Virtue]

9. . . . But a state exists for the sake of a good life, and not for the sake of life only: if life only were the object, slaves and brute animals might form a state, but they cannot, for they have no share in happiness or in a life of free choice. Nor does a state exist for the sake of alliance and security from injustice, nor yet for the sake of exchange and mutual intercourse; for then the Tyrrhenians and the Carthaginians, and all who have commercial treaties with one another, would be the citizens of one state. True, they have agreements about imports, and engagements that they will do no wrong to one another, and written articles of alliance. But there are no magistrates common to the contracting parties who will enforce their engagements; different states have each their own magistracies. Nor does one state take care that the citizens of the other are such as they ought to be, nor see that those who come under the terms of the treaty do no wrong or wickedness at an, but only that they do no injustice to one another. Whereas, those who care for good government take into consideration virtue and vice in states. Whence it may be further inferred that virtue must be the care of a state which is truly so called, and not merely enjoys the name: for without this end the community becomes a mere alliance which differs only in place from alliances of which the members live apart; and law is only a convention, "a surety to one another of justice," as the sophist Lycophron says, and has no real power to make the citizens.

This is obvious; for suppose distinct places, such as Corinth and Megara, to be brought together so that their walls touched, still they would not be one city, not even if the citizens had the right to intermarry, which is one of the rights peculiarly characteristic of states. Again, if men dwelt at a distance from one another, but not so far off as to have no intercourse, and there were laws among them that they should not wrong each other in their exchanges, neither would this be a state. Let us suppose that one man is a carpenter, another a husbandman, another a shoemaker, and so on, and that their number is ten thousand: nevertheless, if they have nothing in common but exchange, alliance, and the like, that would not constitute a state. Why is this? Surely not because they are at a distance from one another: for even supposing that such a community were to meet in one place, but that each man had a house of his own, which was in a manner his state, and that they made alliance with one another, but only against evil-doers; still an accurate thinker would not deem this to be a state, if their intercourse with one another was of the same character after as before their union. It is clear then that a state is not a mere society, having a common place, established for the prevention of mutual crime and for the sake of exchange. These are conditions without which a state cannot exist; but all of them together do not constitute a state, which is a community of families and aggregations of families in well-being, for the sake of a perfect and self-sufficing life. Such a community can only be established among those who live in the same place and intermarry. Hence arise in cities family connections, brotherhoods, common sacrifices, amusements which draw men together. But these are created by friendship, for the will to live together is friendship. The end of the state is the good life, and these are the means towards it. And the state is the union of families and villages in a perfect and self-sufficing life, by which we mean a happy and honorable life.

　　Our conclusion, then, is that political society exists for the sake of noble actions, and not of mere companionship. Hence they who contribute most to such a society have a greater share in it than those who have the same or a greater freedom or nobility of birth but are inferior to them in political virtue; or than those who exceed them in wealth but are surpassed by them in virtue. . . .

BOOK SEVEN

[The Good Ruler]

14. Since every political society is composed of rulers and subjects let us consider whether the relations of one to the other should interchange or be permanent. For the education of the citizens will necessarily vary with the answer given to this question. Now, if some men excelled others in the same degree in which gods and heroes are supposed to excel mankind in general (having in the first place a great advantage even in their bodies, and secondly in their minds), so that the superiority of the governors was undisputed and patent to their subjects, it would clearly be better that once for an the one class should rule and the other serve. But since this is unattainable, and kings have no marked superiority over their subjects, such as Scylax affirms to be found among the Indians, it is obviously necessary on many grounds that all the citizens alike should take their turn of governing and being governed. Equality consists in the same treatment of similar persons, and no government can stand which is not founded upon

justice. For if the government be unjust every one in the country unites with the governed in the desire to have a revolution, and it is an impossibility that the members of the government can be so numerous as to be stronger than all their enemies put together. Yet that governors should excel their subjects is undeniable. How all this is to be effected, and in what way they will respectively share in the government, the legislator has to consider. The subject has been already mentioned. Nature herself has provided the distinction when she made a difference between old and young within the same species, of whom she fitted the one to govern and the other to be governed. No one takes offense at being governed when he is young, nor does he think himself better than his governors, especially if he will enjoy the same privilege when he reaches the required age.

  We conclude that from one point of view governors and governed are identical, and from another different. And therefore their education must be the same and also different. For he who would learn to command well must, as men say, first of all learn to obey. As I observed in the first part of this treatise, there is one rule which is for the sake of the rulers and another rule which is for the sake of the ruled; the former is a despotic, the latter a free government. Some commands differ not in the thing commanded, but in the intention with which they are imposed. Wherefore, many apparently menial offices are an honor to the free youth by whom they are performed; for actions do not differ as honorable or dishonorable in themselves so much as in the end and intention of them. But since we say that the virtue of the citizen and ruler is the same as that of the good man, and that the same person must first be a subject and then a ruler, the legislator has to see that they become good men, and by what means this may be accomplished, and what is the end of the perfect life.

READING 47
_____

*Natural Law**

Thomas Aquinas (1225–1274)

QUESTION 90: THE ESSENCE OF LAW

Law is a rule and measure of acts, whereby man is induced to act or is restrained from acting: for "*lex*" [law] is derived from "*ligare*" [to bind], because it binds one to act. Now the rule and measure of human acts is the reason, which is the first principle of human acts, as is evident from what has

_____
*From Thomas Aquinas, *Summa Theologica*, First part of the second part, Questions 90: 1–2; 91: 1–4; 93: 3; 94: 4; 95: 1.

been stated above; since it belongs to the reason to direct to the end, which is the first principle in all matters of action, according to the Philosopher. Now that which is the principle in any genus, is the rule and measure of that genus: for instance, unity in the genus of numbers, and the first movement in the genus of movements. Consequently it follows that law is something pertaining to reason. . . .

The law belongs to that which is a principle of human acts, because it is their rule and measure. Now as reason is a principle of human acts, so in reason itself there is something which is the principle in respect of all the rest: wherefore to this principle chiefly and mainly law must needs be referred. Now the first principle in practical matters, which are the object of the practical reason, is the last end: and the last end of human life is bliss or happiness, as stated above. Consequently the law must needs regard principally the relationship to happiness. Moreover, since every part is ordained to the whole, as imperfect to perfect; and since one man is a part of the perfect community, the law must needs regard properly the relationship to universal happiness. Wherefore the Philosopher, in the above definition of legal matters mentions both happiness and the body politic: for he says that we call those legal matters "just, which are adapted to produce and preserve happiness and its parts for the body politic": since the state is a perfect community.

QUESTION 91: THE VARIOUS KINDS OF LAW

A law is nothing else but a dictate of practical reason emanating from the ruler who governs a perfect community. Now it is evident, granted that the world is ruled by Divine Providence, that the whole community of the universe is governed by Divine Reason. Wherefore the very Idea of the government of things in God the Ruler of the universe, has the nature of a law. And since the Divine Reason's conception of things is not subject to time but is eternal, according to Proverbs 8:23, therefore it is that this kind of law must be called eternal. . . .

Law, being a rule and measure, can be in a person in two ways: in one way, as in him that rules and measures; in another way, as in that which is ruled and measured, since a thing is ruled and measured, in so far as it partakes of the rule or measure. Wherefore, since all things subject to Divine providence are ruled and measured by the eternal law, as was stated above; it is evident that all things partake somewhat of the eternal law, in so far as, namely, from its being imprinted on them, they derive their respective inclinations to their proper acts and ends. Now among all others, the rational creature is subject to Divine providence in the most excellent way, in so far as it partakes of a share of providence, by being provident both for itself and for others. Wherefore it has a share of the Eternal Reason, whereby it has a natural inclination to its proper act and end: and this participation of the eternal law in the rational creature is called the natural law. Hence the Psalmist after saying: "Offer up the sacrifice of justice," as though someone asked what the works of justice are, adds: "Many say, Who showeth us good things?" in answer to which question he says: "The light of Thy countenance, O Lord, is signed upon us": thus implying that the light of natural reason, whereby we discern what is good and what is evil, which is the function of the natural law, is nothing else than an imprint on us of the Divine light. It is therefore evident that the natural law is nothing else than the rational creature's participation of the eternal law. . . .

A law is a dictate of the practical reason. Now it is to be observed that the same procedure takes place in the practical and in the speculative reason: for each proceeds from principles to conclusions. Accordingly we conclude that just as, in the speculative reason, from naturally known indemonstrable principles, we draw the conclusions of the various sciences, the knowledge of which is not imparted to us by nature, but acquired by the efforts of reason, so too it is from the precepts of the natural law, as from general and indemonstrable principles, that the human reason needs to proceed to the more particular determination of certain matters. These particular determinations, devised by human reason, are called human laws, provided the other essential conditions of law be observed. Wherefore Tully says in his Rhetoric that "justice has its source in nature; thence certain things came into custom by reason of their utility; afterwards these things which emanated from nature and were approved by custom, were sanctioned by fear and reverence for the law." . . .

I answer that, Besides the natural and the human law it was necessary for the directing of human conduct to have a Divine law. And this for four reasons. First, because it is by law that man is directed how to perform his proper acts in view of his last end. And indeed if man were ordained to no other end than that which is proportionate to his natural faculty, there would be no need for man to have any further direction of the part of his reason, besides the natural law and human law which is derived from it. But since man is ordained to an end of eternal happiness which is beyond man's natural faculty , therefore it was necessary that, besides the natural and the human law, man should be directed to his end by a law given by God.

Secondly, because, on account of the uncertainty of human judgment, especially on contingent and particular matters, different people form different judgments on human acts; whence also different and contrary laws result. In order, therefore, that man may know without any doubt what he ought to do and what he ought to avoid, it was necessary for man to be directed in his proper acts by a law given by God, for it is certain that such a law cannot err.

Thirdly, because man can make laws in those matters of which he is competent to judge. But man is not competent to judge of interior movements, that are hidden, but only of exterior acts which appear: and yet for the perfection of virtue it is necessary for man to conduct himself aright in both kinds of acts. Consequently human law could not sufficiently curb and direct interior acts; and it was necessary for this purpose that a Divine law should supervene.

Fourthly, because, as Augustine says, human law cannot punish or forbid all evil deeds: since while aiming at doing away with all evils, it would do away with many good things, and would hinder the advance of the common good, which is necessary for human intercourse. In order, therefore, that no evil might remain unforbidden and unpunished, it was necessary for the Divine law to supervene, whereby all sins are forbidden. . . .

QUESTION 93: THE ETERNAL LAW

The law denotes a kind of plan directing acts towards an end. Now wherever there are movers ordained to one another, the power of the second mover must needs be derived from the power of the first mover; since the second mover does not move except in so far as it is moved by the first. Wherefore we observe the same in all those who govern, so that the plan of government is derived by secondary governors from the governor in chief; thus the plan of what is to be done in a state flows from the king's command to his inferior administrators: and again in things of art the plan of whatever is to be done by art flows from the chief craftsman to the under-craftsmen, who work with their hands. Since then the eternal law is the plan of government in the Chief Governor, all the plans of government in the inferior governors must be derived from the eternal law. But these plans of inferior governors are all other laws besides the eternal law. Therefore all laws, in so far as they partake of right reason, are derived from the eternal law. Hence Augustine says that "in temporal law there is nothing just and lawful, but what man has drawn from the eternal law."

QUESTION 94: THE NATURAL LAW

To the natural law belongs those things to which a man is inclined naturally: and among these it is proper to man to be inclined to act according to reason. Now the process of reason is from the common to the proper, as stated in *Physics I.* The speculative reason, however, is differently situated in this matter, from the practical reason. For, since the speculative reason is busied chiefly with the necessary things, which cannot be otherwise than they are, its proper conclusions, like the universal principles, contain the truth without fail. The practical reason, on the other hand, is busied with contingent matters, about which human actions are concerned: and consequently, although there is necessity in the general principles, the more we descend to matters of detail, the more frequently we encounter defects. Accordingly then in speculative matters truth is the same in all men, both as to principles and as to conclusions: although the truth is not known to all as regards the conclusions, but only as regards the principles which are called common notions. But in matters of action, truth or practical rectitude is not the same for all, as to matters of detail, but only as to the general principles: and where there is the same rectitude in matters of detail, it is not equally known to all. . . .

Consequently we must say that the natural law, as to general principles, is the same for all, both as to rectitude and as to knowledge. But as to certain

matters of detail, which are conclusions, as it were, of those general principles, it is the same for all in the majority of cases, both as to rectitude and as
to knowledge; and yet in some few cases it may fail, both as to rectitude, by
reason of certain obstacles (just as natures subject to generation and corruption fail in some few cases on account of some obstacle), and as to knowledge,
since in some the reason is perverted by passion, or evil habit, or an evil disposition of nature; thus formerly, theft, although it is expressly contrary to
the natural law, was not considered wrong among the Germans, as Julius
Caesar relates.

QUESTION 95: HUMAN LAW

Man has a natural aptitude for virtue; but the perfection of virtue must be acquired by man by means of some kind of training. Thus we observe that man
is helped by industry in his necessities, for instance, in food and clothing. Certain beginnings of these he has from nature, viz. his reason and his hands; but
he has not the full complement, as other animals have, to whom nature has
given sufficiency of clothing and food. Now it is difficult to see how man
could suffice for himself in the matter of this training: since the perfection of
virtue consists chiefly in withdrawing man from undue pleasures, to which
above all man is inclined, and especially the young, who are more capable of
being trained. Consequently a man needs to receive this training from another,
whereby to arrive at the perfection of virtue. And as to those young people
who are inclined to acts of virtue, by their good natural disposition, or by custom, or rather by the gift of God, paternal training suffices, which is by admo-
nitions. But since some are found to be depraved, and prone to vice, and not
easily amenable to words, it was necessary for such to be restrained from evil
by force and fear, in order that, at least, they might desist from evil-doing, and
leave others in peace, and that they themselves, by being habituated in this
way, might be brought to do willingly what hitherto they did from fear, and
thus become virtuous. Now this kind of training, which compels through fear
of punishment, is the discipline of laws. Therefore in order that man might
have peace and virtue, it was necessary for laws to be framed: for, as the
Philosopher says, "as man is the most noble of animals if he be perfect in
virtue, so is he the lowest of all, if he be severed from law and righteousness";
because man can use his reason to devise means of satisfying his lusts and evil
passions, which other animals are unable to do.

As Augustine says "that which is not just seems to be no law at all":
wherefore the force of a law depends on the extent of its justice. Now in
human affairs a thing is said to be just, from being right, according to the rule
of reason. But the first rule of reason is the law of nature, as is clear from
what has been stated above. Consequently every human law has just so much
of the nature of law, as it is derived from the law of nature. But if in any point
it deflects from the law of nature, it is no longer a law but a perversion of law.
But it must be noted that something may be derived from the natural law in

two ways: first, as a conclusion from premises, secondly, by way of determination of certain generalities. The first way is like to that by which, in sciences, demonstrated conclusions are drawn from the principles: while the second mode is likened to that whereby, in the arts, general forms are particularized as to details: thus the craftsman needs to determine the general form of a house to some particular shape. Some things are therefore derived from the general principles of the natural law, by way of conclusions; e.g. that "one must not kill" may be derived as a conclusion from the principle that "one should do harm to no man": while some are derived therefrom by way of determination; e.g. the law of nature has it that the evil-doer should be punished; but that he be punished in this or that way, is a determination of the law of nature.

Accordingly both modes of derivation are found in the human law. But those things which are derived in the first way, are contained in human law not as emanating therefrom exclusively, but have some force from the natural law also. But those things which are derived in the second way, have no other force than that of human law.

READING 48

The Social Contract*

Thomas Hobbes (1588–1678)

CHAPTER 1: OF THE STATE OF MEN WITHOUT CIVIL SOCIETY

1. The faculties of human nature may be reduced unto four kinds; bodily strength, experience, reason, passion. Taking the beginning of this following doctrine from these, we will declare in the first place what manner of inclinations men who are endued with these faculties bare towards each other, and whether, and by what faculty, they are born apt for society, and so preserve themselves against mutual violence; then proceeding, we will show what advice was necessary to be taken for this business, and what are the conditions of society, or of human peace; that is to say, (changing the words only) what are the fundamental laws of nature.

2. The greatest part of those men who have written aught concerning commonwealths, either suppose, or require us, or beg of us to believe, that man is a creature born fit for society. [Since we now see actually a constituted society among men, and none living out of it, since we discern all desirous of congress, and mutual correspondence, it may seem a wonderful kind of

*From Thomas Hobbes, *De Cive,* (1651).

stupidity, to lay in the very threshold of this doctrine, such a stumbling block before the readers, as to deny man to be born fit for society. Therefore I must more plainly say, that it is true indeed, that to man, by nature (or *as man,* that is) as soon as he is born, solitude is an enemy. For infants have need of others to help them to live, and those of riper years to help them to live well, wherefore I deny not that men (even nature compelling) desire to come together. But civil societies are not mere meetings, but bonds, to the making whereof, faith and compacts are necessary. The virtue whereof to children, and fools, and the profit whereof to those who have not yet tasted the miseries which accompany its defects, is altogether unknown; whence it happens, that those, because they know not what society is, cannot enter into it; these, because ignorant of the benefit it brings, care not for it. Manifest therefore it is, that all men, because they are born in infancy, are born unapt for society. Many also (perhaps most men) either through defect of mind, or want of education remain unfit during the whole course of their lives; yet have infants, as well as those of riper years, an human nature. Wherefore man is made fit for society not by nature, but by education. Furthermore, although man were born in such a condition as to desire it, it follows not, that he therefore were born fit to enter into it. For it is one thing to desire, another to be in capacity fit for what we desire. For even they, who through their pride, will not stoop to equal conditions, without which there can be no society, do yet desire it.]

The Greeks call him *political animal,* and on this foundation they so build up the doctrine of civil society, as if for the preservation of peace, and the government of mankind there were nothing else necessary, than that men should agree to make curtain covenants and conditions together, which themselves should then call laws. Which axiom, though received by most, is yet certainly false, and an error proceeding from our too slight contemplation of human nature. For they who shall more narrowly look into the causes for which men come together, and delight in each other's company, shall easily find that this happens not because naturally it could happen no otherwise, but by accident. For if by nature one man should love another, that is as man, there could no reason be returned why every man should not equally love every man, as being equally man, or why he should rather frequent those whose society affords him honor or profit. We do not therefore by nature seek society for its own sake, but that we may receive some honor or profit from it; these we desire primarily, that secondarily: how by what advice men do meet, will be best known by observing those things which they do when they are met. For if they meet for traffic, it is plain every man regards not his fellow, but his business; if to discharge some office, a certain market-friendship is begotten, which has more of jealousy in it than true love, and whence factions sometimes may arise, but good will never. If for pleasure, and recreation of mind, every man is wont to please himself most with those things which stir up laughter, whence he may (according to the nature of that which is ridiculous) by comparison of another man's defects and infirmities, pass the more current in his own opinion; and although this be sometimes innocent, and without offence; yet it is manifest they are not so much delighted with the society, as their own vain glory. But for the most part, in these kind of meetings, we wound the absent; their whole life, sayings, actions are examined, judged, condemned; nay, it is very rare, but some present receive a fling before they part, so as his reason was not ill, who was wont always at parting to go out last. And these are indeed the true delights of society, unto which we are carried by nature; that is, by those passions which are incident to all creatures, until either by sad experience, or good precepts, it so fall out (which in many never happens) that the appetite, of present matters, be dulled with the memory of things past, without which, the discourse of most quick and nimble men, on this subject, is but cold and hungry.

But if it so happen, that being met, they pass their time in relating some stories, and one of them begins to tell one which concerns himself; instantly every one of the rest most greedily desires to speak of himself too. If one relate some wonder, the rest will tell you miracles, if they have them, if not, they will feign them: lastly, that I may say somewhat of them who pretend to be wiser than others; if they meet to talk of philosophy, look how many men, so many would be esteemed masters, or else they not only love not their fellows, but even persecute them with hatred: so clear is it by experience to all men who a little more narrowly consider human affairs, that all free congress arises either from mutual poverty, or from vain glory, whence the parties met, endeavor to carry with them either some benefit, or to leave behind them that same some esteem and honor with those, with whom they have been conversant: the same is also collected by reason out of the definitions themselves, of will, good, honor, profitable. For when we voluntarily contract society, in all manner of society we look after the object of the will; that is, that, which every one of those, who gather together, propounds to himself for good; now whatsoever seems good, is pleasant, and relates either to the senses, or the mind, but all the minds pleasure is either glory, (or to have a good opinion of oneself) or refers to glory in the end; the rest are sensual, or conducing to sensuality, which may be all comprehended under the word conveniences. All society therefore is either for gain, or for glory; that is, not so much for love of our fellows, as for love of ourselves: but no society can be great, or lasting, which begins from vain glory; because that glory is like honor, if all, men have it, no man has it, for they consist in comparison and precellence; neither does the society of others advance any whit the cause of my glorying in myself. For every man must account himself, such as he can make himself, without the help of others. But though the benefits of this life may be much furthered by mutual help, since yet those may be better attained to by dominion, than by the society of others: I hope nobody will doubt but that men would much more greedily be carried by nature, if all fear were removed, to obtain dominion, than to gain society. We must therefore resolve, that the original of all great, and lasting societies, consisted not in the mutual good will men had towards each other, but in the mutual fear they had of each other.

3. The cause of mutual fear consists partly in the natural equality of men, partly in their mutual will of hurting: whence it comes to pass that we can neither expect from others, nor promise to ourselves the least security. For if we look on men full-grown, and consider how brittle the frame of our human body is, (which perishing, all its strength, vigor, and wisdom itself perishes with it) and how easy a matter it is, even for the weakest man to kill the strongest, there is no reason why any man trusting to his own strength should conceive himself made by nature above others: they are equals who can do equal things one against the other; but they who can do the greatest things, (namely kill) can do equal things. All men therefore among themselves are by nature equal; the inequality we now discern, has its spring from the civil law.

4. All men in the state of nature have a desire, and will to hurt, but not proceeding from the same cause, neither equally to be condemned. For one man according to that natural equality which is among us, permits as much to others, as he assumes to himself (which is an argument of a temperate man, and one that rightly values his power); another, supposing himself above others, will have a license to do what he lists, and challenges respect, and honor, as due to him before others, (which is an argument of a fiery spirit): this man's will to hurt arises from vainglory, and the false esteem he has of his own strength; the other's, from the necessity of defending himself, his liberty, and his goods against this man's violence.

5. Furthermore, since the combat of wits is the fiercest, the greatest discords which are, must necessarily arise from this contention. For in this case it is not only odious to contend against, but also not to consent. For not to approve of what a man says is no less than tacitly to accuse him of an error in that thing which he speaks; as in very many things to dissent, is as much as if you accounted him a fool whom you dissent from; which may appear hence, that there are no wars so sharply waged as between sects of the same religion, and factions of the same commonweal, where the contestation is either concerning doctrines, or politic prudence. And since all the pleasure, and jollity of the mind consists in this; even to get some, with whom comparing, it may find somewhat wherein to triumph, and vaunt itself; its impossible but men must declare sometimes some mutual scorn and contempt either by laughter, or by words, or by gesture, or some sign or other; than which there is no greater vexation of mind; and than from which there cannot possibly arise a greater desire to do hurt.

6. But the most frequent reason why men desire to hurt each other, arises hence, that many men at the same time have an appetite to the same thing; which yet very often they can neither enjoy in common, nor yet divide it; whence it follows that the strongest must have it, and who is strongest must be decided by the sword.

7. Among so many dangers therefore, as the natural lusts of men do daily threaten each other withal, to have a care of ones self is not a matter so scornfully to be looked upon, as if so be there had not been a power and will left in one to have done otherwise. For every man is desirous of what is good for him, and shuns what is evil, but chiefly the chiefest of natural evils, which is death; and this he does, by a certain impulsion of nature, no less than that whereby a stone moves downward: it is therefore neither absurd, nor reprehensible; neither against the dictates of true reason for a man to use all his endeavors to preserve and defend his body, and the members thereof from death and sorrows; but that which is not contrary to right reason, that all men account to be done justly, and with right; neither by the word right is any thing else signified, than that liberty which every man has to make use of his natural faculties according to right reason: therefore the first foundation of natural right is this, that every man as much as in him lies endeavor to protect his life and members.

8. But because it is in vain for a man to have a right to the end, if the right to the necessary means be denied him; it follows, that since every man has a right to preserve himself, he must also be allowed a right to use all the means, and do all the actions, without which he cannot preserve himself.

9. Now whether the means which he is about to use, and the action he is performing, be necessary to the preservation of his life, and members, or not, he himself, by the right of nature, must be judge. For say another man, judge that it is contrary to right reason that I should judge of mine own peril: why now, because he judges of what concerns me, by the same reason, because we are equal by nature, will I judge also of things which do belong to him; therefore it agrees with right reason, that is, it is the right of nature that I judge of his opinion; that is, whether it conduce to my preservation, or not.

10. Nature has given to every one a right to all. That is it was lawful for every man in the bare state of nature, or before such time as men had engaged themselves by any covenants, or bonds, to do what he would, and against whom he thought fit, and to possess, use, and enjoy all what he would, or could get. Now because whatsoever a man would, it therefore seems good to him because he wills it, and either it really does, or at least seems to him to contribute toward his preservation, (but we have already allowed him to be judge in the foregoing article whether it does or not, in so much as we are to hold all for necessary whatsoever he shall esteem so) and by the 7 Article it appears that by the right of nature those things may be done, and must be had, which necessarily conduce to the protection of life, and members, it follows, that in the state of nature, to have all, and do all is lawful for all. And this is that which is meant by that common saying, nature has given all to all, from whence we understand likewise, that in the state of nature, profit is the measure of right.

11. But it was the least benefit for men thus to have a common right to all things. For the effects of this right are the same, almost, as if there had been no right at all. For although any man might say of every thing, this is

mine, yet could he not enjoy it, by reason of his neighbor, who having equal right, and equal power, would pretend the same thing to be his.

12. If now to this natural proclivity of men, to hurt each other, which they derive from their passions, but chiefly from a vain esteem of themselves: you add, the right of all to all, wherewith one by right invades, the other by right resists, and whence arise perpetual jealousies and suspicions on all hands, and how hard a thing it is to provide against an enemy invading us, with an intention to oppress, and ruin, though he come with a small number, and no great provision; it cannot be denied but that the natural state of men, before they entered into society, was a mere war, and that not simply, but a war of all men, against all men. For what is war, but that same time in which the will of contesting by force, is fully declared either by words, or deeds? The time remaining, is termed *peace.*

13. But it is easily judged how disagreeable a thing to the preservation either of mankind, or of each single man, a perpetual war is: but it is perpetual in its own nature, because in regard of the equality of those that strive, it cannot be ended by victory. For in this state the conqueror is subject to so much danger, as it were to be accounted a miracle, if any, even the most strong should close up his life with many years, and old age. They of America are examples hereof, even in this present age: other nations have been in former ages, which now indeed are become civil, and flourishing, but were then few, fierce, short-lived, poor, nasty, and destroyed of all that pleasure, and beauty of life, which peace and society are wont to bring with them. Whosoever therefore holds, that it had been best to have continued in that state in which all things were lawful for all men, he contradicts himself. For every man, by natural necessity desires that which is good for him: nor is there any that esteems a war of all against all, which necessarily adheres to such a state, to be good for him. And so it happens that through fear of each other we think it fit to rid ourselves of this condition, and to get some fellows; that if there needs must be war, it may not yet be against all men, nor without some helps.

14. Fellows are gotten either by constraint, or by consent; by constraint, when after fight the conqueror makes the conquered serve him either through fear of death, or by laying fetters on him: by consent, when men enter into society to help each other, both parties consenting without any constraint. But the conqueror may by right compel the conquered, or the strongest the weaker, (as a man in health may one that is sick, or he that is of riper years a child) unless he will choose to die, to give caution of his future obedience. For since the right of protecting ourselves according to our own wills proceeded from our danger, and our danger from our equality, its more consonant to reason, and more certain for our conservation, using the present advantage to secure ourselves by taking caution; than, when they shall be full grown and strong, and got out of our power, to endeavor to recover that power again by doubtful fight. And on the other side, nothing can be thought more absurd, than by discharging whom you already have weak in your power, to make him at once both an enemy, and a

strong one. From whence we may understand likewise as a corollary in the natural state of men, that a sure and irresistible power confers the right of dominion, and ruling over those who cannot resist; insomuch, as the right of all things, that can be done, adheres essentially, and immediately unto this omnipotence hence arising.

15. Yet cannot men expect any lasting preservation continuing thus in the state of nature, that is, of war, by reason of that equality of power, and other human faculties they are endued withal. Wherefore to seek peace, where there is any hopes of obtaining it, and where there is none, to enquire out for auxiliaries of war, is the dictate of right reason; that is, the law of nature, as shall be showed in the next chapter.

CHAPTER 2: OF THE LAW
OF NATURE CONCERNING CONTRACTS

1. All authors agree not concerning the definition of the natural law, who notwithstanding do very often make use of this term in their writings. The method therefore, wherein we begin from definitions, and exclusion of all equivocation, is only proper to them who leave no place for contrary disputes. For the rest, if any man say, that somewhat is done against the law of nature, one proves it hence, because it was done against the general agreement of all the most wise, and learned nations: but this declares not who shall be the judge of the wisdom and learning of all nations: another hence, that it was done against the general consent of all mankind; which definition is by no means to be admitted. For then it were impossible for any but children, and fools, to offend against such a law. For sure, under the notion of mankind, they comprehend all men actually endued with reason. These therefore either do naught against it, or if they do aught, it is without their joint accord, and therefore ought to be excused; but to receive the laws of nature from the consents of them, who oftener break, than observe them, is in truth unreasonable: besides, men condemn the same things in others, which they approve in themselves; on the other side, they publickly commend what they privately condemn; and they deliver their opinions more by hearsay, than any speculation of their own; and they accord more through hatred of some object, through fear, hope, love, or some other perturbation of mind, than true reason. And therefore it comes to pass, that whole bodies of people often do those things by general accord, or contention, which those writers most willingly acknowledge to be against the law of nature. But since all do grant that is done by *right*, which is not done against reason, we ought to judge those actions only wrong, which are repugnant to right reason; that is, which contradict some certain truth collected by right reasoning from true principles; but that wrong which is done, we say it is done against some law: therefore true reason is a certain law, which (since it is no less a part of human nature, than any

other faculty, or affection of the mind) is also termed natural. Therefore the law of nature, that I may define it, is the dictate of right reason, conversant about those things which are either to be done, or omitted for the constant preservation of life, and members, as much as in us lies.

2. But the first and fundamental law of nature is, that peace is to be sought after where it may be found; and where not, there to provide ourselves for helps of war. For we showed in the last article of the foregoing chapter, that this precept is the dictate of right reason; but that the dictates of right reason are natural laws, that has been newly proved above; but this is the first, because the rest are derived from this, and they direct the ways either to peace, or self-defense.

3. But one of the natural laws derived from this fundamental one is this, that the right of all men, to all things, ought not to be retained, but that some certain rights ought to be transferred, or relinquished. For if every one should retain his right to all things, it must necessarily follow, that some by right might invade; and others, by the same right, might defend themselves against them, (for every man, by natural necessity, endeavors to defend his body, and the things which he judges necessary towards the protection of his body) therefore war would follow. He therefore acts against the reason of peace, that is, against the law of nature, whosoever he be, that does not part with his right to all things. . . .

18. No man is obliged by any contracts whatsoever not to resist him who shall offer to kill, wound, or any other way hurt his body. For there is in every man a certain high degree of fear through which he apprehends that evil which is done to him to be the greatest, and therefore by natural necessity he shuns it all he can, and it is supposed he can do no otherwise: when a man is arrived to this degree of fear, we cannot expect but he will provide for himself either by flight, or fight. Since therefore no man is tied to impossibilities, they who are threatened either with death (which is the greatest evil to nature) or wounds, or some other bodily hurts, and are not stout enough to bear them, are not obliged to endure them. Furthermore, he that is tied by contract is trusted, (for faith only is the bond of contracts) but they who are brought to punishment, either capital, or more gentle, are fettered, or strongly guarded, which is a most certain sign that they seemed not sufficiently bound from non resistance by their contracts. Its one thing if I promise thus: if I do it not at the day appointed, kill me. Another thing if thus: if I do it not, though you should offer to kill me, I will not resist: all men, if need be, contract the first way; but there is need sometimes. This second way, none, neither is it ever needful. For in the mere state of nature, if you have a mind to kill, that state itself affords you a right; insomuch as you need not first trust him, if for breach of trust you will afterward kill him. But in a civil state, where the right of life, and death, and of all corporal punishment is with the supreme; that same right of killing cannot be granted to any private person. Neither need the supreme himself contract with any man patiently to yield to his punishment, but only this, that no man offer to defend others from him. If in the

state of nature, as between two cities, there should a contract be made, on condition of killing, if it were not performed, we must presuppose another contract of not killing before the appointed day. Wherefore on that day, if there be no performance, the right of war returns; that is, a hostile state, in which all things are lawful, and therefore resistance also. Lastly, by the contract of not resisting, we are obliged of two evils to make choice of that which seems the greater. For certain death is a greater evil than fighting; but of two evils it is impossible not to chuse the least: by such a compact therefore we should be tied to impossibilities, which is contrary to the very nature of compacts.

19. Likewise no man is tied by any compacts whatsoever to accuse himself, or any other, by whose damage he is like to procure himself a bitter life; wherefore neither is a father obliged to bear witness against his son, nor a husband against his wife, nor a son against his father; nor any man against any one, by whose means he has his subsistence. For in vain is that testimony which is presumed to be corrupted from nature; but although no man be tied to accuse himself by any compact, yet in a public trial he may, by torture, be forced to make answer; but such answers are no testimony of the fact, but helps for the searching out of truth; insomuch as whether the party tortured his answer be true, or false, or whether he answer not at all, whatsoever he does, he does it by right.

CHAPTER 3: OF THE OTHER LAWS OF NATURE

14. As it was necessary to the conservation of each man, that he should part with some of his rights, so it is no less necessary to the same conservation, that he retain some others, to wit the right of bodily protection, of free enjoyment of air, water, and all necessaries for life. Since therefore many common rights are retained by those who enter into a peaceable state, and that many peculiar ones are also acquired, hence arises this ninth dictate of the natural law, to wit, that what rights soever any man challenges to himself, he also grant the same as due to all the rest: otherwise he frustrates the equality acknowledged in the former article. For what is it else to acknowledge an equality of persons in the making up of society, but to attribute equal right and power to those whom no reason would else engage to enter into society? But to ascribe equal things to equals, is the same with giving things proportional to proportionals. The observation of this law is called *meekness*, the violation pleonexia, the breakers by the Latins are styled immodici and immodesti.

29. The laws of nature are immutable, and eternal; what they forbid, can never be lawful; what they command, can never be unlawful. For pride, ingratitude, breach of contracts (or injury), inhumanity, contumely, will never be lawful; nor the contrary virtues to these ever unlawful, as we take them for dispositions of the mind, that is, as they are considered in the court of conscience, where only they oblige, and are laws. Yet actions

may be so diversified by circumstances, and the civil law, that what's done with equity at one time, is guilty of iniquity at another; and what suits with reason at one time, is contrary to it another. Yet reason is still the same, and changes not her end, which is peace, and defense; nor of the mind which the means to attain them, to wit, those virtues we have declared above, and which cannot be abrogated by any custom, or law whatsoever. . . .

31. All writers do agree that the natural law is the same with the moral. Let us see wherefore this is true. We must know therefore, that good and evil are names given to things to signify the inclination, or aversion of them by whom they were given. But the inclinations of men are diverse, according to their diverse constitutions, customs, opinions; as we may see in those things we apprehend by sense, as by tasting, touching, smelling; but much more in those which pertain to the common actions of life, where what this man commends, (that is to say, calls good) the other undervalues, as being evil; nay, very often the same man at diverse times, praises, and dispraises the same thing. While thus they do, necessary it is there should be discord, and strife: they are therefore so long in the state of war, as by reason of the diversity of the present appetites, they mete good and evil by diverse measures. All men easily acknowledge this state, as long as they are in it, to be evil, and by consequence that peace is good. They therefore who could not agree concerning a present, do agree concerning a future good, which indeed is a work of reason. For things present are obvious to the sense, things to come to our reason only. Reason declaring peace to be good, it follows by the same reason, that all the necessary means to peace be good also, and therefore, that modesty, equity, trust, humanity, mercy (which we have demonstrated to be necessary to peace) are good manners, or habits, that is, virtues. The law therefore, in the means to peace, commands also good manners, or the practice of virtue: and therefore it is called moral.

32. But because men cannot put off this same irrational appetite, whereby they greedily prefer the present good (to which, by strict consequence, many unforeseen evils do adhere) before the future, it happens, that though all men do agree in the commendation of the foresaid virtues, yet they disagree still concerning their nature, to wit, in what each of them does consist. For as often as another's good action displeases any man, that action has the name given of some neighboring vice; likewise the bad actions, which please them, are ever entitled to some virtue; whence it comes to pass that the same action is praised by these, and called virtue, and dispraised by those, and termed vice. Neither is there as yet any remedy found by philosophers for this matter. For since they could not observe the goodness of actions to consist in this, that it was in order to peace, and the evil in this, that it related to discord, they built a moral philosophy wholly estranged from the moral law, and inconstant to itself. For they would have the nature of virtues seated in a certain kind of mediocrity between two extremes, and the vices in the extremes themselves;

which is apparently false. For to dare is commended, and under the name of fortitude is taken for a virtue, although it be an extreme, if the cause be approved. Also the quantity of a thing given, whether it be great, or little, or between both, makes not liberality, but the cause of giving it. Neither is it injustice, if I give any man more, of what is mine own, than I owe him. The laws of nature therefore are the sum of moral philosophy, whereof I have only delivered such precepts in this place, as appertain to the preservation of ourselves against those dangers which arise from discord. But there are other precepts of rational nature, from whence spring other virtues. For temperance also is a precept of reason, because intemperance tends to sicknesses, and death. And so fortitude too, (that is) that same faculty of resisting stoutly in present dangers, (and which are more hardly declined than overcome) because it is a means tending to the preservation of him that resists.

CHAPTER 5: OF THE CAUSES, AND FIRST BEGINNING OF CIVIL GOVERNMENT

6. Since therefore the conspiring of many wills to the same end does not suffice to preserve peace, and to make a lasting defense, it is requisite that in those necessary matters which concern peace and self-defense, there be but one will of all men. But this cannot be done, unless every man will so subject his will to some other one, to wit, either man or counsel, that whatsoever his will is in those things which are necessary to the common peace, it be received for the wills of all men in general, and of every one in particular. Now the gathering together of many men who deliberate of what is to be done, or not to be done, for the common good of all men, is that which I call a *counsel.*

7. This submission of the wills of all those men to the will of one man, or one counsel, is then made, when each one of them obliges himself by contract to every one of the rest, not to resist the will of that one man, or counsel, to which he has submitted himself; that is, that he refuse him not the use of his wealth, and strength, against any others whatsoever (for he is supposed still to retain a right of defending himself against violence) and this is called *union.* But we understand that to be the will of the counsel, which is the will of the major part of those men of whom the counsel consists.

8. But though the will itself be not voluntary, but only the beginning of voluntary actions (for we will not to will, but to act) and therefore falls least of all under deliberation, and compact; yet he who submits his will to the will of an other, conveys to that other the right of his strength, and faculties; insomuch as when the rest have done the same, he to whom they have submitted has so much power, as by the terror of it he can conform the wills of particular men unto unity, and concord.

9. Now union thus made is called a city, or civil society, and also a civil person. For when there is one will of all men, it is to be esteemed for one

person, and by the word (one) it is to be known, and distinguished from all particular men, as having its own rights and properties; insomuch as neither any one citizen, nor all of them together (if we except him whose will stands for the will of all) is to be accounted the city. A *city* therefore (that we may define it) is one person, whose will, by the compact of many men, is to be received for the will of them all; so as he may use all the power and faculties of each particular person, to the maintenance of peace, and for common defense.

READING 49

The Rights of Women*

Mary Wollstonecraft (1759–1797)

It is not necessary to inform the sagacious reader, now I enter on my concluding reflections, that the discussion of this subject merely consists in opening a few simple principles, and clearing away the rubbish which obscured them. But, as all readers are not sagacious, I must be allowed to add some explanatory remarks to bring the subject home to reason—to that sluggish reason, which supinely takes opinions on trust, and obstinately supports them to spare itself the labor of thinking.

Moralists have unanimously agreed, that unless virtue be nursed by liberty, it will never attain due strength—and what they say of man I extend to mankind, insisting that in all cases morals must be fixed on immutable principles; and, that the being cannot be termed rational or virtuous, who obeys any authority, but that of reason.

To render women truly useful members of society, I argue that they should be led, by having their understandings cultivated on a large scale, to acquire a rational affection for their country, founded on knowledge, because it is obvious that we are little interested about what we do not understand. And to render this general knowledge of due importance, I have endeavored to show that private duties are never properly fulfilled unless the understanding enlarges the heart; and that public virtue is only an aggregate of private. But, the distinctions established in society undermine both, by beating out the solid gold of virtue, till it becomes only the tinsel-covering of vice; for while wealth renders a man more respectable than virtue, wealth will be sought before virtue; and, while women's persons are caressed, when a childish simper shows an absence of mind—the mind will lie fallow. Yet, true voluptuousness must proceed from the mind—for what can equal the sensations produced by

*From Mary Wollstonecraft, *A Vindication of the Rights of Woman*, (1792), Chapter 13, Section 6.

mutual affection, supported by mutual respect? What are the cold, or feverish caresses of appetite, but sin embracing death, compared with the modest over-flowings of a pure heart and exalted imagination? Yes, let me tell the libertine of fancy when he despises understanding in woman—that the mind, which he disregards, gives life to the enthusiastic affection from which rapture, short-lived as it is, alone can flow! And, that, without virtue, a sexual attachment must expire like a tallow candle in the socket, creating intolerable disgust. To prove this, I need only observe, that men who have wasted great part of their lives with women, and with whom they have sought for pleasure with eager thirst, entertain the meanest opinion of the sex. Virtue, true refiner of joy!—if foolish men were to fright thee from earth, in order to give loose to all their appetites without a check—some sensual wight of taste would scale the heav-ens to invite thee back, to give a zest to pleasure!

That women at present are by ignorance rendered vicious, is, I think, not to be disputed; and, that salutary effects tending to improve mankind might be expected from a *revolution* in female manners, appears, at least, with a face of probability, to rise out of the observation. For as marriage has been termed the parent of those endearing charities which draw man from the brutal herd, the corrupting intercourse that wealth, idleness, and folly, produce between the sexes, is more universally injurious to morality than all the other vices of mankind collectively considered. To adulterous lust the most sacred duties are sacrificed, because before marriage, men, by a promiscuous intimacy with women, learned to consider love as a selfish gratification—learned to separate it not only from esteem, but from the affection merely built on habit which mixes a little humanity with it. Justice and friendship are also set at defiance, and that purity of taste is vitiated which would naturally lead a man to relish an artless display of affection rather than affected airs. But that noble simplic-ity of affection, which dares to appear unadorned, has few attractions for the libertine, though it be the charm, which by cementing the matrimonial tie, se-cures to the pledges of a warmer passion the necessary parental attention; for children will never be properly educated till friendship subsists between par-ents. Virtue flies from a house divided against itself—and a whole legion of devils take up their residence there.

The affection of husbands and wives cannot be pure when they have so few sentiments in common, and when so little confidence is established at home, as must be the case when their pursuits are so different. That inti-macy from which tenderness should flow, will not, cannot subsist between the vicious.

Contending, therefore, that the sexual distinction which men have so warmly insisted upon, is arbitrary, I have dwelt on an observation, that sev-eral sensible men, with whom I have conversed on the subject, allowed to be well founded; and it is simply this, that the little chastity to be found amongst men, and consequent disregard of modesty, tend to degrade both sexes; and further, that the modesty of women, characterized as such, will often be only the artful veil of wantonness instead of being the natural reflection of purity, till modesty be universally respected.

From the tyranny of man, I firmly believe, the greater number of female follies proceed; and the cunning, which I allow makes at present a part of their character, I likewise have repeatedly endeavored to prove, is produced by oppression.

Were not dissenters, for instance, a class of people, with strict truth, characterized as cunning? And may I not lay some stress on this fact to prove, that when any power but reason curbs the free spirit of man, dissimulation is practiced, and the various shifts of art are naturally called forth? Great attention to decorum, which was carried to a degree of scrupulosity, and all that puerile bustle about trifles and consequential solemnity, which Butler's caricature of a dissenter brings before the imagination, shaped their persons as well as their minds in the mould of prim littleness. I speak collectively, for I know how many ornaments in human nature have been enrolled amongst sectaries; yet, I assert, that the same narrow prejudice for their sect, which women have for their families, prevailed in the dissenting part of the community, however worthy in other respects; and also that the same timid prudence, or headstrong efforts, often disgraced the exertions of both. Oppression thus formed many of the features of their character perfectly to coincidence with that of the oppressed half of mankind; for is it not notorious that dissenters were, like women, fond of deliberating together, and asking advice of each other, till by a complication of little contrivances, some little end was brought about? A similar attention to preserve their reputation was conspicuous in the dissenting and female world, and was produced by a similar cause.

Asserting the rights which women in common with men ought to contend for, I have not attempted to extenuate their faults; but to prove them to be the natural consequence of their education and station in society. If so, it is reasonable to suppose that they will change their character, and correct their vices and follies, when they are allowed to be free in a physical, moral, and civil sense.

Let woman share the rights, and she will emulate the virtues of man; for she must grow more perfect when emancipated, or justify the authority that chains such a weak being to her duty. If the latter, it will be expedient to open a fresh trade with Russia for whips: a present which a father should always make to his son-in-law on his wedding day, that a husband may keep his whole family in order by the same means; and without any violation of justice reign, wielding this scepter, sole master of his house, because he is the only thing in it who has reason:—the divine, indefeasible earthly sovereignty breathed into man by the Master of the universe. Allowing this position, women have not any inherent rights to claim; and, by the same rule, their duties vanish, for rights and duties are inseparable.

Be just then, O ye men of understanding: and mark not more severely what women do amiss than the vicious tricks of the horse or the ass for whom ye provide provender—and allow her the privileges of ignorance, to whom ye deny the rights of reason, or ye will be worse than Egyptian task-masters expecting virtue where Nature has not given understanding.

The Clash of Class Interests*

Karl Marx (1818–1883)

[HISTORY AND CLASS STRUGGLE]

The history of all hitherto existing societies is the history of class struggles.

Freeman and slave, patrician and plebeian, lord and serf, guild-master and journeyman, in a word, oppressor and oppressed, stood in constant opposition to one another, carried on an uninterrupted, now hidden, now open fight, a fight that each time ended, either in a revolutionary re-constitution of society at large, or in the common ruin of the contending classes.

In the earlier epochs of history, we find almost everywhere a complicated arrangement of society into various orders, a manifold gradation of social rank. In ancient Rome we have patricians, knights, plebeians, slaves; in the Middle Ages, feudal lords, vassals, guild-masters, journeymen, apprentices, serfs; in almost all of these classes, again, subordinate gradations.

The modern bourgeois society that has sprouted from the ruins of feudal society has not done away with clash antagonisms. It has but established new classes, new conditions of oppression, new forms of struggle in place of the old ones. Our epoch, the epoch of the bourgeoisie, possesses, however, this distinctive feature: it has simplified the class antagonisms: Society as a whole is more and more splitting up into two great hostile camps, into two great classes, directly facing each other: Bourgeoisie and Proletariat.

From the serfs of the Middle Ages sprang the chartered burghers of the earliest towns. From these burgesses the first elements of the bourgeoisie were developed.

The discovery of America, the rounding of the Cape, opened up fresh ground for the rising bourgeoisie. The East-Indian and Chinese markets, the colonization of America, trade with the colonies, the increase in the means of exchange and in commodities generally, gave to commerce, to navigation, to industry, an impulse never before known, and thereby, to the revolutionary element in the tottering feudal society, a rapid development.

The feudal system of industry, under which industrial production was monopolized by closed guilds, now no longer sufficed for the growing wants of the new markets. The manufacturing system took its place. The guild-masters were pushed on one side by the manufacturing middle class; division of labor between the different corporate guilds vanished in the face of division of labor in each single workshop.

Meantime the markets kept ever growing, the demand ever rising. Even manufacture no longer sufficed. Thereupon, steam and machinery revolution-

*From Karl Marx, *Manifesto of the Communist Party* (1848), Chapter 1.

ized industrial production. The place of manufacture was taken by the giant, Modern Industry, the place of the industrial middle class, by industrial millionaires, the leaders of whole industrial armies, the modern bourgeois.

Modern industry has established the world-market, for which the discovery of America paved the way. This market has given an immense development to commerce, to navigation, to communication by land. This development has, in its time, reacted on the extension of industry; and in proportion as industry, commerce, navigation, railways extended, in the same proportion the bourgeoisie developed, increased its capital, and pushed into the background every class handed down from the Middle Ages.

[BOURGEOISIE EXPLOITATION OF LABORERS]

We see, therefore, how the modern bourgeoisie is itself the product of a long course of development, of a series of revolutions in the modes of production and of exchange.

Each step in the development of the bourgeoisie was accompanied by a corresponding political advance of that class. An oppressed class under the sway of the feudal nobility, an armed and self-governing association in the mediaeval commune; here independent urban republic (as in Italy and Germany), there taxable "third estate" of the monarchy (as in France), afterwards, in the period of manufacture proper, serving either the semi-feudal or the absolute monarchy as a counterpoise against the nobility, and, in fact, cornerstone of the great monarchies in general, the bourgeoisie has at last, since the establishment of Modern Industry and of the world-market, conquered for itself, in the modern representative State, exclusive political sway. The executive of the modern State is but a committee for managing the common affairs of the whole bourgeoisie.

The bourgeoisie, historically, has played a most revolutionary part.

The bourgeoisie, wherever it has got the upper hand, has put an end to all feudal, patriarchal, idyllic relations. It has pitilessly torn asunder the motley feudal ties that bound man to his "natural superiors," and has left remaining no other nexus between man and man than naked self-interest, than callous "cash payment." It has drowned the most heavenly ecstasies of religious fervor, of chivalrous enthusiasm, of philistine sentimentalism, in the icy water of egotistical calculation. It has resolved personal worth into exchange value. And in place of the numberless and feasible chartered freedoms, has set up that single, unconscionable freedom—Free Trade. In one word, for exploitation, veiled by religious and political illusions, naked, shameless, direct, brutal exploitation.

The bourgeoisie has stripped of its halo every occupation hitherto honored and looked up to with reverent awe. It has converted the physician, the lawyer, the priest, the poet, the man of science, into its paid wage laborers.

The bourgeoisie has torn away from the family its sentimental veil, and has reduced the family relation to a mere money relation.

The bourgeoisie has disclosed how it came to pass that the brutal display of vigor in the Middle Ages, which Reactionists so much admire, found its fitting complement in the most slothful indolence. It has been the first to show what man's activity can bring about. It has accomplished wonders far surpassing Egyptian pyramids, Roman aqueducts, and Gothic cathedrals; it has conducted expeditions that put in the shade all former Exoduses of nations and crusades.

[BOURGEOISIE EXPANSION]

The bourgeoisie cannot exist without constantly revolutionizing the instruments of production, and thereby the relations of production, and with them the whole relations of society. Conservation of the old modes of production in unaltered form, was, on the contrary, the first condition of existence for all earlier industrial classes. Constant revolutionizing of production, uninterrupted disturbance of all social conditions, everlasting uncertainty and agitation distinguish the bourgeois epoch from all earlier ones. All fixed, fast-frozen relations, with their train of ancient and venerable prejudices and opinions, are swept away, all new-formed ones become antiquated before they can ossify. All that is solid melts into air, all that is holy is profaned, and man is at last compelled to face with sober senses, his real conditions of life, and his relations with his kind.

The need of a constantly expanding market for its products chases the bourgeoisie over the whole surface of the globe. It must nestle everywhere, settle everywhere, establish connections everywhere.

The bourgeoisie has through its exploitation of the world-market given a cosmopolitan character to production and consumption in every country. To the great chagrin of Reactionists, it has drawn from under the feet of industry the national ground on which it stood. All old-established national industries have been destroyed or are daily being destroyed. They are dislodged by new industries, whose introduction becomes a life and death question for all civilized nations, by industries that no longer work up indigenous raw material, but raw material drawn from the remotest zones; industries whose products are consumed, not only at home, but in every quarter of the globe. In place of the old wants, satisfied by the productions of the country, we find new wants, requiring for their satisfaction the products of distant lands and climes. In place of the old local and national seclusion and self-sufficiency, we have intercourse in every direction, universal interdependence of nations. And as in material, so also in intellectual production. The intellectual creations of individual nations become common property. National one-sidedness and narrow-mindedness become more and more impossible, and from the numerous national and local literatures, there arises a world literature.

The bourgeoisie, by the rapid improvement of all instruments of production, by the immensely facilitated means of communication, draws all, even the most barbarian, nations into civilization. The cheap prices of its commodities are the heavy artillery with which it batters down all Chinese walls, with which it forces the barbarians' intensely obstinate hatred of foreigners to capitulate. It compels all nations, on pain of extinction, to adopt the bourgeois mode of production; it compels them to introduce what it calls civilization into their midst, i.e., to become bourgeois themselves. In one word, it creates a world after its own image.

The bourgeoisie has subjected the country to the rule of the towns. It has created enormous cities, has greatly increased the urban population as compared with the rural, and has thus rescued a considerable part of the population from the idiocy of rural life. Just as it has made the country dependent on the towns, so it has made barbarian and semi-barbarian countries dependent on the civilized ones, nations of peasants on nations of bourgeois, the East on the West.

The bourgeoisie keeps more and more doing away with the scattered state of the population, of the means of production, and of property. It has agglomerated production, and has concentrated property in a few hands. The necessary consequence of this was political centralizations. Independent, or but loosely connected provinces, with separate interests, laws, governments and systems of taxation, became lumped together into one nation, with one government, one code of laws, one national class-interest, one frontier and one customs-tariff. The bourgeoisie, during its rule of scarce one hundred years, has created more massive and more colossal productive forces than have all preceding generations together. Subjection of Nature's forces to man, machinery, application of chemistry to industry and agriculture, steam-navigation, railways, electric telegraphs, clearing of whole continents for cultivation, canalization of rivers, whole populations conjured out of the ground—what earlier century had even a presentiment that such productive forces slumbered in the lap of social labor?

We see then: the means of production and of exchange, on whose foundation the bourgeoisie built itself up, were generated in feudal society. At a certain stage in the development of these means of production and of exchange, the conditions under which feudal society produced and exchanged, the feudal organization of agriculture and manufacturing industry, in one word, the feudal relations of property became no longer compatible with the already developed productive forces; they became so many fetters. They had to be burst asunder; they were burst asunder.

Into their place stepped free competition, accompanied by a social and political constitution adapted to it, and by the economical and political sway of the bourgeois class.

A similar movement is going on before our own eyes. Modern bourgeois society with its relations of production, of exchange and of property, a society that has conjured up such gigantic means of production and of exchange, is like the sorcerer, who is no longer able to control the powers of the nether world whom he has called up by his spells. For many a decade past the history of industry and commerce is but the history of the revolt of modern productive forces against modern conditions of production, against the property relations that are the conditions for the existence of the bourgeoisie and of its rule. It is enough to mention the commercial crises that by their periodical return put on its trial, each time more threateningly, the existence of the entire bourgeois society. In these crises a great part not only of the existing products, but also of the previously created productive forces, are periodically destroyed. In these crises there breaks out an epidemic that, in all earlier epochs, would have seemed an absurdity—the epidemic of over-production. Society suddenly finds itself put back into a state of momentary barbarism; it appears as if a famine, a universal war of devastation had cut off the supply of every means of subsistence; industry and commerce seem to be destroyed; and why? Because there is too much civilization, too much means of subsistence, too much industry, too much commerce. The productive forces at the disposal of society no longer tend to further the development of the conditions of bourgeois property; on the contrary, they have become too powerful for these conditions, by which they are fettered, and so soon as they overcome these fetters, they bring disorder into the whole of bourgeois society, endanger the existence of bourgeois property. The conditions of bourgeois society are too narrow to comprise the wealth created by them. And how does the bourgeoisie get over these crises? On the one hand enforced destruction of a mass of productive forces; on the other, by the conquest of new markets, and by the more thorough exploitation of the old ones. That is to say, by paving the way for more extensive and more destructive crises, and by diminishing the means whereby crises are prevented.

[SELF-DESTRUCTION OF THE BOURGEOISIE]

The weapons with which the bourgeoisie felled feudalism to the ground are now turned against the bourgeoisie itself.

But not only has the bourgeoisie forged the weapons that bring death to itself; it has also called into existence the men who are to wield those weapons—the modern working class—the proletarians.

In proportion as the bourgeoisie, i.e., capital, is developed, in the same proportion is the proletariat, the modern working class, developed—a class of laborers, who live only so long as they find work, and who find work only so long as their labor increases capital. These laborers, who must sell themselves piece-meal, are a commodity, like every other article of commerce, and are consequently exposed to all the vicissitudes of competition, to all the fluctuations of the market.

Owing to the extensive use of machinery and to division of labor, the work of the proletarians has lost all individual character, and consequently, all charm for the workman. He becomes an appendage of the machine, and it is only the most simple, most monotonous, and most easily acquired knack, that is required of him. Hence, the cost of production of a workman is restricted,

almost entirely, to the means of subsistence that he requires for his maintenance, and for the propagation of his race. But the price of a commodity, and
therefore also of labor, is equal to its cost of production. In proportion therefore, as the repulsiveness of the work increases, the wage decreases. Nay
more, in proportion as the use of machinery and division of labor increases, in
the same proportion the burden of toil also increases, whether by prolongation
of the working hours, by increase of the work exacted in a given time or by increased speed of the machinery, etc.

Modern industry has converted the little workshop of the patriarchal master into the great factory of the industrial capitalist. Masses of laborers,
crowded into the factory, are organized like soldiers. As privates of the industrial army they are placed under the command of a perfect hierarchy of offi-
cers and sergeants. Not only are they slaves of the bourgeois class, and of the
bourgeois State; they are daily and hourly enslaved by the machine, by the
over-looker, and, above all, by the individual bourgeois manufacturer himself.
The more openly this despotism proclaims gain to be its end and aim, the
more petty, the more hateful and the more embittering it is.

The less the skill and exertion of strength implied in manual labor, in
other words, the more modern industry becomes developed, the more is the
labor of men superseded by that of women. Differences of age and sex have no
longer any distinctive social validity for the working class. All are instruments
of labor, more or less expensive to use, according to their age and sex.

No sooner is the exploitation of the laborer by the manufacturer, so far, at
an end, that he receives his wages in cash, than he is set upon by the other portions of the bourgeoisie, the landlord, the shopkeeper, the pawnbroker, etc.

The lower strata of the middle class—the small tradespeople, shopkeep-
ers, retired tradesmen generally, the handicraftsmen and peasants—all these
sink gradually into the proletariat, partly because their diminutive capital
does not suffice for the scale on which Modern Industry is carried on, and is
swamped in the competition with the large capitalists, partly because their
specialized skill is rendered worthless by the new methods of production.
Thus the proletariat is recruited from all classes of the population.

The proletariat goes through various stages of development. With its birth
begins its struggle with the bourgeoisie. At first the contest is carried on by individual laborers, then by the workpeople of a factory, then by the operatives
of one trade, in one locality, against the individual bourgeois who directly ex-
ploits them. They direct their attacks not against the bourgeois conditions of
production, but against the instruments of production themselves; they destroy imported wares that compete with their labor, they smash to pieces machinery, they set factories ablaze, they seek to restore by force the vanished
status of the workman of the Middle Ages.

At this stage the laborers still form an incoherent mass scattered over
the whole country, and broken up by their mutual competition. If anywhere
they unite to form more compact bodies, this is not yet the consequence of
their own active union, but of the union of the bourgeoisie, which class, in
order to attain its own political ends, is compelled to set the whole

proletariat in motion, and is moreover yet, for a time, able to do so. At this stage, therefore, the proletarians do not fight their enemies, but the enemies of their enemies, the remnants of absolute monarchy, the landowners, the non-industrial bourgeois, the petty bourgeoisie. Thus the whole historical movement is concentrated in the hands of the bourgeoisie; every victory so obtained is a victory for the bourgeoisie.

[COLLISION BETWEEN THE PROLETARIAT AND THE BOURGEOISIE]

But with the development of industry the proletariat not only increases in number; it becomes concentrated in greater masses, its strength grows, and it feels that strength more. The various interests and conditions of life within the ranks of the proletariat are more and more equalized, in proportion as machinery obliterates all distinctions of labor, and nearly everywhere reduces wages to the same low level. The growing competition among the bourgeois, and the resulting commercial crises, make the wages of the workers ever more fluctuating. The unceasing improvement of machinery, ever more rapidly developing, makes their livelihood more and more precarious; the collisions between individual workmen and individual bourgeois take more and more the character of collisions between two classes. Thereupon the workers begin to form combinations (Trades Unions) against the bourgeois; they club together in order to keep up the rate of wages; they found permanent associations in order to make provision beforehand for these occasional revolts. Here and there the contest breaks out into riots.

Now and then the workers are victorious, but only for a time. The real fruit of their battles lies, not in the immediate result, but in the ever-expanding union of the workers. This union is helped on by the improved means of communication that are created by modern industry and that place the workers of different localities in contact with one another. It was just this contact that was needed to centralize the numerous local struggles, all of the same character, into one national struggle between classes. But every class struggle is a political struggle. And that union, to attain which the burghers of the Middle Ages, with their miserable highways, required centuries, the modern proletarians, thanks to railways, achieve in a few years.

This organization of the proletarians into a class, and consequently into a political party, is continually being upset again by the competition between the workers themselves. But it ever rises up again, stronger, firmer, mightier. It compels legislative recognition of particular interests of the workers, by taking advantage of the divisions among the bourgeoisie itself. Thus the ten-hours' bill in England was carried.

Altogether collisions between the classes of the old society further, in many ways, the course of development of the proletariat. The bourgeoisie finds itself involved in a constant battle. At first with the aristocracy; later on, with those portions of the bourgeoisie itself, whose interests have become antagonistic to the progress of industry; at all times, with the bourgeoisie of foreign countries. In all these battles it sees itself compelled to appeal to the proletariat, to ask for its help, and thus, to drag it into the political arena. The bourgeoisie itself, therefore, supplies the proletariat with its own instruments of political and general education, in other words, it furnishes the proletariat with weapons for fighting the bourgeoisie.

Further, as we have already seen, entire sections of the ruling classes are, by the advance of industry, precipitated into the proletariat, or are at least threatened in their conditions of existence. These also supply the proletariat with fresh elements of enlightenment and progress.

Finally, in times when the class struggle nears the decisive hour, the process of dissolution going on within the ruling class, in fact within the whole range of society, assumes such a violent, glaring character, that a small section of the ruling class cuts itself adrift, and joins the revolutionary class, the class that holds the future in its hands. Just as, therefore, at an earlier period, a section of the nobility went over to the bourgeoisie, so now a portion of the bourgeoisie goes over to the proletariat, and in particular, a portion of the bourgeois ideologists, who have raised themselves to the level of comprehending theoretically the historical movement as a whole. . . .

READING 51

The Individual and the Limits of Government*

John Stuart Mill (1806–1873)

CHAPTER 1: INTRODUCTORY

. . . The object of this Essay is to assert one very simple principle, as entitled to govern absolutely the dealings of society with the individual in the way of compulsion and control, whether the means used be physical force in the form of legal penalties, or the moral coercion of public opinion. That principle is, that the sole end for which mankind are warranted, individually or collectively in interfering with the liberty of action of any of their number, is self-protection. That the only purpose for which power can be rightfully exercised over any member of a civilized community, against his will, is to prevent harm to others. His own good, either physical or moral, is

*From John Stuart Mill, *On Liberty,* (1859), Chapters 1, 2, 3, and 4

not a sufficient warrant. He cannot rightfully be compelled to do or forbear because it will be better for him to do so, because it will make him happier, because, in the opinions of others, to do so would be wise, or even right. These are good reasons for remonstrating with him, or reasoning with him, or persuading him, or entreating him, but not for compelling him, or visiting him with any evil, in case he do otherwise. To justify that, the conduct from which it is desired to deter him must be calculated to produce evil to some one else. The only part of the conduct of any one, for which he is amenable to society, is that which concerns others. In the part which merely concerns himself, his independence is, of right, absolute. Over himself, over his own body and mind, the individual is sovereign. . . .

It is proper to state that I forego any advantage which could be derived to my argument from the idea of abstract right as a thing independent of utility. I regard utility as the ultimate appeal on all ethical questions; but it must be utility in the largest sense, grounded on the permanent interests of man as a progressive being. Those interests, I contend, authorize the subjection of individual spontaneity to external control, only in respect to those actions of each, which concern the interest of other people. . . .

. . . This, then, is the appropriate region of human liberty. It comprises, first, the inward domain of consciousness; demanding liberty of conscience, in the most comprehensive sense; liberty of thought and feeling; absolute freedom of opinion and sentiment on all subjects, practical or speculative, scientific, moral, or theological. The liberty of expressing and publishing opinions may seem to fall under a different principle, since it belongs to that part of the conduct of an individual which concerns other people; but, being almost of as much importance as the liberty of thought itself, and resting in great part on the same reasons, is practically inseparable from it. Secondly, the principle requires liberty of tastes and pursuits; of framing the plan of our life to suit our own character; of doing as we like, subject to such consequences as may follow; without impediment from our fellow-creatures, so long as what we do does not harm them even though they should think our conduct foolish, perverse, or wrong. Thirdly, from this liberty of each individual, follows the liberty, within the same limits, of combination among individuals; freedom to unite, for any purpose not involving harm to others: the persons combining being supposed to be of full age, and not forced or deceived.

No society in which these liberties are not, on the whole, respected, is free, whatever may be its form of government; and none is completely free in which they do not exist absolute and unqualified. The only freedom which deserves the name, is that of pursuing our own good in our own way, so long as we do not attempt to deprive others of theirs, or impede their efforts to obtain it. Each is the proper guardian of his own health, whether bodily, or mental or spiritual. Mankind are greater gainers by suffering each other to live as seems good to themselves, than by compelling each to live as seems good to the rest. . . .

CHAPTER 2: OF THE LIBERTY OF THOUGHT AND DISCUSSION

. . . If all mankind minus one, were of one opinion, and only one person were of the contrary opinion, mankind would be no more justified in silencing that one person, than he, if he had the power, would be justified in silencing mankind. Were an opinion a personal possession of no value except to the owner; if to be obstructed in the enjoyment of it were simply a private injury, it would make some difference whether the injury was inflicted only on a few persons or on many. But the peculiar evil of silencing the expression of an opinion is, that it is robbing the human race; posterity as well as the existing generation; those who dissent from the opinion, still more than those who hold it. If the opinion is right, they are deprived of the opportunity of exchanging error for truth: if wrong, they lose, what is almost as great a benefit, the clearer perception and livelier impression of truth, produced by its collision with error. . . .

. . . But it is not the minds of heretics that are deteriorated most, by the ban placed on all inquiry which does not end in the orthodox conclusions. The greatest harm done is to those who are not heretics, and whose whole mental development is cramped, and their reason cowed, by the fear of heresy. Who can compute what the world loses in the multitude of promising intellects combined with timid characters, who dare not follow out any bold, vigorous, independent train of thought, lest it should land them in something which would admit of being considered irreligious or immoral? Among them we may occasionally see some man of deep conscientiousness, and subtile and refined understanding, who spends a life in sophisticating with an intellect which he cannot silence, and exhausts the resources of ingenuity in attempting to reconcile the promptings of his conscience and reason with orthodoxy, which yet he does not, perhaps, to the end succeed in doing. No one can be a great thinker who does not recognize, that as a thinker it is his first duty to follow his intellect to whatever conclusions it may lead. . . .

We have now recognized the necessity to the mental well-being of mankind (on which all their other well-being depends) of freedom of opinion, and freedom of the expression of opinion, on four distinct grounds; which we will now briefly recapitulate.

First, if any opinion is compelled to silence, that opinion may, for aught we can certainly know, be true. To deny this is to assume our own infallibility.

Secondly, though the silenced opinion be an error, it may, and very commonly does, contain a portion of truth; and since the general or prevailing opinion on any object is rarely or never the whole truth, it is only by the collision of adverse opinions that the remainder of the truth has any chance of being supplied.

Thirdly, even if the received opinion be not only true, but the whole truth; unless it is suffered to be, and actually is, vigorously and earnestly contested, it will, by most of those who receive it, be held in the manner of a prejudice, with little comprehension or feeling of its rational grounds. And not only this, but, fourthly, the meaning of the doctrine itself will be in danger of being lost, or enfeebled, and deprived of its vital effect on the character and conduct: the dogma becoming a mere formal profession, inefficacious for good, but cumbering the ground, and preventing the growth of any real and heartfelt conviction, from reason or personal experience. . . .

CHAPTER 3: ON INDIVIDUALITY, AS ONE OF THE ELEMENTS OF WELL-BEING

Such being the reasons which make it imperative that human beings should be free to form opinions, and to express their opinions without reserve; and such the baneful consequences to the intellectual, and through that to the moral nature of man, unless this liberty is either conceded, or asserted in spite of prohibition; let us next examine whether the same reasons do not require that men should be free to act upon their opinions—to carry these out in their lives, without hindrance, either physical or moral, from their fellow-men, so long as it is at their own risk and peril. This last proviso is of course indispensable. No one pretends that actions should be as free as opinions. On the contrary, even opinions lose their immunity, when the circumstances in which they are expressed are such as to constitute their expression a positive instigation to some mischievous act. An opinion that corndealers are starvers of the poor, or that private property is robbery, ought to be unmolested when simply circulated through the press, but may justly incur punishment when delivered orally to an excited mob assembled before the house of a corn-dealer, or when handed about among the same mob in the form of a placard. Acts of whatever kind, which, without justifiable cause, do harm to others, may be, and in the more important cases absolutely require to be, controlled by the unfavorable sentiments, and, when needful, by the active interference of mankind. The liberty of the individual must be thus far limited; he must not make himself a nuisance to other people. But if he refrains from molesting others in what concerns them, and merely acts according to his own inclination and judgment in things which concern himself, the same reasons which show that opinion should be free, prove also that he should be allowed, without molestation, to carry his opinions into practice at his own cost. That mankind are not infallible; that their truths, for the most part, are only half-truths; that unity of opinion, unless resulting from the fullest and freest comparison of opposite opinions, is not desirable, and diversity not an evil, but a good, until mankind are much more capable than at present of recognizing all sides of the truth, are principles applicable to men's modes of action not less than to their opinions. As it is useful that while mankind are imperfect there should be different opinions, so is it that there should be different experiments of living; that free scope should be given to varieties of character, short of injury to others; and that the worth of different modes of life should be proved practically, when any one thinks fit to try them. It is desirable, in short, that in things which do not primarily concern others, individuality should assert itself. Where, not the person's own character, but the traditions of customs of other people are the rule of conduct, there is wanting one of the principal ingredients of human happiness, and quite the chief ingredient of individual and social progress. . . .

CHAPTER 4: OF THE LIMITS TO THE AUTHORITY OF SOCIETY OVER THE INDIVIDUAL

What, then, is the rightful limit to the sovereignty of the individual over himself? Where does the authority of society begin? How much of human life should be assigned to individuality, and how much to society?

Each will receive its proper share, if each has that which more particularly concerns it. To individuality should belong the part of life in which it is chiefly the individual that is interested; to society, the part which chiefly interests society.

Though society is not founded on a contract, and though no good purpose is answered by inventing a contract in order to deduce social obligations from it, every one who receives the protection of society owes a return for the benefit, and the fact of living in society renders it indispensable that each should be bound to observe a certain line of conduct towards the rest. This conduct consists, first, in not injuring the interests of one another; or rather certain interests, which, either by express legal provision or by tacit understanding, ought to be considered as rights; and secondly, in each person's bearing his share (to be fixed on some equitable principle) of the labors and sacrifices incurred for defending the society or its members from injury and molestation. These conditions society is justified in enforcing, at all costs to those who endeavor to withhold fulfillment. Nor is this all that society may do. The acts of an individual may be hurtful to others, or wanting in due consideration for their welfare, without going the length of violating any of their constituted rights. The offender may then be justly punished by opinion, though not by law. As soon as any part of a person's conduct affects prejudicially the interests of others, society has jurisdiction over it, and the question whether the general welfare will or will not be promoted by interfering with it, becomes open to discussion. But there is no room for entertaining any such question when a person's conduct affects the interests of no persons besides himself, or needs not affect them unless they like (all the persons concerned being of full age, and the ordinary amount of understanding). In all such cases there should be perfect freedom, legal and social, to do the action and stand the consequences.

It would be a great misunderstanding of this doctrine, to suppose that it is one of selfish indifference, which pretends that human beings have no business with each other's conduct in life, and that they should not concern themselves about the well-doing or well-being of one another, unless their own interest is involved. Instead of any diminution, there is need of a great increase of disinterested exertion to promote the good of others. But disinterested benevolence can find other instruments to persuade people to their good, than

whips and scourges, either of the literal or the metaphorical sort. . . . But neither one person, nor any number of persons, is warranted in saying to another
human creature of ripe years, that he shall not do with his life for his own benefit what he chooses to do with it. . . .

What I contend for is, that the inconveniences which are strictly inseparable from the unfavorable judgment of others, are the only ones to which a person should ever be subjected for that portion of his conduct and character
which concerns his own good, but which does not affect the interests of others
in their relations with him. Acts injurious to others require a totally different
treatment. Encroachment on their rights; infliction on them of any loss or damage not justified by his own rights; falsehood or duplicity in dealing with
them; unfair or ungenerous use of advantages over them; even selfish abstinence from defending them against injury—these are fit objects of moral
reprobation, and, in grave cases, of moral retribution and punishment.

READING 52

*Justice as Fairness**

John Rawls (b. 1921)

The fundamental idea in the concept of justice is that of fairness. It is this
aspect of justice for which utilitarianism, in its classical form, is unable to
account, but which is represented, even if misleadingly so, in the idea of the
social contract. To establish these propositions I shall develop, but of necessity only very briefly, a particular conception of justice by stating two principles which specify it and by considering bow they may be thought to
arise. The parts of this conception are familiar; but perhaps it is possible by
using the notion of fairness as a framework to assemble and to look at them
in a new way.

1. [TWO PRINCIPLES OF JUSTICE]

Throughout I discuss justice as a virtue of institutions constituting restrictions
as to how they may define offices and powers, and assign rights and duties;
and not as a virtue of particular actions, or persons. Justice is but one of many
virtues of institutions, for these may be inefficient, or degrading, or any of a
number of things, without being unjust. Essentially justice is the elimination of
arbitrary distinctions and the establishment, within the structure of a practice,
of a proper balance between competing claims. I do not argue that the

*From John Rawls, "Justice as Fairness," in *The Journal of Philosophy,* Vol. 54, 1957, pp. 653–662.

principles given below are the principles of justice. It is sufficient for my purposes that they be typical of the family of principles which might reasonably be called principles of justice as shown by the background against which they may be thought to arise.

The first principle is that each person participating in a practice, or affected by it, has an equal right to the most extensive liberty compatible with a like liberty for all; and the second is that inequalities are arbitrary unless it is reasonable to expect that they will work out for everyone's advantage and unless the offices to which they attach, or from which they may be gained, are open to all. These principles express justice as a complex of three ideas: liberty, equality, and reward for contributions to the common advantage.

The first principle holds, of course, only *ceteris paribus*: while there must always be a justification for departing from the initial position of equal liberty (which is defined by the pattern of rights and duties), and the burden of proof is placed upon him who would depart from it, nevertheless, there can be, and often there is, a justification for doing so. One can view this principle as containing the principle that similar cases by judged similarly, or if distinctions are made in the handling of cases, there must be some relevant difference between them (a principle which follows from the concept of a judgment of any kind). It could be argued that justice requires only an equal liberty; but if a greater liberty were possible for all without loss or conflict, then it would be irrational to settle on a lesser liberty. There is no reason for circumscribing rights until they mutually interfere with one another. Therefore no serious distortion of the concept of justice is likely to follow from including within it the concept of the greatest equal liberty instead of simply equal liberty.

The second principle specifies what sorts of inequalities are permissible, where by inequalities it seems best to understand not any difference between offices and positions, since structural differences are not usually an issue (people do not object to there being different offices as such, and so to there being the offices of president, senator, governor, judge, and so on), but differences in the benefits and burdens attached to them either directly or indirectly, such as prestige and wealth, or liability to taxation and compulsory service. An inequality is allowed only if there is reason to believe that the practice with the inequality will work to the advantage of every party. This is interpreted to require, first, that there must normally be evidence acceptable to common sense and based on a common fund of knowledge and belief which shows that this is in fact likely to be the case. The principle does not rule out, however, arguments of a theological or metaphysical kind to justify inequalities (e.g., a religious basis for a caste system) provided they belong to common belief and are freely acknowledged by people who may be presumed to know what they are doing.

Second, an inequality must work for the common advantage; and since the principle applies to practices, this implies that the representative man in every office or position of the practice, when he views it as a going institution, must find it reasonable to prefer his condition and prospects with the inequality to what they would be without it. And finally, the various offices to which special benefits and burdens attach are required to be open to all; and so if, for example, it is to the common advantage to attach benefits to offices (because by doing so not only is the requisite talent attracted to them, but encouraged to give its best efforts once there), they must be won in a fair competition in which contestants are judged on their merits. If some offices were not open, those excluded would normally be justified in feeling wronged, even if they benefited from the greater efforts of those who were allowed to compete for them. Assuming that offices are open, it is necessary only to consider the design of the practices themselves and how they jointly, as a system, work together. It is a mistake to fix attention on the varying relative positions of particular persons and to think that each such change, as a once-for-all transaction, must be in itself just. The system must be judged from a general point of view: unless one is prepared to criticize it from the standpoint of a representative man holding some particular office, one has no complaint against it.

2. [THE ORIGINAL POSITION]

Given these principles, one might try to derive them from a priori principles of reason, or offer them as known by intuition. These are familiar steps, and, at least in the case of the first principle, might be made with some success. I wish, however, to look at the principles in a different way.

Consider a society where certain practices are already established, and whose members are mutually self-interested: their allegiance to the established practices is founded on the prospect of self-advantage. It need not be supposed that they are incapable of acting from any other motive: if one thinks of the members of this society as families, the individuals thereof may be bound by ties of sentiment and affection. Nor must they be mutually self-interested under all circumstances, but only under those circumstances in which they ordinarily participate in their common practices. Imagine also that the persons in this society are rational: they know their own interests more or less accurately; they are capable of tracing out the likely consequences of adopting one practice rather than another and of adhering to a decision once made; they can resist present temptations and attractions of immediate gain; and the knowledge, or the perception, of the difference between their condition and that of others is not, in itself, a source of great dissatisfaction. Finally, they have roughly similar needs and interests and are sufficiently equal in power and ability to assure that in normal circumstances none is able to dominate the others.

Now suppose that on some particular occasion several members of this society come together to discuss whether any of them has a legitimate complaint against their established institutions. They try first to arrive at the principles by which complaints, and so practices themselves, are to be judged. Their procedure for this is the following: each is to propose the principles upon which he wishes his complaints to be tried with the understanding that, if acknowledged, the complaints of others will be similarly tried, and that no complaints will be heard at all until everyone is roughly of one mind as to how complaints are to be judged. They understand further that the principles proposed and acknowledged on this occasion are to be binding on future occasions, Thus each will be wary of proposing principles which give him a peculiar advantage, supposing them to be accepted, in his present circumstances, since he will be bound by it in future cases the circumstances of which are unknown and in which the principle might well be to his detriment. Everyone is, then, forced to make in advance a firm commitment, which others also may reasonably be expected to make, and no one is able to tailor the canons of a legitimate complaint to fit his own special condition. Therefore each person will propose principles of a general kind which will, to a large degree, gain their sense from the various applications to be made of them. These principles will express the conditions in accordance with which each is least unwilling to have his interests limited in the design of practices on the supposition that the interests of others will be limited likewise. The restrictions which would so arise might be thought of as those a person would keep in mind if he were designing a practice in which his enemy were to assign him his place.

In this account of a hypothetical society the character and respective situations of the parties reflect the circumstances in which questions of justice may be said to arise, and the procedure whereby principles are proposed and acknowledged represents constraints, analogous to those of having a morality, whereby rational and mutually self-interested parties are brought to act reasonably. Given all conditions as described, it would be natural to accept the two principles of justice. Since there is no way for anyone to win special advantage for himself, each might consider it reasonable to acknowledge equality as an initial principle. There is, however, no reason why they should regard this position as final; for if there are inequalities which satisfy the second principle, the immediate gain which equality would allow can be considered as intelligently invested in view of its future return. If, as is quite likely, these inequalities work as incentives to draw out better efforts, the members of this society may look upon them as concessions to human nature: they, like us, may think that people ideally should want to serve one another. But as they are mutually self-interested, their acceptance of these inequalities is merely the acceptance of the relations in which they actually stand. They have no title to complain of one another. And so, provided the conditions of the principle are met, there is no reason why they should reject such inequalities in the design of their social practices. Indeed, it would be short-sighted of them to do so, and could result, it seems, only from their being dejected by the bare knowledge, or perception, that others are better situated. Each person will, however, insist on a common advantage, for none is willing to sacrifice anything for the others.

These remarks are not, of course, offered as a proof that persons so circumstanced would settle upon the two principles, but only to show that the principles of justice could have such a background; and so can be viewed as those principles which mutually self-interested and rational persons, when similarly situated and required to make in advance a firm commitment, could acknowledge as restrictions governing the assignment of rights and duties in their common practices, and thereby accept as limiting their rights against one another.

3. [THE DUTY OF FAIR PLAY]

That the principles of justice can be regarded in this way is an important fact about them. It brings out the idea that fundamental to justice is the concept of fairness which relates to right dealing between persons who are cooperating with or competing against one another, as when one speaks of fair games, fair competition, and fair bargains. The question of fairness arises when free persons, who have no authority over one another, are engaging in a joint activity and amongst themselves settling or acknowledging the rules which define it and which determine the respective shares in its benefits and burdens. A practice will strike the parties as fair if none feels that, by participating in it, be, or any of the others, is taken advantage of, or forced to give in to claims which he does not regard as legitimate. This implies that each has a conception of legitimate claims which he thinks it reasonable that others as well as himself should acknowledge. If one thinks of the principles of justice as arising in the way described, then they do define this sort of conception. A practice is just, then, when it satisfies the principles which those who participate in it could propose to one another for mutual acceptance under the aforementioned circumstances. Persons engaged in a just, or fair, practice can face one another honestly, and support their respective positions, should they appear questionable, by reference to principles which it is reasonable to expect each to accept. It is this notion of the possibility of mutual acknowledgment which makes the concept of fairness fundamental to justice. Only if such acknowledgment is possible, can there be true community between persons in their common practices; otherwise their relations will appear to them as founded to some extent on force and violence. If, in ordinary speech, fairness applies more particularly to practices in which there is a choice whether to engage or not, and justice to practices in which there is no choice and one must play, the element of necessity does not alter the basic conception of the possibility of mutual acceptance, although it may make it much more urgent to change unjust than unfair institutions.

Now if the participants in a practice accept its rules as fair, and so have no complaint to lodge against it, there arises a prima facie duty (and a corresponding prima facie right) of the parties to each other to act in accordance with the practice when it falls upon them to comply. When any number of persons engage in a practice, or conduct a joint undertaking, according to rules, and thus restrict their liberty, those who have submitted to these restrictions when required have a right to a similar acquiescence on the part of those who have benefited by their submission. These conditions will, of course, obtain if a practice is correctly acknowledged to be fair, for in this case, all who participate in it will benefit from it. The rights and duties so arising are special rights and duties in that they depend on previous voluntary actions-in this case, on the parties' having engaged in a common practice and accepted its benefits. It is not, however, an obligation which presupposes a deliberate performative act in the sense of a promise, or contract, and the like. It is sufficient that one has knowingly participated in a practice acknowledged to be fair and accepted the resulting benefits. This prima facie obligation may, of course, be overridden: it may happen, when it comes one's turn to follow a rule, that other considerations will justify not doing so. But one cannot, in general, be released from this obligation by denying the justice of the practice only when it falls on one to obey. If a person rejects a practice, he should, as far as possible, declare his intention in advance, and avoid participating in it or accepting its benefits.

This duty may be called that of fair play, which is, perhaps, to extend the ordinary notion; for acting unfairly is usually not so much the breaking of any particular rule, even if the infraction is difficult to detect (cheating), but taking advantage of loopholes or ambiguities in rules, availing oneself of unexpected or special circumstances which make it impossible to enforce them, insisting that rules be enforced when they should be suspended, and, more generally, acting contrary to the intention of a practice. (Thus one speaks of the sense of fair play; acting fairly is not simply following, rules; what is fair must be felt or perceived.) Nevertheless, it is not an unnatural extension of the duty of fair play to have it include the obligation which participants in a common practice owe to each other to act in accordance with it when their performance falls due. Consider the tax dodger, or the free rider.

The duty of fair play stands beside those of fidelity and gratitude as a fundamental moral notion; and like them it implies a constraint on self-interest in particular cases. I make this point to avoid a misunderstanding: the conception of the mutual acknowledgment of principles under special circumstances is used to analyze the concept of justice. I do not wish to imply that the acceptance of justice in actual conduct depends solely on an existing equality of conditions. My own view, which is perhaps but one of several compatible with the preceding analysis, and which I can only suggest here, is that the acknowledgment of the duty of fair play, as shown in acting on it, and wishing to make amends and the like when one has been at fault, is one of the forms of conduct in which participants in a common practice show their recognition of one another as persons. In the same way that, failing a special explanation, the criterion for the recognition of suffering is helping him who suffers, acknowledging the duty of fair play is the criterion for recognizing another as a person with similar capacities, interests, and feelings as oneself. The acceptance by participants in a common practice of this duty is a reflection in each of the recognition of the aspirations of the others to be realized by their joint activity. Without this acceptance they would recognize one another as but complicated objects in a complicated routine. To recognize another as a person one must respond to him and act towards him as one; and these forms of action and response include, among other things, acknowledging the duty of fair play. These remarks are unhappily obscure; their purpose here is to forestall the misunderstanding mentioned above.

The conception at which we have arrived, then, is that the principles of justice may be thought of as arising once the constraints of having a morality are imposed upon rational and mutually self-interested parties who are related and situated in a special way. A practice is just if it is in accordance with the principles which all who participate in it might reasonably be expected to propose or to acknowledge before one another when they are similarly circumstanced and required to make a firm commitment in advance; and thus when it meets standards which the parties could accept as fair should occasion arise for them to debate its merits. Once persons knowingly engage in a practice which they acknowledge to be fair and accept the benefits of doing so, they are bound by the duty of fair play which implies a limitation on self-interest in particular cases.

Now if a claim fails to meet this conception of justice there is no moral value in granting it, since it violates the conditions of reciprocity and community amongst persons: he who presses it, not being willing to acknowledge it when pressed by another, has no grounds for complaint when it is denied; whereas he against whom it is pressed can complain. As it cannot be mutually acknowledged, it is a resort to coercion: granting the claim is only possible if one party can compel what the other will not admit. Thus in deciding on the justice of a practice it is not enough to ascertain that it answers to wants and interest in the fullest and most effective manner. For if any of these be such that they conflict with justice, they should not be counted; their satisfaction is no reason for having a practice. It makes no sense to concede claims the denial of which gives rise to no complaint in preference to claims the denial of which can be objected to. It would be irrelevant to say, even if true, that it resulted in the greatest satisfaction of desire.

4. [AGAINST UTILITARIANISM]

This conception of justice differs from that of the stricter form of utilitarianism (Bentham and Sidgwick), and its counterpart in welfare economics, which assimilates justice to benevolence and the latter in turn to the most efficient design of institutions to promote the general welfare. Now it is said occasionally that this form of utilitarianism puts no restrictions on what might be a just assignment of rights and duties. But this is not so. Beginning with the notion that the general happiness can be represented by a social utility function consisting of the sum of individual utility functions with identical weights (this being the meaning of the maxim that each counts for one and no more than one), it is commonly assumed that the utility functions of individuals are similar in all essential respects. Differences are laid to accidents of education and upbringing, and should not be taken into account; and this assumption, coupled with that of diminishing marginal utility, results in a prima facie case for equality. But even if such restrictions are built into the utility function, and have, in practice, much the same result as the application of the principles of justice (and appear, perhaps, to be ways of expressing these principles in the language of mathematics and psychology), the fundamental idea is very different from the conception of justice as reciprocity. Justice is interpreted as the contingent result of a higher order administrative decision whose form is similar to that of an entrepreneur deciding how much to produce of this or that commodity in view of its marginal revenue, or to that of someone distributing goods to needy persons according to the relative urgency of their wants. The choice between practices is thought of as being made on the basis of the allocation of benefits and burdens to individuals (measured by the present capitalized value of the utility of these benefits over the full period of the practice's existence) which results from the distribution of rights and duties established by a practice. The individuals receiving the benefits are not thought of as related in any way: they represent so many different directions in which limited resources may be allocated. Preferences and interest are taken as given; and their satisfaction has value irrespective of the relations between persons which they represent and the claims which the parties are prepared to make on one another. This value is properly taken into account by the (ideal) legislator who is conceived as adjusting the rules of the system from the center so as to maximize the present capitalized value of the social utility function. The principles of justice will not be violated by a legal system so conceived provided these executive decisions are correctly made; and in this fact the principles of justice are said to find their derivation and explanation.

Some social decisions are, of course, of an administrative sort; namely, when the decision turns on social utility in the ordinary sense: on the efficient use of common means for common ends whose benefits are impartially distributed, or in connection with which the question of distribution is misplaced, as in the case of maintaining public order, or national defense. But as an interpretation of the basis of the principles of justice the utilitarian conception is mistaken. It can lead one to argue against slavery on the grounds that the advantages to the slaveholder do not counterbalance the disadvantages to the slave and to society at large burdened by a comparatively inefficient system of labor. The conception of justice as fairness, when applied to the offices of slaveholder and slave, would forbid counting the advantages of the slaveholder at all. These offices could not be founded on principles which could be mutually acknowledged, so the question whether the slaveholder's gains are great enough to counterbalance the losses to the slave and society cannot arise in the first place.

The difference between the two conceptions is whether justice is a fundamental moral concept arising directly from the reciprocal relations of persons engaging in common practices, and its principles those which persons similarly circumstanced could mutually acknowledge; or whether justice is derivative from a kind of higher order executive decision as to the most efficient design of institutions conceived as general devices for distributing benefits to individuals the worth of whose interests is defined independently of their relations to each other. Now even if the social utility function is constructed so that the practices chosen by it would be just, at least under normal circumstances, there is still the further argument against the utilitarian conception that the various restrictions on the utility function needed to get this result are borrowed from the conception of justice as fairness. The notion that individuals have similar utility functions, for example, is really the first principle of justice under the guise of a psychological law. It is assumed not in the manner of an empirical hypothesis concerning actual desires and interests, but from sensing what must be laid down if justice is not to be violated. There is, indeed, irony in this conclusion; for utilitarians attacked the notion of the original contract not only as a historical fiction but as a superfluous hypothesis: they thought that utility alone provides sufficient grounds for all social obligation, and is in any case the real basis of contractual obligations. But this is not so unless one's conception of social utility embodies within it restrictions whose basis can be understood only if one makes reference to one of the ideas of contractarian thought: that persons must be regarded as possessing an original and equal liberty, and their common practices are unjust unless they accord with principles which persons so circumstanced and related could freely accept.